The Forgotten Kindertransportees

The Forgotten Kindertransportees

The Scottish Experience

Frances Williams

B L O O M S B U R Y
LONDON • NEW DELHI • NEW YORK • SYDNEY

Bloomsbury Academic
An imprint of Bloomsbury Publishing Plc

50 Bedford Square
London
WC1B 3DP
UK

1385 Broadway
New York
NY 10018
USA

www.bloomsbury.com

Bloomsbury is a registered trade mark of Bloomsbury Publishing Plc

First published 2014

British Library Cataloguing-in-Publication Data
A catalogue record for this book is available from the British Library.

ISBN: HB: 978-1-7809-3803-5
ePDF: 978-1-7809-3689-5
ePub: 978-1-7809-3718-2

Library of Congress Cataloguing-in-Publication Data
A catalogue record for this book is available from the Library of Congress.

Typeset by Deanta Global Publishing Services, Chennai, India
Printed and bound in Great Britain

'The Forgotten Kindertransportees' is dedicated in loving memory to my mother, Jenny Williams.

Contents

List of Illustrations

Illustration Acknowledgements

The author and publisher are grateful to Mike Challis for giving permission to reproduce the photographs of William Farinton Drew.

Preface

Introduction

Chapter 2

Abbreviations

Adath	Union of Orthodox Hebrew Congregations
ADRC	Albert Drive Reform congregation
AJA	Anglo-Jewish Association
AJR	Association of Jewish Refugees
BOD	The Board of Deputies
CBF	Central British Fund
CC	Central Council for German Jewry
CREC	Chief Rabbis' Emergency Council
CRC	Czech Minors' Refugee Committee
ERC	Edinburgh Refugee Committee
FDSC	Frankfurt's Domestic Science College
GJRC	Glasgow Jewish Representative Council
GRC	Glasgow Refugee Committee
IAC	Inter-Aid Committee
JCGR	Jewish Council for German Refugees, Glasgow
JAC	Jewish Agricultural Committee
JECJE	Joint Emergency Committee for Jewish Education
JEC	National Council of Jewish Religious Education
KA	Kindertransport Association
NCS	New Central Synagogue

RCM	Refugee Children's Movement
SCC	Scottish Christian Council for Refugees
SCC	Scottish Christian Council
SED	Scottish Education Department
SNCR	Scottish National Council for Refugees
SRC	Scottish Refugee Centre
TUC	British Trade Union Council
WIZO	Women's International Zionist Organization

Preface

Between 1938 and 1939, almost 10,000 unaccompanied minors fled Greater Germany for Britain as part of the *Kindertransport* or children's transport initiative. The outbreak of war prevented their parents from meeting them in Britain and left them dependent upon charitable welfare schemes in order to survive. An estimated 800 of these children were sent north to Scotland. Until now, their story has remained largely forgotten.

The story of Scotland's Kindertransportees has lain dormant for many years and for many reasons, one being that the main historical sources relating to the episode have been scattered around the world in the most unexpected of places. Large quantities of information relating to the Kindertransport in Scotland were found within Southampton University's Parkes Institute and Hartley Library Special Collection. The Glasgow Jewish Archives, the Wiener Library in London, the Leo Baeck/YIVO centre in New York and Washington DC's Holocaust Memorial Museum's archives must also each be credited with filling in the large blanks that have existed in the Scottish Kindertransport story. Information has also been found in Haddington's local archive, Edinburgh's Salisbury Road Synagogue's archive, Yad Vashem of Israel and New York's public archives. Material gathered in these archives includes minute papers, official correspondence, newspapers, private letters, diaries, memoirs, oral testimonies, film, photographs and pamphlets.

Alongside these larger archives, the story of Scotland's forgotten Kindertransportees was brought to life by the private collections located around the world. A most remarkable archive is that of the Challis family's private collection of over 400 negatives, along with private papers, of the late William Farinton Drew. This archive had remained forgotten and undiscovered for over 60 years before being found by Mike Challis, the nephew of Drew. Drew taught English and Chemistry at Whittingehame Farm School, Scotland's pre-*hachsharot.* During his years at Whittingehame, Drew photographed and recorded in letters to his parents the daily lives of resident Kindertransportees. Drew died as a navigator in a Liberator plane, shot down over the Bay of Biscay, on 29 July 1943. Following his death, Mike Challis believes that Drew's collection of photographs and letters was passed on to his father for safekeeping.

Another substantial collection belongs to Ester Golan, a former Kindertransportee and resident of Whittingehame. After making *Aliyah*, Golen settled in Jerusalem, Israel. There she preserved and collected a large archive of school journals, diaries, newspaper clippings and questionnaires relating to her time in Scotland. A number of other surviving Kindertransportees have also shared personal diaries, new and old correspondence, as well as other records of broader life stories.

I am deeply grateful to the Association of Jewish Refugees (AJR) and the Kindertransport Association of Great Britain (KA), whose generosity of funding and support enabled this project to be realized. With their support, I have had unique access to the new and extensive body of compiled questionnaires 'Making New Lives in Britain', which was sent to all known surviving Kindertransportees across the world.[1] In 2006 and 2007, I worked for the KA in association with the AJR to help create this questionnaire, which was disseminated to 2,000 Kindertransportees. One thousand and twenty-five completed questionnaires were returned. This resource has provided a new insight into the minors' personal experiences along with their broader life stories. The completed questionnaires contained multiple-choice answers to a range of questions and have also provided a large body of new memoirs.

The new data provided within the questionnaires have also provided previously inaccessible statistical information. This has enabled a new understanding of patterns that overarch the individual experience. To best utilize this new resource, with funding from the AJR, we formulated an extensive statistical database.[2] Within this database, I imputed over 250 information columns for the 1,025 entries. These resources now enable quantitative analysis of overarching aspects of the Kindertransport as well as of specific case studies. It has allowed questions to be answered that were previously inaccessible: care placement ratios, religious affiliation averages and migratory patterns. One can now assess, for example, the percentage of Scotland's Kindertransportees who were fostered while in Britain and, of those who were fostered, how many experienced this form of care in England or Scotland. Sixty-three per cent of Scotland's Kindertransportees experienced foster care in Britain. Of these, only 58 per cent experienced this form of care within Scotland.

The database's ability to offer new statistical answers to research questions is already correcting existing misinformation that plagues the Kindertransport historiography. One example includes Wolfgang Benz's and Andrea Hammel's study into the trauma associated with the Kindertransport experience. This reiterated the widely held misconception that 'nine out of ten' Kindertransportees did not see their parents again.[3] This particular notion is especially problematic because it has far-reaching implications on discussions about broader life stories and the impact of the Kindertransport on the minors' lives. The database shows that 46 per cent of Kindertransportees were reunited with at least one parent, a vast difference to 10 per cent.[4] Of these 46 per cent, 64 per cent were reunited with both parents. These statistics dramatically transform the outlook of the Kindertransportees' experiences.

Comparisons may also now be drawn between the experiences of minors in Scotland with those in other regions. This has not only allowed new analysis of the Kindertransport in Britain, but also provided access to regional and local variations in experience. The level of Jewish foster homes for Kindertransportees, for example, may be compared in terms of a national or regional picture. The database reveals that in Scotland, of those who were fostered 66 per cent were placed in Jewish homes. In comparison, the national statistic is 30 per cent. Kindertransportees in different regions had very different religious care experiences.

For the use of oral history research, the database has also made it possible to locate Kindertransportees from specific geographic areas and with particular experiences. Eighty-seven were found to have spent time during World War II in Scotland. Within this framework particular care scenarios could be investigated to gather a robust oral history record of the Kindertransportees' experiences in Scotland. Interviews have subsequently been undertaken with a range of Kindertransportees who experienced different living scenarios in Scotland: hostels, foster care, evacuation, pre-*hachsharot* (agricultural training farms for Zionist youth wishing to emigrate to Eretz Yisrael and found a Kibbutz) training, as well as various employment placements and social or economic lifestyles.[5]

Thirty new interviews have been made with Kindertransportees formerly placed in Scotland and who are now located across the world: Britain, United States, Israel and New Zealand. A large number of previously compiled interviews have also been used: Kean College New Jersey Collection, USC Shoah Foundation Institute, the Slate collection, all within Washington DC's Holocaust Museum's archive, the Wiener Library's compilation of Bea Leckowitz's 150 child exile interviews and the Imperial War Museum's Oral History Collection, both in London.

The use of oral history has 'opened the book' for the forgotten story of the Kindertransportees of Scotland.[6] It has provided access to otherwise inaccessible areas of investigation, such as the Kindertransportees' personal interpretation of their experiences in Scotland during the war years.[7] It has revealed the relationship of this experience with broader life stories.[8] In doing so, as Donald Ritchie argues, oral history has proved invaluable in helping to 'remedy the blind spots' of the Kindertransport episode.[9]

The use of oral history and the working dynamics of memory highlight many issues for consideration.[10] The type of narrative that is offered by an interviewee can vary enormously. This can be the result of the collaborative role played by the historian/interviewer in the process of doing oral history.[11] The historian in doing oral history can become a 'ventriloquist', 'director' and editor, and can unintentionally encourage certain responses.[12] This means that a unique dialogue is formed within each interview, dependent on the interviewer as well as on the interviewee.

My personal role as interviewer did impact upon my interviews with Kindertransportees. This was most keenly felt in regards to the personal contact I had with interviewees during the process of organizing and doing the interview. Kindertransportees frequently expressed a keen hospitality and desire to invest a long-term maternal or paternal role in my project. Standing at 5.4 foot and possessing an arguably young appearance, I found that interviewees often received me as a young novice historian who required direction and care. This seemed to lead interviewees to approach storytelling in a manner that they may have adopted with their own grandchildren. This was often characterized by familiarity, trust and acceptance, along with concern that the basic historical outline to the event had been conveyed. This could be frustrating as interviewees struggled to break away from the broader picture and engage with the particular as it related to their personal life experiences. On the other hand, interviewees could become more comfortable with sharing anecdotal information and sensitive personal memories, which they may normally have preferred to keep within the family.

The manner in which I was introduced to my interviewees also established a particular character to my interviewing process. After locating 87 surviving Scottish Kindertransportees from the new database, the KA and the AJR then introduced me to potential interviewees via written correspondence. Further interviewees were found by way of introduction from friends or relatives, some of whom I may already have interviewed. This approach seemed to put interviewees at ease, especially those who continue to express a real concern about Holocaust revisionists. Interviewees were worried about saying the wrong thing to the wrong person. The KA and AJR, along with their friends and family, offered a form of verification of my credentials. This enabled me to begin the interview process with a higher degree of trust and familiarity.

However, the process of introduction via the KA and AJR was not without problems. Upon initially meeting me, Kindertransportees in Scotland expressed suspicion and concern that yet another English Kindertransport story was going to be told. In addition, I found that Kindertransportees who rejected the English or broader popular Kindertransport narrative were agitated to express their criticism and contradictions to the story. Alternatively, other Kindertransportees who believed that an official story was being gathered, in line with popular Kindertransport narratives, expressed agitation to reiterate the grand narrative and to express thanks to Britain.[13]

Interviewees' responses were also shaped by the common presumption that I was both Jewish and Scottish, perhaps due to my affiliation with Edinburgh University in Scotland, Jewish organizations in England and personal interest in a Scottish/Jewish subject matter. Fortunately, after correcting this misunderstanding familiarity had already been established and no hard feelings (albeit slight disappointment or disbelief) was felt. However, as Wendy Ugolini also discovered, the experience of being perceived to be an insider and part of a shared community did mean that interviewees spoke more freely about their personal experiences.[14]

The recording process in interviews can also shape the way in which interviewees choose to narrate their life stories. I chose not to video interviewees, but to use a dictaphone. I felt that this avoided creating too formal an atmosphere. Avoiding visual recording can reduce unease or self-awareness for the interviewee. It also enables anonymity and can help to emphasize dialogue rather than performance.[15] Lawrence Langer has critically argued that the main problem of videotaped survivors' testimonies is that they encourage interviewees to attach the 'grammar of heroism and martydom', as opposed to focusing on private, more mundane daily experiences.[16] By focusing on dialogue rather than performance, I hoped to reduce difficulties that can arise for interviewees in the process of communicating life experiences to a stranger. Barbara Engelking has similarly found that Holocaust testimonies possess particular problems with the language of communication, whereby interviewees may struggle to convey their life story.[17]

Narratives are shaped not only by the personal contact their narrator has had with the subject matter, but also by their current position. Later-life experiences shape perspectives of the past. E. H. Carr has argued that 'to learn about the present in the light of the past means also to learn about the past in the light of the present'.[18] Perception and recollection of history is subject to a subconscious transition over the course of time. Penny Summerfield refers to the influence of 'cultural circuits' upon narratives given by interviewees.[19] This is particularly apparent among Kindertransportees in their process of constructing personal narrative, whereby public discourse or other cultural influences inform personal memories.

Existing public narrative frameworks or current lifestyles of interviewees can impact upon memory and influence the process by which individuals construct narrative from personal experience. The 'composure', or not, of interviewees' testimonies during the giving of an interview can highlight important disparities that may exist between public ideas about a past event and personal memories of the past event.[20] This can throw light upon areas of apparent 'cultural silence'.[21] It can also lead to a degree of uncertainty or frustration for interviewees who feel that their memory contradicts public narrative frameworks.

This is particularly true for the Kindertransport episode, which has experienced a transformation in its position and perceived importance within Holocaust history. The Kindertransport has now become an important emblem within public narratives of Jewish survival and sacrifice during the Holocaust. In becoming a publically recognized historical event, a public Kindertransport narrative framework has been formed. This has meant that a dominant narrative has emerged. As Summerfield has argued, interviewees who may feel that their memories do not tally with this narrative, become uncertain, insecure, reclusive, or simply reconstruct their personal memories to suit the public discourse about the event.

The development of Holocaust historiographies has had other far-reaching implications upon Kindertransportees' narratives. The shadow of Auschwitz and testimonies of 'real' survivors of the Holocaust have influenced and transformed the Kindertransportees' position in Holocaust remembrance and reconciliation. Initially Kindertransportees remained quiet about their experiences, but in recent years they have been able to step out of the shadow of Auschwitz and present their stories as valuable testimonies within the body of Holocaust archives. This has changed narrators' confidence and motivation in the process of telling their stories. Kindertransportees' testimonies may be politically motivated, with the intention of testifying to the tragedy that befell them and their families during the Holocaust. John Murphy has shown the important political role of oral testimonies in constructing public narratives, which in turn influence public inquiries or official apologies.[22] Interviewees have often remarked of the need to record their experiences in order to prevent the Holocaust ever happening again or future generations ever forgetting.[23]

This has also meant that the Holocaust has become a central reference point within Kindertransportees' life stories. Ronnie Landau has shown that the 'central reference point' that can emerge in Holocaust testimonies to the Holocaust in Greater Germany can mean that a black-and-white character of narrative emerges.[24] These testimonies can provide a 'process of reconciliation', whereby clear-cut 'goodies' and 'badies' are created.[25] This can be problematic because it has given 'victim-hood' a central position in many Kindertransportees' narratives. This type of testimony emphasizes loss and trauma in conjunction with the bond of collective 'victim-hood'. Ronnie Landau found, in the case of concentration camp survivors, that a 'grotesque competition in suffering' emerges within testimonies.[26] Barbara Engelking has also pointed to the 'rivalry in martyrology' that she believes has developed among Holocaust testimonies.[27] This problem is not as extreme in the case of the Kindertransportees, yet it does become apparent that degrees of suffering and victimhood emerge as important denominators in narrators' perceptions of the importance of their story, as well as their credentials as a Holocaust survivor. This process has also encouraged the religious experience of Kindertransportees in Britain to be narrated too closely to these historiographies, which are fundamentally concerned with fears for Jewish survival post-Holocaust.[28]

The process of resettlement has also had an important impact upon developing new historical narratives. The transition of the Kindertransportees from being a child to an adult, and from being deemed a foreigner or refugee to being a citizen, are important processes that impose themselves upon narrative. Gopfert argues that those who migrated to the United States or Israel, as opposed to those who remained in Britain, developed more satisfied narrations of their lives.[29] Gopfert puts this down to their early dislocation from the terms 'foreigner' and 'refugee'. This is because in both the United States and Israel migrants constitute the majority of the population, whereas in Britain an accent alone could differentiate someone as 'different'. The result for those remaining in Britain could include a more difficult process of accessing memories due to prolonged upset and agitation over their situation.[30]

The position of the 'Holocaust' in the collective conscious of the community within which Kindertransportees resettled was an important influence on the development of personal narratives in different locations.[31] In the United States the central position afforded to the commemoration of the Holocaust remains in stark contrast to the centrality of military activity in British Second World War memorial days. The different status this gives to survivors within society has a profound effect upon their narrative.[32]

Personal narratives are also subject to change as a result of more personal factors that arise in later years. The Kindertransportees' narratives have undergone a conscious adaptation due to the narrators' personal needs and wants. Andrea Hammel has issued warnings in her work about the process of constructing or 'reconstituting' one's life story.[33] She argues that the need to narrate one's life story is linked to the process of establishing one's place in the world and clarifying who one is: 'we need to narrate our own life story to locate ourselves in the symbolic world of culture.'[34] Jerome Bruner and Susan Weisser call this the 'invention of self'.[35] Murphy also pursues this line of thought and argues that there exists an innate connection between 'memory, identity and public narrative'.[36] Subsequently, memories and narratives are always changing.

The fluidity of memory is particularly relevant as Kindertransportees become older and memories are recalled from further in the past. The increasing distance of the narrator to the event can make it harder to recall memories. This problem has meant that external sources become increasingly valuable to the narrator in their process of recollecting their story.[37] This is particularly true, for example, in the context of Kindertransportees' testimonies of life at Whittingehame. Drew's collection of over 400 photographic negatives, taken during his time at Whittingehame, has in the last 10 years been generously circulated among Kindertransportees. These images have provided a new means for Kindertransportees to reconnect and reimagine past experiences.

These photographs have impacted on Scotland's Kindertransportees' oral testimonies in a number of ways. Testimonies of Whittingehame residents are more coherent, vivid and alive with detail than those given by Kindertransportees who lack photographic reference. A number of dominant and persistent stories have also arisen within this body of oral testimonies. These memories mirror the images found among Drew's collection. This includes, for example, persistent recollections of Charles Maxwell, the second Headmaster, and his infamous Scottish kilt (see Figure 1). It is also of significance that only Maxwell and Drew have been recorded within this photographic archive, and it is only Maxwell and Drew that are well remembered by interviewees (see Figure 2). Another reoccurring anecdote is that of other residents' misbehaviour in the form of climbing out of windows (see Figure 3). The intention of the absailer is not clear from the photograph, but this image is recounted in the vast majority of testimonies as a tendency among misbehaving residents to exit Whittingehame via the windows. This anecdote correlates with Drew's photographs.

The trend to recite visually recorded events has meant that a form of collective memory has developed. This may overshadow personal anecdotes and diversity. Drew's photographs have rejigged forgotten stories and thrown light on angles

Figure 1 Charles Maxwell.
Source: (MCPC/Drew, photographs).

of life at Whittingehame that some Kindertransportees may not otherwise have recorded. They have filtered out less certain recollections and replaced them with stronger visual ideas about a past experience.

Beyond Whittingehame, Kindertransportees' narratives have also developed a particular 'collective' character, which makes it essential to draw out the individual's personal story. This especially occurred following the 50th reunion of the Kindertransport, which saw Bertha Leverton advocating the group identity of the 'kinder'.[38] In connection to the 'collective silence' that existed in the shadow of Auschwitz, Barnett points to the development of a 'collective narrative'.[39] This frequently stresses group thanks to the British nation juxtaposed against commemoration as Holocaust survivors. This has meant that myths and misconceptions that adhere to a general account of the experience have often been reiterated in narratives.

The interviewee's narrative approach can also be determined by the reason why they choose to tell their story and the practice they have had in doing so. Hammel points to two forms of approach to narrative that have subsequently emerged.[40] These adhere either to the linear approach to developments shaped

Figure 2 William Farinton Drew.
Source: MCPC/Drew, photographs.

by a picture of a perfect transition of events or a disjointed narrative with little cohesion and clarity to the process of exile and resettlement. The rehearsed narrator most often offers a linear approach. This is frequently the result of speaking in schools or taking part in other historical projects. A number of Kindertransportees have given testimonies to the Shoah Foundation's archive and similar projects. Thirty-eight per cent of all Kindertransportees have retold their stories at schools. This figure does not change substantially when narrowed to Scotland's Kindertransportees, of whom 32 per cent have spoken at schools. An unusually high percentage of Kindertransportees (40%) have also chosen to write down their story. The process of writing life stories allows for editing and clarifying memories.[41]

These narrators can subsequently become very familiar with the process of telling their stories. These often remain broad in scope, focusing on the larger events that are better known to their audience. In contrast, some Kindertransportees have never previously spoken about their experiences and, as a result, tend not

Figure 3 Kindertransportee climbing out of a window.
Source: MCPC/Drew, photographs.

to approach their story with as much confidence or certainty. Memories are conveyed through numerous unconnected and fragmented episodes; however, these can offer a more personal reflection on minor incidents.

Narratives are also affected by the message or moral of the story that narrators can often wish to convey. This can produce both positive and negative testimonies. The 'successful' narrative is particularly common among Kindertransportees who speak at schools. These are particularly prone to advocating the 'successful' process of resettlement towards complete acculturation and personal achievement. The development of a celebratory narrative often partners the successful interpretation. These are linked to the commemorative era of the Kindertransport and most explicitly expressed in connection with reunions, memorials or public exhibitions that have occurred.[42] This is often expressed at the forefront of accounts as a personal thanks towards Britain or their hosts. As an example, Bentwich, a leading figure in the welfare network for refugees in Britain, recorded an account in 1956 of Britain's reception of refugees. Bentwich approached the subject matter with a substantial degree of jingoism and took efforts to applaud the British Government and Anglo-Jewry without criticism.[43]

The narrator can also be the victim of a selective memory shaped by nostalgia for the 'good times' and this develops a form of comfort narrative. Nostalgia plays a central role in the relationship 'between remembering and forgetting'.[44]

One Kindertransportee, in 'Alice Remembers', reflects upon the powerful role of nostalgia upon her memories of the war years: 'so cold and clear with snow underfoot and we never felt the cold. Ah, for nostalgia!'[45] Miriam Peskowitz interestingly points to the notion of '*maskilim*' (nostalgic comfort) and its power at distorting events to fit new agendas of recollection.[46]

Nonetheless, these personal narratives - oral testimonies, memoirs, diaries, school journals and letters – have provided a unique insight into the minors' lives in Scotland. School journals of Kindertransportees at Whittingehame have recorded friendships, mundane daily activities and their training experiences, such as learning to drive a combine harvester. Diaries highlight social squabbles between minors, heartache and private feelings.

In the process of unearthing the story of Scotland's Kindertransportees a number of issues arose relating to particular concepts and their use within the publication. The overarching consideration is the nature of the reception, care and the process of resettlement for the Kindertransportees in Scotland. This does not seek to gauge the Kindertransportees 'acculturation' of Scottish culture.[47] It also does not wish to stress that two distinct cultures existed: Scottish and migrant, or that the minors moved from one bracket to the other.[48] A 'type' of Scottish or Kindertransportee 'culture' is devoid of meaning and is not presumed.

The terms 'assimilation' or 'acculturation' have often been associated with the idea of refugee resettlement into new communities. Marion Berghahn has struggled with these issues in her work on refugee resettlement in London. She argues that 'appropriation' is a more suitable term for the process of resettlement into the host community.[49] This places emphasis on the simultaneous presence of many different cultural habits from old and new communities.

The term Kindertransport and its associated group identities have also given rise to problematic generalizations or assumptions. The Kindertransport as a common denominator was not widely perceived as a collective identity until the 50th reunion, which was held in London in 1989. Only at this point did many migrant minors discover for the first time that they were not the only ones who had travelled on an organized transport, unaccompanied by their parents, via the Hook of Holland or Hamburg to Britain. At the 50th reunion, Bertha Leverton inaugurated the commemorative era of the Kindertransport with her welcome 'Hello kinder'. The term 'kinder' has since become entrenched in the popular imagination of the group identity of those who used the Kindertransport. This has strengthened the belief in the uniformity of the episode, and the 'kinder' has developed into a by-word for being part of a monolithic kinship group with one identity and experience. The term 'kinder' has therefore consciously not been used. Instead, the term 'Kindertransportee' has been used. This does not intend to suggest a group identity, but merely identify those minors who were allotted a seat on these transports for minors.

*

The story of Scotland's Kindertransportees would have remained largely forgotten had it not been for the help and diligence of a number of people. The Kindertransportees are the backbone to this project, and I am indebted to all the Kindertransportees who have taken the time to preserve their personal archives, complete new questionnaires and respond to my requests to record their stories. Special thanks must go to Hermann Hirschberger, Rosa Sacherin, Ester Golan and Isaac Telem, along with many others. Their generosity of time, historical diligence and unwavering hospitality has made it possible for their story to be told. I am also indebted to Mike Challis for allowing me access to an archival treasure trove.

Enormous gratitude and thanks must be expressed to Dr Louise Jackson and Professor Jill Stephenson of Edinburgh University. Their guidance, support and academic expertise have been of immeasurable help to me during the course of this research project. I am indebted to Professor Tony Kushner, Dr Wendy Ugolini, Dr Adam Budd, Dr Hannah Ewence, Dr Hannah Newton and Dr Christen Ericcson, who gave me guidance, support and friendship over the course of my research. A personal thank you goes to the team at Sunseeker London, notably David Lewis, Christopher Head and Kim Tilley.

A special thank you is due to my step-mother Linda for her unwavering support and tireless proof reading. I could not have done this without her. Thank you also to my husband Gareth for enabling me to finish every day's work with a smile, to Dad for supporting my ambitions and Mum for inspiring them.

Frances Williams
8th April 2013

Notes

1 See appendix 1.

2 See appendix 2.

3 Wolfgang Benz and Andrea Hammel, 'Emigration as Rescue and Trauma: The Historical Context of the Kindertransport', *Shofar: An Interdisciplinary Journal of Jewish Studies*, 23, 1 (Fall, 2004), 4.

4 Kindertransport Association/Association of Jewish Refugees, Worldwide Questionnaire and database. Scottish statistics are based on 87 respondents who were placed in Scotland out of 1026 returned questionnaires (KA: QU/SUP).

5 Despite these methodological opportunities, much of the focus of this evaluation is residential care, rather than foster care. This is largely due to methodological practicalities and limitations. There exists a large body of personal journals, school diaries and letters from Scotland's residential facilities. These sources provide an unusual insight into the day-to-day personal lives of the Kindertransportees. I have not found a comparable archive for Kindertransportees in foster care on a case-by-case basis. These archives will be used in conjunction with new oral testimonies to draw light upon the individual's story.

6 Geoffrey Hartman, *The Longest Shadow* (New York, 2002), 136.

7 Ibid., 133.

8 Alessandro Portelli, 'What makes oral history different', in Robert Perks and Alaistair Thomson (eds), *Oral History Reader* (London: Routledge, 1998), 67.

9 Donald A. Ritchie, *Doing Oral History: A Practical Guide* (Oxford University Press: New York, 2003)

10 Lynn Abrams, *Oral History Theory* (London, 2010), 19, 21, 22, 23, 24. See also Penny Summerfield, 'Culture and Composure: Creating Narratives of the Gendered Self in Oral History Interviews', *Cultural and Social History*, 2004, 1, 65; Eric Hobsbawm, *On History* (London, 1997); Alistair Thomson, 'Unreliable Memories: The Use and Abuse of Oral History', in W. Lamond (ed.), *Historical Controversies* (London, 1998); Barbara Amougal, 'Doubts over Evidence of Camp survivors', *Jerusalem Post*, 17 August 1986, 1.

11 John Tosh, *The Pursuit of History* (Harlow, 2006) 303; Portelli, 'What makes oral history different', 71.

12 Abrams, *Oral History*, 24; Alessandro Portelli, *The Battle of Vale Giulia: Oral History and the Art of Dialogue* (London, 1997), 9.

13 This made it important at an early stage to clarify my independent academic status as a researcher. The KA and AJR were not involved in my project beyond the initial stage of introduction and expressed no desire to influence or direct my research.

14 Ugolini, Wendy, 'The Internal Enemy "OTHER": Recovering the World War Two, Narratives of Italian Scottish Women', *Journal of Scottish Historical Studies*, 24, 2 (2004), 137–58.

15 Portelli, *The Battle of Vale Giulia*, 6.

16 Lawrence L. Langer, *Holocaust Testimonies: The Ruins of Memory* (New Haven, 1991), 165.

17 Barbara Engelking, *Holocaust and Memory* (London, 2001) 304.

18 E. H. Carr, *What is History?* (London, 1961) 62.
19 Summerfield, 'Culture and Composure', 65–93.
20 Ibid., 68.
21 Ibid., 92.
22 John Murphy, 'Memory, identity and public narrative', *Cultural and Social History*, 7, 3 (2010), 299.
23 Dr Frances Williams private collection of interviews (FWPC)/Noah, Sarah. (FWPC interviewees are referred to using a pseudonym).
24 Ronnie Landau, *Studying the Holocaust; Issues, Readings and Documents* (London, 1998), 3.
25 Murphy, 'Memory, identity and public narrative', 298.
26 Landau, Studying the Holocaust, 5.
27 Engelking, *Holocaust and Memory*, 312.
28 Chaim Bermant, *Troubled Eden; An Anatomy of British Jewry* (London, 1969).
29 Rebekka Gopfert, 'Kindertransport: History and memory', *Shofar: An Interdisciplinary Journal of Jewish Studies*, 23 (Fall, 2004), 21–7.
30 Ibid.
31 Ibid.
32 Ibid.
33 Andrea Hammel, 'Representations of Family in Autobiographical texts of child refugees', Shofar: An Interdisciplinary Journal of Jewish Studies, 23 (Fall 2004), 121.
34 Ibid., 122.
35 Jerome Bruner and Susan Weisser, 'The Invention of Self: Autobiography and its Form', in David R. Olson and Nancy Torrance (eds), *Literacy and Orality* (Cambridge, 1991), 141.
36 Murphy, 'Memory, Identity and public narrative', 299.
37 Tosh, *The Pursuit of History*, 1–2.
38 See Anonymous, ROK, *Kindertransport 60 Anniversary; In Deep Gratitude to the People and Parliament of the United Kingdom for Saving the Lives of 10,000 Jewish and other Children who Fled to this Country from Nazi Persecution on the Kindertransport 1938–1939* (London: RoK, 1999) 15–17; see also 'The Reunion', BBC Radio 4 (FM only), 11.15 a.m., 12 September 2010; Association of Jewish Refugees' webpage relating to the Kindertransport Association's activities in Britain, www.ajr.org.uk/kindertransport.htm.
39 Ruth Barnett, 'The Acculturation of the Kindertransport Minors: Intergenerational Dialogue on the Kindertransport Experience', *Shofar: An Interdisciplinary Journal of Jewish Studies*, 23 (2004), 100–10.
40 Hammel, 'Representations of Family', 121.

41 Kindertransportees have been prolific in writing well-edited autobiographies: Gertrude Dubrovsky, *Six from Leipzig: Kindertransport and the Cambridge Refugee Children's Committee* (London, 2003); Vera Gissing, *Pearls of Childhood: The Poignant True Wartime Story of a Young Girl Growing Up in an Adopted Land* (New York, 1988); Eva Hayman, *By the Moon and the Stars* (Auckland, 1992).

42 See Anon, *ROK;* see also 'The Reunion', BBC Radio 4 (FM only), 11.15 a.m., 12 September 2010; 'The Kindertransport Story', BBC broadcast, IPlayer 29 April 2009; Mark Jonathon Harris, *Into the arms of strangers*, film (Washington, 2001); EGPC/Speech transcripts from the 1989 reunion; EGPC/ Reunion documents for Whittingehame Farm School's Kindertransportees.

43 Norman Bentwich, *They Found Refuge; An Account of British Jewry's Work for Victims of Nazi Oppression* (London, 1956).

44 Mary Chamberlain and Paul Thompson (eds), *Narrative and Genre* (London, 1990), 3.

45 'Alice Remembers' in the Whittingehame Farm School reunion brochure, 21.

46 Miriam Peskowitz and Laura Levitt, *Judaism since Gender* (New York, 1997).

47 Frederick Barth (ed.), *Ethnic Group and Boundaries: The Social Organization of Culture Difference* (London, 1970), 10; See also Marion Berghahn, 'German Jews in England; Aspects of the Assimilation and Integration process', in Hirschfield (ed.), *Exile in Great Britain*, 286.

48 A. L. Epstein, *Ethos and Identity* (London, 1978), 92.

49 Marion Berghahn, *Continental Britons; German-Jewish Refugees from Nazi Germany* (London, 1984), 16.

Introduction

The Forgotten Kindertransportees: A Scottish Experience

> *It is not a small thing, in three years of suffering without parallel, to have given to ten thousand children the opportunity to grow up in an atmosphere of decency and normality, to work, to play, to laugh and to be happy and to assume their rightful heritage as free men and women.*[1]
>
> – Dorothy Hardisty

Dorothy Hardisty's confident statement about Britain's humanitarian rescue of 10,000 children provided my first introduction to the 'Kindertransport' episode.[2] Hardisty's congratulatory tone and self-assured belief in the success of the operation provoked a number of questions: Had this rescue operation really provided a better life for 10,000 children? Who were these children? Where were they accommodated in order to guarantee this level of 'decency and normality' and was this even possible during a time of war? Furthermore, had the children in question shared this optimistic view?

It soon became apparent that many levels of complexity encircle Hardisty's zealous statement. In this context, the word 'Kindertransport' is no longer merely a German noun, describing a transport of children to somewhere at some point in time. It has evolved into a powerful historical term and is understood beyond its German linguistic origins. It infrequently requires translation, is rarely italicized and is commonly stripped of its German pronunciation. Why is this? Adopted by the English language, the Kindertransport now denotes Hardisty's historical episode and this has become synonymous with a part of British and Jewish history.

Yet, our understanding of the Kindertransport episode remains limited and largely excludes the experiences of Kindertransportees sent beyond the perimeters of England. The story of Scotland's Kindertransportees has remained largely forgotten. Scotland's Kindertransportees' experiences reveal a much more complicated picture than Hardisty would lead us to believe existed. The very nature of their Scottish experience underlines the complexity and sensitivity of regional placements. There was no typical experience for the Kindertransportees in Britain. Growing up in Scotland had a unique impact upon their lives during the war years, as well as upon their broader life stories.

With this in mind, what was the Kindertransport really all about and who were the children involved? Over 10,000 minors unwittingly became part of this historical episode when they boarded trains from Greater Germany to Britain between December 1938 and September 1939. The unaccompanied minors were of various denominations and ranged in age from 1 to 17 years. They often did not remain together in Britain, but would be distributed far and wide among various types of care facilities such as hostels, foster homes, boarding schools, convents and residential accommodation on farms.

The transport of minors occurred within a turbulent period of mass migration from Greater Germany and was born from the subsequent immigration policies of Britain in response to this crisis. A migrant problem arose because of the progressively overt anti-Semitic and totalitarian legislation implemented within the Third Reich in the 1930s.[3] Following the acquisition of political power by Adolf Hitler in 1933, legislation progressively stripped Jews and dissidents of their civil liberties, culminating in the Nuremberg Laws of 1935. Their social ostracism reached a climax during a state-condoned pogrom on 9 and 10 November 1938, later known as *Kristallnacht* or 'night of broken glass'. By 1938 the pressure for entry permits to Britain was already extensive; following the annexation of Austria in 1938 and later the Sudetenland in 1939, the number of people seeking migration permits grew to new and unprecedented levels.

Britain's approach to tackling the migrant problem from Greater Germany led to the Kindertransport scheme. The legislative response was not informed by altruistic motivations but driven by fundamental concerns to protect British interests and preserve the status quo. These concerns developed pre-existing legislation that had aimed to curtail the influx of undesirable migrants.[4]

Pressure groups including the main institutions of Anglo-Jewry were not opposed to the anti-alien nature of the British Government's immigration policies. Representative bodies of Anglo-Jewry often sought influence over immigration responses to German-Jewish migrants in order to help prevent a 'Jewish problem' arising in Britain. This primarily intended to protect their community's position in Britain.[5] Tony Kushner draws similar links between Anglo-Jewry's immigration policy and the 'emancipation contract'.[6] The 'emancipation contract', Kushner explains, was an unwritten agreement or code of conduct formed between Anglo-Jewry and the British Government or nation as a whole. This required Jews to observe inconspicuous secular lifestyles in exchange for emancipation. This policy discouraged any special categorization or recognition of Jewish migrants as members of a Jewish nation or 'race'.

To uphold this contract, it was important for Anglo-Jewry to remain at the forefront of discussions concerning Jewish immigration policy and protocol in the 1930s. Anglo-Jewry possessed two highly centralized communal institutions: The Board of Deputies (BOD), who represented the national interest of Jews in Britain, and the Anglo-Jewish Association (AJA), who dealt with international affairs and regional institutions that supplied welfare to the community.[7] Anglo-Jewry also developed a number of specifically migrant-orientated representative institutions: the Central British Fund (CBF), the Central Council for German Jewry (CC), later becoming the Central Council for Jewish Refugees, and the Inter-Aid Committee (IAC).[8]

Anglo-Jewry's institutions coordinated efforts in order to take their proposals for tackling immigration from Greater Germany to Parliament. The events of *Kristallnacht* spurred these developments on. With the help of Lord Samuel Hoare, the Home Secretary, on 15 November 1938 they succeeded in orchestrating a preliminary meeting with the Prime Minister Neville Chamberlain to discuss a new approach to immigration protocol.[9] Policy proposals were then taken to the Cabinet for discussion the following day, after which they were presented to the House of Commons for approval.[10] On 21 November Hoare announced the new immigration policy. This broke from previous immigration protocol based on a visa system and established new terms and conditions for entry to Britain.[11]

The crux of the new approach was the concept of the 'trans-migrant'. The trans-migrant emerged from a loophole in the pre-existing system by being based on migrants in transit or temporary refuge in Britain before imminent re-migration abroad. The trans-migrant was perceived as a less troublesome migrant.[12] The conditions of entry were still bolted to the notion of the 'desirable' migrant, but catered for the 'refugee', a term that did not yet exist in British immigration legislation.[13] It was within this loophole that the Kindertransport took shape.

Within the framework of the trans-migrant, block visas were issued which were based on a number of defined categories for admittance. Louise London has noted six defined categories: emigrants in transit, trainees, domestics, people over 60, Czechs and men bound for the Richborough transit camp.[14] Within these distinctions were differentiations between short-term and long-term migrants, but neither allowed permanent entry to Britain. This approach intended to tackle the backlog of applications for entry permits by essentially cutting protocol and speeding up the process of allocating entry permits to suitable candidates. The block visas enabled entry to Britain based on a list of names and the subsequent possession of identity cards, rather than each individual gaining a visa.

The Kindertransports were orchestrated by utilizing the trans-migrant legal framework and subsequent block visa system. This made use of categories enabling youth migration based predominantly on education or training. Subsequently, the scheme required that the migrants were below 17 years of age and underscored the imminence of their re-migration. The scheme was placed under the jurisdiction of a collection of institutions united under the umbrella organization of the CC in Bloomsbury House, London. Within this body, the IAC were given responsibility for the selection process and afforded 1,000 'non-guaranteed' places per month along with an initial unlimited number of 'guaranteed' places. Non-guaranteed minors were incorporated within the pre-existing umbrella guarantee of 1936 given by the CBF for all Jewish migrants entering Britain at this time.[15]

'Guaranteed' minors required a £50 deposit to cover re-migration from Britain. A large variety of personages, groups and institutions worked to organize guarantees for minors. Working within Bloomsbury House, the IAC provided guarantees for 431 minors, the RCM provided a group guarantee for 3,000 minors and Youth Aliyah (a Zionist organization aiming to train Jewish youth for return to *Eretz Yisrael* and life on a *Kibbutz*) sponsored entry permits for a further 700 minors.[16] Kindertransportees were also sponsored by organizations outside the realms of Bloomsbury House. Rabbi Schonfeld independently led the efforts of the Union of Orthodox Hebrew Congregation and sponsored an estimated 100 Orthodox minors.[17] Scottish Kindertransportees also record being sponsored by Austrian Self Aid, Hechalutz, Bachad, the Church of Scotland, small congregations situated across Britain and of various denominations, Jewish Refugee Committees from outside of Scotland, such as Leeds, as well as the *Jewish Chronicle* and Leith Holiday Homes.[18]

Despite the loopholes of the block visa system, the selection process by which the minors were to be admitted to the scheme was time consuming, wrapped with red tape and strict protocol. Various bodies aided the work of the IAC in the organizational process. The Reichsvertretung der Juden in Deutschland and the Israelitische Kultusgemeinde (Jewish Synagogue Association), based in Germany and Austria, respectively, were responsible for allocating places on transports to minors. In Czechoslovakia this was organized by the independent efforts of the Czech Minors' Refugee Committee and individuals, such as Nicholas Winton.[19] Additional Jewish and non-Jewish institutions were also involved in finding suitable minors for the transports.

The result of these various selection processes was a highly varied collection of minors. The body of historical literature that exists for the Kindertransport possesses an active arena of debate concerning the character and background of the Kindertransportees.[20] This has dealt with the Kindertransportees as a group in a variety of ways. Most common is a tendency to treat the minors across Britain as one collective group. Kindertransportees did not arrive from a 'typical' German Jewish background. Tydor Baumel makes this mistake of over emphasizing the group characteristic as Germanic middle-class, professional, bourgeois and urban.[21] The Kindertransportees did not come from one Jewish community or lifestyle in Greater Germany. Claudio Curio has put forward an optimistic perception that a 'special character of childhood exile emerges' and overlooks the abundance of differences among Kindertransportees.[22] Curio's evaluation is based on the presumed enforcement of the strict entry requirements and procedures adhered to by the Refugee Children's Movement (RCM).[23] These considerations gave preference to minors from desirable social, economic and cultural backgrounds: young, female and with little obvious Jewish affiliation.

However, the Kindertransportees and subsequently their experience lacked uniformity or predictability as a group. The Kindertransportees represented a kaleidoscope of different types of people with contrasting backgrounds, including national, regional and local origins, age, gender, religious affiliation and orientation, family background, social and economic circumstance, as well as their contact with anti-Semitism before migration to Britain. Subsequently, a mixed composition of minors arrived in Scotland.

The mixed character of the minors was the result of the mixed character of the organizations that utilized the Kindertransport. These each possessed their own entry criteria for the minors. This included Zionist organizations working for the relocation of *hachsharot* centres. Youth Aliyah's selection process for an allotted place in a *hachsharot* training centre initially considered only ardent members of a Zionist youth movement and prioritized physical strength.[24] Independent philanthropists, who each advocated different agendas, aided the relocation of orphanages and schools through the Kindertransport to Britain. Allocations were also given to minors who simply needed an escort to privately prearranged accommodation in Britain. This meant that the preferred 'type' of migrant minor varied according to how and why they had gained entry onto the Kindertransport.

The organizing bodies utilizing the Kindertransport also possessed an assortment of religious preferences. These organizations shaped specific schemes and their selection criteria, which ranged from non-denominational to Jewish Orthodox. Within the Zionist movement religious affiliation ranged from Hashomer Hatzair's extreme anti-religious Jewish rhetoric to Bachad's fervently observant Jewish Orthodox character. Organizing bodies also included non-Jewish groups, such as the Quakers or Catholic philanthropic groups, who sought non-denominational or non-Jewish minors.

There was also a significant clash in agenda and eventual split between the two chief organizations involved in the bureaucratic orchestration of the Kindertransport. The Chief Rabbi's Emergency Council (CREC) focused on providing Jewish solutions for Orthodox minors and was fervently opposed to the RCM's secular and partisan approach. Curio's evaluations are drawn from the RCM's selection process, which pandered to the old establishment of Anglo-Jewry and their concerns to minimize the 'Jewishness' of immigrants.[25] This did not represent the criteria of all organizations involved in the Kindertransport.

The absence of one approach, orientation or agenda led to the presence of a cross-section of minors among the Kindertransportees.[26] The Kindertransportees' original religious orientation reflected the Jewish kaleidoscope that existed in Greater Germany: Atheist, Agnostic, Reform, Liberal, Conservative, Traditional, Orthodox, Zionist, 'modern', Sephardi and Secular, non-practising and agnostic backgrounds.[27] Kindertransportees also express a mixture of perceived memberships to either the community of the *Ostjuden* or new Eastern European immigrant class, or that of the *Westjuden*, or old establishment.[28]

These findings support the work of Berghahn, Shulamit Volkov and Henry Wasserman, who have taken steps to challenge views that suggest that a type of German Jewry emerged in correlation with a general move towards secular living and the abandonment of religious life.[29] German Jews did not represent a monotype community who had enjoyed a linear move away from religion and towards secular living and 'assimilation' into the German nation. Secular families could maintain traditional religious practices and express their Jewish affiliation in various avenues of life.

The Kindertransportees were also a mix of boys and girls: 54 per cent females and 44 per cent males (2% did not answer).[30] They came from a mixture of national and regional backgrounds. Table 1 reveals the assorted ratio of national origins of Scotland's Kindertransportees.[31] Among these Kindertransportees there also existed a highly varied ratio of nationalities (47% German, 6% Polish, 34% Austrian, 5% Czech and 6% stateless).

The Kindertransportees also arrived from a wide variety of regions within their homelands: from rural locations and villages to large cities or small towns in urban areas, that is, 23 per cent came from Berlin, while 30 per cent came from Vienna; 6 per cent were from Koenigsberg, 5 per cent from Essen and 2 per cent from Frankfurt am Main. Cities of origin within Greater Germany included Dresden, Hanover, Swinemunde, Gelsenkirchen, Guttstadt, Kassel, Brakel, Nuremberg, Dortmund, Ruhla, Breslau, Neuss, Hronov, Glogau, Brandenburg, Adelsheim and Butow. Only 1 per cent of minors came from Prague and 1 per cent from Danzig. 100 per cent of Austrian minors who were sent to Scotland came from Vienna. However, the high ratio of Berliners and Viennese masks a more complex picture of origins. Many Kindertransportees' parents had migrated to these urban centres in the 1930s in response to increased anti-Semitism and a desire for anonymity.

The Kindertransportees cannot be reduced to a type of migrant, minor, Jew or German. They also did not experience a typical type of journey found among Jewish refugees from Greater Germany. Narratives have too frequently grouped the Kindertransportees with an overarching storyline about Jewish refugees during this period. However, the group characteristic of Scotland's Kindertransportees was responsive to different social, economic, cultural, religious and geographic factors pertaining to their origins. These differences

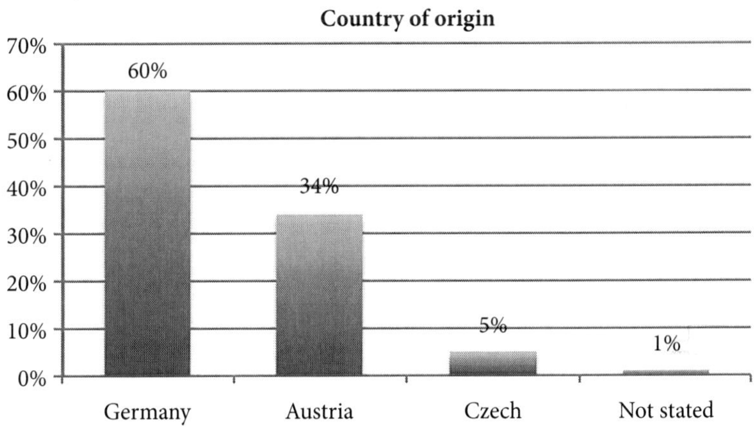

Table 1 Scotland's Kindertransportees' countries of origin.
Source: KA: QU/SUP.

were also heightened by the plurality of the Kindertransport experience once in Britain.

By the close of 1939 an estimated 9,354 minors had arrived in Britain.[32] The first transport of minors took place on 1 December 1938 and consisted of 196 orphans. Following this, an average of 300 minors arrived each week until September 1939. The last transport arrived from Holland in 1940. Upon arrival guaranteed minors were usually dispatched to one of London's main railway stations and on to prearranged destinations; non-guaranteed minors were usually sent to reception camps on the south coast of England.[33] The dissemination of minors in both cases was predominantly short term and led to multiple moves. As a result, in both scenarios Scotland's Kindertransportees had often experienced care in England before or after their arrival in Scotland.

Nonetheless, Scotland played an important role in the reception, care and resettlement story of the Kindertransportees, receiving an estimated 800 dependent minors.[34] Yet, new research continues to marginalize the presence of a Scottish experience among Kindertransportees.[35] Vera Fast's new publication, *Children's Exodus; A History of the Kindertransport,* makes scant reference to Scotland and at one point concludes that the Kindertransportees were indeed the 'strangers within (England's) gates'.[36] Fast fails to provide any detailed information about the varied regional experience in Britain and refers to northern placements as those located in the English midlands. Ruth Barnett's evaluation of experiences of 'acculturation of the Kindertransport minors' actually refers to the national portrait in terms of 'England' and ignores the role of Scotland, Ireland and Wales in this historical episode.[37] This problem has plagued the Kindertransport episode since its conception in 1938. The German Jewish Aid Committee even entitled its published pamphlet for refugee etiquette, 'While you are in England'.[38]

The popularity of a national portrait of the Kindertransport episode has invited an unbalanced body of scholarly work, which focuses on the English-London experience. Past studies have commonly presented a broad national approach, while at the same time offering evaluations that have been drawn from a narrow London experience.[39] Turner's comprehensive investigation into the Kindertransport in Britain focuses on London, along with a select few Jewish hubs in England.[40]

In the wake of the 50th anniversary, Scotland's Kindertransportees chose to form their own commemorative organization, establishing SAROK in 1989, in an effort to prevent the marginalization of Scotland's Kindertransport story.

However, this remained primarily commemorative, focusing on reuniting the 'Scottish contingent'.[41] Rosa Sacherin, a surviving Scottish Kindertransportee and former archivist at Glasgow's Jewish Archives, produced a small commemorative booklet for SAROK.[42] In this, she argues for the need to rectify the prevailing absence of research on the Scottish experience of Kindertransportees. Sacherin continued to try to remedy this hole when she compiled a collection of testimonies from Scottish Kindertransportees.[43]

Despite being linked to national events and a bureaucratic welfare network in England, Scotland's reception and care of the Kindertransportees highlights a particularly Scottish experience and story. The CC, based in London, would oversee the reception, care and eventual re-migration of the vast and ever-increasing numbers of dependent trans-migrants.[44] However, because the CC sought to establish a nationwide welfare network, it pursued a 'system of decentralisation on the lines of the Government Civil Defence Scheme'.

Within this framework, the CC established a number of sub-departments based in London, such as The Refugee Children's Movement (RCM). It also created regional refugee councils and local committees based across Britain, establishing 12 regional headquarters in Britain, with 2 in Scotland (See Tables 2 and 3).[45] The CC's philanthropic system also utilized pre-existing philanthropic networks in Scotland: Jewish and non-Jewish (see Table 4). These were not commercially orientated or state led, but operated within a localized welfare arena, which was regionally fragmented. This system relied on regional bases and local care givers. In doing so, it did not remove the influence of Scotland, its people or its philanthropic legacy.

This approach held similarities to shifts occurring in the philanthropic welfare structure in Britain per se. Finlayson refers to this process as one of an ongoing 'moving frontier'.[46] The process, which tended to graduate towards a centralized system, amalgamated many different organizations, committees and personages. This intended to form a uniform blanket of welfare and philanthropic support across Britain. The process also sought to encourage the transition of power from a smaller voluntary sector to larger state-governed or bureaucratically founded organizations based in London.

The reception policy and procedure afforded to the Kindertransportees on arrival was not fundamentally responsive to their needs. Instead, it was fundamentally reflective of a pragmatic damage control strategy for problematic Jewish migrants, rather than humanitarian concern for Jewish minors suffering persecution in Greater Germany. The Kindertransportees

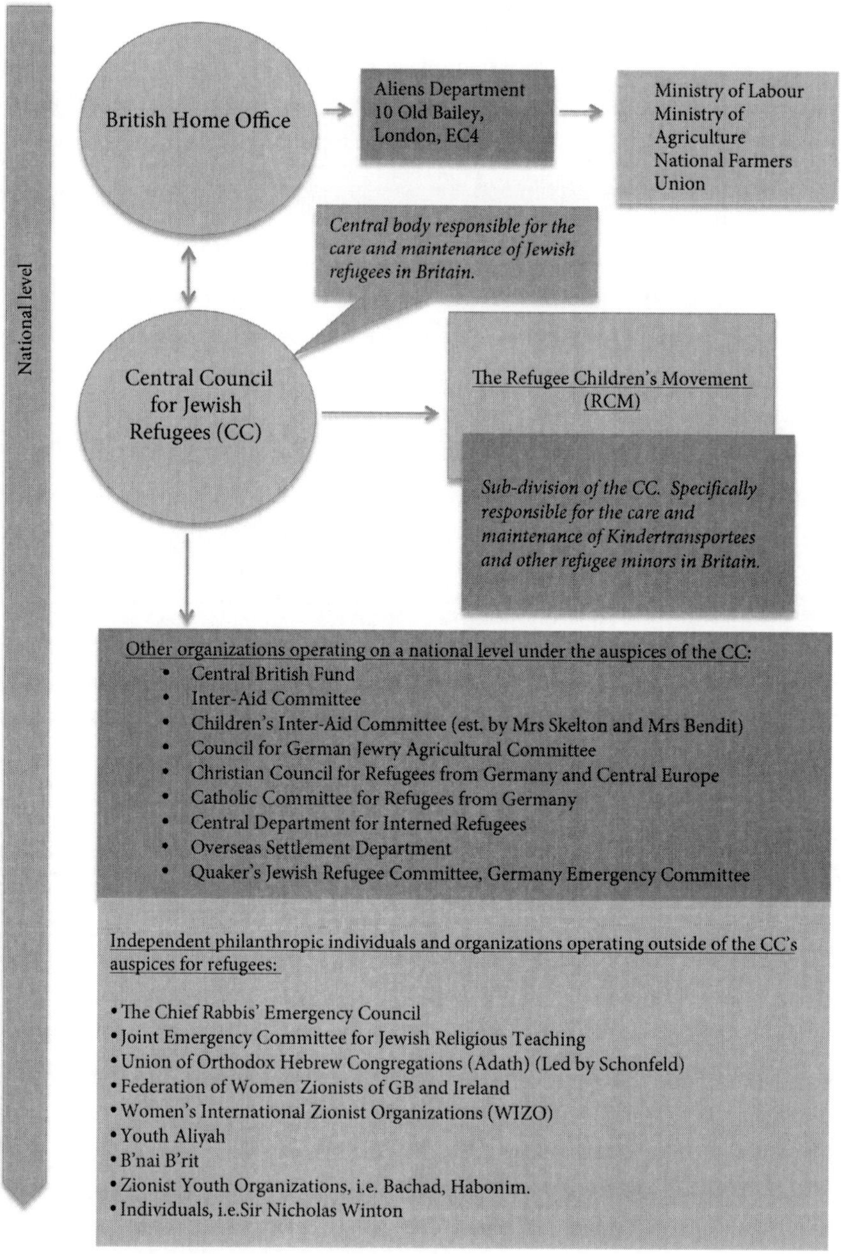

Table 2 Diagrams illustrating the refugee philanthropic welfare network: National level.

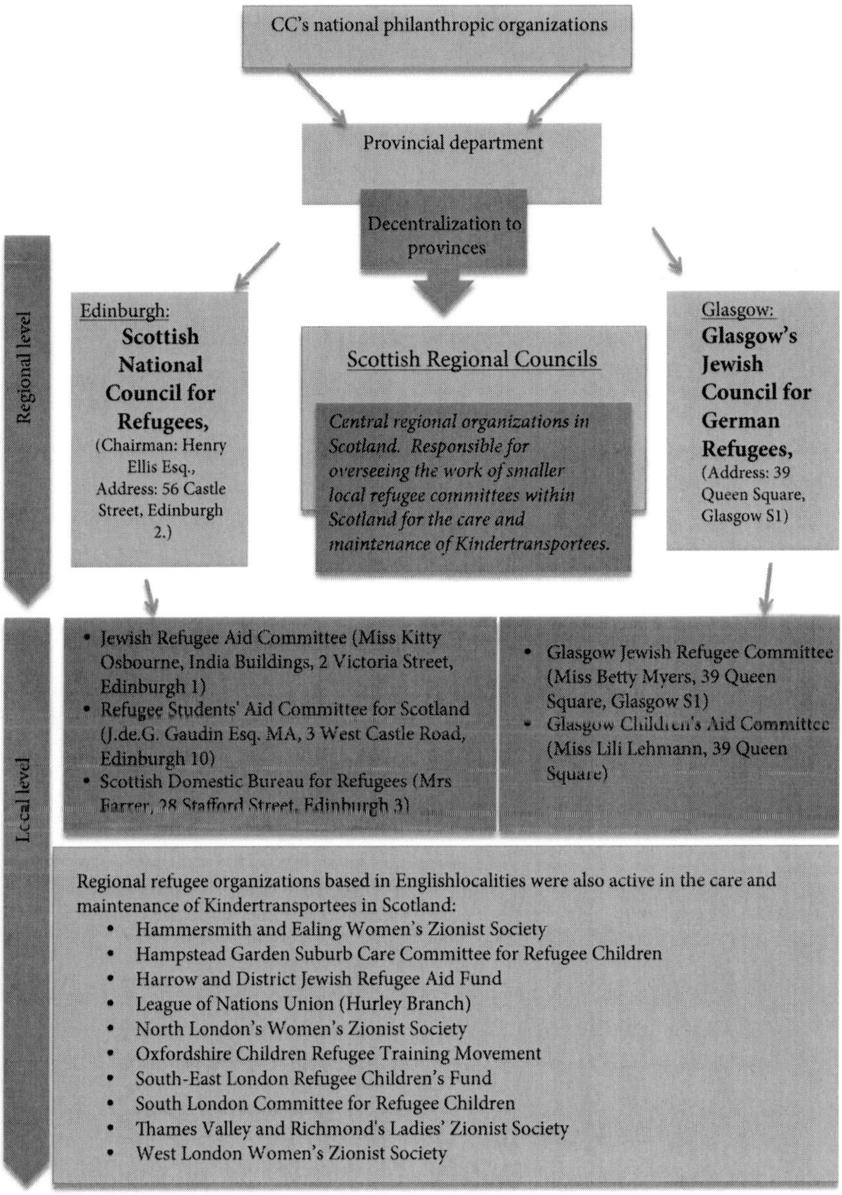

Table 3 Diagrams illustrating the refugee philanthropic welfare network: Regional and local level.

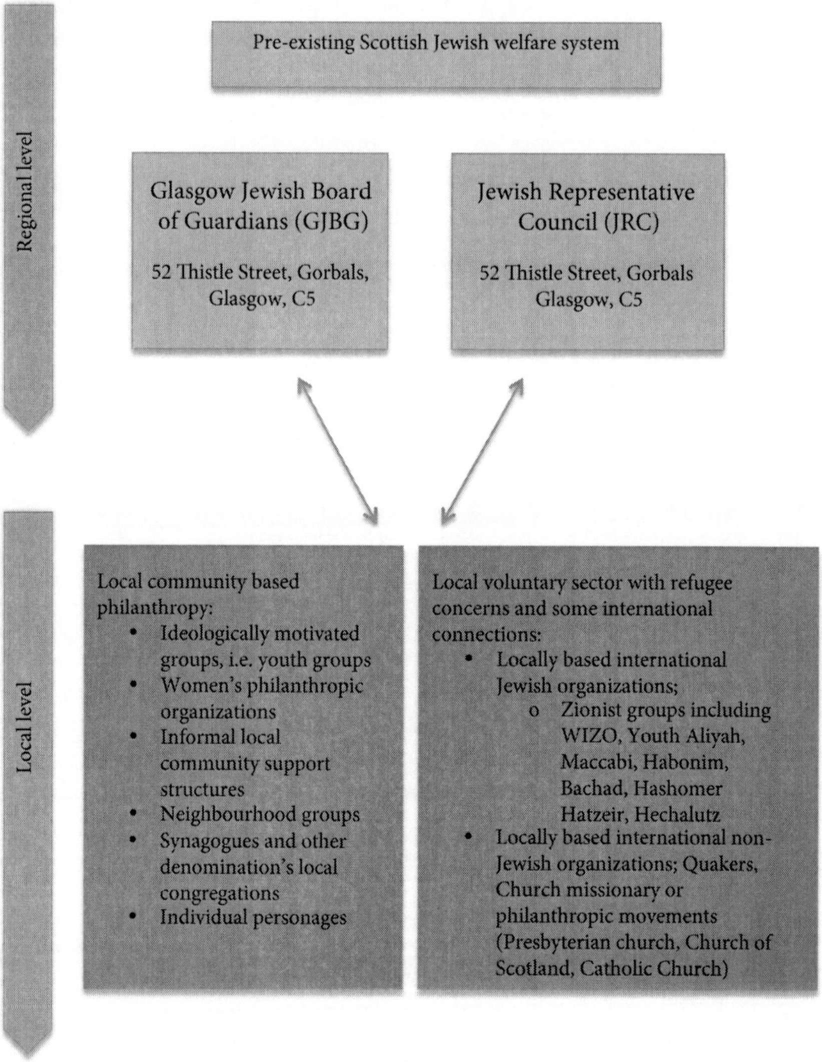

Table 4 Diagrams illustrating the pre-existing philanthropic welfare network in Scotland.

were not received as future British citizens or Scots, nor were they defined as members of a Jewish race.[47] This meant that the Jewish Kindertransportees were first and foremost received in Britain as foreign nationals: German, Polish, Czech or Austrian.[48]

These terms and conditions generated an array of associated labels to their status and these defined how they would be received in Scottish society. These were both positive and negative. As foreign co-religionist, the Kindertransportees were received as a distinctly different Jewish 'type'. This status did not afford them a primary importance to Anglo-Jewry.[49] Anglo-Jewry's institutions remained primarily self-regarding and sought to protect their community interests.[50]

This meant a practical, cautious and pragmatic approach to the reception policy. The Kindertransportee was intended to slot into the community in a manner that would be unnoticed.[51] This focused on distributing the minors far and wide in order to prevent them becoming newsworthy.[52] These efforts did not prevent Kindertransportees from being associated negatively with enemy territories during the war years.[53] They were subsequently also affected by fears concerning the immigrant competitor in the British labour market.[54] Kindertransportees were not to receive any welfare advantages over British citizens.[55]

These assertions do not intend to suggest that there prevailed an ungenerous or scandalous attitude towards refugees in Britain; rather it hopes to underline that the reception and care of the Kindertransportees was responsive first and foremost to the circumstances of the British public and its institutions.[56] With alternative welfare priorities, Kindertransportees became an increasing burden on Jewish communities. The reality of this issue meant that their arrival led to a substantial waning of support and enthusiasm.[57] Flux in support, including Anglo-Jewry, has too often been overlooked in favour of perceptions of Jewish nationalism and Holocaust narratives, which pander to the 'heritage industry's' notion of a unified Jewish people.[58]

In the wake of the outbreak of war, the Kindertransportees' stay in Scotland was temporarily prolonged as they waited for the first opportunity to emigrate. The elongation of their stay meant that their care and nurture in Scotland, during this period of refuge, became an important element of their lives. The secular care and nurture of the Kindertransportees in Scotland drew on a variety of philanthropic ideas and initiatives. However, contrary to popular perceptions, the Kindertransportees' welfare experiences were not necessarily a unique phenomenon. Rather, their care was heavily connected to the surrounding welfare norms and social circumstances during the period. Their care in welfare was a major bridging link for them with Scottish minors.

The Kindertransportees were not cared for within an isolated, self-contained, welfare bubble in Britain. Instead, an enormous range of broader factors within the social, economic and political spheres impacted upon their day-to-day lives. The result of combining a centralized welfare bureaucracy with daily management in Scotland was that clashes, contradictions and lapses in oversight occurred in the Kindertransportees' care.[59] Furthermore, the reality of operating welfare services that lacked adequate infrastructure and operating capabilities left many aspects of their upbringing lacking in anything other than the essentials for survival.[60]

The period was also characterized by experimental approaches to childcare. Criteria for the care of minors or consensus about the meaning of childhood did not yet exist.[61] As a result, care was informed by a haphazard Scottish heritage of preferred approaches to childcare. These approaches to child care in Scotland tended to focus on the physical rather than on the psychological needs of dependents. New initiatives in psychology, psychiatry and psychoanalysis had made little impact, and there remained a persistent ignorance to expressions of psychological problems by care-givers.[62] Instead, care prioritized physical control strategies and solutions to juvenile delinquency.[63] Nonetheless, a distinct lack of supervision and subsequent bad behaviour characterized many Kindertransportees' care experiences.[64]

Middle-class social reforming ideas and a legacy of philanthropic ideology in Scotland played an important role in informing the nurture of the Kindertransportees in Scotland.[65] These influences directed philanthropists to create a care environment deemed suitable for a respectable working-class lifestyle. The result was not only schemes intended to eradicate the working-class ills, but also a lower socio-economic character to provide provisions for Kindertransportees.[66]

The nature of these aforementioned welfare provisions and the manner of care they provided were all moulded by the context within which they occurred. The implications of Britain being at war were far-reaching and overarch Tydor Baumel's theory that the bureaucratic shortcomings were the defining factor in the failure of provisions for Jewish minors during evacuation.[67] The war shaped people's daily lives, creating a unique social situation and a specific position for the Kindertransportee within this scenario. The demands and consequences of war led to a massive disruption in the general pattern of life in Britain. In particular, this created nationwide problems for the community and its institutions and services: welfare, education and hospitals.

The war also affected Jewish life and communal structures. Kushner's evaluation of Anglo-Jewry during this period points to the link between welfare provisions and an overarching breakdown in the very fabric of Jewish life in Britain due to the demands of war.[68] This links to Levin Salmond's evaluation of the 'incalculable' damage by the war to the Jewish social support networks. The war was a catalyst that highlighted pre-existing problems within the community support systems and their institutions' provisions.[69] The war pushed services to their limits and this was particularly true for Jewish education, which suffered an almost total meltdown during the war years. These issues were not remedied during the war years.[70]

Accordingly, living in Scotland during the war had far-reaching implications upon the Jewish lives of the Kindertransportees. The religious life of the Kindertransportees in Scotland was an important aspect of their care and nurturing experience. This aspect of their story has remained highly charged in both the popular imagination and scholarly work about the Kindertransport. At the centre of these debates is the issue of the estrangement of the Kindertransportees from their Jewish roots. This issue has remained one of the main bones of contention in debates about the success or failure of the entire scheme since its formation in 1938. These debates have frequently offered non-pious Kindertransportees an epitaph and mourned this lost generation of Jewish youth due to the religious negligence of their British caregivers.

The religious experience of Kindertransportees in Britain has been narrated too closely to historiographies concerned with fears for Jewish survival post Holocaust.[71] This evaluation is problematic because it has adopted a far too simplistic analogy of the issue by reducing blame to the decision of Jewish or non-Jewish care. Other influences were involved in the Kindertransportees' attachment to their Jewish affiliation. All the Kindertransportees underwent a transition in their Jewish lives and approach to religious piety.

Proselytizing efforts have unhelpfully become entrenched at the forefront of evaluations of non-Jewish care environments. Conversion was a reality and some Kindertransportees did feel pressurized to adopt alternative theologies. However, others found their Jewish life supported and even strengthened in non-Jewish care environments. Furthermore, Jewish care did not guarantee a Jewish life and did not prevent the alienation of Kindertransportees to their Jewish heritage.[72] Jewish care could be found to be inappropriate. German Jewish communities had evolved over time into very different Jewish communities to those found among Anglo-Jewry.[73] The national system for the care of refugees by the dominant Anglo-Jewish communities almost totally excluded the Reform and Liberal synagogues.[74]

The cultural activities of Jewish youth often emerged as the central bond between Kindertransportees and Judaism during the war years. What is often presented as a lost Jewish generation was more accurately a situation in which Kindertransportees adapted to their environments and adopted new bonds to Judaism. Zionism emerged at the forefront of Jewish youth activities in Scotland.[75] The importance of Zionism for Jewish youth during this period has often either been assumed or completely overlooked. It is important to attribute Zionism its proper place in the story of the Kindertransport. The presence of Zionism in the Kindertransport episode and their later lives is not always clear. Zionism was never constant or all-encompassing, and this has caused confusion about its relevance. However, in testimonies it emerges that Zionism was one of the most significant political, social and cultural influences upon many of their lives during and after this period. Zionism created a new understanding of being Jewish within a new social and political framework.[76]

Zionism remained a popular ideology around which care schemes could be tailored. It was not only pushed forward as a suitable approach to the care of the Kindertransportees by ardent Zionist supporters, but was also supported by the mainstream Jewish institutions, such as the BOD and the CC. Pre-*hachsharot* training centres and Zionist youth groups were established across the country to cater for Jewish migrants with the intention of preparing them for making *Aliyah* (emigration) to Palestine. Scotland possessed two pre-*hachsharot* – Whittingehame Farm School and Polton House – and these exclusively catered for Kindertransportees.

Zionism captured the hearts of many of these Kindertransportees. However, for others, the idea of completely shedding their previous lifestyles in order to become pioneers was a terrifying prospect and one that they refused to follow. Many choose to migrate to countries other than Israel, and adopt lifestyles that contradicted the socialist Utopian ideals of the *Olim*.[77]

The fundamental experience of growing up within these residential facilities did, however, have far-reaching implications upon Kindertransportees' life stories. Interviewees argue that they had a particular type of upbringing and nurturing experience due to the specific features of a residential centre. Historians have frequently ignored these issues. Dorit Whiteman and Ruth Barnett have both considered the psychological implications of the Kindertransport upon the Kindertransportees, but failed to connect these impressions to their historical context.[78]

In 1946, the Clyde Report highlighted multifaceted problems that they believed were afflicting Scotland's deprived children living within residential facilities.[79] The report outlined a number of key features that characterized an institutional environment and the likely nurturing experience this would provide for the deprived child. In doing so, the report substantiated previous research by psychiatrists and social theorists, and highlighted a wide array of likely psychological problems that may arise as a consequence of an institutional upbringing.[80] The Kindertransportees' narratives echo the findings of these evaluations.

Kindertransportees use their experiences of residential care to explain the way in which their lives have unfolded. Residential care was felt to have imposed a completely new living environment and upbringing. This was felt to be devoid of familial variables and could not substitute a family or home environment. Kindertransportees believe that their institutional experience was directly responsible for an array of psychological scars.[81] The extent to which these problems actually arose directly because of residential care is not certain, but Kindertransportees do choose to make this connection.

The experience of being a Kindertransportee emerges as an important factor in broader life stories. What is often ambiguous is the particular impact upon Kindertransportees of growing up in Scotland. Kindertransportees often point to the relevance of their specific Scottish geographic locality during the war years. They argue that they possess an important personal connection to Scotland. Yet, they do not claim to be Scottish.

The idea of being 'Scottish' and the Kindertransportees' perception of the meaning of 'Scottishness' is not described in substantive terms or as a certain construct. Instead, Scotland's Kindertransportees reiterate vague, yet powerful popular impressions about all things imagined to represent the 'real' Scotland. These take shape in the form of clichéd symbols of Scottish identity, including consumer items associated with the imagined concept of Scottishness, such as an appreciation of whiskey or tartan.[82] In doing so, Kindertransportees reflect the far-reaching impact that 'Scotland the Brand' and notions of Highlandism have had not only upon tourists, but also upon migrants to Scotland.[83]

Kindertransportees attach themselves to positive public displays of 'Scottishness', most notably linguistic affiliation, whereby, during the course of an interview, an American accent is swiftly reverted to broad Scots. The impression given is that by talking in a Scots accent, the Kindertransportees feel that they swiftly distinguish themselves from English migrants or other migrants, and assert a more authentic Scottish connection. Scots rather than Gaelic is the preferred means to express Scottishness.

Resettlement choices are a useful physical indicator for this evaluation, but they do add to the ambiguity of these connections. Statistical information indicates that the vast majority of Scotland's Kindertransportees (87%) left

Scotland, yet, a range of reasons lie behind their mass exodus.[84] The re-migration of Kindertransportees from Scotland was not only the result of the 'push' factors of Scotland, but, as T. H. Hollingsworth explains, the 'pull' factor also drew many away from Scotland.[85] Forced migration and temporary resettlement in Scotland was not an easy process for the minors. Their integration into their host community in Scotland was by no means a foregone conclusion.[86] During the war years, Kindertransportees often felt homesick and continued to yearn for their homelands.[87] However, the elongation of the Kindertransportees stay in Scotland, due to the continuation of the war, did change their relationship with Scotland. Their migration stories adopted a tri-partite structure, in which they possessed three distinct lives: before migration, Scotland and post-war resettlement.[88] This has had the effect of boosting the importance of Scotland in their life narratives, regardless of whether they chose to remain living within the Scottish borders.

Kindertransportees forged their own lives in new places located across the world. In doing so, they did not forget their Scottish inheritance and often perceive themselves as members of a Scottish diaspora community. Kindertransportees in America, Israel and other distant locations continue to advocate their Scottish roots and heritage. The forgotten Kindertransportees of Scotland cling heartily to the idea of having once been a part of Scotland. They express a profound fondness to all things imagined to be Scottish and a keen abhorrence to all things they perceive as anti-Scottish, most notably the troublesome '*Sassenach*'.

Notes

1 Cited in Barry Turner,. . . . *And the Policeman smiled; 10,000 children escape from Nazi Europe* (London: Bloomsbury, 1990), 1.

2 Dorothy Hardisty was the General Secretary of the Refugee Children's Movement (RCM).

3 See Richard Steigmann-Gall, 'Religion and the churches', in Jane Caplan (ed.), *Nazi Germany; Short Oxford History of Germany* (Oxford: Oxford University Press, 2008), 162; Nikolaus Wachsmann, 'The Policy of exclusion: repression in the Nazi State, 1933–1939', in Caplan (ed.), *Nazi Germany,* 122–43; Sarah Gordon, *Hitler, Germans and the 'Jewish Question'* (Princeton: Princeton University Press, 1984); Marion Kaplan, *Between Dignity and Despair: Jewish life in Nazi Germany* (New York: Oxford University Press, 1998); Kaplan, *Jewish Daily Life in Germany 1618–194* (Oxford: Oxford University Press, 2005); Nicholas Stargardt, *Witnesses*

of War: Children's Lives under the Nazis (London: Jonathan Cape, 2005); Jill Stephenson, 'Nazism, Modern War and Rural Society in Wurttemberg, 1939–45', *Journal of Contemporary History*, 32, 3 (July 1997), 339–56.

4 Geoffrey Finlayson, 'A Moving Frontier: Voluntarism and the State in British Social Welfare, 1911–1949', *Twentieth Century British History*, 1, 2 (1990), 184.

5 See Richard Bolchover, *British Jewry and the Holocaust* (Oxford: Oxford University Press, 2003); David Cesarani (ed.), *The Making of Modern Anglo-Jewry* (Oxford: Blackwell, 1990).

6 Tony Kushner and K. Lunn (eds), *Traditions of Intolerance: Historical Perspectives on Fascism and Race Discourse in Britain* (Manchester: Manchester University Press, 1989), 11.

7 Cesarani, *Modern Anglo-Jewry*, 115.

8 See Turner, *And the Policeman smiled.*

9 PRO/FO/371/22536/250ff, 16 November 1938, cited in Louise London, 'Jewish Refugees, Anglo-Jewry and British Government Policy, 1930–1940', in Cesarani (ed.), *Modern Anglo-Jewry*, 180.

10 PRO/CAB/23/96, 16 November 1938, (Cabinet conclusions, 55(38)5), cited in London, 'Jewish Refugees', 180.

11 *Jewish Chronicle*, 25 November 1938, cited in London, 'British government policy and Jewish refugees, 1933–1945', *Patterns of Prejudice*, 23 (1989/90), 32.

12 Anonymous, *A Defence of the Alien Immigrant* (London: London Committee of the Deputies of British Jews, 1904), 9.

13 See London, *Patterns of Prejudice*; London, 'Jewish Refugees'.

14 London, 'Jewish Refugees', 181.

15 Bolchover, *British Jewry*, 70.

16 Turner, *And the Policeman smiled*, 75; Claudio Curio, '"Invisible" minors; The selection and integration strategies of relief organisations', *Shofar: An Interdisciplinary Journal of Jewish Studies*, 23 (Fall 2004), 44.

17 Turner, *And the Policeman smiled*, 75.

18 (KA: QU/SUP).

19 See Muriel Emmanuel and Vera Gissing, *Nicholas Winton and the Rescued Generation* (England: Vallentine Mitchell Publishers, 1982); see also list of Kindertransportees brought over by Nicholas Winton, http://www.just-powell.co.uk/winton/list.htm.

20 See Curio, '"Invisible" minors'; Benz and Hammel, 'Emigration as Rescue and Trauma', 2–7; Bertha Leverton and Shmuel Lowensohn, *I came alone; Stories of the Kindertransports* (England: The Book Guild, 1990); Turner, *And the Policeman smiled.*

21 Judith Tydor Baumel, 'Twice a Refugee: The Jewish Refugee Minors in Great Britain during Evacuation, 1939–1943', *Jewish Social Studies*, 45, 2 (Spring 1983) 175.

22 Curio, '"Invisible" minors', 42.

23 The RCM's admittance process pandered to fears about providing a catalyst for anti-Semitism in Britain. It was also restricted to criteria of British immigration laws, which welcomed only 'desirable' migrants. Potential foster parents were also at liberty to specify their preferences for particular character traits.

24 *Hadassah, the Women's Zionist Organisation of America; Hadassah and Youth Aliyah* (unknown, 1935); Anonymous, *25 Years of Youth Aliyah* (London: The Children and Youth Aliyah Committee for Great Britain, 1959).

25 Curio, '"Invisible" minors', 55.

26 Alan L. Berger, 'Jewish Identity and Jewish Destiny, the Holocaust in Refugee Writing: Lore Segal and Karen Gershon', *Studies in American Jewish Literature,* 11, 1 (1992) 85.

27 KA: QU/SUP.

28 FWPC/Elijah, Abaigael.

29 See Berghahn, *Continental Britons*; Berghahn, 'German Jews in England'; Todd Endelman, review of Marion Berghahn, 'Continental Britons: German Jewish Refugees from Nazi Germany', *The American Historical Review*, 94, 5 (December 1989), 1389–90; Shulamit Volkov, 'Die Juden in Deutschland 1780–1918', in Lothar Gall A. O. (ed.), *Enzyklopädie deutscher Geschichte*, 16 (Münich, 1994).

30 Ibid.

31 Ibid.

32 Turner, *And the Policeman smiled,* 105.

33 Reception camps included Dovercourt and Lowestoft; See Curio, '"Invisible" children', 46.

34 KA: QU/SUP.

35 Ibid.

36 Vera Fast, *Children's Exodus; A History of the Kindertransport* (London, 2011), 40.

37 Barnett, 'The Acculturation of the Kindertransport Minors', 100–10.

38 HL/MS183/132/4, n.d.

39 E. Baumel, 'The Jewish Refugee Children in Great Britain 1938–1945', Unpublished MA thesis (Bar-Ilan University, 1981); Claudio Curio, 'Verfolgung, Flucht, Retung; Die Kindertransporte 1938/39 nach GroBbritannien', unpublished PhD thesis (University of Berlin, 2006).

40 Turner, *And the Policeman smiled.*

41 Rosa Sacherin, 'SAROK: A history of the Kindertransport in Scotland' (unpublished booklet), 21.

42 See Susan Kleinman and Chana Moshenska, 'Class as a Factor in the Social Adaptation of the Kindertransport Kinder', *Shofar: An Interdisciplinary Journal of Jewish Studies*, 23 (Fall 2004), 28–40; Sacherin, 'SAROK'.

43 SJA/Sacherin's collection of Scottish testimonies; *Scottish Annual Reunion of Kinder: Recollections of Child Refugees from 1938 to the Present* (Glasgow: Scottish Annual Reunion of the Kinder, 1999).

44 HLSC/MS183/384/F1. The CC was an umbrella organization, which incorporated many different philanthropic bodies from across Britain, including Jewish, Quaker and Christian. It also shared its head office with a large number of international philanthropic organizations for Jewish trans-migrants including Youth Aliyah and Bachad. In doing so, the CC was able to maximize its resources and capability to adhere to its guarantee for trans-migrants.

45 HLSC/MS183/384/folder 3, Booklet of Central Council, 1939. See also Appendices 3 and 4.

46 Finlayson, 'A Moving Frontier', 183–206.

47 Bolchover, *British Jewry*, xxvi. The official position adopted by the British Foreign Office and supported by Anglo-Jewry defined Jewish refugees as citizens of a separate European country, not as Jews per se. This was in contrast to their categorization in Greater Germany as members of a separate national and racial group.

48 Geoffrey Alderman, *Modern British Jewry* (Oxford, 1992), 281. In contrast, in Germany to be Jewish was a racial and national categorization.

49 Susanne Hein, 'International Refugee Policy and Jewish Immigration', in Frank Caestecker and Bob Moore (eds), *Refugees from Nazi Germany and the Liberal European States* (New York: Bergahn Books, 2010), 18.

50 Ibid., xii; Alderman, *Modern British Jewry*, 270; Kushner, 'Rules of the Game: Britain, America and the Holocaust in 1944', *Holocaust and Genocide Studies*, 5, 4 (1990), 384; See also Kushner, *The Persistence of Prejudice: Antisemitism in British Society during the Second World War* (Manchester: Manchester University Press, 1989).

51 Kushner, The Persistence of Prejudice, 166, 184; See also Kushner and Katherine Knox, *Refugees in an Age of Genocide: Global, National and Local Perspectives during the Twentieth Century* (London: Frank Cass, 1999), 126–216.

52 Curio, '"Invisible" minors', 41–5; See also Barnett, 'Acculturation of the Kindertransport Minors', 102.

53 London, 'Jewish Refugees', 186.

54 See Richard Anthony, 'The Scottish Agricultural Labour Market, 1900–1939: A Case of Institutional Intervention', *The Economic History Review*, New Series, 46, 3 (August 1993), 558–74; J. Parr, 'The skilled emigrant and her kin: gender, culture and labour recruitment', *Canadian Historical Review*, 68 (1987), 529–51; Alison MacEwen, *Gender Segregation and Social Change; Men and Women in Changing Labour Markets* (Oxford: Oxford University Press, 1994).

55 M. L., Buck, 'Feeding A Pauper Army: War Refugees and Welfare in Britain, 1939–42', *Twentieth Century British History*, 10, 3 (1999), 328.

56 Bolchover, *British Jewry*, 54; Finlayson, 'A Moving Frontier', 1.
57 Tydor Baumel, 'Twice a Refugee'.
58 Kushner (ed.), *The Jewish Heritage in British History; Englishness and Jewishness* (London: Frank Cass & Co, 1992), 1–4.
59 Cesarani, *Modern Anglo-Jewry*, 115.
60 See Lynn Abrams, *The Orphan Country; Children of Scotland's Broken Homes from 1845 to the Present Day* (Edinburgh: John Donald, 1998).
61 Tydor Baumel, 'Twice a Refugee', 181; Bernard Steinberg, 'Jewish Education in Great Britain during World War II', *Jewish Social Studies*, 29, 1 (January 1967), 27. See also Hugh Cunningham, 'Histories of Childhood', *The American Historical Review*, 103, 4 (October 1998); Karin Cavert, *Children in the House: The Material Culture of Early Childhood, 1600–1900*, (Boston, 1992), cited in High Cunningham, 'Histories of Childhood'; Stephen Lassonde, review of Peter N. Stearns', 'Childhood in World History' (New York, 2006), Kriste Lindenmeyer, 'The Greatest Generation Grows Up: American Childhood in the 1930s' (Chicago, 2005); Nicholas Sammond, 'Babes in Tomorrowland: Walt Disney and the making of the American child, 1930–1960' (Durham, 2005), in *Journal of Social History* (Summer, 2007); Anne-Marie Ambert, 'An International Perspective on Parenting: Social Change and Social Constructs', *Journal of Marriage and Family*, 56, 3 (August 1994), 529.

In the 1930s, 'childhood' had emerged in popular imagery and ideology as a distinct and important life period, separate from 'adulthood'. Karin Cavert has argued that the process of change developed over a long period of time between 1600 and 1900: shifting from the 'inchoate adult' to the 'natural child' and then to the idea of the 'innocent child' by 1900. Stephen Lassonde explains that these shifts fundamentally were paving the way towards the development of the modern model of childhood. This is linked to a perception of the child not as a fixed entity and prelude to a predictable adulthood, regardless of care or treatment during this time of maturation, but instead as a view that childhood experiences create the adult. Hugh Cunningham argues that notions of childhood continued to flux between the idea of the child as an agent or as biological determined adults. Even so, by the 1930s, in addition to their economic input, children's emotional contribution and development had emerged as important considerations in the concept of childhood. Children were increasingly viewed as 'malleable creatures subject to socialisation' (Lassonde, review, 1019).

The 1930s represented an important era in which childhood was officially defined. This was partnered by a greater degree of state regulation of the family and childhood. Subsequently, children were increasingly officially distinguished as different from adults. Children tended to be treated as children, rather than young adults. Prohibitions on economic activity, as well as compulsory schooling and emphasis on maternal care developed in an effort to protect childhood.

Nevertheless, unofficially within informal social channels, the cultural invention of childhood continued to be constructed and reconstructed, varying region to region. As a result, the Kindertransportees' experiences as 'children' did not always reflect official policy towards the notion of childhood.

62 Ute Benz, 'Traumatization through Separation: Loss of Family and Home as Childhood Catastrophes', *Shofar: An Interdisciplinary Journal of Jewish Studies*, 23 (2004), 85–99; Macnicol, 'The Effect of the Evacuation', 3–31; John Welshman, 'Evacuation and Social Policy During the Second World War: Myth and Reality', *Twentieth Century British History*, 9, 1 (1998), 28–53.

63 David Smith, 'Official Responses to Juvenile Delinquency in Scotland During the Second World War', *Twentieth Century British History*, 18 (2007), 78–105.

64 See Tammy Proctor, '(Uni)Forming Youth: Girl Guides and Boy Scouts in Britain, 1908–39', *History Workshop Journal*, 45 (Spring 1998), 103–34.

65 John Macnicol, 'The Effect of the Evacuation of Minors on Official Attitudes to State Intervention', in Harold L. Smith (ed.), *War and Social Change* (Manchester: Manchester University Press, 1986), 3–31; See Abrams, *The Orphan Country*. For information on the Environmentalism movement, see Linda Bryder 'Wonderlands of Buttercup, Clover and Daisies; Tuberculosis and the open-air school movement in Britain, 1907–39', in Roger Cooter (ed.), *In the Name of the Child; Health and Welfare, 1880–1940* (London: Routledge, 1992), 72–91.

66 Macnicol, 'The Effect of the Evacuation', 3–31.

67 Tydor Baumel, 'Twice a Refugee', 177.

68 Kushner, 'The impact of British anti-Semitism', 115–37.

69 Abrams, *The Orphan Country*, 170.

70 Ibid.

71 Bermant, *Troubled Eden*.

72 For details on Anglo-Jewry see Todd Endelman, *The Jews of Britain; 1656 to 2000* (London: University of California Press, 2002); C. Hutt & HL. Kaplan (eds), *A Scottish Shtetl – Jewish Life in the Gorbals, 1880–1974* (Glasgow: Unknown, 1984).

73 Miri Freud-Kandel, *Orthodox Judaism in Britain since 1913; An Ideology Forsaken* (London: Vallentine Mitchell, 2006).

74 Steinberg, 'Jewish Education', 39.

75 Braber, *Jews in Glasgow*, 117.

76 Laurence Silberstein, 'Toward a Postzionist Discourse', in Miriam Peskowitz and Laura Levitt (eds), *Judaism since Gender* (New York: Routledge, 1997), 93.

77 Olim were trained pioneers who were to make Aliyah to Israel and establish *Kibbutzim*.

78 Dorit Bader Whiteman, *The Uprooted: A Hitler Legacy: Voices of Those Who Escaped Before the 'Final Solotion'* (New York: Insight Books, 1993); Ruth Barnett, 'The Other Side of the Abyss: A Psychodynamic Approach to Working with

Groups of People who Came to England as Children on the Kindertransporte', *British Journal of Psychotherapy,* 12, 2 (1995), 178–94.

79 See Bob Holman, 'Fifty Years Ago: the Curtis and Clyde Reports', *Children and Society,* 10 (1996).

80 See also John Bowlby, *Maternal Care and Mental Health* (London: Northvale, 1950).

81 Ruth Barnett, *By the Rivers of Babylon: A Kindertransportee's Experience of Uprooting, Exile and Reconciliation* (unknown) 2; See also Berghahn, *Continental Britons*, 300.

82 Emma Combes, Sally Hibbert, Gillian Hogg, Richard Varey, 'Consuming Identity: The Case of Scotland', *Advances in Consumer Research*, 28, 328.

83 Ibid., 330.

84 KA:QU/SUP.

85 Rowland Berthoff, review of T. H. Hollingsworth, 'Migration: A Study Based on Scottish Experience between 1939 and 1964', *International Migration Review*, 5, 4.

86 Berghahn, *Continental Britons*, 9; Berghahn, 'German Jews in England', 288.

87 Peter Gay, *Freud, Jews and other Germans: Masters and Victims in Modernist Culture* (New York: Oxford University Press, 1978), 95.

88 An earlier version of Chapter 6 concerning the migration of the Kindertransportees appears in the collective volume of Andrea Hammel and Bea Lewkowicz (eds), *The Kindertransport to Britain 1938/9: New Perspectives* (Rodopi: Amsterdam, 2012).

1

Protecting the Status Quo: The Reception of the Trans-migrants

> [Scottish people] they were delightful, people say they are very stingy, but that is not true at all they are really generous.[1]
>
> It was shocking, we were ill-treated. When we arrived we were searched and stripped and everything in our cases was taken out and misappropriated . . . it was pretty poor . . . from a hygiene point of view, a few people were very badly injured . . . it was not nice, it was traumatic.[2]

The reception of the Kindertransportees in Britain has often been portrayed as an emblem of the altruistic nature of British philanthropy and publicly celebrated as an example of the nation's humanitarian spirit.[3] This, it has been argued, set Britain apart, as a heroic nation which embraced thousands of desperate Jews from Greater Germany in their time of need.[4] This narrative often vilifies nations that did not admit as many refugees as Britain – the United States, South Africa, Canada or Australia – and presents the Kindertransport as a badge of honour for Britain. It has also ignored the relevance of anti-Semitism or alien hostility from the host nation to the new arrivals. In doing so, it has perpetuated certain images of the child migrants themselves and their reception experience in Britain. These images, which were also used during the period, promote the idea of the desirable migrant and nurtured a celebratory concept of the migration experience.

The dominant narrative that has emerged advertises the migrant as one abounding with gratitude and loyalty to Britain.[5] It has encouraged the emergence of celebrated figures, such as Nicholas Winton, towards whom gratitude and an uncritical celebratory narrative are given.[6] This unbalanced interpretation of the event and the experience have been perpetuated by films and television broadcasts, which celebrate the 'heroism' and underline the overall success story of the Kindertransport.[7] Caroline Sharples has debated the need to go 'beyond the celebratory' narrative and challenge popular images of the 'smiling policeman', in order to form a more critical understanding of the Kindertransportees' reception in Britain.[8] Kushner has also argued that there is an absence of 'critical reflection' and that this has led to a high degree of 'irredeemable sentimentalism' to emerge in the narrative of the Kindertransport episode.[9] This tends to detail a monolithic, successful reception experience in Britain as well as the heroic work of the refugee organization.[10] The 'happy ending' storyline dominates these evaluations and this has reduced evaluations to the issue of good over evil.[11] Sharples believes that this has produced a 'safe story' with 'clear-cut heroes and villains'.[12]

These tendencies have also established a form of competition within Kindertransport narratives. Supporters of the positive 'reassuring narrative framework' have sometimes actively sought to prevent Kindertransportees or researchers contradicting their preferred narrative.[13] Sharples' critical article in *History Today* received a dogmatic reply from Leonard Smith, who entitled his reply 'Thank God for the Kindertransport' and argued that 'by any standards, the efforts of a dedicated band of people in Britain . . . was a cause for celebration'.[14] Ugolini's research has shown that this tendency is not uncommon, whereby the 'elite discourse gains dominance' and interviewees express apprehension of saying the wrong thing.[15]

The uniformity of this positive interpretation has prompted some alternative, more critical, minority views to be put forward. These are predominantly in the form of Kindertransportee testimonies rather than critical academic evaluations. These tend to aggressively challenge the authenticity of positive Kindertransportee testimony and subsequent histories of the Kindertransport. Murphy has shown that this often emerges when participants of a historical episode feel that 'their story was not being represented'.[16] This is particularly true among Scottish Kindertransportees, who express frustration that their Scottish experience has not been included in the 'English' Kindertransport story.[17] Such testimonies often seek to criticize the 'English' story and its prevalence for expressing 'deep gratitude to the people and Parliament of the United Kingdom'.[18]

These approaches, overtly positive or critical, are both problematic, because they form an unbalanced interpretation. They have formed a gulf between interpretations of the Kindertransport. This has encouraged the oversimplification and relegation of interpretations and narratives into two camps. These tend to focus on the level of altruism among their British hosts. Critical narratives stress an unsuccessful reception experience due to inadequate and un-humanitarian characteristics of British philanthropy. In contrast, successful narratives stress the generous welcome and heroic hospitality of hosts. The Kindertransportees' reception in Scotland was far more complex and multifaceted than both these interpretations have previously credited.

It is particularly important to clarify these interpretations because, as the Kindertransport has received increasing media coverage and commemorative authority, an increasingly naïve collective narrative about the episode has emerged in the public imagination.[19] The Kindertransport now possesses its own collection of memorials, most notably in Britain the 1999 statue erected outside Liverpool Street station. These reiterate the preferred image and narrative of the Kindertransport episode: vulnerable children rescued by the British Government. Kushner has referred to this situation as the result of the dangers of the 'heritage industry', which lends itself to the romanticization and distortion of historical episodes.[20] Cesarani has also touched on the problem of the 'commercial exploitation' of nostalgia, which is a particular problem within the public commemorations of the Kindertransport episode.[21] Current events, such as the 50th, 60th and 70th anniversary celebrations of the Kindertransport, have perpetuated this positive lopsided narrative.[22]

Minority views have become ostracized from these national events, mainly because they seek to cut against the grain of the moral of the story. The moral has emphasized a positive lesson learnt by the trans-migrant experience. In contrast, critical interpretations of the Kindertransport have become increasingly popular within Holocaust commemorations and related cinematic explorations.[23] This has encouraged the Kindertransport to be portrayed in a melodramatic form.[24] They have become aligned with Holocaust narratives that stress trauma, loss and victimhood during this period.

Neither the celebratory nor the critical narrative offers a representative evaluation of the event and experience. The Kindertransportees' reception experience in Scotland points to some aspects of both the celebratory and critical narratives, yet it also shows a less exclusive and theatrical episode, moulded by the broader picture in Britain. This was fundamentally shaped by a number of terms associated with their status in Britain. These were ascribed to them officially and unofficially. These associations were not always positive and determined particular features of their reception in Scotland.[25] These features were not unkind nor were they purely altruistic.

New additions to the 'Jewish problem'

The reception of the Kindertransportees in Scotland was shaped by priorities to protect the national, economic and social status quo. Britain's reception of 'Jewish refugees' provided no special favours for the migrants.[26] Instead, it was rooted in 'caution and pragmatism', which was shaped by British wants and needs.[27] The Kindertransportees were not received as 'Kindertransportees', but were deemed trans-migrants from foreign, later enemy territory, and of the Jewish persuasion, an association that carried a multitude of potential dangers for Britain.

Anglo-Jewry were particularly concerned about the impact that an influx of destitute Jewish migrants could have upon their status quo. Anti-Semitism, or the threat of anti-Semitism, was a real concern for Anglo-Jewry at the time.[28] This meant that a fear of anti-Semitism became a central feature in the official reception afforded to the Kindertransportees. Anglo-Jewry felt threatened by the potential consequences of a mass influx of Jewish migrants into Britain.[29] They united to protect themselves against the perceived danger that threatened to provoke hostility.[30] Defensive action was led by a small group of Anglo-Jewry's elite men, who shared a vested interest in protecting their acquired gains in Britain.[31] Anglo-Jewry focused efforts on placating the gentile community and their concerns about Jewish immigrants, along with preventing any future provocation of hostilities.[32] In an interview in 2007, John Grenville argued that Anglo-Jewry's defensive behaviour was relatively normal and to be expected.[33] Grenville argued that as an 'established minority', they felt 'threatened' by the large influx of 'the same minority who are not yet assimilated'. This produced a practical, cautious and pragmatic approach to the Kindertransportees' reception in Britain, which was motivated by self-preservation.

Concern for the prevention of anti-Semitism led to a desire to express the desirability of the new arrivals and the limited impact they would have on the British public. In 1941, the CC disseminated a circular across Britain intended to tackle misconceptions about Jews, entitled 'Jews Some Plain Facts'.[34] The popular press was another important tool for influencing the reception of the new arrivals. It provided a means for promoting certain images and a particular public understanding of the Kindertransportees. Articles sought to underline that the Kindertransportees would not be a financial burden on the British taxpayer. Press reports emphasized that it was the Jewish community that would be financing the new arrivals.[35] In July 1938, the *Scotsman* reported the success of the 'Glasgow Appeal', whereby 'Glasgow-Jewry raised £10,000 for the relief of refugee Jewish children' at a luncheon by B'nai B'rith.[36] In December 1938, the *Scotsman* also highlighted the 'abundance of gifts' for the newcomers, suggesting that they would not require any additional supplies.[37] Later in the month a report of the arrival of Kindertransportees in Edinburgh emphasized that even the 'poorest' members of the Jewish communities were caring for the new arrivals.[38]

Anglo-Jewry also prioritized discretion in the reception process and dictated that the Kindertransportees should be received inconspicuously with minimal public attention. This was in line with normal national protocols for dealing with refugees. If exclusion of refugees was not possible, then the desired alternative was that they should remain 'invisible'.[39] To achieve this, Kindertransportees tended to be scattered to reception areas across Scotland to avoid refugee enclaves. Kushner refers to this as a 'policy of dispersal', whereby Kindertransportees would be filtered individually into various neighbourhoods, with few amenities to enable them to regroup.[40] Their reception would preferably create social isolation for an individual in a private home in a remote location.

Jan was born to Orthodox Jewish Polish parents and grew up in Frankfurt, Germany, before escaping to Scotland upon the Kindertransport. She was fostered by a wealthy Jewish Orthodox family in Pollokshields, Glasgow. She attended the local school before, first, being evacuated to the countryside and later withdrawn from schooling in order to provide her guardian with domestic help and assistance in his garment factory. Despite her lengthy attendance at one local school, Jan was shocked to learn that other Kindertransport children had attended the same school in Pollokshields.[41] She recalls that no effort was made to connect her to other refugee children who lived in close proximity. Jan recalls that she felt contact with other Kindertransportees was 'frowned upon'.[42]

Benson arrived from a small town near Prague, Czechoslovakia, where he had lived with his non-religious, non-practising and totally secular Jewish parents. On arrival, he was fostered in Glasgow. Cared for by an elderly Jewish and Zionist lady, Benson felt totally absorbed into the family and his new community. He attended his local school and joined local youth groups such as Habonim. Benson recalls that, although Kindertransportees lived in relative close proximity, he did not have contact with them: 'I knew one or two of my foster aunt's friends had taken in a Kindertransport child, but the meetings were . . . no'.[43] Kindertransportees in urban hostels were also not encouraged to form enclaves with other local trans-migrants.

Rachel originally lived in Berlin with her politically active and Orthodox Jewish family. At the age of 13 she left on the Kindertransport to Britain. Upon arrival, Rachel was first sent to Dovercourt reception camp, before being sent to a boarding school in Edinburgh. After a short stay at the boarding school, she was first fostered by a poor Jewish family, before being sent to a wealthier Jewish family in Edinburgh. Her second foster family expected her to work as a maid. After running away from this family, she arrived in Glasgow and stayed in the Quaker's Renford Street hostel for girls. The hostel was in close proximity to the Garnethill synagogue, however Rachel recalls having minimal interaction with the neighbouring Kindertransportees:

> I had to begin with no contact with Glasgow's Jewish community. When I stayed in the hostel, only once do I remember going up to the boys' hostel for Passover, a Seder meal.[44]

A fear that the new arrivals might provoke undue hostility towards Jews meant that efforts were made to minimize the relevance of their Jewish heritage.[45] A concern for the link between anti-Semitism and the growth in strength of National Socialism encouraged support for this strategy. Articles frequently referred to the children as 'non-Aryans' rather than Jews.[46] The *Scotsman* devoted articles to explain the existence of non-Jewish Jewish refugees.[47] These reports suggested the accidental and limited strength of their Jewish association. In November 1938, the *Scotsman* reported the plight of 'a little Austrian boy of partly Jewish blood'.[48] In May 1939, the *Scotsman* explained that a significant number of German 'Jews' had never previously realized that they were Jewish and that many of these people had previously been members of the Hitler Youth and soldiers in the German army.[49] In later years, when the popular press sought financial support and hospitality from the general public, it focused on the Christian Kindertransportees.[50]

This strategy meant that the Kindertransportees were labelled and received primarily as refugees and foreigners. *The Times* almost totally excluded references to the Kindertransportees' Jewish affiliation in reports about their settlement in Britain. Instead, articles solely referred to the new arrivals as the refugees of various foreign origins.[51] Between 1938 and 1946, only 6 articles appear with reference to the 'Jewish refugees', while 159 reported on the 'refugees'.[52] In February 1939, *The Times* referred to the 'Polish refugee children' entering Britain, with only one discreet reference to their Jewish affiliation.[53]

Furthermore, Anglo-Jewish and Scottish Jewish communities did not receive the Kindertransportees as Jewish brethren. The Kindertransportees possessed different cultural, social, economic and religious orientations to Scotland's

Jewish communities. Emil Fackenheim was an independent German Jewish refugee in Scotland. Fackenheim has written about the enormity of tackling the sense of alienation towards Jewish hosts and the significance of local prejudices held against refugees by these Jews in Scotland.[54]

This meant that their reception experience was entangled with prejudices held by the Jewish communities. Fundamentally, these remained rooted in the perceived distinction between the *Ostjuden* and the *Westjuden* Jewish communities.[55] Simplistically, the former was based on one's connection to an Eastern European Jewish heritage and one's affinity with *shtel* culture and strict Orthodoxy. *Westjuden* tended to define a secular non-pious Jew. Collins' research has argued that there existed in Glasgow an ongoing level of tension between the *Ostjuden* and *Westjuden* communities.[56] The former, for example, believed that the *Westjuden* had taken too many steps away from Orthodoxy and lost their Jewishness. Collins has described this social conflict as one of 'mutual contempt', whereby each felt superior to the other.[57] Existing animostities were intensified with the arrival of German Jews who possessed a very distinct Jewish culture to Anglo-Jewry.[58]

As German Jews, the Kindertransportees could feel snubbed by both Anglo-Jewry's *Westjuden* and *Ostjuden* communities. The Kindertransportees were predominantly *Westjuden,* yet a significant number did come from an *Ostjuden* background. Both types of associated Jewish communities received the Kindertransportees in Scotland. A number of more secular, or *Westjuden,* Kindertransportees were fostered within the *Ostjuden* Glasgow communities in the Gorbals or Pollokshields. These Kindertransportees recall being received with suspicion. The children were in some cases suspected or accused of not being Jewish because of their liberal religious preferences or secular physical appearance.[59]

Elijah was born in 1924 in Warsaw, Poland, and grew up in a small rural village, before later moving with his family to Danzig, Germany. He had a non-Orthodox Jewish upbringing and attended the local Polish school in Germany. Before arriving at Whittingehame in Scotland, Elijah was fostered by a strictly Orthdox Jewish family and struggled to integrate into the pious lifestyle of Anglo-Jewry. Elijah believes he was ostracized and experienced prejudice towards him because of his *Ostjuden* characteristics.[60] Gertrude Goldberg was born in Vienna, Austria, in 1930. She was one of Schonfeld's rescued children who used the Kindertransport to reach safety. She was initially sent to Sunderland and recalls the impact of her 'continental clothes' in defining her alien non-Jewish background.[61]

The reception of the Kindertransportees by Anglo-Jewry was also marked by preconceptions concerning their German Jewish origins and social or economic backgrounds. Anglo-Jewry was predominantly of *Ashkenazi* origin. John Grenville has argued that the Anglo-*Ashkenazi* community was acutely aware of the *Sephardi* legacy of the German Jewish elite and a legacy of prejudiced behaviour to their native community. This, Grenville clarifies, was expressed in resentment towards the new arrivals as 'stuck up German Jews' from middle-class families. Kindertransportees had gained their place on the Kindertransport because they had been vetted as desirable migrants. In many cases, this was based on their privileged social or economic status in Greater Germany. Rachel's first foster family were poor and of *Ostjuden* heritage. Rachel believes her reception by the family was coloured by class prejudices.

> I think the problem was these people originally came from Poland . . . they always felt that the German Jews did not treat them well and that came across. There was no feeling towards me. It was resentment more than anything else . . . they made us feel very inferior. . . . I felt hurt within myself because I was considered not worthwhile . . . it doesn't leave you ever.[62]

Refugees, enemy aliens and foreigners

In the absence of Jewish associations, the label 'refugee' was chosen as a more appropriate categorization for the Kindertransportees. At the Annual Refugee Conference of 1942, discussions focused on the 'ideological war' that was being fought by the refugee organizations in order to prevent the general public from perceiving the refugees as enemy aliens or new members of a 'Jewish problem'.[63] In Scotland, extensive regional planning and consideration for a suitable term was granted to reduce their impact. The Scottish National Council (SNC) afforded a large amount of time to clarify the correct public designations to be used in reference to the new trans-migrants in the region.[64] In an effort to clarify them as different from 'German Germans', the SNC agreed that the description 'Refugee from Nazi (or Fascist) Oppression' was self-explanatory.[65] It was felt that this was sufficient to combat enemy alien associations with the new arrivals without drawing unnecessary attention to their Jewish heritage.

Unfortunately, this exposed Kindertransportees to the stigma associated with being a refugee. Interviewees have stressed the relevance of their associated status as dependent poor refugees in Scotland upon their reception experience into Scottish society. This label was felt to carry a heavy load of social stigmas and class-related prejudices. In March 1944, the *Scotsman* entitled a report 'Asylum to Refugees; Scotland's Share and Problems'.[66] This reported that, although the public attitude to refugees was not 'anti-refugee', it remained essential to foster better relations by way of 'mutual and reciprocal contacts'. This report is a good indication of the limited level of social engagement by Scots with their local refugees and the subsequent level of 'otherness' this encouraged. In 1944, Joseph Sachs argued that to counter these social divisions the central goal should be to 'make the refugee cease to be a refugee in the shortest possible time'.[67]

Kindertransportees recall the associated stigma they felt attached to their refugee status as that of being of a poor immigrant class. Max Milner was an adult trans-migrant in Scotland during the war years and attended Edinburgh University. He recalls an incident of being rejected by a member of the local Jewish community because of the derogatory status his landlady afforded him, describing him as a 'penniless Jewish refugee from Germany'.[68]

Kindertransportee Edna came from an Orthodox German Jewish family. Using the Kindertransport, she travelled directly to Whittinghame. After 2 years at Whittinghame, Edna was sent to a domestic work placement in a rural location in East Lothian. During this time, she recalls feeling very isolated and being treated unfavourably, 'like a refugee'.[69] When introducing Jan to friends, her foster family in Pollockshields referred to her as 'our refugee'.[70] Jan interpreted this relationship negatively and felt that the use of the term deemed 'something inferior to the average person'.[71]

The stigma associated with being a refugee was felt by some Kindertransportees to have been interpreted with fear and assumptions about their bad character. Rachel, who was fostered in Edinburgh before moving to a hostel in Glasgow, remembers that 'fear of immigrants coming into the community' led to 'quite a lot of anti-refugee feeling . . . you were warmongers'.[72] As a result, Rachel states that she 'always felt an outsider, I always felt that I had to be very careful and I never felt part of it, I couldn't, I knew I was a refugee and I knew there were limitations to what I could expect and what I could demand'.[73]

Michael Warton was born in Könnigsberg, East Prussia, to Orthodox Jewish parents. He attended the local Gymnasium before being forced to leave due to anti-Semitism. His Zionist mother had always sought migration to Palestine, but was forced to send Michael on the Kindertransport to foster parents in Glasgow. In Glasgow, Michael lived with a wealthy Jewish man and attended the local grammar school. At age 15 he took an apprenticeship in a furniture factory in Glasgow. During this time, he lived in the Jewish-run Garnethill boys hostel and attended night school. Michael explains that the issue of being a refugee greatly affected his relationship with the Glasgow Jewish community:

> The people that we got to know . . . they called us refugees and they looked at us as refugees, whether we were Jewish refugees was something else . . . they didn't necessarily ascribe the Jewish aspect to us, but we were refugees and no matter what we did, whatever employment we were seeking that was the tag that was attached to us.[74]

The term 'refugee' did not detach the Kindertransportees from associations with foreigness or being deemed alien immigrants. *The Times* predominantly referred to the Kindertransportees as 'Polish refugees' or 'German refugees', with emphasis on their countries of origin.[75] The minors' foreign origins, rather than Jewish affiliation, defined them as outsiders to the wider community. In contrast to Kushner's perception of the close relationship between being Jewish and experiencing xenophobia, in Scotland the connection between religion and alien status was predominantly directed against members of the Catholic faith.[76] Ugolini has shown that Italian immigrants experienced this double bind in being both foreign nationals and Catholics, leading to xenophobia and prejudice in Scotland.[77] This, Ugolini argues, prevented them from being accepted during the wartime as anything other than the 'enemy "other"'.[78] Abrams's work also draws attention to the focus in Scotland on the disparity between the Scottish Presbyterian community and the 'foreign' Catholic community.[79] This does not appear to be the case for the Jewish Kindertransportees, whose otherness was predetermined by their foreign national origins.

The Kindertransportees were German, Czech, Polish and Austrian, and this feature defined who they were in Scotland, namely foreign migrants. Fear and distrust of foreigners was prevalent across Scottish society during this time period.[80] There was a prevalence of anti-alienism in Glasgow against all immigrants, most especially towards the Irish and Italians.[81] This culminated in 1940 with violent anti-Italian riots, enforced relocation of migrants or internment.[82] Such cases of violent outbursts and everyday antagonisms worked as a reminder to migrants that they held a vulnerable position in Scottish society and continued to possess an alien status in Scotland.[83] In 1939, Neville Laski of the Board of Deputies of British Jews stated that 'the English are not a people who take easily to foreigners' and this appeared true also for the Scots.[84]

The Kindertransportees' foreign origins are frequently highlighted in interviews as remaining to be a barrier to their authentic 'Scottishness' in later life. Edna believes that she was considered 'not so much as a refugee but as a foreigner'.[85] Kindertransportees reiterate the idea of needing to have been 'born and brought up' in Scotland to qualify as a real Scotsman.[86] The terms 'birth, blood and belonging' have been underlined as determinants to authenticity of a true Scottish identity.[87] The Kindertransportees' stress that they lacked these credentials and stress the endurance of their foreign accents prevented them from ever being a proper Scot.[88]

Kindertransportees argue that Scottish Jewry shared these beliefs, along with others linked to Scottish nationalism. This, it has been argued, created a unique tribal identity among Scottish Jews. Rachel, who has remained in Glasgow to the present day, still feels the pressure of exclusivity of the 'Scottish club' and particularly the 'Scottish Jewish club':

> When people ask me what I am I say "I am British", there is no question about it, but I cannot say that "I am Scottish", I find that for one reason difficult. I feel secure being British. Scottish have got a . . . they are really quite clannish. So I don't say I am Scottish . . . people will say "well you are not really Scottish are you" . . . being British you can hide a great deal.[89]

The Kindertransportees were not Scottish-born and did not feel that they were invited to be members of the 'club'.

As non-Scots there arose issues connected to their reception as alien immigrants who may one day seek employment. This included a concern about the collective impact they could have, given the opportunity, as a cheap labour force. The popular press offers an interesting insight into the depth of concern felt in Scotland towards the new migrants and those seeking to gain permits to enter Britain. In January 1938, the *Scotsman* wrote of the need for protection against the potential immigrant 'invasion' of the labour market.[90] In July 1938, Sir Samuel Hoare explained that immigration restrictions needed to remain stringent 'for economic reasons'.[91] These concerns questioned the 'absorptive capacity' of Britain and the subsequent impact this could have on 'existing standards of living and labour, or create unassimilable alien communities'.[92]

Concerns about the damaging immigrant were paramount in the formal negotiations between Anglo-Jewry and the British Government, and these subsequently shaped national strategies for the Kindertransportees' reception in Britain.[93] The Aliens Acts of 1905 and 1919 defined the conditions for their entry to Britain. At the forefront of these terms were concerns about the British economy and the rights of the native labour market against foreign competition.[94]

In 1939, the British Trade Union Council (TUC) declared their 'fears of unfair alien competition' and sought a new cap on the number of refugees admitted to Britain.[95]

A reception policy would adhere to pre-existing restrictions and prohibitions for immigrants to Britain per se. This dictated the fundamental nature of the Kindertransport, that of being a 'children's' transport. This would only be open for those undergoing either education or training. It also prohibited minors over the age of 17 who would pose an immediate potential threat to the labour market. The assumption was that they would have left Britain before they reached an employable age. The Kindertransportees were also to be unaccompanied by their parents, who could also challenge British workers' jobs. British citizens and the economic well-being of the nation took precedence over concerns for refugees from Greater Germany.

These restrictive conditions came to the forefront of the Kindertransportees' reception experience in Scotland. This was especially significant as their stay became elongated and their need to seek employment became inevitable. Britain was only gradually recovering from mass unemployment and a financial downturn during the 1930s.[96] The Kindertransportees were a potential threat to Britain's workforce and the unemployed seeking work. The Central Councill (CC) cautioned Jewish migrants not to threaten the labour market or undertake any activity that might remove an opportunity from a British national.[97] Migrants were to be received into a limited pool of working environments, with heavy restrictions on the conditions of work. These opportunities were in industries that lacked a labour force, such as domestic service and agriculture.[98] The CC enforced terms and conditions for the way in which trans-migrants could enter work and how they should behave in this environment.[99] This emphasized their secondary position to any British citizen.[100]

The Kindertransportees' status in Britain, as a restricted migrant labour work force, did not prevent them being received as a surplus of cheap unregulated labour. This proved to be appealing to employers and potential caregivers. Foster carers have been recorded as seeking to exploit the Kindertransportees for cheap labour. Female Kindertransportees were sometimes received into families as domestic help, rather than as new members of the family.[101] Rachel recalls that upon arrival at her foster home in Edinburgh, 'I then became a maid . . . a domestic . . . no more schooling . . . schooling was finished'.[102] Another Kindertransportee recalls that her experiences at the first two foster homes in Glasgow were awful as she was used first as a domestic help and then as a nanny.[103]

Kindertransportees could also supplement the family's income if they left school early and found outside employment. Many Kindertransportees were expected to begin full-time employment at 14, the legal school-leaving age until 1947. Isabel lived in a small agricultural village in Germany with her large, yet poor, Conservative Jewish family. Her parents sent her and her two sisters to Aachen to avoid anti-Semitism, and eventually put them on the Kindertransport. On arrival in Britain she was sent to numerous foster homes in England. She was evacuated with one of her foster mothers to Kemnay, Scotland. Isabel recalls that she was educated until she was 16, when she was expected to go to work.[104]

Hano Fry lived in Hamburg, Germany, with his non-practising and non-religious parents. After his parents divorced, he moved with his mother to Berlin, where he attended the local Gymnasium. He left on the Kindertransport to a prearranged foster placement with a parson of the Church of Scotland in Scotland. Fry felt that his foster family returned him to Glasgow because he refused to provide them with an extra household income.[105] Thereafter he lived at the Garnethill hostel in Glasgow. Farmers would also utilize Kindertransportees as cheap labour hands, especially during harvest times.[106] Kindertransportees who attended both Whittingehame Farm School and Polton House recall their experiences working on neighbouring farms in East Lothian with little if any financial reward.[107]

Living in Scotland during the war years meant that as refugees and foreigners the Kindertransportees also became suspected enemy aliens. Bernard Gainer's research has stressed that the public reaction to the 'Alien invasion' during World War I developed into extreme forms of Germanophobia, whereby Dachshunds were found disembowelled.[108] This situation emerged once again during World War II.[109] This became increasingly overt as contingency plans for safeguarding Britain's home front from the enemy during wartime developed. This prioritized the control and policing of any potential enemy alien spies.

The fear of the 'alien invasion' peaked in May 1940 and public support shifted towards internment of all foreign nationals. The popular press suggests that during this period there was little opposition to the move. In August 1940, one reader of the *Scotsman* wrote that he knew a refugee who feared 'Nazi agents in this country' were watching him.[110] The writer concluded that, due to this threat, he believed it was also in the refugee's interest to be interned. *The Times* had already declared by 14 September 1939 that 'it is indeed right that the public should be ceaselessly on their guard, but they need not constitute themselves unofficial bloodhounds'.[111] In May 1940, a meeting of the philanthropic refugee organizations at Bloomsbury House underlined their support for the Government's internment policy.[112] In the summer of 1940, the CC had instructed refugees to spy on one another.[113]

Much of the official reception policy for the Kindertransportees during the war years was based on these national security concerns, and was heavily marked by a period of distrust by the general population, Jewish and non-Jewish. For 9 per cent of Scotland's Kindertransportees, this feature of their reception experience in Scotland was epitomized in their eventual classification as enemy aliens and by internment.[114] In July 1940, 11 Kindertransportees at Whittingehame Farm School who had turned 16 were required to 'appear before a Tribunal' in Edinburgh.[115] A teacher at Whittingehame, Drew, wrote in 1940 of the distrust by the tribunal of the training schools' *Kupah* (communal bank).[116] Norman Bentwich recorded that of Whittingehame's 40 male students, over 16 were eventually interned in a 'barricaded racecourse' in Edinburgh.[117] Nathan lived in Vienna, Austria, before leaving on the Kindertransport for Britain. Upon arrival he was initially sent to Dovercourt reception camp, before being sent to Whittingehame Farm School. Nathan was one of the unlucky residents at Whittingehame who were interned.[118]

Kindertransportees living in private foster care were also subject to internment. Ariel grew up in Vienna, Austria, with his Jewish parents. His father worked as a banker and lawyer. Via the Kindertransport, he was sent to a non-Jewish, male, Danish, immigrant, foster parent in Edinburgh. His foster father helped his parents escape Germany, where they initially worked in Birmingham as domestics. Due to fears concerning the alien migrant, Ariel and his father were interned. Ariel was sent to York Internment camp. Fry was interned for 3 months in 1940 before being released to continue his studies.[119]

The second quotation used to open this chapter is from an interview with Henry Wuga and recounts his traumatic reception experience during internment.[120] Wuga lived in Nuremburg, Germany, before leaving for Britain on the Kindertransport. On arrival he was fostered by a Jewish lady in Glasgow. Following the designation of Perth as a protected area, Wuga, at age 16, was expected to register as an alien. Failing to do this led to his internment. Wuga was shunted around various internment facilities. These included St Vincent Street remand home, which was also used for those awaiting sentence as juvenile offenders or children in need of care and protection, Mary Hill's Barracks in Glasgow with a number of German prisoners of war, Donaldson School in Edinburgh, an institution for deaf and dumb children, York Race Course internment camp and later Warth Mills internment camp, before finally being sent to Peel camp on the Isle of Man. Wuga recalls the whole experience of incarceration as being traumatic and unsettling. Wuga gave the opening quotation for this chapter in reference to his reception at Warth Mills camp, a disused cotton mill.

Kindertransportees in remote and relatively isolated hostels or training farms also recall feeling that anti-alienism became an influencing factor in their daily lives. Edna, a pupil at Whittingehame, recalls that 'anti-Semitism was not a factor, but as soon as war broke out anti-alienism was felt very strongly by us. . . . In Germany we were considered as Jews and in Britain we were considered as Germans, as enemy aliens'.[121] Leslie Brent, who was cared for in Bunce Court in England, believes that his reception was marked by a lack of distinction between a 'German German who was potentially a spy or potentially a Nazi and a Jewish German, who had just escaped from Germany as a refugee and who was as anti-German as they were'.[122] Many Kindertransportees who were deemed friendly aliens were still received as potential spies and threats to the national interest. This developed a varied pattern of 'tolerance and intolerance'.[123]

Temporary migrants become dependent minors

The trans-migrant status of the Kindertransportees was another central feature to their reception experience in Scotland. Essentially they were being received as temporary charges and not as permanent migrants. Information given to the general public about reception facilities, such as Whittingehame, reiterated their fundamental goal for training the young migrants for life abroad and their 'imminent departure'.[124] The British Government also made efforts to promote a general understanding of the temporary nature of the trans-migrants' entrance to Britain. In November 1938, the Home Secretary, Sir Samuel Hoare, explained his stance on refugees, declaring that 'refugees who intend to be trans-migrants are generously treated and special consideration is given to young children'.[125] Herbert Morrison, appointed as Home Secretary in October 1940, underlined that the Kindertransportees were to rejoin their parents abroad as soon as possible.[126] As early as November 1938, the *Scotsman* reported that assurances had been secured that the entry of 200 children on a temporary basis was not 'the thin edge of a wedge to open the door to extra Jewish migrants'.[127]

The temporary aspect of being a 'trans-migrant' was therefore at the forefront of the Kindertransportees' reception experience. As trans-migrants they were received as temporary visitors and were not expected to remain in Britain for very long. Their further migration was widely viewed as imminent. The *Scotsman* repeatedly reported the 'temporary' basis of their stay and predicted their imminent departure overseas to join their parents.[128] Only gradually does the popular press express a growing awareness of the elongation of the refugees' stay in Britain. In December 1938, the *Scotsman* predicted that at the most 'some may remain in the capital as long as two years'; however, most would have migrated by then.[129]

The outbreak of war temporarily suspended migration plans, but it did not end the intentions of the scheme to direct the trans-migrants to other countries as soon as possible. Strategies to aid onward migration from Britain remained extremely important.[130] In January 1941, the *Scotsman* reported that the Kindertransportees at Whittingehame continued to be trained for migration to Palestine despite the temporary impossibility of this plan because of the war.[131] Even as late as March 1944, with the close of war in sight, public discussions revolved around the notion that the refugees would be returning to their homelands.[132]

The Kindertransportees were not received as future British citizens. This meant that little attention was paid to forming lasting relationships with a local community. Kindertransportees frequently reflect that the local synagogue, rabbis or members of a Jewish community made no noticeable effort to contact them while in Scotland.[133] Reception placements were predominantly arranged as temporary solutions.[134]

The elongation of the Kindertransportees stay in Britain made developments and changes necessary to the structure and workings of the philanthropic network that was to receive them in Scotland. These changes were important in defining their reception experience. Anglo-Jewry and the British Government had agreed that the new migrants were not to burden the British taxpayer. Accordingly, the CBF and representatives of Anglo-Jewry provided pledges for the trans-migrants' financial needs while they remained in Britain.[135] This financial guarantee enabled more trans-migrants to gain entry permits to Britain as group certificates were issued. The Kindertransport scheme was one such group certificate. Subsequently, Anglo-Jewry became the guarantors of a large number of dependent trans-migrants.

In response to the heavy burden that the new migrants posed, a nationwide refugee welfare network was established. This was centrally structured around the CC in Bloomsbury House, London. The CC maintained primary control and authority over the migrants' welfare in Britain through the guise of various specific sub-departments.[136] The Refugee Children's Movement (RCM) was specifically responsible for the social welfare of the trans-migrant minors in Britain and the Kindertransportees fell under its jurisdiction. In order for migrants to be dissemintated beyond the feasible scope of BH in London, responsibility and management were disseminated to regional councils and local committees across Britain.[137] In Scotland, two regional councils were formed, the Jewish Council for German Refugees (JCGR) in Glasgow and the Scottish National Council for Refugees (SNCR) in Edinburgh. These councils were responsible for overseeing the activities of ten locally based committees across Scotland.[138] A further ten locally based committees were established in the regions. In Glasgow, for example, these included the Glasgow Refugee Committee (GRC) and the Glasgow Children's Aid Committee (GCAC). Edinburgh also possessed committees, most notably the Edinburgh Refugee Committee (ERC).

Pre-existing philanthropy in Scotland was also utilized by the CC for regional care solutions.[139] In Glasgow, the local welfare network was relatively united by 1939. The Glasgow Jewish Board of Guardians (GJBG) and the Glasgow Jewish Representative Council (JRC) collectively supervised the pre-existing Jewish welfare system at 52 Thistle Street, Gorbals. The GJBG/JRC oversaw a network of community-based activities, undertaken by many different individuals, groups and organizations on a local level. By the 1930s, this was a relatively united social welfare network with a functional support structure that included successful fund-raising operations.[140]

Despite the egalitarian picture, this suggests, the system developed a hierarchical philanthropic structure. This closely mirrored an ongoing process that was occuring in Britain, in which philanthropic jurisdiction was shifting from the local and voluntary sector towards a centralized and more bureaucratic structure. The Kindertransportees' reception was responsive to this new philanthropic system.

The emergence of a philanthropic hierarchy brought with it power struggles and new political negotiations. The Kindertransportees' reception was shaped by these political developments, which had resulted in an atmosphere of ongoing tensions and competing agendas. Tensions existed within Jewish philanthropy as a result of the rise of a new immigrant class.[141] The rise of a new *Ostjuden* political elite within Jewish philanthropy and representative organizations introduced new Orthodox Jewish orientations and overt Zionist agendas.[142] These cut against the preferences of the 'cousinhood', the old Jewish political elite. Most notably, the Jewish Board of Deputies experienced a coup by the Zionist lobby. This new faction openly derided the 'cousinhood's' preference for discretion and apologist approaches to politics. This political competition was also locally alive in Scotland. In Glasgow there occurred an important rise in the population size and political significance of the Russian and Polish Jewish communities.[143] This resulted in the relocation of the leading philanthropic organizations, the GJBG/JRC, from Garnethill to the Gorbals, the domain of new Jewish settlers.

These political movements were challenging the old establishment's monopoly over philanthropic agendas and policies. This meant that policies and agendas for the Kindertransportees' reception often appeared contradictory or in conflict. Arieh Handler worked within the CC and orchestrated the reception of Kindertransportees in Britain. He recalls that there was 'a lot of friction' within the community, which led to clashes over policy and protocol. Rabbi Schonfeld and the Chief Rabbi's Emergency Council (CREC) condemned the RCM for their openly non-denominational policy for receiving Kindertransportees in Britain. Schonfeld felt their pragmatic approach to religious care did not give enough weight to Orthodoxy or Jewish environments.[144] The reception of the Kindertransportees was caught in the middle of this tug of war for control. Schonfeld and the CREC even went as far as 'kidnapping' Kindertransportees from non-denominational care placements by the RCM, in order to relocate them to Orthodox facilities.[145]

There were also ongoing power struggles between different philanthropic organizations incorporated within the CC's umbrella. The concept of the CC was ambitious, because it sought to unify a complex web of fragmented and sporadic, local and regionally based, philanthropic administrative systems from across Britain. Philanthropic organizations in Scotland adhered to an array of different orientations and agendas: refugee, Jewish, Zionist, secular or Christian. This created a chaotic and often overlapping welfare network for the Kindertransportees' reception in the region. London states the prolific occurrence of cross-membership and 'co-options' within the CC.[146] The geographic distance of Scotland to the CC in London made the situation more complicated.[147] This meant, as Gottlieb also argues, that regional bodies were active in Scotland, but none enjoyed real authority and no regional centre of control emerged to offer governance to their activities.[148] In this environment, it was difficult for the national system to provide efficient leadership or direction for a reception policy in Scotland.

The superficiality of binding a fragmented philanthropic network and the limitations to the CC's reach into Scotland meant that the Kindertransportees' reception was shaped by confusion and a lack of governence. The CC had removed Scotland's philanthropic autonomy and disabled its ability to direct a regional Jewish welfare network for migrants. Scottish schemes for migrants were formulated and approved in London by the CC. Protocol, decision-making and management strategies were made by a small body of London's male Jewish elite.[149] Cesarani refers to this power structure as one of 'oligarchy and plutocracy'.[150] Within the CC's reports, Scotland continued to be recorded as a subheading under England and to be treated as a regional rather than as a national unit.[151] Decisions and procedures were made in London and relayed to Scotland. This created an official reception policy that was formal, impersonal and English.

The governing monopoly that the CC held over the reception of trans-migrants also meant that state interests were infused into localized Scottish philanthropy. The CC's contract with the British Government for entry certificates and visas meant that particular national agendas based on state interests had to be adhered to by local philanthropists. The existing 'mixed economy of welfare' in Britain per se was moving towards a greater degree of centralized state regulation.[152] This sought to implement regulated and approved standards of care across Britain. In accordance, national protocols and formalities were filtered down the philanthropic hierarchy of the CC to Scotland for the reception of the Kindertransportees. This meant that the Kindertransportees' reception received an added layer of red tape and official procedure.[153]

The RCM also maintained an autocratic role in determining the reception of the Kindertransportees in Scotland at the expense of local caregivers. This again determined that the official policy for the Kindertransportees' reception in Scotland was more reflective of national agendas and English welfare preferences than of Scottish preferences. There existed important distinctions between Scotland's philanthropic heritage and England's preferences.[154] Scotland possessed a unique legacy of short-term boarding-out placements, rural crofting relocations of urban delinquents and small-scale residential care. Scotland was unable to challenge English directives because it did not possess an organization comparable in size to the CC.[155] The pre-existing Jewish representative bodies of Scotland – Glasgow's Jewish Board of Guardians and the Jewish Representative Council – had also failed to reach spheres of influence comparable to the Board of Deputies in London before the mid-1930s. Subsequently, the Kindertransportees' reception had to respond to English procedures and protocol. It was therefore an 'official' English policy of reception, not a Scottish one.

However, the RCM's bureaucratic predominance was coupled with a limited level of jurisdiction or information being disseminated to Scottish caregivers. This meant that the Kindertransportees in Scotland were received with a lack of knowledge. The Kindertransportees' personal records were kept in Bloomsbury

House, London, except for a period of evacuation when they were relocated to another location in southern England. The CC refused to 'transfer papers of refugees from London to regional committees'.[156] Any specific information had to be requested from London on a case-by-case basis. This affected the day-to-day decision-making about the care of the children and important decisions continued to be redirected to London.[157]

The RCM also never afforded Scotland's Kindertransportees a figure *in locos parentis*. In May 1939, a conference was organized in Edinburgh to consider a 'local children's guardian committee', something that had already been established in other cities.[158] This committee was to supervise the Kindertransportees in the locality, 'to try to find guarantee homes . . . to examine the bona-fides of a family offering to take a child . . . and to provide whole or in part for the children who came in as "non-guaranteed.[159] The committee was formed from 18 societies, with Lord Russell as President and James Watt as Chairman. However, this committee never possessed actual guardianship of the Kindertransportees and, as indicated above, lacked information to do so. Steps to clarify the Kindertransportees' official guardian in Britain were not taken until 1944, before which guardianship had been unofficially assumed by the RCM.[160] However, guardianship of the Kindertransportees in Scotland was never resolved. In 1944, Kindertransportees in England and Wales were legally placed under the sole guardianship of the RCM's Chairman, Lord Gorell.[161] However, in Scotland Gorell was only appointed 'tutor' to the Kindertransportees.[162] The failure to clarify guardianship of Scotland's Kindertransportees meant that their reception was marked by uncertainty about Scotland's responsibility to or liabilities for the individual minor.[163]

Furthermore, the transition to a centralized and nationwide philanthropic welfare system, based in London, actually worsened care standards and financial weaknesses. The CC sought to incorporate pre-existing welfare facilities and philanthropic organizations to create a nationwide blanket of trans-migrant welfare. This would envelope regional infrastructures in order to enlarge reception options for the CC. The result in Scotland was that pre-existing facilities and philanthropic organizations, mainly in Glasgow and Edinburgh, became overloaded with dependent minors. This weakened an already overstretched and small Jewish welfare system.[164] Anglo-Jewry failed to take active measures to enlarge provisions in response to the increased demands from trans-migrants.[165] The added pressure led to the almost total collapse of their financial strength.

The CC's effort to establish a more uniform and equal blanket of welfare financially weakened Scotland's main centres of Jewish philanthropy – Glasgow and Edinburgh – because it required funds from wealthier areas to support under-funded areas. In order to do this, the CBF, the central financial division for the CC, amalgamated the fund-raising efforts of the Jewish communities across Britain into one financial resource. This meant that Scotland's funds, which had previously been channelled directly into local Jewish welfare facilities, were now sent to London before being redistributed across Britain. This created a financial deficit for Scotland.

This was felt to be particularly unfair in Glasgow, where philanthropic fund-raising had continued to yield successful revenue. The Glasgow communities were extremely active in fund-raising. The *Jewish Echo* advertised fund-raising ventures, such as 'Glasgow Aid for Whittingehame House'.[166] This appeal brought in £7,000 from the Women's Appeal Committee. The Glasgow community promised 140 covenants and pledged £25,000 for the Kindertransportees.[167] This was a disproportionate amount, which could have provided handsomely for the reception of the Kindertransportees in Glasgow had it not been siphoned off to London.

The deficit in Scotland, after the redistribution of monies, meant that the region received the Kindertransportees with limited resources. Despite Glasgow's appeal channelling £1800 to London, they had received only £737 85s in return by 1940.[168] Additional expenses needed to be claimed in writing by the regional committees and organizations directly to London.[169] In November 1942, the schedule of claims for 'Scottish maintenance' was recorded and included claims for projects such as Polton House, amounting to £127 17s, and for organizations such as Scottish Xian, amounting to £107 30s.[170] Because Glasgow received the largest proportion of refugees in Scotland and consequently undertook far more initiatives and incurred greater costs, it in particular developed a deficit. In November 1942, the expenses claimed by Aberdeen amounted to just £9 15s, while Edinburgh claimed £24 13s. In comparison, Glasgow claimed £132 21s.[171]

Subsequently, a tenuous relationship developed between the regional philanthropic organizations and the CC. This was worsened when more Kindertransportees were sent to Scotland. In 1941, the GJRC estimated that an average of £520/month was required for the maintenance, welfare and administration costs of the refugees.[172] Reports of the CC record that 'towards the end of the last year correspondence took place between the Glasgow Committee and the London office in which the former alleged that under an arrangement made between Sir Maurice Bloch and Mr I. M. Sieff, 50 per cent of the money collected in Glasgow was to be retained by them for the maintenance of local refugees'.[173] Mr Bakstansky and Mr Stephany of the CC questioned the legitimacy of this arrangement and would not authorize it. Subsequently, a shortfall in finances continued for Glasgow, despite their formidable fund-raising.

These difficulties meant that it was not in the interest of Scotland to receive more Kindertransportees. The Kindertransportees had to be received in a manner that would keep costs low and the burden of care as manageable as possible. In contrast to Gottlieb's perception that considerations for practical maintenance of refugees came before financial practicalities, it emerges that for the Kindertransportees in Scotland financial considerations and limitations remained core to the character of their reception and care.[174] Decisions were based on an evaluation of cost and financial feasibility. The lack of funds meant that care was based on minimal expense.

A lack of funds meant that foster care continued to be the preferred care solution by both the GJBG/JRC and the JCGR. Philanthropy focused on 'mutual aid' and community 'self-help', whereby the 'private individuals would bear the expense'.[175] The *Scotsman* reported that the trans-migrants were themselves to take responsibility for generating financial 'self help'.[176] Kindertransportees who could not be channelled into self-supporting facilities, such as foster care, were sometimes returned to London. By 28 March 1939, Beatrice Latter of the Glasgow Jewish Council wrote to 'Mrs Rosenfelder' that she was 'sorry to say, that at the moment we have so many applications on our books that it is impossible to take on any more. . . . As a matter of fact we have found it necessary to return a number to London'.[177]

The financial pressure caused by the costs involved in organizing care placements meant that Kindertransportees often recall feeling that they were only reluctantly accepted, or chastised for adding extra costs when they required relocating. Rachel decided to leave her second foster family in Edinburgh because she felt she was being exploited as domestic help. She arrived uninvited in Glasgow and consequently experienced a disapproving reception. She recalls:

> They were livid with me for arriving in Glasgow and they said you had better go back into domestic work. . . . They were really angry with me. That was the Glasgow Jewish Refugee Committee. I gave them extra work . . . it cost money for me to be in Glasgow. What business had I to come to Glasgow when I had had a bed to sleep in, in Edinburgh.[178]

Shifts in opinion

It is important to note that the reception of the trans-migrants by Scottish society was not uniform or consistent. Public attitude changed towards the trans-migrants between 1938 and 1945. Their reception was at times marked by overt expressions of humanitarian concern and sympathy for the problems afflicting Jews in Greater Germany, while at other times it reflected a greater degree of indifference, intolerance or even hostility. These shifts were not linear and progressive, but fluctuated in both directions during the period.

Initially, attention was focused on the desirable nature of the young migrants. Support and enthusiam for the scheme required that the Kindertransportees be viewed as good children, innocent victims and potential supplements to families without children. Anglo-Jewry placed extensive care on the selection process for the Kindertransport scheme. This sanctioned only 'desirable' migrants to be included on the transport to Britain.[179] This policy was 'self-regarding' rather than 'other-regarding'.[180] These differentiations meant that the selection process was marked by prejudice against the 'undesirable' child.[181] Bentwich argues that 'everything possible' was done to restrict entry to desirable young minors who would suit foster care-givers' wish lists, rather than prioritizing the urgency of each child's case.[182]

The reception policy of the Kindertransportees intended to uphold the high standard of migrant procured through the strict entry process and subsequently maintain favourable public opinion towards the migrants. The RCM's criteria and process of elimination included psychological and physical verification.[183] This involved a medical examination, along with an investigation into previous behavioural habits. This included school reports and character references. This system was prevalent within the wider migrant selection process, which allowed only certain 'types' of Jews to be helped.[184] Rigorous examinations were also used in the organization of the Basque evacuation to Britain. The 4000 Basque migrant minors underwent a second medical examination on arrival in Southampton and would be designated coloured ribbons according to their condition: 'clean', 'verminous' or 'infectious'.[185] Once in Britain various strategies sought to prevent any slip into deviancy or ill health.

The popular press was used to stress the desirable social backgrounds of the children. In December 1938, the *Scotsman* reported of the good appearance and social quality of the Kindertransportees.[186] Kushner has highlighted the tendency within Mass Observation reports to present the Kindertransportees as well-behaved children, settling into their new homes successfully.[187] In December 1938, the *Scotsman* reported that 'happy children' arrived in the city of Edinburgh, emphasizing the notion that as children they were automatically good, happy and desirably natured.[188]

The Kindertansportees were also portrayed as children, with little focus given to the teenage migrants. By the 1930s the concept of the 'child' as distinct from the 'adult' had developed in informal and formal channels of child care.[189] This led to the child being increasingly viewed as innocent and in need of protection.[190] Appeals for public support nurtured this image to best exploit humanitarian sympathies for the innocent child victim. Reports in the popular press, such as the *Scotsman*, stressed that fund-raising was for the 'children'.[191] The media and *Picture Post* presented the Kindertransportees as happy, grateful and 'utterly innocent' vulnerable children.[192]

The Kindertransportees were also received as potentials for adoption. The popular press and Jewish organizations promoted the image of the vulnerable child orphan. In December 1938, the *Scotsman* reported on the young migrants' orphan status.[193] By January, the *Scotsman* had reported that the Government did not allow adoption 'at this stage', suggesting that the door was open for future adoption of foster children.[194] Rabbi Schonfeld, the leading Orthodox Jewish philanthropist for the Kindertransportees, wrote in January 1939 that 'most of our children are partly orphans as their parents are in a living tomb'.[195] The presentation of the Kindertransportees' bleak parental future makes it unsurprising that there were many requests for orphans.[196]

Nonetheless, archives of various journals, such as *The Times* and the *Scotsman*, reflect a lull in general enthusiasm and attention from the British population towards the new arrivals following the outbreak of war. For the most part, between November 1938 and September 1939, the popular press avidly followed the story of the Kindertransportees' arrival in Britain. The frequency of reports suggests an initial high level of interest from the general public, while the tone is indicative of a significant level of philanthropic ambition for the trans-migrant children's cause. In July 1938, a group of Scottish citizens wrote to the *Scotsman* to express their sense of, what Kushner has referred to as, Christian 'philo-Semitism'.[197] They wrote that they felt 'morally responsible for the sufferings of our fellow-men' and that 'Christianity and democracy dare not let slide this chance of acting together for the good of all mankind'.[198]

However, following the outbreak of the Second World War in September 1939, there is a notable absence of attention or interest in the migrants. At this point, ambivalence appears to become the most suitable adjective to describe public opinion towards the trans-migrants.[199] Reports become preoccupied with matters of the war effort and British citizens' daily lives. This temporarily changes in May 1940, when agitation about aliens in Britain dominates headlines, with scaremongering stories and subsequent responses.

This pattern was also partnered by shifts in the level of opposition towards the trans-migrants. It is important to note that as support fluctuated so too did opposition to the trans-migrant cause. Archives of leading journals reflect ongoing conversations and debates between members of the community. A significant number of scare stories emerge in the popular press that report undesirable behaviour of trans-migrants. *The Times* frequently reports on various examples of criminal activity by 'refugees'.[200] Alternatively, reports emerge that stress the positive contribution being made by refugees to the war effort. In April 1944, the *Scotsman* reported on the successful integration into the war effort and loyalty to Britain of the trans-migrants. At the same time, Kindertransportees' testimonies also express the growing anxiety by hosts due to their charges' extended stay and the reluctance of hosts to receive Kindertransportees.

Scotland's host community were neither altruistic nor uncharitable in the reception of the Kindertransportees. Subsequent philanthropy was not characterized by a kindred spirit and humanitarian crusade for refugees, yet, nor was it shaped purely by uncharitable gestures or uncompromising policies. It is unhelpful to reduce these evaluations into two opposing camps that advocate either British altruism or Kindertransportee victimhood.

The reception of the Kindertransportees in Scotland was based on an acceptance criteria for migrants shaped by 'self-serving motives of countries' and their citizens.[201] This does not mean that Britain's policy towards the Kindertransportees was ungenerous or lacking in moral attributes, rather that these terms have limited relevance in this discussion. The practical process of receiving the trans-migrants could be driven by sympathies and humanitarian goals, but at the root were greater humanitarian concerns for British citizens, especially during a time of war.

Notes

1 FWPC/Ranita.

2 Wiener Library, Association of Jewish Refugees oral history collection, 150 interviews by Bea Leckowitz (WL/BL), no. 74.

3 Stephen Adams, 'Sir Nicholas Winton the British Schindler meets the Holocaust survivors he helped save', *The Telegraph,* 4 September 2009.
4 'WWII Rescue train trip recreated', BBC News, 4 September 2009.
5 See Bentwich, *They found refuge*; 'The Kindertransport Story', BBC broadcast, IPlayer 29 April 2009; John Presland, 'A Great Adventure; The story of the Refugee Children's Movement', *RoK*; FWPC/Sarah, Noah.
6 Robert Hall, 'Czech evacuees thank their savior,' BBC News, 4 September 2009; Stephen Adams, 'Sir Nicholas Winton the British Schindler meets the Holocaust survivors he helped save,' *The Telegraph,* 4 September 2009.
7 'WWII Rescue', BBC; 'Into the Arms of Strangers'.
8 Caroline Sharples, replies. *History Today* 54 (May 2004), 5.
9 Kushner, 'The Kinder: A Case of Selective Memory?', in Kushner (ed.), *Remembering Refugees, Then and Now* (Manchester: Manchester University Press, 2006), 144.
10 Turner, 'Policeman smiled'; Alan Gill, *Interrupted Journeys: Young Refugees from Hitler's Reich* (Sydney: Simon and Schuster, 2004), 156.
11 Ibid., 144–5.
12 Sharples, 'Kindertransport; Terror, Trauma and Triumph', *History Today*, 54 (March 2004), 3.
13 Ugolini, 'The Internal Enemy "OTHER"', 143.
14 Leonard Smith, 'Thank God for the Kindertransport', *History Today* 54 (May 2004) 5.
15 Ugolini, 'The Internal Enemy "OTHER"', 143.
16 Murphy, 'Memory, Identity and public narrative', 310.
17 FWPC/Rachel, Edna, Marthe.
18 *RoK* (title page); FWPC/Josephina, Rachel.
19 'The Kindertransport Story', BBC (2009).
20 Kushner, 'The end of the 'Anglo-Jewish Progress Show: Representations of the Jewish East End, 1887–1987', in Kushner (ed.), *The Jewish Heritage in British History; Englishness and Jewishness* (London: Frank Cass & Co, 1992), 97.
21 Cesarani, 'Dual Heritage or Duel of Heritages? Englishness and Jewishness in the Heritage Industry', in Kushner (ed.), *The Jewish Heritage,* 29.
22 *RoK.*
23 'The Reunion', BBC Radio 4 (FM only), 12 September 2010; 'The Kindertransport Story', BBC (2009).
24 Sharples, 'Kindertransport'.
25 See Louise London, 'British government policy and Jewish refugees, 1933–1945', *Patterns of Prejudice*, 23 (1989/90), 26–43; Kushner, 'The impact of British anti-Semitism'.

26 London, 'Jewish Refugees', 164; See also London, *Whitehall and the Jews, 1933–1948: British Immigration Policy, Jewish Refugees and the Holocaust* (Cambridge: Cambridge University Press, 2001).

27 Ibid.

28 Kushner, 'British anti-Semitism', in Cesarani (ed.), Modern Anglo-Jewry, 192; Endelman, The Jews of Britain, 198.

29 Dolf Michaelis and Eva Michaelis-Stern, *Emissaries In Wartime London; 1938–1945* (Jerusalem: Unknown, 1989) 14.

30 Ibid.

31 Eugene Black, *The Social Politics of Anglo-Jewry: 1880–1920* (Oxford: Blackwell, 1998), 389.

32 Kushner, *The Persistence of Prejudice*, 66.

33 WL/BL/150.

34 HLSC/MS183/384/F1, Circular No. 125 of CC, April 1941.

35 *Scotsman*, 28 December 1938.

36 Ibid., 26 July 1938.

37 Ibid., 3 December 1938.

38 Ibid., 27 December 1938.

39 HLSC/MS183/381/F1, circular no.121 of Central Council, 2 December 1941; Kushner and Knox, *Refugees in an Age of Genocide*, 126–216; Kushner, *Remembering Refugees*, 145.

40 Kushner, *Remembering Refugees*, 145.

41 FWPC/Jan.

42 Ibid.

43 FWPC/Benson.

44 FWPC/Rachel.

45 Kushner, *The Persistence of Prejudice*, 153.

46 *Scotsman*, 8 November 1938.

47 Ibid., 8 May 1939.

48 Ibid., 8 November 1938.

49 Ibid., 8 May 1939.

50 Ibid., 8 November 1938, 16 March 1939.

51 *The Times*, 11, 28 January 1939, 16 February 1939.

52 *The Times* digital archive.

53 *The Times*, 16 February 1939.

54 Emil Fackenheim, *Epitaph for German Judaism; From Halle to Jerusalem* (Wisconsin: The University of Wisconsin Press, 2007), 97.

55 David Brenner, 'Promoting East European Jewry: "Ost und West", Ethnic Identity and the German Jewish Audience', *Prooftexts*, 15, 1 (January 1995), 63.

56 Collins, *Aspects of Scottish Jewry*, 74.

57 Ibid., 75.

58 Rainer Kömel, 'German-Jewish Refugees in Scotland', in Collins (ed.), *Aspects of Scottish Jewry*, 74.

59 Chaim Bermant, 'Memoir of an E-European immigrant to Glasgow,' *Tenth Anniversary Magazine; Patterns and Images of Jewish Immigration in Scotland* (Glasgow, 1997).

60 FWPC/Elijah.

61 WL/BL/51.

62 FWPC/Rachel.

63 HLSC/MS183/384/F1, Report of Annual Refugee Conference, 18–19 January 1942.

64 HLSC/MS183/384/F2, minutes of Refugee Joint Consultative Committee, 17 July 1941.

65 Ibid.

66 *Scotsman*, 21 March 1944.

67 Ibid.

68 WL/BL/3.

69 FWPC/Edna.

70 FWPC/Jan.

71 Ibid.

72 FWPC/Rachel.

73 Ibid.

74 WHMMA/USC, 02/12/96.

75 *The Times*, 16 February 1939, 11 January 1939.

76 Kushner, 'The impact of British anti-Semitism', 197.

77 Ugolini, 'The Internal Enemy "OTHER"', 148.

78 Ibid.

79 Abrams, The Orphan Country, 44.

80 Buck, 'Feeding A Pauper Army', 323.

81 Braber *Jews in Glasgow,* 35; Ugolini, 'The Internal Enemy "OTHER"', 137–58.

82 Ugolini, 'The Internal Enemy "OTHER"', 140.

83 Ibid.

84 EGPC: newspaper clippings.

85 FWPC/Edna.

86 McCarthy, 'Scottish National Identities', 201.

87 Kiely, Bechhofer and McCrone, 'Birth, blood and belonging', 150–71.

88 FWPC/Rachel, Noah.

89 FWPC/Rachel.

90 *Scotsman*, 5 January 1938.

91 Ibid., 6 July 1938.

92 Ibid., 13 July 1938, 3 December 1938.

93 See Richard Bolchover, *British Jewry and the Holocaust* (Oxford: Oxford University Press, 2003); Alderman, *Modern British Jewry*; London, 'British government policy', 26–43.

94 Kushner, *The Persistence of Prejudice*, 89.

95 Ibid.

96 See W. H. Marwick, Scotland in Modern Times; *An Outline of Economic and Social Development since the Union of 1707* (London: Frank Cass, 1964); A. J. P. Taylor, *English History, 1914–1945* (Oxford: Oxford University Press, 1965).

97 HLSC/MS183/289/2/F1.

98 HLSC/MS183/289/2/F1. Employment report, March 1940; HLSC/MS183/290/F1, Letter from Home Office, 21 June 1943; HLSC/MS183/290/F1, Minutes from Central Council, 1 May 1940.

99 MS183/132/4; Pamphlet for refugees entitled 'While you are in England'.

100 HLSC/MS183/384/F1, Quarterly Report of Jewish Refugee Committee, January – March 1942; HLSC/MS183/384/F1, Circular No.106 of Central Council, 21 July 1941.

101 FWPC/Rachel, Edna.

102 FWPC/Rachel.

103 KA:QU/SUP: 134.

104 KA:QU/SUP:2160/I06/08; FWPC/Isabel.

105 WHMA/USC:31378.

106 HLSC/MS116/157/AJ396/5, 21 March 1939.

107 WHMA/USC:36790; FWPC/Elijah.

108 Bernard Gainer, *The Alien Invasion* (London, 1972), 207.

109 HLSC/MS183/384/F1, Circular no. 12 of CC, 29 December 1941; Alderman, *Modern British Jewry*, 270.

110 *Scotsman*, 12 August 1940.

111 *The Times*, 14 September 1939.

112 Kushner, *The Persistence of Prejudice*, 174.

113 Ibid.

114 KA:QU/SUP.

115 MCPC, William Farinton Drew, letter, 23 July 1940.

116 Ibid.

117 Norman Bentwich, *Jewish Youth Comes Home; The Story of the Youth Aliyah, 1933–1943* (London: Hyperian Press, 1944).

118 FWPC/Nathan.

119 WHMA/USC/31378. (USC interviewees are first refferred to with their full name, thereafter using only their surname).

120 WL/BL/74.

121 FWPC/Edna, e-mail correspondence, 8 July 2010.

122 WL/BL/72.
123 Bernard Wasserstein, *Britain and the Jews of Europe 1939–1945* (New York: Oxford University Press, 1979), 79.
124 *Scotsman*, 6 December 1938.
125 Ibid., 22 November 1938.
126 HLSC/MS183/290/F1.
127 *Scotsman*, 21 November 1938.
128 Ibid., 13 July 1938, 21 November 1938, 23 December 1938, 8 May 1939.
129 *Scotsman*, 28 December 1938.
130 HLSC/MS116/157/AJ396/5.
131 *Scotsman*, 16 January 1941.
132 Ibid., 21 March 1944.
133 FWPC/Jan, Rachel, Edna.
134 The short-term approach to care placements and the resulting lack of permanency afforded to the Kindertransportees will be discussed in more detail in Chapter 2.
135 The Central British Fund was the financial arm of the refugee welfare network.
136 HLSC/MS183/384/F1.
137 HLSC/MS183/384/folder 3, Booklet of Central Council, 1939; See appendices 3 and 4.
138 Ibid.: Scotland was designated region 11, with committees established in Edinburgh, Glasgow, Aberdeen, Ayr, Dundee, Perth and St Andrews.
139 *Jewish Echo*, 10 February 1939: these included the Senior Women Zionists, Hadassah, and the Garnethill Women's Zionist Society; See appendix 5.
140 See Collins, *Glasgow Jewry*; Collins, *Second City Jewry*. See also *Jewish Echo*, 10 February 1939: these included the Senior Women Zionists, Hadassah, and the Garnethill Women's Zionist Society.
141 Cesarani, 'The Transformation of Communal Authority in Ango-Jewry, 1914–1940', in Cesarani (ed.), *Modern Anglo-Jewry*, 116.
142 Ibid., 126.
143 Collins, *Second City Jewry*, 223.
144 WL/BL/25; See Chapter 3 for a detailed discussion on the religious care of the Kindertransportees.
145 Turner, ... *And the Policeman smiled*, 253.
146 London, 'Jewish Refugees', 168.
147 Black, review of Gottlieb, *Men of Vision*, 1805–06.
148 Amy Zahl Gottlieb, *Men of Vision; Anglo-Jewry's Aid to victims of the Nazi Regime 1933–1945* (London: Weidenfeld and Nicolson, 1998), 131.
149 Cesarani, *Modern Anglo-Jewry*, 116.
150 Ibid.
151 HLSC/MS183/289/2/F1, Report of JRC, March 1940.

152 Finlayson, 'A Moving Frontier', 185.
153 Shatzkes, *Holocaust and Rescue,* 12.
154 Abrams, *The Orphan Country,* 39.
155 Braber, *Jews in Glasgow,* 35.
156 HLSC/MS183/384/F1, Circular No.95 of CC, 10 April 1941.
157 FWPC/Levi.
158 *Scotsman*, 6 May 1939.
159 Ibid.
160 HLSC/MS183/290/F1, Interview with Mr Herbert Morrison, 6 July.
161 HLSC/MS183/290/F1, Letter from the Home Office, 21 June 1943.
162 Bentwich, 72.
163 HL/SCMS183/290/F1, Solomon Schonfeld, 'Scriptural points in Mr Cooper's letter' (July 1943).
164 Alderman, *Modern British Jewry*, 79.
165 Ibid.
166 Jewish Echo, 10 February 1939.
167 HLSC/MS116/157/AJ396/5, Report of CC, 31 December 1939.
168 HLSC/MS116/157/AJ396/5, Minutes of CC, 15 May 1941.
169 HLSC/MS116/157/AJ396/5, Report CC, 31 December 1939.
170 HLSC/MS183/384/F1, CC, *The Care of German and Austrian Refugees*, November 1942.
171 Ibid.
172 HL/MS183/384/F1, Report of CC, 1941.
173 Ibid.
174 See Gottlieb, Men of Vision.
175 Finlayson, 'A Moving Frontier'; HLSC/MS183/53/F2, Minutes, 19 December 1938.
176 *Scotsman*, 21 March 1944.
177 HLSC/MS116/157/AJ396/2, Letter from JCGR, 28 March 1939.
178 FWPC/Rachel.
179 Alderman, *Modern British Jewry,* 270, 275; See also Curio, '"Invisible" children', 41–56.
180 Finlayson, 'A Moving Frontier',184.
181 Ibid.
182 Bentwich, *They Found Refuge*, 66.
183 See Curio, '"Invisible" children'.
184 Bolchover, *British Jewry,* 49; London, 'Jewish Refugees', 175.
185 Dorothy Legarreta, *The Guernica Generation: Basque Refugee children of the Spanish civil war* (Nevada: University of Nevada Press, 1984) 108.
186 *Scotsman*, 3 and 28 December 1938.
187 Kushner, *Remembering Refugees,* 154.

188 *Scotsman*, 27 December 1938.
189 See James, Jenks and Prout, *Theorizing Childhood*; Henrick, 'Constructions and reconstructions of Britain childhood', 35–59; Aries, *Centuries of Childhood*; Strandell, review, 395–98.
190 Lassonde, review, 1019; See also Cavert, 'Children in the House'.
191 *Scotsman*, 26 July 1938.
192 Kushner, *Remembering Refugees*, 152.
193 *Scotsman*, 3 December 1938.
194 Ibid., 3 January 1939.
195 HLSC/MS183/53/F2, letter from Schonfeld, 9 January 1939.
196 Ibid.
197 *Scotsman*, 12 July 1938, letter from H. W. Austin, Phyllis Bottome, Arnold Lunn and Geraldine Drummond; Kushner, *Persistance of Prejudice*, 70.
198 *Scotsman*, 12 July 1938.
199 Ibid., 21 March 1944.
200 *The Times*, 5, 16, 20 January, 20 February, 11 April, 13 June 1939.
201 Deborah Dwork and Jan Van Pelt, *Flight from the Reich: Refugee Jews, 1933–1946* (New York: Robert W. W. Norton & Co., 2009).

2

The Making of an Invisible Trans-migrant: Kindertransportee Care

> Scottish people are not very fond of children; they are very fond of animals. They're crazy about their animals; children they send to the boarding school when they can afford it. If they cannot afford it they put a latchkey around their neck and let some roam the street. They do not on the whole look terribly well after their children. If they have a dog and anything happens they go absolutely hysterical.[1]

Gertrude Black, a refugee to Edinburgh from Greater Germany, gives a frank and largely derogatory statement about her impression of Scotland's approach to childcare and welfare during World War II. Unique characteristics do emerge in Scotland's welfare provisions for the child-in-care and these informed particular care experiences for the Kindertransportees in Scotland during the period 1939–45.[2]

The Kindertransportees were accommodated within many different types of welfare services and facilities: foster homes, evacuation centres, trans-migrant hostels, agricultural training centres, orphanages, approved schools, boarding schools and convents. These facilities were not part of a national grid of state-sponsored care, but tended to be sporadic philanthropic schemes adherent to an overlapping collage of welfare networks. These intended to aid vulnerable and needy children in Britain based on an array of welfare agendas.

The Jewish community of Scotland possessed a collection of welfare services for Jewish children and the Kindertransportees were incorporated into these schemes, including the Gertrude Jacobson Orphanage.[3] Other denominations' pre-existing facilities also absorbed Kindertransportees, including the Convent of the Sacred Heart, Aberdeenshire. Kindertransportees were also integrated into secular philanthropic facilities for poor working-class children: The Priory (Selkirk's Children's Home) and remand homes, such as St Vincent Street's Home, Edinburgh.[4] Residential facilities were predominantly centres of care designed for Scotland's poor or delinquent children. However a number of Kindertransportees did live within accommodation designed to school Scotland's fee-paying and financially privileged youth: St Trinnean's School (evacuated from Edinburgh to Galashiels), St Columbia's College (St Bushey's) and St Hilary's (Edinburgh).[5]

The care solutions for Kindertransportees were not all pre-existing. Some were newly formed welfare solutions in response to the experiences and demands of war. These included the evacuation hostels, such as Birkenward hostel in Skelmorlie, Ayrshire, Ernespie House and Castle Douglas hostel in Dumfriesshire.[6] Kindertransportees were also cared for within schemes created specifically to cater for the dependent trans-migrant minor after 1938. These included Garnethill hostel, Salisbury Road hostel, Whittingehame Farm School and Polton House.[7] All these welfare services were geographically stretched across Scotland: Glasgow, Clydebank, Edinburgh, Aberdeenshire, Ayrshire, Dunfermline and elsewhere.[8]

Care schemes for the trans-migrant minor

The manner of care given to the Kindertransportees while living within these facilities was greatly shaped by the philanthropic motivation of Jewish refugee organizations. Anglo-Jewry desired to find solutions for the dependent trans-migrant minor, while at the same time resolved to protect the status quo and maintain good relations with the gentile community. This meant that care strategies focused on maintaining a good opinion of the temporary migrants during their stay in Britain.[9] The CC tailored care schemes so that they would best create useful and, subsequently, desirable 'good' migrants.[10]

Aiding the British war effort was perceived as the most valuable role that the Kindertransportees could play during this period. The CC promoted the utilization by the Government of the valuable surplus of trans-migrants in Britain, in order to bolster Britain's strength on the home front.[11] Agriculture was initially one of only a few avenues open to trans-migrants in aiding the war effort. This opportunity was not missed by the CC and conversations followed between the Government and the Central Agricultural Committee, a subdivision of the CC. These discussions sought to assist 'refugee men and women to secure agricultural training or employment'.[12] Handler recorded that Bachad intended to direct its charges towards helping the war effort through agriculture.[13] Handler estimated that about 3,000 youth (boys and girls) aided British harvests and agricultural requirements of war.[14]

As the war continued, the Kindertransportees were gradually afforded a wider scope of war-work opportunities. Government training centres, which intended to ameliorate skills' shortages, were opened to refugees in early 1941 and this broadened Kindertransportees' opportunities.[15] Gerald Jayson was sent, via the Kindertransport, to Bachad's *Hachsharot* called Millsie Farm in Northern Ireland. He recalls that he was encouraged to pursue useful training to help the war effort, which led him into the airforce at the age of 15.[16] In 1944, John Presland noted that an estimated 800 Kindertransportees were now within HM Armed Forces.[17]

Kindertransportees were also encouraged to participate in defence-of-the-realm options in Scotland. Stefan Ruff arrived in Britain on the second Kindertransport from Vienna. He was initially housed in Lowestoft, Warner's holiday camp, before being sent to a Jewish Old Age home that was being used for minors in Walton-on-Naze. Ruff recalls that he failed to meet the selection criteria of visiting potential foster parents and was eventually transferred to Clayton House, near Ipswich. Ruff was eventually fostered by a Christian family and then later sent to a Jewish family in Galloway. He was then sent to Glasgow and lived in the Garnethill hostel. He recalls that he became an active member of the Officer Training Corps while at university in Scotland.[18]

The British Air Raid Wardens (ARP) was another popular choice among Kindertransportees. Abaigael lived in Vienna, Austria, and enjoyed a Traditional Jewish upbringing before emigration to Britain on the Kindertransport. On arrival in Britain, she was first sent to a reception camp, before being dispatched to a poor foster family in Lincoln. The family could not afford to keep her and she was eventually sent to Whittingehame in Scotland. At Whittingehame, Abaigael recalls late night ARP patrols under the supervision of their teacher Drew.[19] Drew took photographs of his training sessions with Kindertransportees at Whittingehame. Figures 4, 5 and 6 capture Kindertransportees undertaking practical training for the protection of Britain on the home front.

The CC promoted the useful roles and occupations for the British war effort undertaken by the trans-migrants. In 1944, the *Scotsman* reported that 'most of the boys [from Polton House] joined the forces at calling up age or before'.[20] In March 1944, the *Scotsman* reported Sir Cecil Weir's statement:

> The majority of refugees in this country with whom the Scottish National Council was concerned had been here since before the war and a very large number had

Figure 4 ARP training.
Source: MCPC/Drew, photographs.

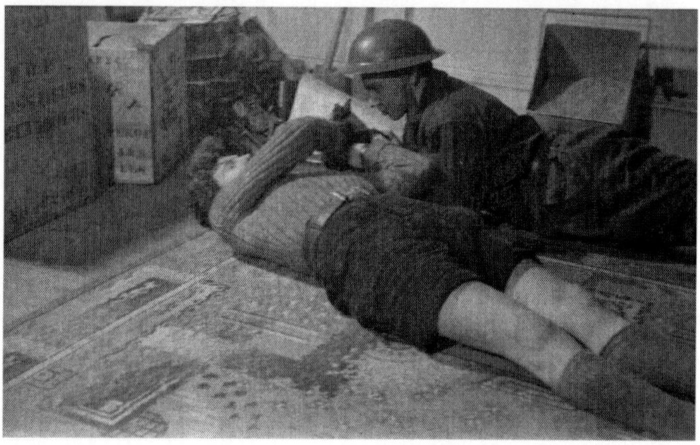

Figure 5 ARP training.
Source: MCPC/Drew, photographs.

> been absorbed in British Industry . . . a very useful and profitable experience with the refugees . . . they were now doing work of importance in the national effort.[21]

Despite the desire to promote the Kindertransportees as useful migrants, the directives were cautiously formulated and burdened with heavy restrictions based on the Kindertransportees' status in Britain as trans-migrants. No education, training or employment advantage was to be given to migrant children over a British national.[22] The Kindertransportees' care emphasized their secondary position to British citizens. Policy makers responded to pressure to appease British citizens' fears that refugees were being given all the advantages.[23] A Kindertransportee recalls being asked at Dovercourt camp what they wanted

Figure 6 ARP training.
Source: MCPC/Drew, photographs.

to be and the great displeasure of the administrator when they said they wished to be a doctor:

> The woman who was filling the form in said: "I can't put that down – you must remember that you are a refugee."[24]

The trans-migrant status of Kindertransportees in Britain did, however, provide them with an abundance of opportunities devised to promote further migration.[25] The Government was reluctant to enable refugees to feel like permanent citizens in Britain during the war years.[26] Herbert Morrison, the Home Secretary, remained stalwart in his stance that migrants from Greater Germany were not expected to remain in Britain.[27] In 1944, Presland stated that the intention of the CC was 'to maintain, educate, train and re-emigrate the 9,341 children under its care'.[28]

Subsequently, the CC's care initiatives often focused on education and training that would provide the Kindertransportees with an advantageous position for migration. Training intended to equip them with a life skill that would be in demand in an overseas destination, such as agricultural and manual labouring skills.[29] This meant that academic ambitions were not given priority.[30] Agricultural or manual labouring skills were in demand by a large number of potential target countries for migration, including Palestine, Australia, Canada, South Africa and the United States (see Chapter 4 for a detailed examination of the agricultural training facilities in Scotland).[31]

Despite these intentions, the majority of the Kindertransportees were unable to undertake further migration from Britain before 1945. This meant that for the duration of their elongated stay in Britain their care intended to aid invisibility and discretion in their integration into local communities.[32] This put emphasis upon their isolation, invisibility and extensive distribution across Britain to avoid ghettos of Jewish migrants.[33] Unlike the care of the Basque refugee minors from Spain in the early 1930s, the CC sought to prevent colonies of migrants or enclaves that could draw attention to their presence.[34] The crux to this distinction was the Kindertransportees' integration into British welfare services, rather than the emphasis on 'colonies' and separate services. Karen Gershon, a Kindertransportee who was cared for at Whittingehame, has gathered a collection of testimonies from Kindertransportees cared for across Britain. These testimonies underline the CC's aversion to the urban hostels or residential care facilities in close proximity to British communities because they resembled 'foreign colonies'.[35]

The desire for discretion meant that care initiatives sought to speed up the processes by which Kindertransportees acclimatized and Anglicized themselves in their new environments.[36] This was in stark contrast to care initiatives for the 4,000 Basque children, which sought to avoid Anglicization in order to protect and maintain their separate Spanish and Basque identity.[37] Black has called Anglo-Jewry's care policy 'the pressure-cooker' for Anglicization.[38] This immediately required an introduction to the British 'way-of-life' and language. Kindertransportees' testimonies have pointed to the pressure they felt to adopt the English language and drop their Germanic characteristics.[39] The Kindertransportees were directed not to use their original Germanic language publicly.[40] They were also to be discreet about their national origins, religious affiliations and migrant circumstances. During the war years, some also chose to exchange their Germanic names for British ones.[41]

An important aspect of Anglicization was the adoption of British imperial and patriotic values. This was especially important during the war, when a fear of the enemy alien in Britain's midst encouraged the CC to promote the refugees' loyalty to Britain. The desire to present the trans-migrants as loyal citizens was reignited in 1944 with the close of war in sight. At this point in time, the British Government had still not confirmed the future status of refugees in Britain and discussions about repatriation provoked fear and loathing among refugee organizations.[42] In 1944, a report in the *Scotsman* recorded a meeting with the Association of Jewish Refugees (AJR) and their member Dr Adler-Rudel, who was seeking British citizenship.[43] This report is indicative of the representative organizations' desire to emphasize the trans-migrants' complete and successful integration into Britain, along with their total loyalty to Britain. This policy, which has been referred to as the 'Anglo-Saxon imperial' project, would not have been unfamiliar to Kindertransportees, especially for 16 per cent who attended a Gymnasium in Germany, which was prone to advocating German imperialism.[44] All the Kindertransportees under 14 were supposed to attend school in Britain and became subject to this form of national propaganda.

Schools instilled 'good' British values, which would make 'good' citizens.[45] In doing so, schools would teach youth to become a national asset and loyal subject.[46] This practice continued into the late 1950s as the Scottish Education Department (SED) advocated the role of schools in the training for citizenship.[47] Primary schooling was to teach 'personal hygiene, clear speech, road safety, good manners and conduct', while secondary schooling introduced minors to a successful way of life in the outside world.[48]

To speed up integration, outside of their daily schooling, Kindertransportees were encouraged to adhere to a secular lifestyle and maintain daily interaction with a local community. Participation with local community centres and youth groups was encouraged by the CCC. They provided a controlled environment for gradual integration of trans-migrants into the local community. In Glasgow, Kindertransportees joined the local youth refugee club, referred to as 'the House on the Hill', on 358 Sauchiehall Street.[49] The club aided their integration into the local Scottish community.[50] On 23 August 1941, the club's Kindertransportees participated in a local celebration called the 'Festival of Nations' day in support of the unified British effort against Hitler.[51] Wuga recalls that Kindertransportees would participate in 1 May marches alongside Scots and that they would tour Scotland in order to raise money for Clementine Churchill's national fund.[52] He also remembers the dominant role of the Scottish Trades Union movement in Glasgow for connecting Kindertransportees to local Scottish people.[53] Rachel has expressed the important role these clubs played in connecting their members to local political movements and events.[54] In doing so, they were able to meet native Scots.

Kindertransportees in residential facilities outside of the city centres were encouraged to participate in local leisure pursuits. It was believed that Anglicizing influences could come from many directions, including playing with other children, reading, watching films at the cinema, attending social functions, such as dances, and participating in sports or clubs.[55] Figures 7 and 8 show a football match at Whittingehame. Similar matches were organized with the local community.

Despite these Anglicizing influences, residential facilities could inhibit Kindertransportees from naturally immersing themselves into the social networks in their local communities. The CC was concerned that this could weaken their speedy integration process. Handler has recalled his concern that

Figure 7 Football matches at Whittingehame.
Source: MCPC/Drew, photographs.

Figure 8 Kindertransportee playing with a football.
Source: MCPC/Drew, photographs.

Kindertransportees in residential facilities would struggle to become good citizens in Britain because they lacked a normal socializing process.[56]

As a result, for Kindertransportees isolated in rural residential facilities, a curriculum would also be used to substitute artificially the 'normal' socializing process. This would establish a new normative frame of reference with a theology that was felt to be compatible with life in Britain and that would make good British citizens.[57] These strategies sought to re-educate residents based on a preferred model. In Whittingehame, Kindertransportees recall their headmaster Charles Maxwell seeking to transform residents into 'English gentlemen' with attributes he associated with Eton College's aristocratic pupils.[58]

Welfare initiatives concern to install good citizenship also included a preoccupation with eliminating 'hedonistic girls and non-heroic boys'.[59] Boys were to express an affinity to the 'ideals of manly heroism and physical vigour'.[60] These qualities would be in tune with the war effort. Youth movements were an important resource to instil these nationalistic values into the Kindertransportees. The Scout movement was especially infused with jingoism and encouraged members to embrace an enthusiasm for the British Empire. Between 1941 and 1944, membership of the Boy Scouts in Scotland rose by 25 per cent.[61] This remained a popular choice among Kindertransportees.

Whittingehame possessed an active Scout group, led by Drew. This group built their own clubhouse on the grounds, organized outdoor pursuits and sought to emulate the aspirations of Robert Baden-Powell for British youth living the British 'way-of-life'. Figure 9 shows the semi-constructed Scout clubhouse at

Figure 9 Scout clubhouse.
Source: MCPC/Drew, photographs.

Figure 10 Interior of Scout clubhouse.
Source: MCPC/Drew, photographs.

Figure 11 Interior of Scout clubhouse 2.
Source: MCPC/Drew, Photographs.

Whittingehame, while Figures 10 and 11 reveal the interior of the clubhouse with images displayed of Robert Baden-Powell and King George VI. The Scouts played an important role in teaching youth the social roles and values of the British Empire, if only by way of their pledge: 'To do my duty to God and to the King'.[62]

Middle-class virtues and working-class problems

Although specific care initiatives were formulated for the Kindertransportees, the CC more commonly utilized pre-existing welfare facilities. In doing so, they often failed to offer tailor-made provisions for the Kindertransportees' specific needs as foreign trans-migrant minors. This approach to the Kindertransportees' care seems to have been most acutely felt within schooling. Filtered into mainstream schooling, services were often unable to cater for foreign migrants' specific requirements. The linguistic barriers experienced by Kindertransportees were frequently left unattended or dealt with by them being placed with lower age groups in school.

Walter Nachtigall was born in Vienna, Austria, to an observant Jewish family. At the age of 8 he left Austria on the Kindertransport with his sister. On arrival they were sent to Edinburgh to separate foster families: Nachtigall to a Jewish physician. He experienced very poor care with the physician. During one of the physician's holidays, Nachtigall was sent to a non-Jewish family in rural Dysart, Scotland. He remained with the family for the remainder of the war years. During the course of his schooling in Scotland, Nachtigall found that he was placed in a lower grade because he was unable to communicate with the teacher in his correct tier group.[63] Warton was also downgraded at school and recalls this experience as extremely disturbing.[64] Wuga was sent to Belhousey Boys' School, a lesser school for educationally challenged minors, because he could not speak English well.[65]

This approach to the Kindertransportees' care may best be viewed as one of integration by total immersion.[66] Kindertransportees were normally treated in the same manner as dependent British minors entering welfare. The most immediate problem with this approach was the linguistic adjustment Kindertransportees had to achieve. Elsie was born in Vienna, but grew up in a little village on the Czech border until 1938. Her Jewish family had converted to Catholicism, and she attended a Catholic convent school before migrating to Britain on the Kindertransport. It was through the contacts of her Catholic aunt, that she gained a place at the Catholic convent school of the Sacred Heart in Aberdeen, Scotland. She grew up in the convent for 16 years. On arrival at the convent, Elsie recalls the communication problems she encountered:

> My first order of business was to find out where the bathroom was . . . my first trauma was to find the word for bathroom. The German word is "closet" and they would show me broom closets and china closets and all kinds of closets. That was a traumatic happening. . . . The children and nuns were wonderful but we just could not communicate.[67]

Except for those in specific migrant residential care, Kindertransportees were often not given English lessons. Elsie eventually learnt English because she needed to survive in her new environment. Even for those in trans-migrant residential care, linguistic problems were not always attended to. Elijah lived in Poland until he was 5 when his Polish parents moved to Danzig, Germany. In Germany, he attended the local Polish school and recalls that he could still not speak German when he arrived in Britain. This caused a linguistic barrier for him with other Kindertransportees at Whittingehame. It meant that he found adjustment to life in Scotland extremely difficult and lonely:

> I had difficulties, as I did not speak German very well . . . my mother language was Polish. There were hardly any kids from Poland. There were Czech kids. There were no Polish kids as much as I remember. It was mainly German, Austrian, Czech. . . . They could only speak the English they knew, some knew English as they learnt it at school, but most did not, so we spoke German.[68]

The reliance of the RCM upon pre-existing welfare facilities and provisions of care for all dependent minors in Scotland has meant that the Kindertransportees' care cannot be viewed as a solitary or unique event, but must be placed within the Scottish context of welfare services. The pre-existing welfare networks that were used to care for the Kindertransportees were already infused with British welfare values, ideas and approaches to philanthropy.

Much like wider British philanthropic activity, Scottish philanthropy was motivated and driven by a middle-class social-reforming heritage. Despite the rise of self-help initiatives and the increased presence of a new working-class philanthropy, for the most part philanthropy remained the domain of the upper echelons of British society. This meant that the care of the Kindertransportees was shaped by middle-class social reforming ideals and expectations for a working-class community. Philanthropy became an important link between the rich and the poor, as the upper echelons of society utilized reforming tools to police the lower echelons of society.[69] Evacuation policies in Britain were organized by military, middle-class, male minds for working-class communities.[70] Bourgeois women were also particularly active in the philanthropic arena and established an alliance with care-giving agencies.[71]

Despite the pressures of war on domestic welfare, middle-class philanthropists were still preoccupied with the 'abnormalities' of working-class family life.[72] Evacuee problems reinforced 'conservative, behavioural interpretations of poverty', which placed blame upon poor parenting and social inadequacy.[73] British philanthropy sought to instil middle-class ideas about morality, lifestyle expectations and respectability upon the working classes. This created a form of

British philanthropic heritage entrenched in class racism in which the working classes were being 'ethnicized'.[74]

Reforming initiatives were largely based on a concern for the five pillars of evil: want, disease, ignorance, squalor and idleness, reported by Beveridge, as well as a legacy of philanthropic ideologies in Scotland.[75] Three dominant ideas existed in Scotland during this period – Calvinism, environmentalism and class eugenics.[76] Scottish philanthropists remained diligent Calvinists and Presbyterians throughout the war years.[77] Together these ideas shaped the particular character of welfare initiatives for Kindertransportees.

British philanthropy sought to break dependency and aid self-help. In 1944, Joseph Sachs was quoted in an article, published in the *Scotsman*, saying that the chief goal of welfare for dependent refugees was that they should 'cease to be a refugee in the shortest possible time'.[78] In reference to the Basque migrant minors in Britain, Adrian Bell similarly argues that 'self-sufficiency is the common requisite of all those who are to survive in exile'.[79]

The care of the Kindertransportees was not indulgent, but rooted in concerns about preventing long-term dependence on welfare.[80] Kushner has described this approach as 'scientifically-based charity', whereby Anglo-Jewry would prefer to refuse support rather than to allow dependence.[81] Two refugee social centres were established in Glasgow as a means to generate refugee self-help and independence.[82] This tendency meant that reluctance to provide support often emerges as a common denominator to Kindertransportees' experience of care in Scotland. Kindertransportees who were sent to the Gertrude Jacobson Orphanage were reluctantly accepted and cared for.[83] They were received as a burden and viewed as foreign paupers.[84] The atmosphere of care could subsequently be one of resentment and limited value for those who continued to seek aid.

When welfare was provided, it was designed as a temporary solution only and rested on short-term plans. This meant that Kindertransportees often experienced multiple care placements across Britain. This tendency was deeply entrenched in Scottish philanthropic traditions.[85] Scotland's residential care facilities were intended for short durations of 1 or 2 years, while foster care was perceived as a temporary measure and adoption rarely sought. The length and term available within foster placements was not central to the placement.[86] This continued during the war years and there continued prolific instances of billeting and re-billeting of evacuees between 1940 and 1941.[87] Thirty per cent of evacuees were moved from their first homes between 1940 and 1944, and in one case relocated eight times.[88] Kindertransportee Lore Segal's recollection of five different foster homes does not seem that peculiar or unique in comparison.[89]

Residential facilities established for Kindertransportees adhered to this short-term strategy. Whittingehame and Polton House only provided a 2-year training course, while the Garnethill hostel catered for boys only during their schooling or training in Glasgow. Furthermore, Kindertransportees cared for outside of the refugee perimeter of welfare also recall many different homes and placements. Elsie was sent to a different home for each school holiday.[90] Rachel recalls her hostel in Glasgow closing during the war years and receiving minimal support to find new accommodation.[91] She felt her experience reflected a lack of care or concern for providing permanency or stability to dependent trans-migrants. Little thought seems to have been given to providing a regular dependable environment.

Idleness was perceived as a fundamental cause of long-term dependency on British philanthropy. Initiatives that sought to tackle idleness were an important feature of the Kindertransportees' care experience in Scotland. The Scottish Poor Law took a tough stance towards able-bodied unemployed.[92] This approach was adopted by the CC. As a result, refugees could find themselves in a poverty trap after finding employment, because they were immediately removed from 'war refugee' status and further aid.[93] The CC prioritized helping Kindertransportees gain early employment experience. This included not only training, but also one-off loans and incentives to break dependency.

Lola Sprinzeles lived in Vienna with her observant Conservative Jewish family. She received a very patriarchal upbringing from her father who was a teacher and ordained Rabbis. She went to a fee-paying Jewish high school. After arriving in Britain on the Kindertransport, Sprinzeles was adamant that she did not wish to be fostered. Instead, she was sent to Whittingehame. On completion of her 2-year course, she received a leaving package of £3.[94] This contribution was meant to temporarily support Kindertransportees who decided not to pursue further *hachsharot* training, but instead sought independent employment.[95] Fry was given a loan of £10 in 1943 when he migrated to London to undertake employment.[96] Table 5 indicates that the CC was successful in the objective to push Kindertransportees into early employment. Statistics suggest that the majority of Kindertransportees gained their first job between the ages of 14 and 17.

The Kindertransportees were also affected by the legacy of the class Eugenics movement in Britain and its influence within welfare services. This responded to middle-class concerns about national degeneration, especially within the lower classes of British society.[97] Subsequent care initiatives aimed at providing

	Age 13	Age 14	Age 15	Age 16	Age 17	Age 18	Age 19	Age 20	Age 21	Age 22
Series1	2%	14%	14%	17%	17%	12%	10%	5%	7%	2%

Table 5 Kindertransportees' age at first employment.
Source: KA: QU/SUP.

a healthy working-class lifestyle. These schemes were rooted in class concerns rather than in racial biological prejudices, and prescribed 'preventative and interventionist' methods.[98] The immediate concern was policing the good health of the nation. The legacy of the ill health of recruits during the South African Boer War, World War I and then during the period in World War II drew attention to the weakness and vulnerability of the nation.[99] Young people were seen to represent the strength of the nation.[100] Accordingly, importance was placed upon healthy citizens for a strong nation.[101]

As a result, the child-in-care received a certain level of health care in Scotland. Tuberculosis and rickets were a major concern. A new category termed *pre-tuberculous* developed for children with weak health.[102] Attention was focused on improving the health of the child through schools. School medical inspections and milk provisions intended to improve basic health and nutrition, while later in 1931 the Board of Education required that primary schools should aid the health and happiness of their pupils.[103] Despite these advances, many people continued to be shocked at the 'verminous' nature of the children evacuated from cities.[104]

The migrant in Britain was the recipient of particularly extensive eugenic scrutiny and criticism. This was aimed at protecting the health of British citizens by way of only admitting 'desirable' and healthy migrants. The CC would go to great lengths to weed out the 'feeble-minded' and weak child from transits from Greater Germany.[105] Once admitted to Britain, the CC was keen to maintain the health of the trans-migrants. The CC wished to maintain this standard through basic medical check-ups to their physical health. Basic health provisions were provided specifically for the Kindertransportees in residential facilities. Jayson recalls that at the Millsie camp in Northern Ireland 'we had a dentist. . . . I remember him pulling eight teeth in one go . . . there was a doctor, but he did not come all that often.'[106] Figure 12 shows that dentists visited the Kindertransportees at Whittingehame.

Environmentalism was another social reform ideology that strongly coloured the Kindertransportees' care experience in Scotland. Environmentalism focused on remedying social ills and promoting physical health by way of providing particular environments deemed 'normal', respectable and healthy. Environmental causes continued to be emphasized as the causes of bad citizenship, juvenile delinquency and other working-class misdemeanours.[107] Schemes tended towards an aversion to city life and the promotion of a rural lifestyle. Seebohm Rowntree's reports of 1901 and 1936 had, for example, highlighted severe problems afflicting city children.[108] Rowntree's report, along with widespread impressions of a lice-infested evacuee, generated a negative image of city life among philanthropists and led to the desire to remove children from the urban environment.[109]

The desire to create a healthier living environment led to schemes that intended to introduce 'fresh air' into the daily lives of minors. The open-air school movement, which developed between 1907 and 1939, promoted fresh air within city schools and rural breaks for urban dwellers.[110] By 1937 there were 155

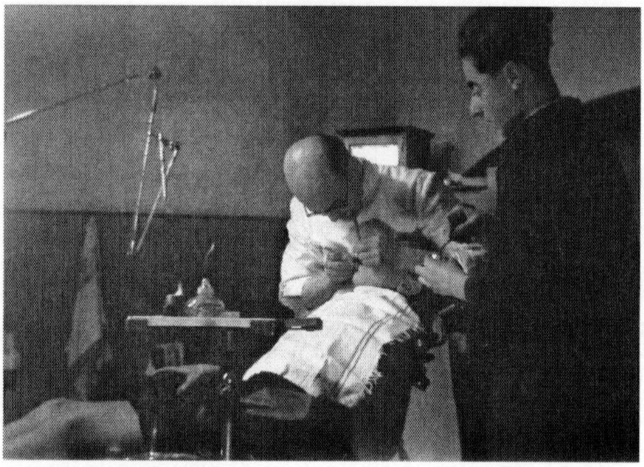

Figure 12 Dentist at Whittingehame.
Source: MCPC/Drew, photographs.

open-air schools, with 16,500 pupils, and 40 out of Glasgow's 221 local schools adhered to 'open-air' principles by 1935.[111] In 1943, the SED advocated 'open-air life'.[112] When Kindertransportee Nachtigall's foster parent went on holiday, he was accommodated by a family in Dysart, Fife, within the 'fresh-air' fund's scheme to relocate Edinburgh's urban children to the rural areas of Scotland for short breaks.[113]

The principles of the fresh-air movement were more widely adhered to, and Kindertransportees were recipients of moves to push minors into outdoor pursuits. The 1937 Physical Training and Recreation Act encouraged physical exercise, outdoor pursuits and membership of youth clubs, such as the Scouts. These all intended to promote ideals of the rural outdoor life. The Kindertransportees joined an array of youth groups, including Maccabi clubs for sports, and the Scouts or Zionist youth groups for rural excursions and outdoor pursuits.[114] There was also support for residential facilities based in rural areas. Whittingehame and Polton House both promoted rural lifestyles through agricultural training within a rural setting. The *hachsharot*'s intention was to teach children to embrace a rural, physical and outdoor lifestyle.[115]

The care of Kindertransportees was also shaped by the social and economic horizon placed on welfare ambitions by its middle-class creators. This decreed an approach and level of care based upon presumptions about respectable working-class lifestyles and expectations. Subsequently, Kindertransportees' care and nurture in Scotland possessed a working-class basis, character and content. Foster homes were frequently working-class.[116] Nachtigall was initially without a bed and 'put in a storage room' because his foster family lacked facilities to cater for him.[117] He remembers that his later foster family in Dysart was even poorer.[118]

Residential facilities frequently reflected ideas about working-class needs. Ernst Flesch was born in Vienna, Austria, before migrating to Britain on the Kindertransport. On arrival he was sent to the Gertrude Jacobson Orphanage in Glasgow, a care home established by Glasgow's Jewry in 1913 for poor Jewish orphans. He recalls that the orphanage embodied its intention to provide for 'poor Jewish kids'.[119] The orphanage was based in a poor district of Glasgow, supervised by persons of a poor economic background, and provided facilities equivalent to a poor household.[120] The accommodation was physically poor, financially overstretched and lacked adequate resources to cater for its growing number of inmates.[121] Flesch recalls that food in the orphanage was not good and the institution was comparably inferior to the neighbouring Garnethill hostel for Kindertransportees.

Despite Flesch's envious perception, residential facilities established specifically for Kindertransportees in Scotland, such as the Garnethill hostel, also suffered from a similarly low level of care. Kindertransportees recall that Garnethill hostel lacked many necessities, space and any comforts.[122] Ruff remembers Garnethill hostel's 'institutional' character.[123] Whittingehame is also recalled as a basic facility. Alice Hubbers was born in Vienna, Austria, an only child to Traditional Jewish parents. Her parents ran a wholesale perfumery shop and they lived in a large apartment. She left on the Kindertransport with her friend Lotte and both girls were allocated to a poor foster family in Lincoln. The family could not afford to look after the girls and new placements were found for them. Hubbers was sent to Whittingehame. She recalls that the condition of Whittingehame was extremely basic, large and impersonal.[124]

The nature of these care provisions do reflect a trend within residential facilities to provide only necessities, exclusive of variety or luxuries, yet this scenario was shaped by the restrictions caused by the war. Wartime circumstances led to a chronic lack of resources and supplies for existing schemes. This meant that care facilities were of a low standard and unable to make improvements. There existed widespread poverty and disruption to normal home life across Scotland due to the war.[125] Organizations were unable to remedy problems because of the persistent and widespread lack of the necessary commodities, including accommodation, staff, food and equipment.[126]

The subsequent working-class living environments were often felt by the Kindertransportees to be of a much lower standard of living to their past lifestyles. Susan Kleinman, Chana Moshenska, Buck, Macnicol, Titmuss and Welshman collectively place too much faith in the class-conscious ethos of British society and its subsequent insurance that the appropriate placement was found for evacuees and trans-migrant minors based on social status.[127] Kleinman and Moshenska argue that 'wealthy, educated and cultured kinder were sent to English, gentile families with similar class identities; working-class minors were sent to working-class families, Jewish or gentile'.[128] Buck has also argued that a class-conscious Britain prevented Kindertransportees from being placed in lower socio-economic circumstances.[129] Buck argues that the Kindertransportees were matched with class appropriate care environments. Instead, it seems that Kindertransportees' socio-economic circumstances in Britain were predominantly 'pot-luck' and responsive more to availability than to suitability.

The minors experienced both social and economic elevation and lowering in their position in society. The Kindertransportees arrived from a highly varied type of social and economic backgrounds. A significant number did arrive from middle-class, professional and relatively wealthy backgrounds.[130] Yet, the majority of Kindertransportees found they were now living in a lower working-class social and economic circumstance, whether this was within institutional facilities or foster homes. Elsie experienced a drop in her social and economic living environment during her school holidays when she was sent to an array of poor families. Of one placement in Brea Mar, Elsie recalls:

> Well the word poor does not do . . . they were poor in material things, very working-class.[131]

The working-class character of the Kindertransportees' care frequently meant that they were nurtured towards a very different future lifestyle, which possessed contrasting expectations to their previous lives in Greater Germany. Experiences were often marked by a need or demand from hosts to earn a wage and contribute to the household finances. The middle-class values that shaped care programmes did intend to encourage the Kindertransportees to adopt respectable working lives. This entailed their absorption into skilled manual or trade work, rather than into unskilled irregular employment, which was perceived as a plague for working-class communities.

As a result, a certain pattern of employment emerges among Kindertransportees. Training opportunities did tend to be based upon demand and practicality and very much a 'luck-of-the-draw'.[132] Kindertransportees, such as Wuga, stress their unintended careers as a result.[133] Nevertheless, the tendency was not to filter youth into the lowest employment positions in the community, but rather to channel Kindertransportees into skilled blue-collar work. There existed a real aversion towards employment opportunities that were viewed as unskilled, dirty work and associated with low social status.[134] Girls were encouraged to become domestics, rather than factory workers, an occupation deemed suitable for the lowest echelons of British working society.[135] This concern prevented many females from joining munitions factories or the ATS during the war years. Similarly, few boys became Bevan Boys and worked in the mines.[136]

Initiatives also intended to deter boys from employment deemed to be unreliable or irregular, such as street trading, and strictly deter girls from prostitution.[137] Instead, boys were encouraged to become farm workers, disciplined servicemen or skilled in a reliable trade. In 1941, the agricultural committee estimated that by 1944, 1,000 refugee children would be employed on farms and 800 Kindertransportees serving in the armed forces.[138] Some

Kindertransportees were able to find white-collar employment, but these too tended to follow a trend of being within service industries, such as shop work, commercial employment, including bookkeeping or shorthand, typing, nursing or teaching for girls.

In order to adopt these respectable working-class lives, Kindertransportees were expected to gain a certain level of education and training. This required the acquisition of certain life skills suitable for respectable employment in Britain. In 1943, the SED's report stated that:

> Good citizenship is rarely possible unless suitable and satisfactory occupations have been found, and unless the individual has the ability, training and experience to carry them on . . . employment therefore lies behind any scheme of continued education.[139]

In line with these objectives, technical training, trade skills and apprenticeships dominated Kindertransportees' care experience. This was also true for the Scottish child-in-care, who was intended to adopt an 'honest and industrious' life based upon knowledge of a trade.[140] Minors in Scotland were also encouraged to undertake 'day continuation classes' up to the age of 16, after compulsory schooling, in order to push minors into craft and commercial occupations.[141] Schemes would teach trade skills through technical training or practical experience. The SED recorded a system of 'pre-employment' courses intended to give vocational training for specific occupations.[142]

Specific initiatives formulated by the CC were also imbued with these objectives and training strategies. In 1944, Presland of the CC stated that 'the general rule of the Movement is that at about 16 the young people shall enter some vocational training to fit them for a future which must, in the best circumstances, be arduous'.[143] Fry went to Paisley Technical School and believes that 'irrespective of whether they are Jews or refugees, [people] take the view that you are more likely to earn a living if you do technical studies'.[144] He comments that technical school offered a relatively inexpensive yet efficient training option for employment compared to university (25 shillings to £9, respectively).[145]

Whittingehame promoted trade skills for boys – carpentry, draughtsmanship, shoemaking and wood work – and domestic service or servicing roles for girls – cooking, laundry and dressmaking – although these gender lines were not rigid.[146] The approach to training at Whittingehame resembled that of residential schools in Scotland, whereby students would follow a 'half-time' system.[147] This divided their schooling between practical and academic learning. In pursuit of respectable employment, many Kindertransportees also undertook practical experience options in the form of apprenticeships. At the age of 15, Warton became an apprentice within a furniture factory and learnt the trade skills of a cabinet-maker.[148]

The focus on practical respectable employment for the working-class member did mean that few Kindertransportees found their academic ambitions were supported. Before migration, the majority of the Kindertransportees of age had begun to undertake education aimed at higher academic involvement. Table 6 illustrates that the highest number of respondents attended a Gymnasium before migration. Gymnasiums were designed to prepare students for a university education. In contrast, in Scotland, as previously mentioned, Kindertransportees were only expected to obtain a basic education. Kindertransportees were to acquire academic education up to the point of the school-leaving certificate, or lowers in Scotland.[149] The majority of Kindertransportees would attend state schooling, along with Jewish education after school. At Polton House residents were sent to Bonnyrigg School.[150]

Academic expectations were not encouraged beyond the compulsory schooling age of 14 and 'only those with special gifts' were allowed to pursue full-time study after the age of 16. Despite the *Scotsman*'s report to the contrary, I have been unable to find any Kindertransportee at Polton House who recalls being given the option to attend night school at Heriot-Watt College, Edinburgh.[151]

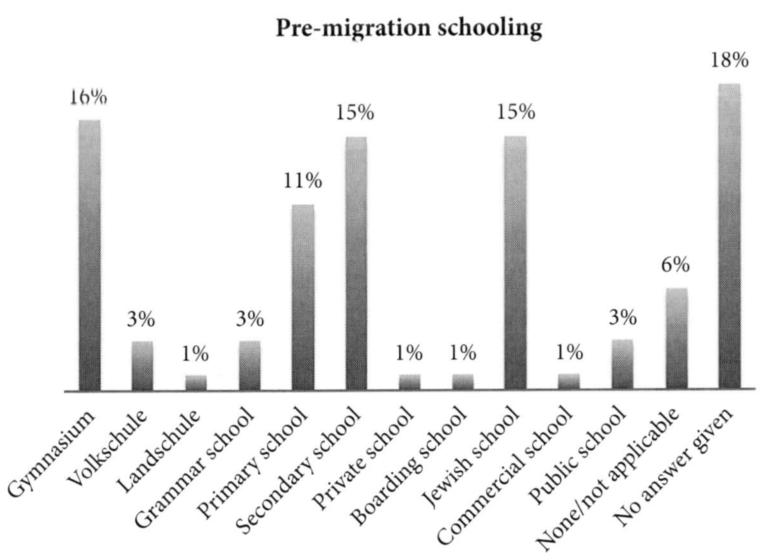

Table 6 Pre-migration schooling.
Source: KA:QU/SUP.

In July 1944, the *Scotsman* also reported that Polton House currently possessed one girl who was 'working for her MA'.[152] However, this seems to have been the exception rather than the rule. Miss M. C. Cowan, the Chairman of the Children's sub-committee in Edinburgh, reported that of the 325 children on their list 'educational measures were being applied as strictly to refugee children as to Scottish children'.[153]

When academic education was provided in care facilities – residential and foster – it tended to be of a low standard. Edna notes that the quality of teaching and education at Whittingehame was poor.[154] Josephine came from Berlin, Germany. Her parents were non-observant Orthodox Jews, but she did attend Jewish school. Aged 16, she left on the Kindertransport and was sent directly to Whittingehame. After Whittingehame, she joined the David Eder farm, an adult *hachsharot* in England, before making *Aliyah* to Palestine with Youth Aliyah. She later joined the British Army and returned to England. Josephine dwells on her 'lost career' as a pianist due to her limited education and training options in Scotland.[155]

In foster care, Kindertransportees often found that their carer's education expectations were low. Ruff was sent to his local secondary school in Woodsire and recalls that his foster family had completely different expectations for education and employment based upon the local schooling system:

> At that time, school-leaving age was 14. There was a very different approach, English Chemists were, if you like, not of the same class as Austrian chemists. I mean it was a nice enough family, but the thought of me going to school after 14 or even going to university never entered their head. As far as they were concerned, as soon as I was 14, I didn't need to go to school and I needed to find somewhere to work.[156]

Nurtured by caregivers with lower educational expectations, Kindertransportees frequently express their struggle to complete even their basic schooling.[157] Fry refused to undertake employment and was eventually evicted by his foster family.[158] In 1944, Eleanor Boll argued that children cared for within unskilled working-class homes were unlikely to pursue education beyond compulsory schooling age.[159] Few Kindertransportees were able to immediately pursue further full-time academic education after the age of 14. The point at which compulsory schooling ended became a watershed that brought to an end full-time education.[160]

Poor education opportunities were also due to the disruptions of war and a subsequent retarded educational system for all Scottish minors during the period.[161] Air bombardments and blackouts, the loss of trained teachers or caregivers to war work, and the general shortages of resources or suitable premises made it difficult for all Scottish minors to gain access to a good education.[162] Makeshift schools with haphazard teaching standards that lacked resources were the result. Boll described the situation in 1944 as a 'sketchy affair'.[163] Between 1939 and 1945 hundreds of thousands of children were living without education and basic schooling services including free milk and health care.[164] It has been estimated that by May 1940 10 per cent of school children in England and Wales were without elementary education services, and that by April 1941 210,000 children were not receiving full-time education.[165] In 1944, H. C. Dent described four clear stages of education during the war: 'Disintegration, recuperation, adaptation and fermentation'.[166]

Subsequently, the education experience for many of the Kindertransportees was poor and shaped by limited contact hours, substandard tuition and irregular attendance. Fry recalls that he wished to study physics in 1941, but that there was no teacher available at Paisley Technical School to teach physics.[167] Whittingehame depended on the staff's knowledge to shape the curriculum, rather than being able to source staff to fill specific subject posts. This meant that education was uneven and could not easily cater for the student's specific subject interests. Flesch recalls the impact of war upon his schooling:

> Then, in Scotland again, I did my first year of Secondary school in the hostel. But then these teachers were called up, you see, or took the place of those who were called up in Glasgow and so on. So, after that, we had only people who were Hebrew teachers. They didn't know how to deal with kids.[168]

There was also the problem of a lack of fellow students in schooling. This meant that a number of Kindertransportees were cared for in unorthodox education environments that lacked the normal classroom dynamics. Flesch recalls that in his local grammar school in Greenock he was the only student in his German class.[169]

Despite the prevalence of limited education for school-aged minors during the war, further education was important to Kindertransportees and 59 per cent did achieve further qualifications. However, it is important to note that this was most often undertaken in later life after employment had been found. Night school and part-time study were the most popular forms of further education for Kindertransportees.[170] The majority (58%) could not and only 32 per cent were able to pursue full-time university education.[171] In 1939, there were only 70,000 students undertaking higher education in Great Britain and Kindertransportees did not constitute many of these places.[172]

Raising a child in care: A Scottish tradition

There existed no national guideline for childcare services concerning the nurturing needs of minors while in care, yet there did exist an assortment of theories that informed approaches.[173] This meant that there was an experimental character to welfare provision in Britain and a lack of conformity.[174] The very nature of Kindertransportee care was not based on any grounded guidelines and was thus a learning curve for all involved. Furthermore, the care of Kindertransportees under Scottish welfare was by no means uniform. Various strategies were advanced in an *ad hoc* manner.

During this period, the public were particularly concerned about the threat of juvenile delinquency in Britain and this fear shaped elements of the Kindertransportees' nurture in Scotland. There existed a perceived rise in offences by juveniles. This was less a demarcation of the escalation of juvenile delinquency during the period, and more a reflection of the increased public awareness and concern about the offender.[175] The unattached youth was believed to be roaming unmolested around Britain, terrorizing good citizens. Fear of the dangerous adolescent led to the emergence of welfare strategies to police this section of society.[176] The SED's 1943 report was heavily weighted in concerns for youth.[177] In 1944, Boll reported the perceived magnitude of the problem during the war years. Boll states that in the 'first 12 months of the war, juvenile delinquency had increased 41%' in Britain.[178] In Scotland, a Youth Advisory Committee, under the chairmanship of Lord Keith, was established to tackle concerns about youth problems.[179]

The subsequent strategies designed to combat the juvenile delinquent developed a number of features and focuses. Juvenile delinquency was perceived as a male phenomenon and focused on those aged between 12 and 17 years. Attention focused on the dangerous 'unattached' youth and their potential for unsupervised bad behaviour. The desire to prevent delinquency and reform male youths led to the merging of territory between juvenile punishment, provisions for youth leisure and welfare in Scotland during the war.[180] Three issues remained the focus of juvenile reformers: poor parenting, environment of care and lack of recreational activities.[181] These concerns led to welfare strategies aimed at maintaining the supervision of youth and directing them towards solutions for the proper use of their leisure time. Schemes also worked to push youth into early employment to avoid delinquency and anti-social habits.

The desire to police youth was particularly central to the Kindertransportees' care because of their unsupervised status in Britain. There is a common narrative within Kindertransport historiographies, which overlooks the significance of their situation in Britain as a large number of unaccompanied youth who were prone to misbehaving (see Chapter 5 for information about Kindertransportee behaviour).[182] The CC was concerned that they prevent negative publicity surrounding any Jewish migrant in Britain. Accordingly, they sought to quell any potential problems with Kindertransportees' bad behaviour. In 1939, the CC wrote of the fear surrounding minors who proved 'difficult to raise' and the impact they would have on placing 'normal' children.[183] The CC feared that difficult children would scare off potential guarantors. In 1944, Presland recorded the problems of managing a surplus of adolescent males:

> One of the problems of hospitality, which manifested itself, was that of the older boys and youths. A large number of these had been included in the earlier transports because of the danger they ran of being sent to concentration camps, but it is clearly more difficult to find hospitality for an adolescent, with all the problems arising from his age, than for a young child who can be fitted into the life of a family.[184]

To tackle these problems, care schemes drew strategies from a legacy of Behaviourism. This focused on managing and controlling the minor, with predetermined rules and punishments.[185] It is possible to distinguish four main features to the Kindertransportees' care, which were prescribed by Behaviourism: regimentation, routine, discipline and strict punishment.[186] These were all felt to best manage, police and control the potential dangerous juvenile in every youth. Behaviourism also prescribed remedial management techniques. Scotland had progressed from initially removing the juvenile from the home environment and placing them in places of detention, to establishing remedial residential institutions to reform minors.[187] This led to the use of day industrial schools and residential reformatories during the nineteenth century. These operated by way of purposeful daily management strategies. These would enable the complete control of the unattached youth by occupying every hour of their day.

Regimentation of residents' daily lives was at the heart of the remedial care strategy. Kindertransportees have reflected on the centrality of regimentation to their upbringing in Scottish residential facilities. Edna recalls that everyone at Whittingehame was allowed the same amount of material possessions.[188] At Whittingehame, Kindertransportees were also given a morning roll call and daily life was based upon an organized rotation system.[189] The training programme adhered to a strict tri-partite structure encompassing the trainees' entire day. Each day was divided between certain hours designated for practical work, academic education and cultural pursuits.[190] Little time was left over for the children to choose a personal activity.

This approach prioritized a fully encompassing daily routine. A regimented daily structure afforded little time for the minors to spend freely. Elsie was cared for in the Convent of the Sacred Heart, Aberdeen, and recalls of her life that:

> Everything was regimented including your dining. . . . You got up too early, 6.30, did your bed, wash etc, and had to be downstairs 7.30am ish, then there was mass, then breakfast, then housework or what ever your assignment was like dusting or moping, and then you went to class until lunchtime. After lunch you had one hour or recreation, which was usually a supervised activity. Maybe walking, having a baseball game, going to a field to practise hockey and then back to class until 4.00pm. Then tea time and then study hall, then rosary, then homework, and you had so much homework, which you had to drive yourself to get done before dinner time, about 6.30pm, then after supper there was an hour or half of recreation, such as Scottish country dancing . . . then by 9.00pm you were dead to the world.[191]

Care schemes also adopted a paternalistic approach and sought to police the juvenile by way of entrenching the minor's daily life in a blanket of firm discipline.[192] This strategy was rooted in the presumption that minors could be taught to behave in certain ways by rewards and punishments.[193] Institutions used a blanket code of behaviour to discipline the resident body. These regulated boundaries were often static and unlike rules that can be renegotiated in small family environments.

The isolated cloistered character of residential facilities meant that rules and regulations would encroach on every hour of the Kindertransportees' daily lives. Elsie recalls discipline in the convent in Aberdeen:

> In those days it was a cloistered order and very strict. You were not supposed to speak except during meals at certain times between the bells and when you were spoken to at class.[194]

However, this aspect of the Kindertransportees' care is often recalled as one of the most familiar aspects of their upbringing, mirroring their lives before migration. Isabel recalls that her father led a strictly patriarchal family unit. After the Nazi party came to power and anti-Semitism became a reality in daily life, her parents moved to a big city and later sent Isabel to Aachen to live with her two aunts. Isabel points to the strict and regimented habits of her German family and especially her two aunts who supervised her before migration on the Kindertransport.[195] Edna states that she was 'used to discipline . . . you had to make your bed, you had to be punctual, you had to do your jobs'.[196]

Despite some similarities, the forms of punishment used in residential facilities were often very different to those used by parents. Interviewees have emphasized the use of parental authority and individual accountability to enforce self-discipline in the family environment.[197] Few suggest that their parents used physical force to discipline them as minors.[198] Corporal punishment continued to be utilized in some Scottish residential facilities during this period.[199] Mahood has found one extreme incident that occurred within a Scottish Roman Catholic reformatory between 1927 and 1934, where a boy was beaten so severely that he could not get up for 9 days.[200] The striking of children with a cane continued to be used in remand homes and other residential facilities.[201] However, it did become less common during this period and Smith argues it gradually only equated to '1% of cases' in which punishment was sought.[202]

Kindertransportees' testimonies do not suggest that corporal or extreme bodily punishment was enforced. Nevertheless, physical forms of punishment were used against Kindertransportees. In Whittingehame, headmaster Maxwell is recalled by Kindertransportees as wielding a slipper against misbehaving residents.[203] Another resident recalls being smacked across the face in the dining area by a member of staff.[204] This physical approach to discipline was often unfamiliar to Kindertransportees.

The threat of certain punishment was also used to discipline Kindertransportees by way of a deterrent. Edna refers to the disciplinary approach at Whittingehame as very different to that normally issued within *hachsharot:* 'obedience out of fear that you would be punished (rather than) self discipline for the collective'.[205] Ernespie House's male hostel supervisor enforced a strict disciplinary regime, which few Kindertransportees dared to challenge.[206]

Collective management strategies were also used to control the Kindertransportees. These used forms of collective punishment, such as prohibitions that prevented residents' activity or threats of expulsion from the care environment. The latter was particularly unique to an institution because it emphasized the insecure, temporary nature of the facility, unlike the home. Levi was born in Berlin, Germany, to Polish parents and received an observant Orthodox Jewish upbringing. In October 1938 his father was expelled as a Polish Jew and soon afterwards Levi left on the Kindertransport to Britain under the auspices of Youth Aliyah and B'nai B'rith. On arrival he was sent to Whittingehame. During his time at Whittingehame he agitated for a greater degree of religious observance and Zionist support, including the appointment of Madrichem to guide the minors. His actions eventually led to his expulsion. Levi recalls his emotional upset after being expelled and his relief when he was allowed to return.[207] On another occasion, Levi was 'gated' after misbehaving, meaning that he could not go beyond the school perimeters for an outing.[208] This was a form of collective punishment because as a group leader it meant that his whole group was prohibited from leaving the grounds. Elijah recalls the significant impact of this approach in the punishment of the Kindertransportees: 'One of the punishments was they could not go on an outing and an outing was very very important to us as we were closed in all the time'.[209]

Despite the importance placed on supervising youth and controlling juveniles, discipline of the Kindertransportees in care, in reality, often proved to be weak.[210] This was largely due to a lack of information, accountability and/or adequate staff. Supervisors of Kindertransportees were often unable to respond to individual problems because of the minimal priority and time given by the RCM to disseminating information about individuals. The CC sought to maintain jurisdiction and control over regional philanthropy. This meant that their central subdivision, the RCM, did not send Kindertransportees' personal records to local caregivers or regional committees. As a result, caregivers had limited information about their charges and this made it difficult to offer intimate care.

Such problems also afflicted the majority of non-refugee residential facilities in Britain.[211] There existed a general ignorance of hosts to their charges' needs due to the failure of non-refugee organizations to provide this information.[212] In some cases caregivers were reduced to relying on numbers rather than on individual names.[213] Numbers were used for the Kindertransportees during transit to Britain, but this tactic does not seem to have been continued in care. However, that caregivers worked in ignorance was even more acute because of the Kindertransportees' foreign backgrounds and particular circumstances.[214]

The weak level of supervision and discipline of Kindertransportees was also due to the lack of clear accountability or responsibility for charges.[215] Official guardianship was never completely clarified for Scotland's Kindertransportees.[216] Handler felt that there were problems of misbehaviour among Kindertransportees because there was a lack of accountability among organizations for the individual minor and limited authority when problems arose.[217]

Weak and limited discipline was also due to an increasingly limited pool of persons available to provide supervision. The disruptions caused by war challenged traditional resources within a Scottish society for supervising youth. Boll also argued that a situation of inadequate supervision and care existed due to mobilization and evacuation.[218] The development of mass British migration during this period, including evacuation and drafting into the army, impacted heavily on a domestic and international level.[219] Mass population movements led to the disintegration of communities and the breakdown of their traditional informal frameworks for supervising youth. It broke family units and weakened the stability of the private sphere of the community. Minors experienced multiple losses of familial support and 'normal' supervising social structures.[220] Basque minors in Britain experienced a similarly limited level of supervision due to actual shortages in available people during wartime.[221] The CC expressed their anxiety at the absence of a family unit or close community, normally relied upon to govern youth.[222]

This situation was not easily rectified and led to limited availability or permanency of staff to educate or supervise Kindertransportees.[223] Education or residence facilities were forced to rely on inexperienced staff or were forced to close, leaving Kindertransportees without access to basic schooling or daily supervision. This situation was not unique to Scotland. Ann Essinger at Bunce Court, England, experienced difficulties in finding staff during the war years.[224] This resulted in inappropriate and unsuitable supervisors. Flesch recalls that a substitute teacher 'had lived in Italy and he told us he was in the Fascist youth in Italy', while the other substitutes just 'couldn't deal with us'.[225]

A lack of adequate supervision also meant that Kindertransportees often experienced care marked by accidents or management problems. Accidents did occur when Kindertransportees were left to guide themselves on a daily basis. This was a particular problem afflicting Kindertransportees working within agricultural training centres. At Whittingchame, Kindertransportees were left unsupervised in charge of agricultural machinery, including a combine harvester. This could result in accidents. In September 1940, one such Kindertransportee lost his leg after stepping into the thrashing machine.[226]

The breakdown of traditional means for supervising youth meant that importance was placed on youth groups and recreational activities to attach the 'unattached' juvenile. Philanthropists were preoccupied with finding distractions or 'counter-attractions' for youth.[227] Efforts were made to extend leisure facilities, which could provide healthy pastimes.[228] The youth group was seen as a remedy to improper use of leisure time and unsupervised juvenile free time after school.[229] The youth movement became central to the policing of youth in the 1930s and 1940s.[230] In 1942, the SED sought to register youth between 16 and 17 years of age in order to determine the extent of the problem of the 'unattached' youth, those not affiliated with a youth group.[231] The results showed that 'unattached'

Scottish youth aged 16 constituted 47.2 per cent of boys and 71.4 per cent of girls. In order to uncover the root of the problem, 683,000 unattached youth were interviewed. Boll underlines that not only money and long working hours prevented recreational participation in youth groups, but also the popularity of 'unattached' social activities, such as 'cinemas, dance halls, billiard saloons, company of the opposite sex and hanging out'.[232]

Youth movements accordingly emerged as a dominant force in the supervision and care experience of youth in Scotland. Kindertransportees became involved in youth groups of various affiliations and orientations. Kindertransportees' choices tended to be based on financial feasibility. Some groups required uniforms or membership subscriptions, while others did not. Popular choices included the Scouts or the Jewish Lads Brigade, the Zionist youth groups – Habonim, Bachad or Hashomer Hatzair – or Communist or Socialist groups. Benson joined multiple youth groups at any one time with his friend in Glasgow.[233]

Within their chosen groups the Kindertransportees would participate in recreational and cultural enrichment activities. Dena was born in Poland, but grew up near to Vienna, Austria, with her parents who were Orthodox Jews. She attended the local Gymnasium until the Anschluss, when she was moved to a Jewish Zionist school. Dena migrated to Britain on the Kindertransport after her father was killed in Dachau in 1938. On arrival she was sent to Lowestoft reception camp, England, before being taken to Whittingehame. At Whittingehame Dena belonged to the Habonim youth group. She recalls that within their chosen group the Kindertransportees would participate in a range of activities and weekend excursions.[234] Flesch would be invited on Highland weekend retreats with his Habonim group.[235] Garnethill's hostel directed its residents to join the Maccabi clubs in Glasgow, which would supervise physical health and sporting activities in the evenings on a weekly basis.[236]

Refugee cultural centres were also popular choices among Kindertransportees in Scotland. These centres intended to relieve the cultural isolation of the foreign migrants and occupy them in a controlled environment during their free time.[237] In Glasgow, Kindertransportees joined the Sauchiehall club.[238] At the club, Wuga recalls that 'we learnt a lot' and members participated in lectures, music and discussion groups.[239] Fry recalls the access this club granted them to cultural and educational resources under the supervision of the adult migrant community:

> It was run by somewhat older people . . . who were essentially political refugees, some of them may have been Jews but did not admit it, . . .there were quite a lot of

> Czech students . . . quite a few were studying to be doctors . . . and there were a lot of more impressionable people and we had a lot of discussions about politics and philosophy and took part in acting, which they wrote, which was very anti-fascist, but was somewhat communist dominated, so it tended to follow the party line and it provided a lot of interest and I suppose support to all of these young people.[240]

The Sauchiehall club was closely connected to the Scottish Refugee Centre (SRC), which opened in 1941.[241] The SRC coordinated its activities with other refugee clubs in Glasgow, including the Freie Deutsche Jugen (Free German Youth), established in 1943, and the Freier Deutscher Kulturbund (Free German Cultural Union) established in 1942. The youth clubs played an important role in the trans-migrants' care in Scotland. Some provided alternative education courses, while others helped to prepare young people for migration.[242]

The welfare strategies aimed at preventing the emergence of dangerous juveniles also included moves to promote good mothering. There existed a keen pro-natalist climate of opinion in Scotland during this period, which identified the neglectful or deficient mother as being responsible for rearing delinquent sons.[243] To rectify the problem, schemes focused on reforming young girls into model female prototypes. While boys were perceived as the danger and efforts were made to reform their wicked ways, girls were perceived as the root cause and prescribed a number of specific remedies to prevent them producing more delinquents.[244]

Concerns for female virtue meant care aimed at protecting normative values for female morality and chastity. Scottish welfare facilities reinforced gender roles by way of education, training and employment directives. These all tended to focus on placing girls within protective living environments. This hoped to guard female 'respectability' by way of restricting girls' exposure to corruptible vices from the outside world.[245] The 'home' was deemed the safest place for females and this encouraged a tendency to support domestic service roles for girls.[246] This tendency informed the CC's policy for female Kindertransportees' care and employment placements in Britain. It was viewed that girls could be placed more easily in domestic positions in London and therefore fewer girls were sent to Scotland.[247] Many of those that were sent to Scotland were also directed into domestic work. Rachel was placed as a domestic in Edinburgh, while Edna was sent into domestic work after completing her training at Whittingehame.[248]

The Kindertransportees' care was also directed by concerns to teach minors against immoral lifestyles. Anglo-Jewry was concerned to prevent negative stories emerging about Jewish females and their role in British society.[249] This was linked to the myth of the Jewish prostitute and her danger to the Gentile man. Trans-migrant residential facilities possessed a strict code of conduct rooted in middle-class moral standards. Edna believes that Whittingehame, a coeducational facility, possessed 'an extremely high moral standard'.[250] Drew wrote to his parents of his role as housemaster in protecting the girls' chastity.[251] Drew's bedroom was located at the entrance to the girls' dormitories, which allowed him to guard the girls from unwarranted male visitors.

Remedies would place importance upon traditional domestic roles for girls in preparation for their future roles as mothers. Girls were to learn to adopt supporting roles for men and possess virtues that would enable them to rear good citizens in the future. Education and training services adhered to specific ideas about correct gender roles. Schools played an important role in teaching minors their class and gender-related place in society.[252] In 1943, the SED advocated that females should be 'occupied at home' and therefore 'home-making and keeping must form an important part of the future training'.[253] By 1958, the SED's position had not changed and continued to advocate 'handicraft' for boys and 'homecraft' for girls.[254] This approach focused on teaching girls 'mothercraft' and skills required for managing a household.[255] Esther Breitenbach, Alice Brown and Fiona Myers have argued that this has led to the marginalization of females in Scotland.[256]

Residential facilities structured their training programmes to adhere to these traditional patriarchal codes of behaviour for girls. Training facilities habitually utilized gendered curriculums. At Whittingehame, this was not imposed along a solid immovable line, but it did set a normative benchmark for initial placements of female and male trainees. Girls were able to undertake practical farm work, including fieldwork and harvesting, but they were most commonly occupied with domestic service and servicing roles. Abaigael explains the delicate balance adhered to in Whittingehame between pragmatically allowing everyone to 'muck-in' and the maintenance of gender roles based on female domesticity:

> There were two jobs the girls never did, one was attend the boilers and the kitchen range because that was done with coal . . . also the heating, that all had to be done and then we had a cobbler's shop where only the boys went. . . . Girls went into the kitchen, into the laundry, and we went into the sewing room . . . the boys didn't go into the sewing room, but they had to go into the laundry . . . the girls had to do more housework and cooking, but we all had to go out onto the fields, come summer or winter and do field work, agricultural work as well as the boys, except the boys were sent to do harder jobs. They went with a forester.[257]

Figure 13 Kitchen work.
Source: MCPC/Drew, photographs.

Figures 13, 14 and 15 capture the usual gender ratio in different occupations within Whittingehame. Girls dominated the sewing rooms, kitchens and laundry, while the boys were greater in numbers within physical farm labouring jobs outside. A similar *hachsharot* centre based in Essex outlined its gender policy in its prospectus:

> Most girls are expected at some time or other during their course of instruction, to learn one or more of the various branches of housekeeping, i.e. cooking, laundry and housework. Girls who show a special inclination and aptitude for agricultural work will normally be allowed to remain on this work during their entire course.[258]

In 1944, the *Scotsman* reported of Polton House that boys were in handicrafts and girls in domestic subjects. That 'cooking and sewing occupy a good deal of the time of the older girls, but washing up is strictly rationed' between boys and girls'.[259] At Whittinghame, this structure meant that the majority of girls divided

Figure 14 Laundry work.
Source: MCPC/Drew, photographs.

Figure 15 Kindertransportees feeding chickens.
Source: MCPC/Drew, photographs.

their time between fulfilling domestic duties within the house, the care and maintenance of the other children, their instruction in domestic or servicing spheres, and the care of the poultry yards or fieldwork. They received instruction from the previous headmistress of Frankfurt's Domestic Science College, Mrs Laquer, and her deputy, Ruth Fishall.[260]

Alice Hubbers was born in Vienna, Austria, and lived with her Traditional Jewish parents. Her maternal grandparents were originally from Slovakia and her grandmother was a strict Orthodox Jew. Hubbers was sent to Whittingehame and recalls that half of the day was devoted to 'laundry, housework' and either the mending or making of clothes, shoes and other necessary items for the children.[261] The girls also received cooking lessons, learning to make jams and other essentials such as butter. Horticultural experience was provided, but this tended to be limited to managing the dairy and the small plot of land set aside for the girls.[262] A number of female Kindertransportees did acquire training beyond the boundaries of domesticity; however, these too adhered to preferred gender roles in Scotland that would not compete with male roles. Most commonly, these included clerical work, nursing or teacher training.[263]

The boys at Whittingehame were given a wider scope of training opportunities and different daily chores to the girls. Edna recalls that at Whittingehame 'they tried hard to give the boys a profession in which they could work in, but not for the girls'.[264] Edna believes that this meant the boys' daily instruction surrounded agricultural work in the fields, the maintenance of farm machinery and becoming proficient in a trade: carpentry, mechanics or draughtsmanship. Drew photographed the male residents undertaking their training and daily duties on the workshops. Figure 16 shows two boys

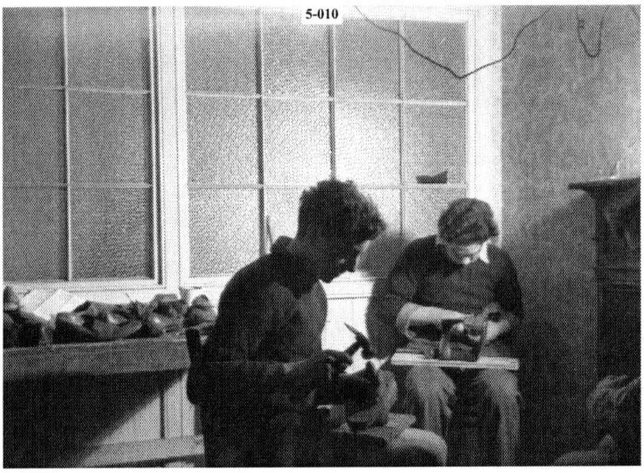

Figure 16 Cobbler's shop.
Source: MCPC/Drew, photographs.

undertaking cobbler's training. The boys were also responsible for the physical restoration and alterations needed to maintain the accommodation.[265]

The physical care of the dependent trans-migrants in Scotland was also shaped by preconceptions about gender requirements, and this prioritized the need to accommodate male youths. It was felt to be easier to place girls in domestic service, while adolescent males posed a real placement problem. Garnethill hostel was established to accommodate boys, while the girls were belatedly incorporated into a Quaker-run hostel nearby.[266] Whittingehame admitted a smaller percentage of girls than boys, accommodating the maximum of 40 girls out of the 200 places.[267]

Scottish philanthropy was also enveloped in a heritage of concern for helping the vulnerable child. Concepts of 'childhood' and 'family' have changed over time and played an important role in directing policy.[268] The concept of the vulnerable child and the importance of 'childhood' emerged within the middle classes in the nineteenth century.[269] However, the notion of the child as vulnerable and the 'victim' had not yet been formally implemented into welfare services, concern for protecting children in need of care continued to develop through the 1930s. This situation especially progressed following the Morton Committee's formulation of Scotland's Children and Young Persons Act in 1932.[270] This extended the responsibility of welfare for helping such minors.

Scotland possessed a unique heritage of Calvinist theology, which pointed philanthropists towards particular concerns and strategies for protecting the vulnerable child. Combined with ideas of Environmentalism, these concepts encouraged stricter policing of the family and a practice of removing minors from unsuitable families and home environments. Protecting the vulnerable child took on a new level of importance during wartime, when they were perceived as future assets to the nation.[271] This led to a number of new protective schemes.[272]

British philanthropy's concern to protect the vulnerable child led to legislation designed to police levels of care and the family.[273] The 'child-saving-movement' intervened in private spheres of life and imposed a new form of regulation upon family life.[274] This led to the emergence of the inspector, who became responsible for visiting residential centres and home environments. Philanthropists' interest in controlling and inspecting the home grew in the 1930s, pushing the home to become the institution liable for regulation.[275] All Scottish residential facilities were also subject to a governing board and regular inspections.[276] The CC established inspectors to check on the children within foster homes under the auspices of the RCM. However, the impact of both systems was limited. Both lacked manpower and efficiency.[277] Scotland suffered from a weaker and less developed system of inspection than England.[278] This was the result of a long preference for short-term welfare options and boarding-out, rather than residential care solutions.[279] The CC also relied upon untrained, inexperienced volunteers.[280] Inspectors often questioned children in front of foster parents. Subsequently, Kindertransportees do express a varied care experience that lacked regulation. Despite these disparities with England and general weaknesses, Scotland's Kindertransportees were still afforded a degree of legality and a number of formal supervisory schemes.

The preoccupation with protecting the endangered and vulnerable child could not always ensure a happy home life, but it did promote a common care experience for Kindertransportees sheltered from the realities of war. This was by way of mass evacuation and the censorship of war news by adult supervisors. Tydor Baumel refers to the 'pied piper' migration of 1,473,000 evacuees on 31 August 1939.[281] Kindertransportees were incorporated into the mass evacuation schemes and shared similar experiences of billeting, relocation and makeshift reception centres as other Scottish children. During the war, 37 per cent Kindertransportees were evacuated and only 39 per cent state that they were not evacuated.

Scotland's Jewish communities of Glasgow and Edinburgh orchestrated a number of coordinated evacuations to designated Jewish reception areas. The majority of Glaswegian Jews relocated to Ayrshire during evacuation. Twenty-seven Jewish evacuees relocated to Troon, 26 to Largs and Lockerbie, and 100 families and many Jewish servicemen to Ayr.[282] Kindertransportees were included in the Jewish migration to these areas and individual billets were organized. Warton, who was fostered by a cantor in Glasgow, was later evacuated to a billet in Ayr.[283] He recalls that 'it was like a summer resort, which had a very good high school'.[284]

The Kindertransportees were also incorporated into the large residential Jewish evacuation schemes established in Scotland during the war years. These aimed at protecting and sheltering the vulnerable child from war on the home front.[285] Castle Douglas hostel, Kirkcudbrightshire, and Birkenward hostel, Skelmorlie, accommodated up to 160 Kindertransportees.[286] Ruff was evacuated with the Jewish community to the Castle Douglas hostel, after being initially fostered by a Christian family in Glasgow.[287] The Gertrude Jacobson Orphanage and the Garnethill hostel were both evacuated to these centres.

Bert's family originated in Poland, but he was born in Prague, Czechoslovakia.[288] His Jewish family was Ultra-Orthodox. His parents were very poor and in 1934 it was decided that they could not afford to care for him anymore. He was sent to Vienna, Austria, and adopted by his uncle and aunt. In light of increasing anti-Semitism, he was sent on the Kindertransport to Britain. On arrival he was sent to the Gertrude Jacobson Orphanage, Glasgow, and was later evacuated to Birkenward. He recalls that the evacuation hostel was filled mainly with Austrian and German minors.

These Jewish evacuation hostels became important hubs of Jewish activity in Scotland.[289] Jewish educational facilities were also relocated to evacuation areas and Kindertransportees were not excluded from these facilities.[290] Glasgow's *Talmud Torah*, along with its two teachers, relocated to Ayr. Jewish education initially took place twice a week on Saturday and Sunday with 40 children, including six evacuees from Troon, in attendance.[291] Bert recalls that while at Birkenward he was 'bussed to school every morning'.[292]

These efforts meant that the Kindertransportees' care in Scotland was heavily marked by a period of evacuation and an overarching care policy for their protection from the realities of war. As a result, Ruff believes he subsequently never heard 'a shot fired, neither a bomb dropped, never, nothing'.[293] Elsie recalls that being cloistered in Aberdeen meant that she remained unaware of the war and only received censored news deemed suitable by her supervisors, which was very little.[294] Debbie was born in Frankfurt and grew up in Berlin, Germany. She lived with her non-Orthodox Jewish parents and attended a Jewish school. She was sent via the Kindertransport to a pre-arranged foster care placement with an Ultra-Orthodox Jewish family in London. She was later evacuated with her school to Windsor, before being sent to Polton House, Scotland. She remembers that her time at Polton House was uninterrupted by the events of war.[295] Nachtigall remained with his 'fresh-air' foster family in Dysart due to the evacuation of children from Edinburgh and, as a result, remained sheltered from any experience of the war.[296]

*

The Kindertransportees' experiences of care in Scotland do not truly reflect Gertrude Black's derogatory impression of Scottish peoples' approach to looking after their children. Rather, their care experience in Scotland was infused with a wide variety of ideas, preconceptions, agendas and realities. These were not all unique to a Scottish experience, but they were drawn from new, old and developing circumstances that uniquely surrounded the Kindertransportees in Scotland. Care experiences were incredibly varied in response to these specific circumstances and relevant issues. They are reflected upon by Kindertransportees in both positive and negative tones. The common experience that does emerge is that welfare solutions were not sympathetic to the foreign child, but instead encouraged integration and adaptation to their new Scottish surroundings by way of total immersion.

Notes

1 WL/AG/76.

2 See Buck, 'Feeding A Pauper Army'; Richard Titmuss, *History of the Second World War: Problems of Social Policy* (London: HMSO, 1976); John Welshman, 'Evacuation and Social Policy During the Second World War: Myth and Reality', *Twentieth Century British History*, 9, 1 (1998), 28–53.

3 SJA: Jack Cowen, recollections of the Gertrude Jacobson Orphanage, 24 September 1995; Collins, *Be Well!*, 68.

4 KA: QU/SUP.

5 Ibid.

6 Ibid.; SJA: Memoirs, letters from evacuated Kindertransportees, photographs and reunion documents of evacuation centres in Scotland.

7 KA: QU/SUP.

8 Ibid.

9 Geoffrey Alderman, 'The defence of an image', in Alderman (ed.), *Modern British Jewry*; HLSC/MS116/157/AJ396/5; HLSC/MS183/384/F1.

10 HLSC/MS183/384/F1, Circular No100 of CC, 6 June 1941; Ibid. Quarterly report of JRC, January – March 1942.

11 HLSC/MS183/289/2/F1, Minutes of CC, 11 April 1940, 5.

12 Ibid. List of forms of employment, 15, 16.

13 WL/BL/25.

14 Ibid.

15 Buck, 'Feeding A Pauper Army', 336.

16 WL/BL/26.

17 Presland, *A Great Adventure*, 21.

18 WL/BL/50.

19 FWPC/Abaigael.

20 *Scotsman*, 26 July 1944.

21 Ibid., 21 March 1944.

22 Curio, 'Invisible children', 54; See also Kushner and Knox, *Refugees in an Age of Genocide*, 126–216.

23 See also Kushner, 'The Kinder: A Case of Selective Memory?', in Kushner (ed.), *Remembering Refugees,* 141–80.

24 Karen Gershon, *We Came as Children: A Collective Autobiography of Refugees* (London: Harcourt Brace and World, 1966), 40.

25 Jill Rutter, *Refugee Children in the UK* (New York, 1999), 57; See also Nina Glick Schiller, Linda Basch, Cristina Szanton Blanc, 'Immigrant to Transmigrant: Theorising Transnational Migration', *Anthropological Quarterly*, 68, 1 (January 1995), 48–63; Curio, 'Invisible children'; Alderman, *Modern British Jewry.*

26 Anthony Grenville, *Jewish Refugees from Germany and Austria in Britain, 1933–1970: Their Image in AJR Information* (London: Vallentine Mitchell, 2010), 67–74; London, *Whitehall and the Jews,* 261; London, 'Jewish Refugees', in Cesarani (ed.), *The Making of Anglo-Jewry* (Oxford: Oxford University Press, 1990), 164; Kushner, *The Persistence of Prejudice,* 11.

27 Grenville, *Jewish Refugees,* 52.

28 Presland, *A Great Adventure*, 26.

29 HLSC/MS183/384/F1, Quarterly Report of JRC, January – March 1942.

30 Curio, 'Invisible children', 54.

31 HLSC/MS183/289/2/F1, Minutes of CC, 25 April 1940.

32 Grenville, *Jewish Refugees,* 60.

33 Kushner and Knox, *Refugees in an Age of Genocide,* 126–216; See also Curio, 'Invisible children'.

34 Adrian Bell, *Only for 3 months; The Basque Children in Exile* (Norwich: Mousehold Press, 1996), 143; Natalia Benjamin (ed.), *Recuerdos: Basque Children Refugees in Great Britain* (Oxford: Mousehold Press, 2007), 45; Rutter, *Refugee Children,* 59.

35 Gershon, *We Came as Children*, 42.

36 Kushner, *The Jewish Heritage in British History: Englishness and Jewishness* (London: Frank Cass, 1992), 14.

37 Bell, *Only for 3 months*, 143.

38 Black, *The Social Politics of Anglo-Jewry,* 390.

39 WHMA/USC: 36790.

40 HLSC/MS183/132/4, Pamphlet for refugees entitled 'While you are in England'.

41 KA: QU/SUP.

42 Grenville, *Jewish Refugees,* 52.

43 *Scotsman*, 25 April 1944.

44 London, 'British government policy and Jewish refugees', 40; KA:QU/SUP; See also Stachura, *The German Youth Movement.*

45 Hugh Cunningham, *The Invention of Childhood* (London: BBC books, 2006), 179.

46 Smith, 'Official Responses to Juvenile Delinquency in Scotland', 100.

47 Scottish Education Department; *Public Education in Scotland* (Edinburgh: Her Majesty's Stationery Office, 1958).
48 Ibid., 34.
49 SJA:Unknown Newspaper clipping, 25 February–3 March 1989; See also Collins, *Aspects of Scottish Jewry*, 77–8.
50 Ibid.
51 WL/BL/74.
52 Ibid.
53 Ibid.
54 FWPC/Rachel.
55 Rosalyn Livshin, 'The Acculturation of the Children of Immigrant Jews in Manchester, 1890–1930', in Cesarani (ed.), *The Making of Anglo-Jewry*, 79.
56 WL/BL/25.
57 Scottish Education Department, *Public Education in Scotland*, 34; See also London, 'Jewish Refugees', 115–37; Cunningham, *Children and Childhood in Western Society since 1500* (London: Longman, 1998).
58 FWPC/Levi, Abaigael.
59 Smith, 'Official Responses to Juvenile Delinquency', 103.
60 Ibid.
61 Ibid.
62 Tammy M. Proctor, 'On My Honour: Guides and Scouts in Interwar Britain', *Transactions of the American Philosophical Society*, New Series, 92, 2 (2002), 6; Linda Mahood, *Policing Gender, Class and Family; Britain, 1850–1940* (London: UCL Press, 1995); see also Proctor, '(Uni)Forming Youth', 103–34.
63 WHMA/KC/RG-50.002*43.
64 WHMA/USC: 23855.
65 WL/BL/74.
66 FWPC/Elsie.
67 Ibid.
68 FWPC/Elijah.
69 Mahood, *Policing gender*, 7.
70 See Macnicol, 'The effect of evacuation'.
71 Mahood, *Policing Gender*, 6; See also Jacques Donzelot, *The Policing of Families* (New York: Pantheon Books, 1979).
72 Smith, 'Official Responses to Juvenile Delinquency', 104.
73 Welshman and Stewart, 'The Evacuation of Children in Wartime Scotland', 102.
74 Mahood, *Policing Gender*, 13.
75 NA/PREM/4/89/2.
76 Mahood, *Policing Gender*, 25.

77 Smout, *Punishment and Welfare* (Aldershot, 1985) 153; see also Mahood, *Policing Gender*, 30.

78 *Scotsman*, 21 March 1944.

79 Bell, *Only for 3 months*, 184.

80 Black, *The Social Politics of Anglo-Jewry*, 390.

81 Kushner, *Anglo-Jewry Since 1066: Place, Locality and Memory* (Manchester: Manchester University Press, 2009), 183.

82 Ibid.

83 Braber, *Jews in Glasgow*, 32.

84 See Buck, 'Feeding A Pauper Army'.

85 Mahood, *Policing Gender*.

86 June Thoburn, 'Trends in Foster Care and Adoption', in Olive Stevenson (ed.), *Child Welfare in the UK* (Oxford: Blackwell Science Ltd, 1999), 122.

87 Tydor Baumel, 'Twice a Refugee', 180.

88 Patricia Lin, 'National Identity and Social Mobility: Class, Empire and the British Government Overseas Evacuation of Children During the Second World War', *Twentieth Century British History*, 7, 3 (1996), 333.

89 Lore Segal, *Other People's Houses* (New York: Harcourt, 1964).

90 FWPC/Elsie.

91 FWPC/Rachel.

92 Richard Anthony, 'The Scottish Agricultural Labour Market, 1900–1939: A Case of Institutional Intervention', *The Economic History Review*, New Series, 46, 3 (August 1993), 559.

93 Buck, 'Feeding A Pauper Army', 329.

94 WHMA/USC: 43932.

95 Ibid.

96 WHMA/USC: 31378.

97 See Francis Galton, *The Possible Improvement of the Human Breed, under the Existing Conditions of Law and Sentiment* (London: Eugenics Education Society, 1909); Donald MacKenzie, 'Eugenics in Britain', *Social Studies of Science*, 6, ¾ (September 1976) 499–532; Emel Aileen Gökyiğit,'The Reception of Francis Galton's "Hereditary Genius" in the Victorian Periodical Press', *Journal of the History of Biology*, 27, 2 (Summer 1994), 215–40.

98 Mahood, *Policing Gender*, 13; Cathy Urwin and Elaine Sharland, 'From bodies to minds in childcare literature; advice to parents in inter-war Britain', in Roger Cooter (ed.), *In the Name of the Child; Health and Welfare, 1880–1940* (London: Routledge, 1992), 174.

99 Cunningham, *The Invention of Childhood*, 178.

100 Proctor, 'On My Honour', 7.

101 See Priscilla Robertson, 'The home as a nest', in Lloyd de Mause (ed.), *The History of Childhood* (London, 1976), 427.
102 Bryder, 'Wonderlands of Buttercup', 76.
103 Richard Ellis, 'Effects Of War On Child Health', *The British Medical Journal,* 1, 4544 (7 February 1948), 241; Bryder, 'Wonderlands of Buttercup', 76.
104 Ellis, 'Effects Of War', 241; see also John Welshman and Stewart, J., 'The Evacuation of Children in Wartime Scotland: Culture, Behaviour and Poverty', *Journal of Scottish Historical Studies*, 19 (2006), 28–53.
105 Curio, 'Invisible children', 45.
106 WL/BL/26.
107 Smith, 'Official Responses to Juvenile Delinquency', 104.
108 B. Seebohm Rowntree, report: *Poverty: A Study of Town Life* (1901) based on York and follow-up study in 1936. These both pointed to the extent of children living in poverty in Britain.
109 Cunningham, *Invention of Childhood,* 185.
110 See Bryder, 'Wonderlands of Buttercup'.
111 Ibid., 88.
112 Thomas Johnston, *Scottish Education Department; Compulsory Day Continuation Classes; Fourth Report of the Advisory Council on Education in Scotland* (Edinburgh. His Majesty's Stationary Office, 1943), 18.
113 WHMA/KC/RG-50.002*43.
114 FWPC/Benson, Levi, Abaigael.
115 Erica Simmons, '"Persecuted, Uprooted": Youth Aliyah and the Rescue of European Jewish Children', *Hadassah and the Zionist Project* (Oxford: Rowman & Littlefield Publishers, 2006), 115.
116 Abrams, *The Orphan Country*, 19, 24.
117 WHMA/KC/RG-50.002*43.
118 Ibid.
119 WL/BL/137.
120 Ibid.
121 Collins, Be Well!, 70; See also SJA: Jack Cowen (24 September 1995).
122 WHMA/USC: 31378.
123 WL/BL/50.
124 WHMA/USC: 43138.
125 Abrams, *The Orphan Country*, 173; see also Titmuss, *History of the Second World War.*
126 Stewart and Welshman, 'Evacuation and Social Policy During the Second World War: Myth and Reality', *Twentieth-Century British History,* 9, 1 (1998), 28–53.
127 Susan Kleinman and Chana Moshenska, 'Class as a Factor in the Social Adaptation of the Kindertransport Kinder', *Shofar: An Interdisciplinary Journal of*

Jewish Studies, 23 (2004), 31; Buck, 'Feeding A Pauper Army', 326; Macnicol, 'The Effect of the Evacuation', 3–31; Titmuss, *History of the Second World War,* 103; Welshman, 'Evacuation and Social Policy', 28–53.

128 Kleinman and Moshenska, 'Class as a Factor', 31.

129 Buck, 'Feeding A Pauper Army', 326.

130 WHMA/USC:23855; FWPC/Marthe; WHMA/31378.

131 FWPC/Elsie.

132 Rutter, *Refugee Children,* 60.

133 WL/BL/74.

134 Ibid., 29.

135 Penny Summerfield, *Women Workers in the Second World War; Production and Patriarchy in Conflict* (London: Croom. Helm, 1984), 55.

136 KA: QU/SUP.

137 Mahood, *Policing Gender*, 117.

138 *Ibid*; HLSC/MS183/384/F1, Report of CC, 1941.

139 Johnston, 'Continuation classes', 5.

140 Ibid., 89.

141 Ibid., 6.

142 Scottish Education Department; Public Education in Scotland, 40.

143 Presland, *A Great Adventure,* 26.

144 WHMA/USC: 31378.

145 Ibid.

146 HLSC/MS116/157/AJ396/5, Report, 21 March 1939.

147 Mahood, *Policing Gender*, 86.

148 WHMA/USC: 23855.

149 See B. J. Elliott, 'Early Examination Reform in Scotland and the Crisis in History 1888–1939', *Journal of Educational Administration and History*, 1478–7431, 24, 1 (1992), 47–57.

150 *Scotsman*, 26 July 1944.

151 Ibid.

152 Ibid.

153 *Scotsman*, 21 March 1944.

154 FWPC/Edna.

155 FWPC/Josephina.

156 WL/BL/50.

157 FWPC/Jan, Josephina, Edna; WHMA/USC: 31378.

158 WHMA/USC: 31378.

159 Eleanor S. Boll, 'Britain's Experience with Adolescents', *Annals of the American Academy of Political and Social Science*, 236 (November 1944), 77.

160 Cunningham, *Children and Childhood,* 172.

161 Kröger, 'Child Exiles', 8–20.
162 Steinberg, 'Jewish Education', 44.
163 Boll, 'Britain's Experience with Adolescents', 77.
164 Steinberg, 'Jewish Education', 30; Titmuss, *History of the Second World War,* 147.
165 Steinberg, 'Jewish Education', 37.
166 H. C. Dent, *Education in Transition* (London: Routledge, 1944), 38.
167 WHMA/USC: 31378.
168 WL/BL/137.
169 Ibid.
170 KA: QU/SUP; Rutter, *Refugee Children in the UK*, 60.
171 KA: QU/SUP.
172 Peter G. Moore, 'The Next Decade', *Journal of the Royal Statistical Society*, Series A (General), 146, 3 (1983), 213.
173 Finlayson, 'A Moving Frontier', 195.
174 Tydor Baumel, *Twice a Refugee,* 181; Steinberg, *Jewish Education,* 27; Abrams, *The Orphan Country*; Hildegard Feidel-Mertz and Andrea Hammel, 'Integration and Formation of Identity: Exile Schools in Great Britain', *Shofar: An Interdisciplinary Journal of Jewish Studies*, 23 (2004), 81.
175 Smith, 'Official Responses to Juvenile Delinquency', 85.
176 Boll, 'Britain's Experience with Adolescents'; See also Mahood, *Policing Gender.*
177 Johnston, 'Continuation classes'.
178 '*The Spectator,* 'Juvenile Delinquency', 166, 5895 (20 June 1941), cited in Boll, 'Britain's Experience with Adolescents'.
179 Johnston, 'Continuation classes', 4.
180 Smith, 'Official responses to Juvenile Delinquency', 78.
181 Ibid., 104.
182 WL/1368/2/2/1-166, Reunion of the Kindertransport Documents 1987–2002.
183 (Letter from CC, 22 June 1939) cited in Curio, 'Invisible children', 49.
184 Presland, *ROK*, 23.
185 Urwin and Sharland, 'From bodies to minds in childcare literature', 180, 188; see also Cunningham, *Invention of Childhood,* 192.
186 Ibid.
187 See Mahood, *Policing Gender*; Abrams, *The Orphan Country.*
188 FWPC/Edna.
189 Ibid.
190 HLSC/MS116/157/AJ396/5; see also Jewish Echo, 10 February, 24 March 1939.
191 FWPC/Elsie.
192 Mahood, *Policing Gender*, 7.
193 Cunningham, *Children and Childhood,* 175.
194 FW/PC/Elsie.

195 FWPC/Isabel.
196 FWPC/Edna.
197 FWPC/Rachel.
198 WHMA/USC: 3679.
199 Mahood, *Policing Gender,* 97.
200 Ibid.
201 Smith, 'Official responses to Juvenile Delinquency', 98.
202 Ibid.
203 FWPC/Levi.
204 Ibid.
205 FWPC/Edna.
206 SJA: Ernestpie House reunion documents.
207 FWPC/Levi.
208 Ibid.
209 FWPC/Elijah.
210 Buck, 'Feeding A Pauper Army', 329.
211 Titmuss, *History of the Second World War,* 103.
212 Ibid.; Abrams, *The Orphan Country*, 59.
213 Cunningham, *The Invention of Childhood,* 178.
214 Rainer Kölmel, 'Problems of Settlement; German-Jewish Refugees in Scotland', in Gerhard Hirschfield (ed.), *Exile in Great Britain; Refugees from Hitler's Germany* (London: Allen & Unwin, 1984), 257.
215 HL/SC/MS116/157/AJ396/5.
216 HL/SC/MS183/290/F1/GEN.473/6/4/CEC/SS/E.
217 WL/BL/25.
218 Boll, 'Britain's Experience with Adolescents', 81.
219 Macnicol, 'The Effect of the Evacuation'; Welshman, 'Evacuation and Social Policy', 28–53; Tydor Baumel, 'Twice a Refugee', 179.
220 Ibid.
221 Legarreta, The Guernica Generation, 126.
222 Presland, *ROK,* 24.
223 Buck, 'Feeding A Pauper Army', 329.
224 Anna Essinger, *Bunce Court School, 1933–1943,* 3, cited in Gopfert, 'Kindertransport: History and memory', 61.
225 WL/BL/137.
226 MCPC/Drew, Letters, 6 February 1943.
227 Smith, 'Official responses to Juvenile Delinquency', 100.
228 Ibid., 99.
229 Scottish Education Department: Public Education in Scotland, 40.
230 Proctor, 'On My Honour', 6; Cunningham, *Invention of Childhood,* 203.

231 The Board of Education, Scottish Education Department, *The Youth Registration in 1942* (1943), cited in Boll, 'Britain's Experience with Adolescents', 80.
232 Ibid., 76.
233 FWPC/Benson.
234 FWPC/Elijah, Dena.
235 WL/BL/137.
236 HLSC/MS183/384/F1.
237 Collins, *Aspects of Scottish,* 77–8.
238 Ibid.
239 WL/BL/74.
240 WHMA/USC:31378.
241 *Jewish Echo*, 11 June 1941.
242 Collins, *Aspects of Scottish Jewry,* 80.
243 Smith, 'Official responses to Juvenile Delinquency', 87.
244 Ibid., 103.
245 Mahood, *Policing Gender*, 25.
246 *Jewish Echo*, 9 May 1941.
247 HLSC/MS116/157/AJ396/2, Letter from GCJR.
248 FWPC/Rachel, Edna.
249 Kushner, *The Persistence of Prejudice,* 67.
250 FWPC/Edna.
251 MCPC/Drew, Letter, 25 April 1940.
252 Mahood, *Policing Gender,* 11, Harry Hendrick, *Images of Youth: Age, Class and the Male Youth Problem, 1880–1920* (Oxford: Oxford University Press, 1990), 123; Mahood, *Policing Gender,* 12.
253 Johnston, *Continuation Classes,* 6.
254 Scottish Education Department, Public Education in Scotland.
255 Cunningham, *Invention of Childhood,* 190.
256 Esther Breitenbach, Alice Brown, Fiona Myers, 'Understanding Women in Scotland', *Feminist Review*, 58, International Voices (Spring 1998), 45.
257 FWPC/Abaigael.
258 HL/PL/*Bachad Farm Institute: The Lodge*, Prospectus, 3.
259 *Scotsman*, 26 July 1944.
260 WHMA/USC: 43138.
261 Ibid.
262 Michael Cohen, 'Report from Kfar Hanasi', in Hashannah; The Scottish Jewish Year Book; 1957–58 (Glasgow 1955–56), 17.
263 Mahood, *Policing Gender,* 131.
264 FWPC/Edna.
265 *Jewish Echo*, 10 February 1939.

266 FWPC/Rachel.
267 *Jewish Echo*, 24 March 1939.
268 See Abrams, *The Orphan Country*.
269 See Mause, *The History of Childhood*, 420; Cunningham, *Children and Childhood;* Cunningham, *The Invention of Childhood.*
270 Smith, 'Official Responses to Juvenile Delinquency', 80.
271 Cunningham *Children and Childhood*, 172.
272 Abrams, *The Orphan Country*, 62.
273 Mahood, *Policing Gender*, 8.
274 Ibid.
275 Smith, 'Responses to Juvenile Delinquency', 81.
276 SJA: SOC0004, Fay Cohen Stein, Memoir, 5 January 1995.
277 Harry Ferguson, 'Cleveland in History; The abused child and child protection, 1880–1914', in Cooter (ed.), *In the Name of the Child*, 148, 164.
278 FWPC/Benson, Sarah.
279 Abrams, *The Orphan Country*, 3.
280 HLSC/MS183/50/F2.
281 Tydor Baumel, *Twice a Refugee*, 175.
282 Abrams, *The Orphan Country*, 52.
283 WHMA/USC: 23855.
284 Ibid.
285 Steinberg, 'Jewish Education', 58.
286 Abrams, *The Orphan Country*, 53; Steinberg, 'Jewish Education', 58.
287 WL/BL/50.
288 FWPC/Bert.
289 Steinberg, 'Jewish Education', 58.
290 Abrams, *Caledonian Jews*, 51.
291 FWPC/Bert.
292 Ibid.
293 WL/BL/50.
294 FWPC/Elsie.
295 FWPC/Debbie.
296 WHMA/KC/RG-50.002*43.

3

Scottish Care for the Jewish Minor: Kindertransportees' Adaptation to a New Jewish Life

> [To be Jewish] . . . is it racial inheritance – or a self-chosen ethnic identity? Does it require synagogue affiliation, or does identifying with Maureen Lipman suffice?
>
> Is support for Israel relevant – and do financial contributions count? Is being Jewish constituted by our moral standards and ethical behaviour? Or is it to do with the food we eat – or choose not to eat? Is my Jewishness defined by whom I marry? Or if I marry?
>
> Is it connected to belief in God? Or following the *halachah* (Jewish law)? Or reading the *Jewish Chronicle*? Or is it a sick feeling in the stomach when you hear the word "yid" on the tongue of a stranger? . . . What constitutes our Jewish identity is, in the end, a very personal response we formulate for ourselves . . . determined by experiences.[1]

Between 1938 and 1939, 9,354 minors were brought over by the RCM and 7,482 of these were deemed to be 'Jewish'. The Chief Rabbi's Religious Emergency Council (CREC), directed by Rabbi Solomon Schonfeld, sought to provide a proactive Orthodox Jewish force aimed at preventing the widespread estrangement from Judaism of these Jewish refugee youth during their stay in Britain. In 1944, the Union of Orthodox Hebrew Congregations (Adath) published Schonfeld's report, entitled 'The Child-Estranging Movement'.[2] The report was an exposé of the 'alienation of Jewish refugee children in Great Britain from Judaism' and intended to 'defend the religious rights of Jewry's orphans'.[3] The major contention was that the non-denominational RCM, officially responsible for Kindertransportees' care in Britain, was failing to prevent Jewish Kindertransportees being placed within both non-Orthodox and non-Jewish care environments. Schonfeld claimed that the RCM had adopted a *laissez-faire* policy in relation to the religious life of the Kindertransportees and was forcing them into non-Jewish homes and lifestyles, which inevitably led to their estrangement from Judaism.

The RCM claimed that it had adopted a non-denominational approach to all care placements, but did still wish to maintain a Jewish upbringing for Jewish children when it was possible, particularly for Orthodox children.[4] The RCM's placement policy was pragmatic and strategic in character. It was realistic in the restricted circumstances. The RCM prioritized saving children by placing them in every available home, rather than restricting numbers on account of Jewish authenticity.[5] This meant members remained in constant conflict with the Orthodox community, CREC and Adath.[6]

The battle that ensued during the war years regarding the RCM's placement policy has been continued in latter-day discussions about the success or not of the entire Kindertransport scheme. The main bone of contention remains the perception that the lax placement protocol of the RCM did not protect the Kindertransportees' Jewish heritage. Critics argue that this alienated a large number of Kindertransportees from Judaism.[7] These current debates have perpetuated the notion that non-exclusive Jewish care of Kindertransportees inevitably exposed them to proselytizing and mass conversion. In 2003, Handler stated he believed that 'out of the 10,000 Kindertransport people a maximum of 3000 or 4000 remained in the Jewish fold'.[8] In 1999, during the 60th anniversary of the Kindertransport, Bertha Leverton offered an epitaph to the lost Kindertransportees: 'I realised that, like myself, many had been sent to non-Jewish homes and got sadly lost to our faith and tradition. Only the arrival of our parents saved us from that same fate.'[9]

Such perceptions neglect the broader picture and can pander to naïve assumptions, such as that the Kindertransportees had initially been attached to Judaism. It also assumes that all Kindertransportees' felt that piety to religious traditions was important, or that they even wanted to maintain a high degree of religious observance. Sixty-one per cent of Scotland's Kindertransportees felt that they were able to maintain the correct level of religious observance while in care, compared to 18 per cent who felt they were not.[10] These statistics should not be assumed to suggest that the correct level of care meant a strictly observant, Orthodox Jewish lifestyle. It could also mean that the Kindertransportees experienced a suitable absence of piety. Five per cent stated that this question was not applicable, suggesting the irrelevance of a religious upbringing. The prevalence of such presumption has encouraged an unhelpful narrative within Kindertransport literature. This narrative groups the Kindertransportees into a monolithic Jewish type, who were firmly within the Jewish fold before migration. It also ignores a wide spectrum of other, often more important, influences on the Kindertransportees' religious lives. These influences both pushed and pulled upon their Jewish affiliation.

What emerges is a separation between the meaning of being Jewish and being connected to Judaism. These features were two different aspects of the Kindertransportees' Jewish lives in Scotland. The former refers to the social, cultural or political connotations of being Jewish, while the latter relates to religious piety, spiritual faith and ritual observance. The Jewish experience of Kindertransportees during the war years was much more complex than has previously been suggested. Conversion was a reality in Scotland, but there was no linear flood of Jewish youth abandoning Judaism for Christianity. Instead, various factors influenced youth to rethink their relationship with Judaism and the Jewish people. The religious experience of Kindertransportees in Britain has been narrated too closely to historiographies concerned with fears for Jewish survival post-Holocaust.[11] What has been overlooked is the migration of many Kindertransportees away from Judaism towards a more secular Jewish lifestyle.

Changes to Jewish life in Greater Germany

Prior to migration, the Kindertransportees' Jewish lives were already in transition and many had experienced upbringings in families that were already estranged from Judaism. Jews from Greater Germany reflected a kaleidoscope of different types of affiliation to Judaism. Table 7 shows that there was a wide spectrum of Jewish types, as well as non-Jews, among the Kindertransport group. Many of these religious preferences and affiliations contradicted the Orthodox basis of the CREC's arguments for Kindertransportee religious care. The findings suggest that only 29 per cent of Scotland's Kindertransportees were Orthodox, while 32 per cent were Liberal, 3 per cent were Traditional and 23 per cent were Jewish but with no particular association.[12] Furthermore, not all Kindertransportees considered themselves to be Jewish.[13] Only 91 per cent believe that they were Jewish on arrival, while 3 per cent note that they were non-Jewish on arrival and a further 4 per cent had no religious faith.[14] Fay Cohen Stein, daughter of the Governor of Whittingehame Farm School, recalled that many of the Jewish Kindertransportees lacked any kind of religious observance.[15]

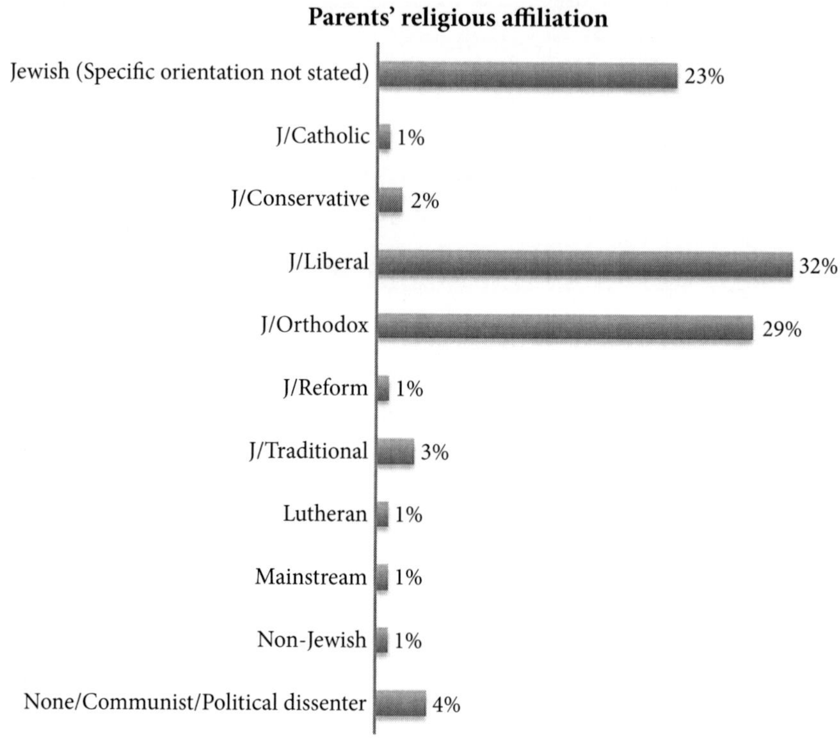

Table 7 Parents' religious affiliation.
Source: KA: QU/SUP.

These findings reflect a correlation with wider trends among Jews in Greater Germany. There had been great concern for the popularity among German Jews for a secular, non-spiritual lifestyle. German-Jewish publications, such as *Ost und West,* sought to ameliorate German Jewry's estrangement from Judaism and promote *Ostjuden* pious and non-secular traditions.[16] The term *Trotzjudentum* was even applied by the Nazis to the prevalence of secular, non-practising, assimilated Jews in Germany.[17] Emil Fackenheim termed such German Jews as '*Konfessionlose* Jews'.[18] Many of the Jews in Germany considered themselves to be Germans rather than Jews.[19]

Many Kindertransportees' religious lifestyles reflected these developments within the Jewish communities of Greater Germany. Fry recalls that, despite his parents' Jewish origins, his family was non-practising and his mother had actually been baptized at birth.[20] Jacob arrived via the Kindertransport from Herlingham, a small village in southern Germany. His parents were not religious, but he did attend a Jewish school.[21] Benson remembers his Czechoslovakian family as not at all religious, but 'totally secular'.[22] Living a secular lifestyle, Abaigael's family did not observe the Sabbath and worked on Saturdays.[23] Ruth, a Kindertransportee who was cared for in England, states that 'I really did not have a tradition . . . we didn't practise anything'.[24] At the point of departure from Greater Germany, many Kindertransportees already reflected a greater attachment to a secular lifestyle.

Before migration, the Kindertransportees also personally underwent transitions in their Jewish life and their understanding of being Jewish. For a significant number of Kindertransportees, their Jewish identity was newly acquired, an unexpected result of classification by the Third Reich. Many had had no previous connection with Judaism or a Jewish community. Elsie remembers the shock she experienced when she discovered that she was Jewish and was subsequently ostracized from her school and friends.[25]

Other Kindertransportees knew they were Jewish, but this had played no role in their lives before the Third Reich emerged. Josephine recalls: 'I knew I was Jewish but it was not important, it was nothing, until Hitler came'.[26] The pressures of Nazism meant that to be a Jew increasingly defined who you were, where you could go and how you could get there.[27] The most immediate aspect of this process was the Jews' ejection from non-denominational schools. For some, this meant that they had to attend Jewish schools for the first time.[28] Josephine was forced to leave her Gymnasium and attend the very religious local Jewish Hadassah School.[29] John Grenville was born in 1928 and lived in Berlin, Germany, with his Jewish family. He recalls his shock when he moved to a Jewish school after *Kristallnacht*.[30]

Nazi family policy often led to a Jewish community revival and the rediscovery for Germans of their Jewish identity.[31] Dena believes that fellow Kindertransportees, from 'quite assimilated houses, . . . all of a sudden became religious' because of Hitler's new laws.[32] Kindertransportees remember that Jewish life had also become increasingly limited and inward looking.[33] Warton felt that, after *Kristallnacht*, Jewish life was completely transformed.[34] Communities shrank daily and readjustments in services and provisions had to be continually renegotiated.[35] *Kashrut* (Jewish dietary laws) became increasingly difficult. Prohibitions on the slaughtering of kosher food meant that fewer families could find suitable supplies. Isabel's family could no longer observe *Kashrut* after ritual slaughtering was prohibited and supplies from Frankfurt were found always to be off.[36]

Jewish life also became increasingly sectarian as an ever-deepening divide emerged between 'gentiles' and Jews in Germany during the 1930s.[37] Isabel recalls that secular 'life really stopped for a Jewish child, there was nothing'.[38] Warton recalls that, after being 'closed off from fraternising with German people, . . . we stuck with our own people as far as Jewish friends were concerned . . . we had our own plays and activities'.[39] After 1933, he had minimal contact with non-Jewish children except neighbours.

Interaction with non-Jewish people became increasingly negative and even violent. Warton recalls that 'it was not uncommon to have stones thrown at you'.[40] Rachel recalls that as a child, 'I didn't really have non-Jewish friends. . . . I learnt early on that we were not wanted'.[41] Ruth desired to avoid contact with her Jewish heritage due to this fear of persecution.[42] Ugolini has shown similar tendencies among Italian immigrants' children.[43] She argues that minors experienced prejudice and bullying due to their Italian 'otherness' and many subsequently wished to dissociate themselves from their foreign status as 'Italians'.[44]

These changes also meant that some Kindertransportees had begun to migrate towards other denominations. Jewish children were being placed in convents, monasteries and Catholic homes for safety across Europe.[45] These strategies would have created a new religious lifestyle for the Kindertransportees before migration.[46] Elsie's parents baptized her and sent her to a Catholic school.[47] It was through this placement and the Catholic connections her family developed that Elsie was able to join the Kindertransport to Britain. Ruth's family also chose to send her to a Catholic school.[48] She recalls that growing up in a small Catholic village meant that she never felt any difference from Catholics. Martha Bauer was born in Kassel, Germany, and after her parents divorced, she grew up with her extended family. At the age of 10, her uncle and aunt sent her to the Catholic High School.[49] Fry's parents chose to send him to a Catholic school because they believed it was a friendlier and safer schooling environment.[50] Such Kindertransportees were already exposed to new rituals and beliefs and had already developed a religious normality in life that did not include Jewish observance.

Furthermore, not all of the Kindertransportees' parents wished for their children to be placed in Jewish care homes. Elsie recalls that in Czechoslovakia her parents did not want to send her to a Jewish school because she 'knew nothing about Judaism'.[51] They felt that she would feel estranged from that environment compared to the Catholic convent. Elsie remembers that, although she came from a Jewish background, her family observed Christian rituals:

> We believed in Chris Kindle (Father Christmas), the Christ child who brought presents at Christmas time . . . believed in Wusterhausen, the Easter Bunny who brought eggs and presents. We believed in Saint Nicholas who came 25 December and brought presents.[52]

She remembers 'no Jewish connections at all' before leaving her parents.[53] Elsie's aunt was a Catholic and encouraged her parents to convert and to begin Elsie's Catholic life with a baptism in Vienna. Elsie had always questioned whether these were truly the wishes of her parents, yet she discovered that when her parents were deported they chose to remain within the Catholic group. Elsie was sent via the Kindertransport to a Catholic convent in Scotland. On arrival in Britain, Adath's Jewish care ambitions were not suitable or appropriate for 'Jewish' Kindertransportees such as Elsie.

Non-Jewish care

The central concerns of Adath and CREC for the Kindertransportees were that they were placed within a Jewish, preferably Orthodox, care environment, in close proximity to a local Jewish community and receiving Jewish education. It was believed that these provisions would protect Jewish youth from proselytizing efforts and would maintain their connection with Judaism. Nevertheless, not all Kindertransportees in Scotland had access to these three requirements.

Despite clashing with CREC and Adath, the RCM continued to utilize non-Jewish care environments for Kindertransportees across Britain. Sixty-six per cent of Scotland's Kindertransportees were sent to Jewish homes, compared to 25 per cent who were cared for in non-Jewish foster homes. This shows that in Scotland the majority of Kindertransportees placed in foster homes were kept within Jewish households. Nevertheless, 25 per cent were required to be allocated to non-Jewish foster homes. It is interesting to note that in England, the proportion of Kindertransportees sent to non-Jewish homes was over twice as high (57%) as it was in Scotland (25%). Only 30 per cent of Kindertransportees fostered in England lived in Jewish homes.

This scenario existed because insufficient numbers of Jewish homes were available. Schonfeld initiated a decree, requesting rabbis across the country to 'influence members of their respective communities to take over immediately as many refugee children as possible, in order to prevent such [Jewish] children from being placed in non-Jewish homes'.[54] Despite these efforts, in 1944, Presland (who worked for the RCM) wrote about the lack of Orthodox Jewish homes for the number of Orthodox parents applying in Germany and the subsequent necessity of utilizing non-Orthodox and Christian homes.[55]

To tackle these shortfalls, the RCM sought to identify Orthodox children and prioritize Jewish care for them; non-Orthodox Kindertransportees would be readily sent to non-Jewish care homes. Presland recalls that in the reception camps 'the children were divided into Orthodox Jewish children, who needed special food and arrangements, and non-Orthodox and Christian'.[56] The problem with this policy was that many Kindertransportees could not certify exactly what affiliation their parents preferred. Eva Michaelis Stern, who worked with the RCM and Youth Aliyah, recalls the Kindertransportees' confusion when asked to clarify their religious orientation.[57] When asking one child 'whether he would like to live in an Orthodox group', he answered that he wanted to paint. Another child could not offer any information about what her family would do on a Friday night.[58] As a consequence, Orthodox Kindertransportees were also at times sent to non-Jewish care environments.

Non-Jewish care environments could pose a problem for Jewish Kindertransportees' connection to Judaism, especially when proselytizing activities were present. Turner has argued that in Britain 'the conversion rate to Christianity was well into double figures'.[59] However, new data do not suggest that the figure was quite so high, but conversion was a reality. An estimated 4 per cent of Scotland's Kindertransportees converted to Christian denominations, including the Anglican Church, the Church of Scotland, Roman Catholicism and the Episcopalian church.[60] This figure is still below the average 10 per cent rate of conversion among Germany's Jews between 1800 and 1933.[61]

Scotland did possess missionary organizations and persons who sought to convert the Kindertransportees. Orthodox Calvinist or Presbyterian ideas had a strong influence on Scottish philanthropists' activities.[62] Scotland possessed a deep heritage of evangelical schemes, which traditionally targeted the new Jewish immigrants by way of providing welfare support.[63] Although by 1940 the focus of missionary activity had shifted towards friendship and a support of Zionism, activities still sought to spread the Christian Gospel.[64]

In 1941, Reverent David McDougall wrote a 'Chronicle of the Jewish Mission of the Church of Scotland', which pointed to the less overt proselytizing processes active in Scotland.[65] He stated that its purpose 'for the Evangelization of the Jewish people of Scotland' would encourage the gradual conversion of Scottish Jewry to Christianity by way of communal integration.[66] McDougall was involved in the establishment of the Scottish Christian Council for Refugees (SCC), which would later work with the Scottish National Council (SNC) in order to help the Kindertransportees in Scotland. The SCC represented all the churches of Scotland, including the Catholic Church.

Linked to this was the 'Church of Scotland's Jewish Mission Committee' in Edinburgh. Reverend George Knight oversaw the committee's activities and produced a booklet 'For Christians only – About the Jew'.[67] As Lewis Cameron has argued, the purpose of these publications was to aid the integration of Jews into the Christian community 'through intimate contact with the local church and school'.[68] This process, it was thought, would nurture a 'Christian character' among Jews and form strong bonds between the communities.[69] Kindertransportees, such as Rachel, predominantly remember experiencing these integrationist and less dogmatic approaches to conversion.[70]

Under the auspices of the RCM, the SNC was the leading regional organization supervising Kindertransportees' care in Scotland and was seen as a potential source of proselytizing. In 1944, Schonfeld reported his fears to CREC:

> The Scottish Council has taken over from The Movement of the Care of Jewish Refugee Children (RCM). The Movement has taken no drastic action against conversionist activities among refugee children within the Scottish Council.[71]

Schonfeld was particularly concerned that there was a serious lack of 'Jewish oversee' in Scotland.[72] He believed that exposure 'to conversionist intentions' would threaten the Kindertransportees' ability to 'uphold their Jewish traditions and customs'.[73] It is not clear whether Schonfeld was justified in his concerns.[74]

The CREC believed that Christian foster homes posed the greatest risk.[75] This was because foster homes could potentially isolate the children from any Jewish environment. They could also influence and coerce Kindertransportees to participate in Christian rituals. In 1941 Jewish evacuees were found to be under direct proselytizing influences in foster homes.[76] This was viewed as mainly due to foster parents who claimed the price of conversion in return for their kind hospitality.[77] The limited resources of the Jewish organizations, as well as the delay until 1941 of efforts by CREC to remedy the situation, meant that supervision of these evacuee care placements was limited and little was done.[78] By the time efforts were made, contact had been lost with many of the children.

Kindertransportees remember feeling pressurized to submit to Christianity because of dependency, gratitude, or even a desire to fit in and join in. Sunday church attendance was often a regular family ritual and community event. Some Kindertransportees did not want to miss out on this event. Christmas and other Christian festivals were also attractive to Kindertransportees. Marthe grew up in Kassel, Germany, with her Jewish parents. Her father worked for a Jewish social care organization. Marthe was sent, via the Kindertransport, to a pre-arranged Christian foster placement in Edinburgh at the age of 6. She recalls that after her foster parents moved to Collington, she swiftly made friends and became a member of the Church of Scotland.[79] She went to Brownies and Girl Guides, and was drawn into the local Christian community, despite never being forced to attend church. Nachtigall's Christian foster family never attempted to convert him, but he chose to accompany them to church every Sunday and ingratiate himself with the local Christian community.[80] Nachtigall's foster mother, May Salmond, recalls his overwhelming joy on Christmas Day, when his foster family and friends in the community gave him many gifts:

> I can still see your face on Christmas morning, you not knowing anything about Christmas, I think all of Dysart gave you a present.[81]

Conversion could also be dogmatically advocated and difficult to avoid. Black, an adult trans-migrant, remembers that in Glasgow she befriended a non-Jew who would invite her to his house and then preach to her that she must convert.[82] On meeting a fellow Jew who had converted, Black was told, should she convert, she would receive 'pocket money every week'.[83] Kindertransportee Fry lived with a Scottish parson's family of the Church of Scotland.[84] Fry recalls that he was sent to church twice on Sunday to listen to sermons. He was eventually asked to leave after refusing to convert. Fry believes:

> Their major motive for taking me was quite clearly that they wanted to convert me to Christianity and I wasn't amenable.[85]

Rachel also experienced pressure to convert in return for support and guidance after moving to Glasgow.[86] She recalls that she had no other form of support and relied heavily on a minister and his wife. Rachel had been introduced to the couple by her sister and gradually found the minister's wife forceful in her efforts to convert her. This process included her being introduced to their church, choir and rangers' social club. She recalls on her eventual refusal to convert that 'Mrs MacDonald could never forgive me . . . that was a very difficult time, it was not easy'.[87]

Aside from proselytizing, non-Jewish care could also be problematic because it potentially isolated Kindertransportees from Jewish or other denominational communities. In 1944, Schonfeld expressed his fears that many Jewish children had been placed in good Christian homes, but that these lacked 'any Jewish contacts'.[88] Fry's brother, fostered by a family of Plymouth Brethren, lived in an isolated village called Hardgate, near Clydebank.[89] Fry believes that the puritan sect was 'terribly limited and backward, they condemned going to the theatre or the cinema', and enforced a very sectarian isolated lifestyle on his brother.[90] His brother was cut off from all outside influences and was not able to maintain Jewish or secular links during this period.

Being isolated from Jewish communities could cause an array of problems for the Kindertransportees' Jewish lifestyle. Non-Jews dominated non-Jewish areas and were often ignorant of Jewish traditions. Jacob recalls being asked 'who he was' by a Scottish woman.[91] When he told her that he was Jewish, she replied: 'I thought you people had horns'.[92] Such ignorance about Jews was not unique to Scotland, but affected Kindertransportees across Britain. One Kindertransportee points to the extent of naïvety that could exist when she recalls her first evening meal with her non-Jewish foster parent in England:

> On our first evening we were served fried bacon with fried bread . . . "we can't eat that" I said
> "why not?" asked Mrs Noble
> "because we're Jewish"
> "that's impossible!"
> "why?"
> "because you haven't got a tail!" and that was that![93]

Nachtigall recalls that in the remote Scottish village of Dysart, Fife, he was somewhat of a novelty: 'not only was I the only Jew in that town, I think that most people never knew or had encountered a Jew'.[94] Isabel was sent to Kemnay, a village north of Aberdeen, and doubts that the community 'had ever seen a Jew, if they thought we had horns I don't know. . . . I didn't come into any contact with any Jews except my aunt, until I went back to London'.[95]

Prejudiced ignorance could be a problem for Kindertransportees in non-Jewish care homes. Rachel was sent to the Quaker-run Renfield Street Hostel, Glasgow, for female Kindertransportees and other trans-migrants.[96] She found a lack of understanding among the staff and felt that the warden was anti-Semitic. She recalls the warden verbally abusing her and a friend when they were passing time in an air-raid shelter: '"how dare you people laugh when our people are being killed . . . what Hitler is doing to the Jews is quite right" '. Anti-Semitism or ignorance about Jews was felt to be such a problem in Britain that Woburn House published a booklet in 1941, entitled 'The Jews; some plain facts'.[97] This intended to challenge myths and stereotypes thought to be widely held by non-Jews about Jews:

> There is not a single Jew on the Board of the Bank of England nor is any Jewish controlled firm represented on it. . . . Jews do not control the Press.[98]

Isolation from Jewish communities could lead Kindertransportees to lose their understanding of Judaism and Jewish life, even if they did not convert to another denomination. Kindertransportees living in non-Jewish environments could find it difficult to maintain rituals and observances, which were not supported in their surrounding community. Kindertransportees could be forced to travel on the Sabbath or find that kosher food was unavailable in such environments.[99] Isabel decided to buy a live chicken when she visited her sister in England, in order to enjoy kosher food.[100] Schonfeld's correspondence draws attention to the problems Jews faced in secular employment for regular observance.[101] Marthe believes that she was at a disadvantage to Glasgow's Kindertransportees because they had contact with a Jewish community and were therefore able to maintain their 'heritage'.[102] She states that:

> A couple of times a year I go to synagogue, but I don't really know anything about it. . . . I was really never in touch with Jewish people. I would follow people who were talking in a strange accent.[103]

Marthe regrets that she is no longer able to pass her heritage on to her children, because she has forgotten it.

Failing to maintain Jewish traditions and not gaining an understanding of Jewish liturgy could permanently ostracize Kindertransportees from Jewish communities. Kindertransportees found it hard to reconnect with their Jewish families because of their non-Jewish experiences. Elsie's Catholic upbringing, 16 years in the Convent of the Sacred Heart, caused a problematic relationship for her with her Jewish aunt.[104] Elsie recalls that when she first moved in with her aunt in America, she hung her 'rosary over the bed post, it almost gave her [aunt] a heart attack'.[105]

Other problems for future Jewish lifestyles, stemming from non-Jewish care, included marrying non-Jewish partners. This could permanently ostracize Kindertransportees from Jewish communities who opposed 'marrying out'. Hans lived in a small town near Berlin, Germany, before migrating to Britain via the Kindertransport. On arrival, he was put on the 'flying Scotsman' to Edinburgh, where he was met by his non-Jewish foster family. They lived in Portobello and he attended the local non-Jewish school. During his time living with the family, Hans had some contact with Jewish people and the Jewish community of Edinburgh. However, he chose to marry a non-Jew and felt excluded from the local Jewish community after 'marrying out'.[106]

The adoption of additional beliefs in conjunction with Judaism could also be problematic. Ani originally lived in a small village in Odenwald, Germany. Her Jewish family later relocated to a city for anonymity. She was allocated a place on the Kindertransport with the help of Bertha Bracey and the Quakers. In Britain, she was sent to a number of Quaker-run hostels. She states that she is a 'cross with the Quakers . . . they do not convert folk. . . . I call myself a Jewish Quaker, or a Quaker Jew. It feels all right'.[107]

However, non-Jewish care did not automatically mean that Kindertransportees were exposed to Christianity, proselytizing influences, or experienced a loss of 'Jewishness'. Jewish piety and contact with a Jewish community could also be nurtured in non-Jewish care environments. The Presbyterian traditions of the Church of Scotland meant that some Kindertransportees recall receiving religious education appropriate to their Jewish backgrounds while living with non-Jews. Marthe recalls that at school in Scotland she had to learn bits out of the Bible, but her teachers would only give her sections from the Old Testament.[108] Nachtigall's church visits every Sunday with his foster family were followed by a session with the local minister to recite the *Shomar.*[109] Nachtigall recalls that Presbyterian traditions meant that the minister could help him with his Hebrew and Old Testament studies. The compatibility of the traditions of Scotland's Presbyterians and Judaism is also suggested by the adoption of Presbyterian traditions by some of Scotland's Jewish congregations. Garnethill's congregation adopted certain Presbyterian customs.[110]

Kindertransportees placed in non-Jewish care homes could also experience more Jewish nurturing than they were previously accustomed. Hans' non-Jewish family sent him to the Salisbury Road synagogue, Edinburgh, every weekend.[111] During this period, he attended Jewish education classes until he was *Bar Mitzvah'd*. Before Scotland, Hans had never been to a synagogue and his family did not adhere to any Jewish traditions. His non Jewish foster family also had various connections with Jews in Scotland and he eventually became apprenticed to one of these contacts. Hans' schooling was also connected to the Jewish community. He recalls that upon receiving an anti-Semitic remark from a teacher at the school, the large Jewish body at the school ensured that the teacher was removed. He also had close Jewish friends.[112]

Not all non-Jewish caregivers possessed a particular faith or offered an alternative to Judaism. Ariel was fostered in Edinburgh by a non-Jewish man and remained ignorant of any religious affiliation he may have possessed.[113] The standard of care in a non-Jewish home could also sometimes potentially be better than its Jewish alternative, offering long-term, stable, and loving, home environments. Nachtingall had moved from a Jewish home in Edinburgh, where he was very unhappy, to a non-Jewish family, where he felt happy and asked to stay.[114]

Non-Jewish care environments were not necessarily the final influence on Kindertransportees' connection to Judaism. Kindertransportees often re-established their connection with a Jewish community or their Jewish faith in later years. Elsie lived a devout Catholic life in Scotland for 16 years before migrating to America to rejoin her family.[115] She recalls that at that time she was a 'very religious Catholic' and even considered becoming a nun.[116] In America, Elsie discovered Judaism for the first time. She recalls that her first serious boyfriend was Jewish, followed by her husband, and that through these connections she learnt about being Jewish:

> For the first time in my life I went to a service and learnt about the Jewish holidays. I was being exposed to something I had never had.[117]

She does not currently practice regularly, but remains affiliated with the local temple and married in a Jewish ceremony. Elsie reflects that her experiences have meant that she feels a close affinity and warmth with Catholics, but also feels that she is Jewish.

Jewish care

There are a large number of features that determine a pious Jewish lifestyle. Jason Heppell has suggested a list of important traditions to be adhered to by an observant Jew: including regular attendance of a synagogue on the Sabbath, definite observance of the main religious festivals – *Yom Kippur, Rosh Hashanah, Pesach, Shavuot, Purim* – prayers by the father at least once a day, kosher food, Friday night family meals, attendance of a *Cheder* for Hebrew instruction, *Bar Mitzvah*, daily prayers and synagogue attendance for boys, *Yeshiva* education and a Jewish social life.[118] Jewish care provisions operating in Scotland did not automatically allow Kindertransportees access to all of these activities or safeguard their commitment to piety.

The Kindertransportees were placed in a number of Jewish care environments in Scotland. These included foster homes, pre-*hachsharot* facilities, orphanages, evacuation centres and hostels. Steinberg notes that five Jewish hostels were established by 1943 in order to cater for 193 evacuated Jewish children.[119] In Scotland, two Jewish evacuation centres, Castle Douglas and Kirkcudbrightshire, accommodated about 100 Jewish youth including Kindertransportees, while Birkenward hostel, Skelmorlie, cared for 60 minors.[120] Two hostels were also established specifically for the Kindertransportees: Glasgow's Garnethill hostel and Edinburgh's Salisbury Road hostel. The pre-existing Jewish Gertrude

Jacobson Orphanage also admitted Kindertransportees. Whittingehame and Polton House were also established specifically for trans-migrant Jewish youth.

Despite the relatively small size of Scotland's Jewish population, contact with a local Jewish community was feasible for most Kindertransportees. Beyond the two main traditional centres of Jewish life in Scotland – Glasgow and Edinburgh – there were also Jewish congregations in Aberdeen, Dumfermline, Falkirk, Greenock and Inverness.[121] In 1936, Aberdeen is recorded as having 25 Jewish families, Dumfermline possessed nine families in 1937, Falkirk had 62 families in 1945 and Greenock five families in 1933.[122] These centres, especially Ayr, were boosted in numbers and vibrancy by evacuation during the war years, especially from Glasgow and Edinburgh, as well as by Jewish servicemen. Scotland's Jewish communities had developed a strong infrastructure to support religious piety and a Jewish community life, including *Talmud Torah, Cheder, Chevra Torah*, youth clubs, community centres, Orthodox boarding houses, *shuls* and *Shechita*.[123] Competing congregations emerged within most of these centres; 17 synagogues emerged in Glasgow.[124]

The CREC and Adath directed local rabbis to encourage their congregations to engage with the trans-migrants on a regular basis. Kindertransportees in Jewish foster care tended to adhere to the normal preference for attending the closest synagogue. Benson was fostered in the south side of Glasgow and so never joined Kindertransportees of Garnethill hostel at the Garnethill synagogue.[125] Instead, he attended the local Pollokshields synagogue. Congregations could sometimes extend social invitations to the Kindertransportees after the service. The Kindertransportees at Whittingehame were invited to Glasgow to perform for the local congregation at Garnethill.[126] Rachel remembers being invited by the local rabbi, Dr Crossgrove, the minister at Garnethill, for *Shabbat* at his house.[127] Individual members of the congregation sometimes formed close relations with Kindertransportees. Hans recalls that an elderly Jew 'sort of took me under his wing, a fellow call Levi'.[128] Levi's son invited Hans to become a companion to his son and later suggested that he join his knitwear company.

Alongside contact with their local Jewish communities, Kindertransportees who lived within Jewish residential care facilities did have additional advantages for maintaining their Jewish connections by merely being housed together. Handler recalled his eagerness to benefit the minors' Jewish upbringing simply by ensuring that they were kept together.[129] Jewish residential facilities also benefited from unique connections with their local synagogue and Jewish communities. The Gertrude Jacobson Orphanage's president was Reverend

Phillips, who had previously been the minister of Garnethill congregation and remained an important leader of the community.[130] Garnethill and Salisbury Road hostels were both directly linked to their respective local synagogues.

Residential care homes sought to offer a high level of Jewish piety and enable daily interaction with Jewish guidance counsellors and caregivers. Flesch recalls that the Gertrude Jacobson Orphanage was 'very Jewish', run by Jewish staff.[131] Whittingehame was provided with its own rabbis, Joseph Hans Heinemann and, headmaster, Reverend Bernard Cherrick.[132] Both Heinemann and Cherrick provided guidance and oversaw day-to-day religious activity in the centre. At Whittingehame, Edna also remembers Pummy Engel, the Madrich (Zionist guidance councillor) of Bachad, who offered 'long conversations about God and creation'.[133]

Rabbi Salis Daiches, of Salisbury Road synagogue, Edinburgh, was also closely involved with the religious management of Whittingehame. Eli Fachler was born in 1923 in Berlin, Germany, and his parents were observant Orthodox Jews.[134] He came to Britain on the Kindertransport under the auspices of Youth Aliyah and on arrival was sent directly to Whittingehame. He recalls Daiches' involvement in the preparations after *Pesach* for *Shavuot* and his advice about religious etiquette; Fachler had kept growing his beard over *Pesach*, but was unaware that he was allowed to shave over the 5 days between *Rosh Chodosh* and *Shavuot*, until Daiches advised him otherwise.

Jewish facilities, such as Whittingehame, were established as independent centres for Jewish life. Whittingehame was located in an isolated rural location in East Lothian and a *shul* was established on the estate. Drew, a former teacher at Whittingehame, wrote to his parents detailing the religious traditions and observances followed by the trainees.[135] These he recorded as being the main festivals *of Purim, Pesach, Roshannah, Chanukah* and *Yom Kippur*. For *Purim*, the trainees put on a play emanating from Eastern Jewish theology and 'mysticism'.[136] Figure 17 shows *Pesach* observance at Whittingehame. For *Pesach* all corn and flour products were locked away, new crockery was brought out to be used, 'the kitchen range was raised to red-heat to purge it of previous impurity', blessings were performed, and *matzoth*, parsley and horseradish eaten, along with 'an egg roasted' and a shank-bone roasted in cinders.[137] Elijah recalls that for *Yom Kippur* Kindertransportees would fast.[138]

On a daily basis, residential facilities offered Kindertransportees an opportunity to maintain observances to Jewish traditions. Drew recalls the *Hora* and 'other peculiar Jewish dances' being performed.[139] The Sabbath was also adhered to, and Abaigael recalls that no work was performed during this time.[140] Josephine

Figure 17 Pesach at Whittingehame.
Source: MCPC/Drew, Photographs.

remembers that teachers and other staff at Whittingehame made a special effort on the Sabbath to uphold traditions, including the lighting of candles.[141] Fachler, who later provided religious support for Kindertransportees at Polton House, recalls that Whittingehame was 'run on strictly Orthodox lines'.[142] Hubbers recalls that the kitchen was set up to adhere to *Kashrut*.[143] Separate washing-up areas and utensils were established for meat and for milk, and grace and 'all the appropriate blessings were made'.[144] Cohen Stein recorded that 'those very observant children who took *kashrut* very, very seriously' would receive their ice cream treat at a different time to the other children at Whittingehame.[145] This was because they could not eat dairy products for several hours if they had had meat for dinner.

A Jewish scriptural education was deemed another central ingredient to a Jewish upbringing and most important for the maintenance of Kindertransportees' connection with Judaism.[146] Centres of Jewish learning sought to teach an array of subjects, including '*Talmud, Mishnah, Pentateuch* with commentaries, Prophets, Hebrew language and literature, Jewish history, Jewish religion, history of Zionist and Palestinography', along with classes in *Dinim* (Jewish laws).[147] Kindertransportees were commonly enrolled in Jewish education facilities local to their original placements. These could include attendance of a *Yeshiva, Cheder* or private Jewish tuition.

Some Kindertransportees experienced Rabbinical training or preparation for *Bar Mitzvah*. In Polton House, a tutor from Edinburgh was found for a group of boys in preparation of their *Bar Mitzvah*.[148] Fachler was also employed to provide Jewish education.[149] In Whittingehame, Rabbi Heinemann provided private lessons in Judaism alongside Reverend Cherrick.[150] Rabbi Daiches from

Edinburgh supervised the Orthodoxy of Whittingehame. In 1939, Daiches reported to Schonfeld that 'the teaching of Hebrew as a vernacular, Jewish history, religion, etc, would form an important part of the curriculum'.[151]

Jewish education led some Kindertransportees on to deeply devout Orthodox Jewish lives in later life. Immanuel Jakobovits was a former resident of Whittingehame and eventually became the Chief Rabbi of Great Britain.[152] This is an indication of the success of the Orthodox education given to the Kindertransportees. Jakobovits was able to pursue higher education and attended *Etz Chaim Yeshiva* in London, the Jew's College and the University of London. By 1949, he was appointed Chief Rabbi of Ireland at the young age of 27. However, Jakobovits' life story seems to be the exception rather than the rule.

Kindertransportees living outside the residential facilities had a more sporadic Jewish educational experience. No comprehensive national Jewish education service existed during this period, so Kindertransportees in foster care were reliant on *ad-hoc* RCM initiatives and local community provisions. The RCM decreed that Kindertransportees in non-Jewish foster homes, outside of Jewish areas, were to undertake correspondence courses, while Kindertransportees living within Jewish areas were to enjoy group celebrations of Jewish Holy Days and study groups, organized by their regional committees.[153] The Maccabi and Habonim groups were to be utilized to offer education in Jewish social pursuits. These objectives were not widely experienced, and I have yet to find a Kindertransportees in Scotland who recalls undertaking a correspondence course.

Nonetheless, Scotland's Jewish communities did possess pre-existing Jewish education services to support the RCM's suggested education policy for Kindertransportees. In the 1920s, the Scottish Area Council for Jewish Education was established and Boards of Jewish Education were created in the main Jewish centres. Kindertransportees in Glasgow benefited from a particularly strong infrastructure. In 1935, the *Talmud Torah* became part of Glasgow's Board of Jewish Education. Bar Kochba sports clubs had been established in Glasgow in 1933 and these became connected to the British Maccabi Association. In Glasgow, there also existed a Jewish Fresh Air Fund, which undertook schemes to take urban Jewish children into the countryside for short breaks.[154] Edinburgh also possessed well-established education facilities. Edinburgh's *Talmud Torah* was established in 1894 and before 1914 was held in the basement of the Orthodox Graham Street Synagogue before moving to Sciennes School.[155] Classes in Edinburgh were daily between 5 p.m. and 7 p.m. Herbert Adler, the

Director of the JEC, made regular inspections of Scotland's various education facilities.[156]

Nonetheless, Jewish education remained weak, sporadic and did not reach all of the Kindertransportees. The situation was made worse by the demands of the war, most notably by the mass evacuation of minors. In December 1939, the Joint Emergency Committee for Jewish Education in London created 90 new centres of Jewish education for 3,000 evacuated children.[157] This rose to 129 in 1940. However, this had little impact on the Kindertransportees in Scotland. In 1940, Frank Samuel wrote to Anthony de Rothschild about the continued failures to provide a religious education to evacuated Jewish children.[158] By the close of war the education system had virtually broken down.[159] In 1940, the *Jewish Chronicle* reported that an estimated 70 per cent of Jewish children in Britain were still not receiving a Jewish education.[160] In May 1941, the CC recorded that 'more than 5,000 children' under the RCM still received 'no organised religious education'.[161] It was also estimated that Habonim (a socialist Zionist youth movement) was only providing an education service to 500 children in Britain in 1939.[162]

Education provisions were never unified, and there continued to be a fragmented collection of competing Jewish education facilities, each affiliated to a corresponding synagogue. The system in Scotland continued to be part-time and lacked funds, staff, supplies and access to pupils.[163] In 1942, the Chief Rabbi wrote to the Home Office requesting that the CREC be given authority over the Kindertransportees' Jewish education.[164] Hertz argued that the Kindertransportees were receiving inadequate and 'sporadic attempts' at education, which at best provided them with a 'minimum of religious instruction'.[165]

Furthermore, Jewish care and education provisions for Kindertransportees suffered a number of weaknesses due to the unique regional theological and practical character it possessed.[166] This meant that Kindertransportees experienced a different and sometimes alien Jewish education or upbringing. Kindertransportees arrived from many different types of Jewish and non-Jewish backgrounds, communities and synagogues. They represented the whole spectrum of preferences and affiliations: Ultra-Orthodox, Orthodox, Misrachi, German Jewish Reform, Liberal, Conservative, non-practising, secular and even atheist.[167] Their orientations were also strongly coloured by their national origins, varying from German (56%), Austrian (34%), Czech (6%) and Polish (4%).[168]

The vast majority of Kindertransportees did not arrive with a shared Orthodox pious ideal to that offered by CREC.[169] Adath's interpretation of appropriate Jewish care for Jewish children was derived from Anglo-Jewry's

Orthodox theology and ritual traditions. Yet, there existed fundamental differences between Jewish orientations established in Germany and those formed in Britain. Leo Baeck Institutes were established in 1955 in Jerusalem, New York and London, specifically to preserve the unique type of Judaism preferred by German Jewry.[170]

These regional and national disparities caused confusion over Jewish terms, such as Liberalism, Reform or Orthodoxy, and their comparable congregations in Britain. German Liberalism was not comparable with Britain's Liberal congregations, which tended to be more conservative and formal. German Reform was also very different to congregations born out of reforming movements in Britain. In 1944, Schonfeld reported his belief that the trans-migrants were a very different religious community to Anglo-Jewry.[171] Schonfeld wrote:

> In Germany "orthodox" meant only the few strictly observant groups. Yet the "Konservativ" were almost as orthodox, and the "Liberalen" were observant of traditional Jewish rites and customs, as is the bulk of the orthodox Anglo-Jewish community. Yet any child described on the questionnaire as being other than "orthodox" was and is regarded as outside the responsibility of the general Anglo-Jewish community.[172]

Schonfeld's statement underlines the problems of translating German Jewish orientations to a British counterpart. I have not identified a Kindertransportee who expresses having found that they were placed in a comparable Jewish care environment to their past.[173] Jan lived with her Polish parents in Frankfurt, Germany. Her Orthodox Jewish family was wealthy and owned a fabric menswear business. She was sent to Glasgow, via the Kindertransport, to a prearranged Jewish foster family. Her foster family was Orthodox and lived in a wealthy area of Pollokshields. She recalls the different type of Orthodoxy that her Jewish foster family possessed:

> They were Orthodox, not as Orthodox as me, we have variations of it, they did certain things on the Sabbath that I didn't do, but I had to just fit in.[174]

Kindertransportees recall feeling alien to the Scottish Jewish theology and approach to piety. Josephine emphasizes in her narrative the differences she felt between herself and the Scottish Jews.[175]

Despite 32 per cent of Kindertransportees having arrived from Liberal Jewish backgrounds and 1 per cent from Reform homes, their Jewish care and education remained dominated by Orthodox or Traditional Jewish approaches to Judaism. In 1894, John Simon Oswald wrote of 'Reformed Judaism' that there was a fundamental difference between 'those who may be described as Rabbinical and as Reform Jews'.[176] Oswald describes this difference as a contrast in 'mental attitude' and basic approach to Judaism, whereby 'Reformed Judaism recognises an inherent distinction between ritualism and spirituality'.[177]

Adath's Orthodoxy represented a 'type' of Judaism that was fundamentally opposed to German Jewry's reforming tendencies and preferred liberal theology. Reformers desired to introduce rationalism and interpretative discussion into Judaism and this led to clashes with their local Orthodox communities. Orthodox teaching assumed the uncritical, literal approach to the interpretation of the *Talmud Torah*. This adhered to the notion of the divine revelation of oral and written *Torah* and the immutability of tradition. The Reform and Liberal congregations prefer a more critical interpretation.[178]

Max Milner, an independent trans-migrant, recalls his struggle to engage socially with Scotland's Jewry, whom he found lacked the habit of discussion and debate in their Jewish theology and daily lives as Jews.[179] Milner believes this made it imperative for trans-migrants to establish a Progressive Liberal or Reform Judaism movement in Britain.[180] Nonetheless, little progress was made in Scotland during the war years in establishing congregations based on these German-Jewish preferences. The influence of German settlers in the nineteenth century had declined swiftly and trends were not preserved after the 1890s.[181] Garnethill took reforming steps, but never adopted Liberal or Reform affiliations. In 1931, the Albert Drive Reform Synagogue (The Progressive Synagogue) (ADRC), in Govanhill, Glasgow, was established, but this congregation only began to grow with the influx of trans-migrants from Greater Germany and never achieved significant support in Glasgow.[182] I have not identified one Kindertransportee who attended this synagogue.[183] There was little alternative to a Traditional or Orthodox approach to Judaism in Scotland.[184]

Welfare schemes for Kindertransportees excluded British Reform or Liberal impetus as Orthodox and Traditional congregations of Anglo-Jewry sought to protect their monopoly over service provisions. There existed a legacy of deeply rooted divisions and clashes in opinion between the Orthodox and reforming congregations in Britain.[185] Adath and the CREC viewed these movements as a 'deadly peril threatening our traditional Jewish life'.[186] The Chief Rabbi was fervently opposed to any influence the Liberal or Reform movements may have in Britain.[187]

In Glasgow, the New Central Synagogue (NCS) clashed with the ADRC.[188] The NCS objected to the ADRC's contact with the Glasgow Jewish Representative Council (GJRC) and made efforts to exclude them from future contact with welfare schemes. The ADRC was also barred from *Shechita* (communal board).[189] This situation was not exclusive to Scotland. Across Britain, Reform or Liberal congregations were being actively excluded from Jewish philanthropy. Hertz initially excluded the Liberal and Reform congregations from the National Council of Jewish Religious Education (JEC), while the Board of Orthodox Education and the CREC offered exclusively Orthodox education provisions.[190]

Subsequently, the Reform or Liberal movements remained ostracized from Scottish Jewish welfare provisions, financially weak and of little significance to the Kindertransportees' religious care. Instead, the Traditional Orthodox congregations of Garnethill synagogue, Glasgow, and the Graham Street Synagogue, Edinburgh, decreed the correct type of provisions for a Jewish environment for Kindertransportees in Scotland. The religious style and approach to worship this afforded could be far removed from Kindertransportees' previous religious orientations. For example, in Germany, Reforming Jews sought *Bildung* (or secular education).[191] In contrast, in Britain Jewish minors from Liberal, Reform or other alternative affiliations were forced to attend exclusively Ashkenazi Orthodox Jewish classes during the war.[192] At Whittingehame, 'lectures in Jewish tradition, in Hebrew, in religion' were provided, and Sprinzeles believes that these 'were taught in a Traditional manner'.[193]

The Orthodox approach to services could be very different. Linguistic preferences of Scotland's congregations were different to reforming congregations, which tended to adopt the national language, such as English. The *Talmud Torah* in Glasgow continued to use Yiddish for instruction, a language that many Kindertransportees did not understand. Kindertransportees also recall lacking knowledge of Hebrew, which meant that they were unable to understand liturgy and participate in services.

Kindertransportees tended to be more familiar with the larger synagogue approach.[194] This adhered to more formal structures for worship, with regular opening times and disciplined approaches to services. The newer Jewish communities from Eastern Europe in Scotland maintained a preference for informal small congregations of worship. These included *Chevrot* (fraternities) or *Beth Hamedrash* (prayer houses).[195] In Glasgow's Gorbals, the *Chevra Kadisha* and *Beth Jacob* congregations remained loyal to this tradition. Rabbi Daiches had struggled in Edinburgh to unite the community because of these aversions to large united synagogues, perceived as '*der englisher shul*'.[196]

The larger *shuls* that had emerged in Scotland often still maintained strict Orthodox approaches to services. In the Gorbals, these included the Great Synagogue and Central Synagogue. In Edinburgh, the Edinburgh Independent

Hebrew Congregation was formed to cater for strictly Orthodox orientations. These services would maintain Hebrew or Yiddish services, rather than English, segregated congregations, and specific prayers or rituals abandoned by Liberal/Reform congregations. Ministers were also drawn from Eastern Europe. The Crosshill synagogue, Glasgow, appointed Rabbi Mosche Dryan from Poland in 1935 to lead their congregation.

The older Jewish communities who had migrated to Scotland from Western Europe predominantly adhered to Traditional Judaism. This also offered Kindertransportees a new type of Jewish lifestyle. Chaim Bermant recorded that the 'Anglo-Jewish community had many virtues, but its ways were alien to the newcomers from Germany, as they had been to those from Poland and Russia.'[197] Traditional Judaism offered a new approach to theology and piety from strict Orthodoxy, taking tentative steps to modernize some of the stricter forms of worship. Garnethill and the Graham Street Synagogues led efforts to modernize certain aspects of Scottish Jewry's approach to piety. They were perceived as the '*Englisher shuls*' and followed some reforms introduced by the United Synagogue of Britain.[198]

These reforms made the Traditional congregations milder in temperament than their Orthodox co-religionists.[199] However, their ties to an Orthodox community prevented any radical departures from the orthodox Traditional approach.[200] The *Amida* (long devotional prayer) was reintroduced in Garnethill in 1922 and Rev M. Simmons was eventually forced out after trying to make further changes. Simmons moved to Pollokshields, where he again found resistance to any modernizing overtures. The Graham Street Synagogue also made limited amendments, due to Dalches' desire to appease the Orthodox community, who held him in suspicion for being too modern.[201]

Cultural disparities also existed within and between the Kindertransportees and the host Jewish communities. The Kindertransportees express their experiences of entering a new type of Jewish lifestyle in the community. On a day-to-day basis in the community, the Kindertransportees' approach to Jewish life was fundamentally different from Anglo-Jewry's. Rather than possessing the synagogue at the heart of the community, German Jews tended to congregate at the café.[202] German Jews remained proud of their distinct German culture in Scotland. Edna recalls:

> To the best of my knowledge we were not very well understood by British-Jewry. The German style of religion (however varied it was within Germany) was distinctly different from the British, which was more of an "Ostjuden" and a mixture of Yiddish. It greatly differed from the German style.[203]

Isabel recalls that 'Jewish Germans formed groups . . . they had social events . . . they all were German Jews it seemed like, I think we were just drawn to each other'.[204] Jewish trans-migrants in Scotland eventually established their own self-help society – The Society of Jewish Refugees (SOJR) – in 1940.[205] This was a refugee welfare organization, which intended to enable aid and cultural support for trans-migrants by trans-migrants. SOJR even offered continental food to satisfy the trans-migrants' common food cravings.[206]

A dichotomy also existed within Jewish communities between *Ostjuden* and *Westjuden* lifestyles, or between Jews with origins in either Eastern or Western Europe. This division had been present in Greater Germany, meaning that many Kindertransportees arrived in Britain with an acute awareness of their particular community membership.[207] Geographic origins had formed a polarization in cultural heritage and practices. In Germany, *Ostjuden* could be marked out by their distinctive appearance, including black clothing, side locks and *yarmulkes* [Kippah], among others.[208] Drew wrote to his parents about the divisions among the children at Whittingehame, between those who were *Ostjuden* and 'who have led a narrow ghetto life for generations' and the non-Orthodox Kindertransportees. Drew noted:

> Our Poles are as a Jewish race apart, disliked by the others . . . their laws differ often in particulars. The non-Orthodox, whose parents are non-Orthodox or "Liberal", are as other normal children in all matters. Even the Orthodox from Southern Germany and Austria have not this warped outlook on life.[209]

These divisions invited a revival of old prejudices between Jewish communities.[210] *Polnische or Galizische Schnorrer* became terms used against Jews from Eastern Europe, who preferred strict Orthodoxy.[211] Viewed as superstitious backward fanatics, they were not secular enough for *Westjuden* communities' preferences. On the other hand, reforming Jews were perceived suspiciously as being closer to Gentiles than the Jews.

Scotland possessed a number of sizable and vibrant, strictly Orthodox *Ostjuden* communities. These communities were derived from Eastern European immigrants from the 1890s. They tended to be located in poorer districts and preferred sectarian approaches to Jewish life. In Glasgow, the Gorbals was still the heart of the Orthodox community.[212] Kindertransportees, such as Benson, were fostered within this community.[213]

The *Ostjuden* communities in Scotland continued to draw their day-to-day lifestyles from Eastern European *shtetl* culture.[214] A former resident of the Gorbals, originally from a small Latvian *shtetl*, recalls that during this period the Gorbals 'offered the sights, sounds and smell of home . . . one heard Yiddish in the streets, saw Jewish names on the shop-fronts, and Jewish food on the counters. Fogels sold the best Russian bread'.[215] The laws of *Halakha*, which govern Orthodox life, could impact on the Kindertransportees' lives in a number of ways.[216] Female Kindertransportees could find themselves in more restrictive and prohibitive environments. Married women could be expected to wear the *sheitel* (wig).[217] Women's role in religious life could become increasingly peripheral and segregated.[218] Orthodox synagogues used a *mechitza* (women's section) and traditionally only boys would be expected to attend *Cheder* and be *Bar Mitzvah'd*. This was not compatible with many of the Kindertransportees' religious ambitions and expectations.[219]

The Kindertransportees could also find the local Jewish life inappropriate and this could lead to friction and difficult relationships with their hosts. Without adopting new customs, the Kindertransportees could find it difficult to ingratiate themselves with their host community. One independent trans-migrant recalls that he found it difficult to accept and adapt to the new type of Jewish community because they 'had all sorts of customs and we just couldn't relate . . . it was like a completely different world'.[220] Rachel was placed with an Orthodox family in Dalkeith, Edinburgh, and found that her German-Jewish heritage caused tensions with her hosts, who originated from Poland.[221]

Furthermore, despite efforts to encourage the local Jewish communities to engage with the Kindertransportees, the local Jewish communities were not automatically hospitable. Not all Kindertransportees recall having had interaction and some express their sense of exclusion from its activities. The strictly Orthodox *Ostjuden* community did not always accept the Kindertransportees as Jews because of these disparities in cultural heritage. Kindertransportees could find themselves involuntarily ostracized and estranged from their local community.[222] A member of Glasgow's Gorbals' community recorded that the arrival of the Kindertransportees and other trans-migrants was a shock to the local residents, who felt that 'they didn't look or sound Jewish, because they went around with their bare heads and spoke German, rather than Yiddish. Some of them weren't even circumcised and I suspected they were frauds'.[223] Rachel recalls the clash that occurred in Glasgow between the trans-migrants and the native Scottish Jews because the latter felt that the former 'were not Jews'.[224]

Jewish communities could be inward looking and unreceptive to the new arrivals. Rachel felt that the Edinburgh community was 'cold' to her.[225] When she moved to Glasgow, she also struggled to make contact with the community. Hans recalls that he had no other contact with the Salisbury Road congregation other than his friend Levi.[226] Rachel recalls that during her stay with a Jewish foster family in Edinburgh she was excluded from all social engagements with the Jewish community.

> I wasn't really much part of Edinburgh or Glasgow Jewish community . . . as far as Edinburgh was concerned the only contact that I had was when I went to Synagogue and back again . . . it was a time that I was extremely lonely, I didn't have anyone to talk to. . . . I used to go to the library and get books out. . . . I created my own dream world.[227]

Kindertransportees also remember being rejected by members of Scotland's Jewry because of their foreign refugee status. Jan was rejected by a Jewish suitor because she lacked family credentials and as a refugee was not perceived in a favourable light by his parents.[228]

Exclusion from the Jewish communities in Scotland also occurred because of a number of broader factors. Kindertransportees argue that they were in many cases too poor, too young and too busy to become involved in Jewish community life. Being minors meant that the Kindertransportees were excluded from a number of areas of Jewish social life. The Albert Drive Synagogue, which was the only congregation affiliated with the Reform Movement in Glasgow, had an associated social club, the '306 Club'. However, 'no person under the age of 21' was admitted without their parents' consent.[229] Jan remembers that 'the Scottish community was a nice vibrant community, but I was not part of it because I was a child'.[230] Rachel recalls that only when her mother joined her in Glasgow, did she begin to have contact with the Glasgow community:

> The first time I did [meet the Jewish community] was when my mother came in 1947 . . . because she went to synagogue and was much more involved with the Jewish people. . . she had more in common with them . . . but I didn't have that.[231]

However, Jan believes that had she been older, she would still not have been able to participate because she was too busy working to survive in her new environment: 'I had to work at the age of 16. . . . I really was very busy'.[232] Membership of certain aspects of Jewish community life also demanded money, which the Kindertransportees lacked. Garnethill still required 'seat holder rates' and this prevented the poorer Jews in the community from attending.[233]

People often preferred philanthropy rather than personal engagement with the trans-migrants. Fachler recalls that at Whittingehame, the governors, drawn from Glasgow and Edinburgh's Jewish communities, would remain at a distance, only asking specific questions.[234] Rachel lived on Renfield Street in a hostel for girls, run by the Quakers, and only once recalls joining the boys at Garnethill hostel for Passover and a *Seder* meal.[235] Her impression of the local Glasgow community was that, because of the war, they were inward looking and desired to tackle their own problems first. Ariel lived in Edinburgh, fostered by a non-Jewish man.[236] He believes that he was never contacted by Scotland's Jewry and thought that Edinburgh did not have a synagogue or Jewish community.

The disparities that existed between the Kindertransportees and their Jewish hosts, in cultural heritage and religious affiliation, meant that when they did receive Jewish care, guidance or education, they did not inevitably engage with Judaism. Care facilities adhered to a 'one-size-fits-all' and an 'all-or-nothing' approach to Jewish care provisions and did not cater for Kindertransportees floating in the middle of the religious spectrum. The result was that the majority of the children did not receive the correct level, orientation or type of religious care for their needs. The atheist or secular children still received too much religion, as they participated in Holy Day celebrations and adhered to *Kashrut* and the Sabbath. Those whose families had observed some customs or who were of non-Orthodox backgrounds received the wrong kind of religious care. Of those who were previously observant, but of an alternative affiliation and who therefore felt compelled to remain outside the smaller and in many ways alien, strictly observant Orthodox group, they experienced a sharp break in their religious interaction.

This meant that Kindertransportees could become ostracized, opt out or rebel against a Jewish lifestyle while living within a Jewish residential facility. Sprinzeles recalls that 'there was no rigidity about it . . . there was as much as you wanted to observe . . . it was very liberal'.[237] Being unrepresentative and non-mandatory led some Kindertransportees to choose to opt out. Subsequently, in Whittingehame, the residents became increasingly fragmented and divided, split between the pious and non-pious. Kindertransportees stuck to certain groups and Drew wrote to his parents of the divisions that developed between the observant and non-observant groups.[238]

Nathan lived in Vienna, Austria, with his observant Orthodox Jewish family. On arrival in Britain, he was first sent to Dovercourt reception camp in England, before being sent to Whittingehame. At Whittingehame, he joined the religious Orthodox Bachad youth group and recalls that two separate dining rooms emerged.[239] Only the religious dining room adhered strictly to Jewish law, such as not mixing meat and milk. Abaigael recalls that Kindertransportees in the non-religious dining area were not required to pray before meals.[240] Elijah opted out of a pious lifestyle and remembers that the Orthodox trainees at Whittingehame 'kept to themselves'.[241] Elijah never attended the synagogue at Whittingehame. Kindertransportees who chose to opt out also had the option to join the Scouts, under the guidance of the non-Jewish Drew. Drew's protégés express little recollection of any Jewish interaction. Sprinzeles does not remember having been in contact with any religious Kindertransportees, despite the high number of observant students at the school.[242]

Rebelling against the new imposed living environment and consciously rejecting piety, when they were at liberty to do so, was not uncommon. Kindertransportees were adolescents and would rebel against new prohibitive lifestyle. Benson was from a non-practising Jewish family and fostered by a 'moderately' observant Jewish family in Glasgow.[243] He recalls that he was expelled from the *Yeshiva* in Glasgow after rebelling against its impositions on his lifestyle. Benson was accused of eating ice cream on *Yom Kippur* and happily accepted his expulsion. In Whittingehame, Kindertransportees challenged Daiches' strict approach to Sabbath observance. The matron recalls the trainees' enjoyment of 'mixed bathing', which Daiches opposed.[244] Drew also recorded an ongoing debate within the school concerning the use of lamplight to read during the Sabbath.[245] Levi recalls non-observant children eating and cooking for themselves outside the school building on Holy Days when everyone else had to fast.[246]

Alternatively, Kindertransportees who did not opt out, wishing to maintain a Jewish life, often found that they had to compromise their Jewish orientation and adopt the new prescribed approach. Edna came from an Orthodox German family. She decided to join Bachad and the strictly Orthodox Kindertransportees at Whittingehame because she felt that otherwise she was not receiving any Jewish support: 'I had the feeling that the only place I could keep up my religion was Bachad'.[247] Edna's mother wrote to her objecting to her decision, believing it to be a different type of Jewish affiliation to her upbringing.[248] Rachel believes that as a result of a different type of Jewish care, she 'had moved away from' the Jewish life her parents had preferred.[249]

In care environments, over-zealous Jewish care, especially if it adhered to a strict Orthodox approach, could also overwhelm and alienate Kindertransportees. Higher levels of piety and prohibitive laws could appear daunting and scary. In such cases, Kindertransportees felt that a Jewish lifestyle was being 'imposed versus embraced'.[250] Elijah was initially sent to a family in England who assumed that he would be suitable for a *Yeshiva*.[251] Elijah recalls that his family in Poland 'were not overly religious . . . we were not Orthodox religious . . . [in

England] they wanted to put me into a *Yeshiva*. I was not a religious person and when I saw this *Yeshiva*, I just ran. It frightened me'.[252] Elijah went on to join the non-religious group at Whittingehame. Flesch was sent to the Gertrude Jacobson Orphanage and recalls that the religious experience pushed him away from Judaism:

> Lots of prayers . . . and we went to *Cheder* and on Holy days we went to synagogue of course. So it was very Jewish . . . a bit too much . . . they shoved it down our throats, which didn't improve our piety . . . they wanted us to stay Jewish . . . which we did up to a point. We had *Bar Mitzvah* . . . we had services in the hostel. In fact all the time, too much. . . . I was gradually losing my connections really with the religion. When we got away from there, of course, I can't remember anybody going to synagogue ever, of my friends after, when we got to London.[253]

Flesch's reflection is a frank testimony of the problems of estranging Kindertransportees from Judaism as a result of over-zealous Jewish care.

The Jewish residential facilities also transformed the role of Judaism in the Kindertransportees' daily lives by way of institutionalizing Jewish life. The Kindertransportees' engagement with Judaism was no longer within a small private family setting, but instead now took place within public communal activities. Handler has testified to his concerns at the time about the impact of 'institutionalised religion' for the young people within Britain's *hachsharot*.[254] Important events occur within the family setting and these were not continued in the Kindertransportees' lives within Jewish residential care: 'a *Seder*, a Friday-night meal, a birthday, an anniversary, or that symbolic inauguration of the marital relationship: a Jewish wedding'.[255] The participation of family generations in Jewish life was missing in residential care homes.[256] Sprinzeles missed out on her *Bat Chayil* (Orthodox ceremony for girls) because, without her close family support, she lacked a sponsor or guidance.[257] Evelyn Cowan's memoir of growing up in the Gorbals as a child underlines the centrality to a child's life of religious festivals within the home, such as *Chanukah*.[258]

Jewish foster care was not a guarantee of inclusion within a Jewish family life. Kindertransportees could be ostracized and excluded from participation in Jewish activities, within private and public domains. This could be caused by class prejudice and xenophobia, which led foster parents to relegate Kindertransportees to domestic service and servicing roles.[259] Rachel was fostered in Edinburgh by a Jewish family and was expected to provide domestic service in return for her lodgings.[260] Other than accompanying them to the local synagogue, she was excluded from all Jewish activities.

Intentions to provide a fully encompassing Jewish living environment were further weakened by the reality that a Jewish care environment was never exclusively Jewish and nearly always possessed a significant non-Jewish presence. Kindertransportees in Jewish foster homes engaged with non-Jews on a daily basis in Scotland.[261] Kindertransportees were not always sent to Jewish schools by Jewish caregivers, but were frequently enrolled in secular local schools. The Kindertransportees at Garnethill hostel attended the local Garnetbank Primary School.[262] Jan's Jewish foster parents sent her to a local secular school, which was a culture shock because she had never been with non-Jewish children.[263] The Kindertransportees' schooling was especially significant to their religious upbringing, because many of the local schools tended to adhere to either Catholicism or Protestantism in Scotland.[264]

Christian missionaries were also active in Jewish communities, providing philanthropy and welfare. Evangelical missionaries were active in the Gorbals of Glasgow and provided various forms of welfare benefits to entice Jews to convert.[265] Alexander Levison was active in the Independent Hebrew Congregation of Edinburgh, but also worked to convert Jews.[266]

Non-Jews also worked within Jewish care facilities and could challenge or compromise the Jewish environment. Whittingehame utilized a large number of non-Jewish staff, including the headmaster, Maxwell, his deputy Drew, estate workers, and Lord and Lady Traprain, on whose estate the school was established.[267] Drew wrote to his parents about incidents at Whittingehame, when non-Jewish staff challenged the religious rules of the school. One instance included Drew and the Matron deciding to eat a lobster caught by one of the boys, despite shellfish being prohibited by the rules of *Kashrut*.[268] Drew also received parcels of food from his parents, which allowed him to enjoy 'entirely non-Jew meals' with Maxwell.[269] Whittingehame's Rabbi Heinemann clashed with Drew after discovering that he had allowed the cows in the dairy to be milked on the Sabbath.[270] The Rabbi banned the boys from drinking the subsequent supply of milk. Drew wrote to his parents about his frustration about the Rabbi, 'a narrow-minded spineless little stickler for orthodoxy'.[271]

Kindertransportees in Jewish residential care were also introduced to the local Christian community. Drew took Whittingehame's resident Kindertransportees to see the Rector of Whittingehame Church, resident in the adjacent Manse. Whittingehame Church is located just outside the grounds of the estate and could be accessed quickly and directly by a pathway through the estate's gardens.[272] Lady Traprain played an important role in the daily lives of the Kindertransportees. The *Haddingtonshire Courier* reported her activities, introducing Kindertransportees to Christian festivals.[273] On 6 January 1939, she took Kindertransportees to the local public hall, where Christmas festivities took place.[274] Their visit was coordinated with members of the local parish and non-Jewish children, from Tynepark Home and Morham Vale Home. The Kindertransportees gave recitations under the direction of 'Mrs Myles' and listened to the other children singing festive songs. Father Christmas presented the Kindertransportees with gifts and Reverend Marshall Lang was present.

The Jewish committees responsible for the care of Kindertransportees in a Jewish environment also utilized the help of non-Jewish organizations. In 1940, a report by the CC recorded that 'relations with the Christian Council . . . (was) one of the happiest features' of their work.[275] In 1939, the *Jewish Echo* reported that the refugee hostels in Glasgow were working in co-operation with the Scottish Christian Council (SCC).[276] Reverend Robert Smith led the SCC in Edinburgh.[277] Non-denominational youth organizations, such as the Scouts, were also permitted within Jewish care environments. These often had links to local non-Jewish congregations.

Kindertransportees who express that they had limited religious engagement with Judaism do not necessarily mean that they were no longer engaged with a Jewish life. Jewish youth groups or clubs, providing recreational activities, became an important component of Jewish life for the Kindertransportees. This point is often overlooked. These organizations advocated social, cultural and national connections to being Jewish. These sometimes overtly opposed religiosity, yet they tended to encourage a strong association with a Jewish community.

This trend had already been established for many Kindertransportees before migration. The German youth movement had become an important aspect of the lives of young people, and each denomination possessed its own related cluster of clubs.[278] Youth groups tended to be affiliated with a local church or synagogue.[279] Prohibitive social legislation, combined with the desire of Jewish youth for extra-curricular past-times, meant that Jewish youth groups became enormously important in daily lives. Reicha Freier's Youth Aliyah, as well as Habonim, Bachad, Hashomer Hatzair and other Zionist youth groups, emerged as important sources of socialization for Jewish minors.[280] Each youth movement catered for three age groups: *Bonim* (age, 9–12), *Tsofim* (age, 13–15) and *Vatikim* (age, 16 and above).[281]

In Scotland, this trend continued as Kindertransportees chose to become affiliated with a range of different Jewish youth groups. The Maccabi club became popular among Kindertransportees and offered non-religious sports pursuits.[282] In Glasgow, this club was associated with Garnethill's congregation. While at Garnethill, Fry joined 'a youth organisation . . . equivalent of the Scouts and some Jewish sports club. . . . I learnt boxing . . . these were Jewish sports organisations'.[283]

Zionist youth groups captivated many Kindertransportees and provided an important alternative connection to Judaism and the meaning of being Jewish. Zionism displaced previously held notions about the meaning and expression of being Jewish.[284] Zionist groups advocated the political and national significance of being 'Jewish'.[285] In 2003, Handler argued that regardless of whether the Kindertransportees were affiliated with religious or non-religious Zionism, they were still Jewish per se and so strict piety was not as important a factor for their connection to being Jewish.[286]

Zionism became the central component of Scottish Jewish identity.[287] To be Jewish was no longer understood in religious terms, but became a national, political and social connection.[288] Edna recalls that, at Whittingehame, the trainees adopted a national significance to their 'Jewishness' and that Zionism took precedence over religion.[289] These shifts led many Kindertransportees to express an atheist or agnostic connection to their Jewish heritage.

Scotland's vibrant Zionist youth movement played a central role in Kindertransportees' lives in the region. Ruby Ockrent established a Habonim group in Edinburgh, and there also existed groups for Bachad, Hashomer Hatzair and Bnei Keive.[290] Bachad and Bnei Keive remained the religious options for youth, while Hashomer Hatzair was particularly anti-religious. A socialistic communist movement, Kindertransportees who joined Hashomer Hatzair vehemently veered away from piety. Habonim also challenged the religious connections of the Kindertransportees. Habonim was a socialist trade union-orientated group, which, in Britain, had traditionally been affiliated with its local synagogue. However, the influence of the German Habonim youth pushed the group further away from this relationship and towards a more 'irreligious' secular orientation.[291]

Elijah was a member of Habonim at Whittingehame and recalls that the youth group 'did quite a lot of Zionist things . . . not religious at all'.[292] Benson recalls that he consciously rejected piety in favour of his Habonim youth group.[293] He initially would go to meetings of Habonim and Bnei Keive with no particular preference. Ending up in Habonim, he describes it as a Jewish Scouts with no religious observance. Benson followed his *Gar'in* (group of Zionist youth, who will make *Aliyah* together) to Amiad, Israel, a non-religious kibbutz. Milner believes that the Habonim group offered trans-migrants an important alternative to Jewry's religiosity and Orthodox theology.[294]

Broader life stories: Jewish lives lost and found

> My confusion was threefold. Firstly for years I could not be sure if I was German or English, Jew or Gentile. I used to say that I got sore from sitting on the fence. In recent years however, I have resolved these problems and at last come to terms with myself.[295]

This statement is indicative of the lack of clarity felt by the Kindertransportees in relation to their Jewish connection in their later lives. The meaning of being Jewish became entwined in an important dichotomy between a pious Jewish connection and a secular Jewish lifestyle. Previous evaluations have focused on piety and this has invited inflated figures for the number of 'lost' Jewish youth to Judaism. These have too often ignored those who chose only to engage in secular, non-pious Jewish pursuits, yet who continue to consider themselves as Jewish. Table 8 demonstrates the continued presence of Jewishness among the Kindertransportees in later life. This shows that there was a slip in Jewish affiliation from 91 per cent to 70 per cent. However, this does not indicate that there was a mass loss of Jewish youth from Judaism. Eighteen per cent state that they have no religious faith, suggesting theological confusion and uncertainty,

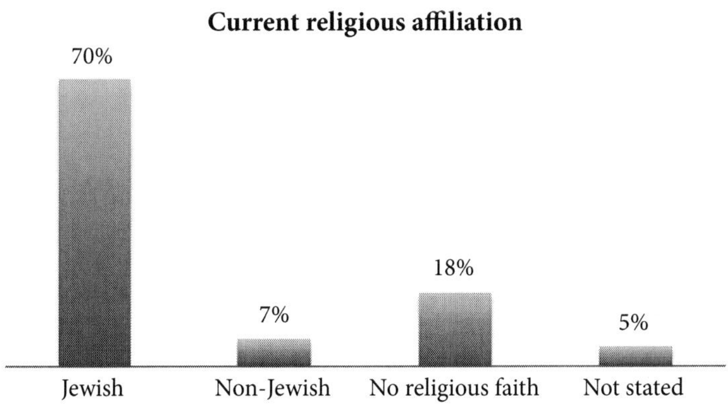

Table 8 Current religious faith.
Source: KA: QU/SUP.

rather than conversion to an alternative faith. The non-Jewish contingency has only risen by 4 per cent.

This suggests that evaluations have tended to put forward too confidently the Orthodox interpretation of Jewish life and disqualify the atheist or agnostic Jew. The whole question of the extent to which Kindertransportees remained in the Jewish fold, or became estranged from Judaism, seems too simplistic. It is not possible to suggest a benchmark for the level of piety Kindertransportees had had and then lost. There was no monolithic type of Jew that they had once been and were no more. In later life (shown in Table 9), Kindertransportees state nine different types of Jewish affiliation: Liberal, Orthodox, Reform, Conservative, Secular, Traditional, Havurah, non-practising, Liberal/non-practising and Jewish with no orientation.[296]

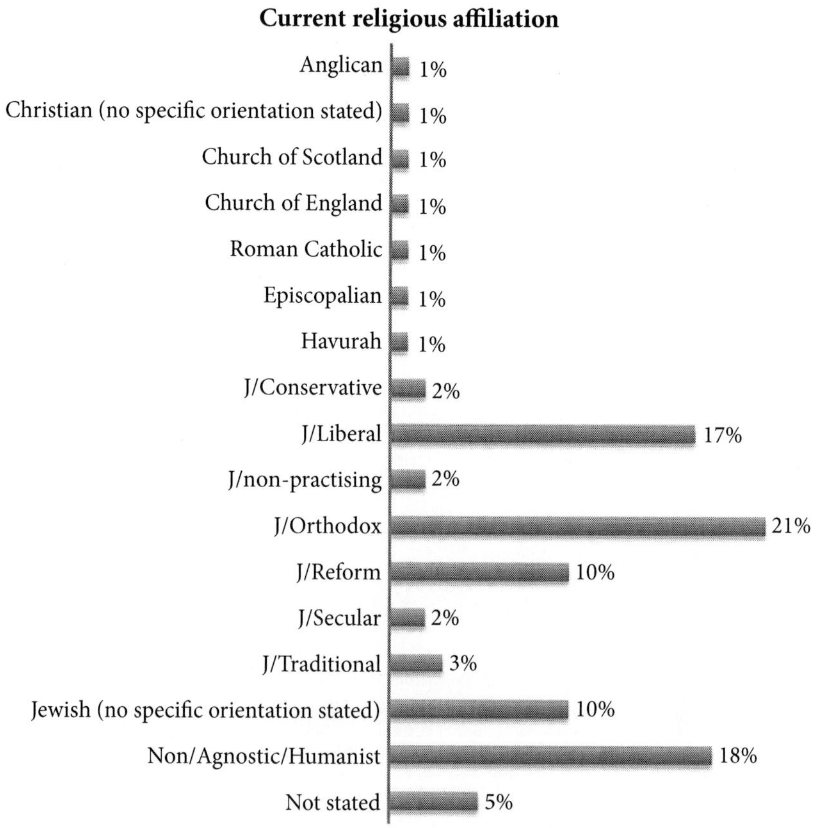

Table 9 Current religious affiliation.
Source: KA: QU/SUP.

Those who no longer state that they are Jewish by religion do not all profess a Christian conversion; among them is a Humanist, and 18 per cent who profess no religion, including atheists and agnostics.[297] This migration was also not a linear motion away from Judaism. Kindertransportees could adopt greater piety or return to Judaism in later life. Twenty-one per cent of Kindertransportees now state that they are now Jewish Orthodox. Of these, only 83 per cent had previously been Jewish Orthodox.[298] Others absorbed additional theologies and incorporated them within their understanding of Judaism. For some the experience in Scotland was so alien and unfamiliar that it had limited impact on their lives as Jews. After the war, they re-imagined and recreated the Jewish customs and traditions their parents had preferred in Greater Germany.

Fundamentally, Kindertransportees experienced a change in their connection to Judaism under all circumstances. Kindertransportees could drop their pious traditions, but remain connected to certain aspects of a Jewish lifestyle. Some chose to opt out of a Jewish association altogether, while others adopted new Anglo- or Scottish Jewish religious orientations.

'Estrangement' is the wrong word to use in this discussion. The Kindertransportees underwent a 'change' in their Jewish lifestyles. They experienced a transition from a Jewish life characterized by their Jewish community in Greater Germany and their home lives before migration to one shaped by their position and environment in Scotland, and then formed by their broader life stories.

Notes

1 Howard Cooper and Paul Morrison, *A Sense of Belonging; Dilemmas of British Jewish Identity* (London: Weidenfeld & Nicolson, 1991), 51.

2 HLSC/MS183/344/10, '"The Child Estrangement Movement"; An Expose on the alienation of Jewish Refugee Children in GB from Judaism', Pamphlet, January 1944.

3 Ibid.

4 HLSC/MS183/384/F2, Report of CC, 'Religious Teaching of Refugee Children'; see also HLSC/MS183/53/2.

5 HLSC/MS183/290/F1.

6 Turner, ... *And the Policeman Smiled,* 235.

7 FWPC/Sarah, Edna.

8 WL/BL/25, Arieh Handler.

9 Bertha Leverton, in *ROK,* 4.
10 KA: QU/SUP
11 See Bermant, *Troubled Eden.*
12 KA: QU/SUP.
13 Flora Hogman, 'The experience of Catholicism for Jewish minors during World War II', *Psychoanalytic Review* (1963), 75, 4 (Winter, 1988), 512.
14 KA: QU/SUP.
15 *Jewish Echo*, 24 March 1939.
16 Brenner, 'Promoting East European Jewry', 63.
17 Ibid., 67.
18 Fackenheim, *Epitaph for German Judaism,* 12.
19 Gay, *Freud, Jews and other Germans,* 29.
20 WHMA/USC: 31378.
21 FWPC/Jacob.
22 FWPC/Benson.
23 FWPC/Abaigael.
24 FWPC/Ruth.
25 FWPC/Elsie.
26 FWPC/Josephina.
27 See Nicholas Stargardt, *Witnesses of War: Children's Lives under the Nazis* (London, 2005), 12.
28 WHMA/USC: 23855; FWPC/Rachel.
29 FWPC/Josephina.
30 WL/BL/150.
31 Lisa Pine, *Nazi Family Policy, 1933–1945* (Oxford: Berg Publishers, 1997), 155.
32 FWPC/Dena.
33 Marion A. Kaplan, *Between Dignity and Despair; Jewish Life in Nazi Germany* (New York: Oxford University Press, 1998), 51.
34 WHMA/USC: 23855.
35 Ibid; FWPC/Jan, Ariel.
36 FWPC/Isabel.
37 Stargardt, *Witnesses of War,* 12; Kaplan, *Between Dignity and Despair,* 51.
38 FWPC/Isabel.
39 WHMA/USC: 23855.
40 Ibid.
41 FWPC/Rachel.
42 FWPC/Ruth.
43 Ugolini, 'The Internal Enemy "OTHER"', 156.
44 Ibid.
45 Hogman, 'The Experience of Catholicism', 511.

46 Ibid., 513.
47 FWPC/Elsie.
48 FWPC/Ruth.
49 WHMA/SC: 1349–36.
50 WHMA/USC: 31378.
51 FWPC/Elsie.
52 Ibid.
53 Ibid.
54 HLSC/MS183/53/2.
55 Presland, 'A Great Adventure', in *ROK*, 21.
56 Ibid., 23.
57 Eva Michaelis Stern, *Children in the Searchlight* (Jerusalem, 1946), 2.
58 Ibid.
59 Turner, ... *And the Policeman Smiled*, 241.
60 KA: QU/SUP.
61 Gordon, *Hitler, Germans and the 'Jewish Question'*, 16.
62 Smout, *Punishment and Welfare*, 153; See also Mahood, *Policing Gender*, 30.
63 Elisabeth Imber, 'Saving Jews: The History of Jewish-Christian relations in Scotland – 1880–1948', unpublished MA thesis (Brandeis University, 2011), 64.
64 Ibid., 84.
65 See David McDougall, *In Search of Israel; A Chronicle of the Jewish Mission of the Church of Scotland* (New York: Nelson, 1941).
66 Ibid.
67 NYL/George Knight, *'For Christians Only – About Jews'* (Edinburgh, 1939–45); See also James Wells, *United Free Church of Scotland; Our Jewish Mission* (Scotland: Unknown, 1905).
68 Lewis Cameron, *The Challenge of Need: A History of Social Service by The Church of Scotland 1869–1969* (Edinburgh, 1971), 41.
69 Ibid.
70 FWPC/Rachel.
71 HLSC/MS183/344/10, Schonfeld (1944), 5.
72 Ibid.
73 HLSC/MS183/223/F1, Schonfeld, report of 'The Jewish Relief Association'.
74 Unfortunately, the archives for the Scottish National Council, which may clarify this point, remain unfit for viewing and can therefore not be accessed. (HLSC/MS183/481/2).
75 HLSC/MS183/344/10.
76 Steinberg, 'Jewish Education', 37.
77 Ibid., 53.
78 Tydor Baumel, 'Twice a Refugee', 180.

79 FWPC/Marthe.
80 WHMA/KC/RG-50.002*43.
81 Ibid. Letter by May Salmond, 8 February 1989.
82 WL/BL/76.
83 Ibid.
84 WHMA/USC: 31378.
85 Ibid.
86 FWPC/Rachel.
87 Ibid.
88 HLSC/MS183/344/10, Schonfeld (1944), 3.
89 WHMA/USC: 31378.
90 Ibid.
91 FWPC/Jacob.
92 Ibid.
93 Leverton, and Lowensohn, I came alone, 354.
94 WHMA/KC/RG-50.002*43.
95 FWPC/Isabel.
96 FWPC/Rachel.
97 HLSC/MS183/384/1, *The Jews; Some Plain Facts*, booklet (London, 1941).
98 Ibid., 41.
99 Zahl Gottlieb, *Men of Vision*, 174.
100 FWPC/Isabel.
101 HLSC/MS183/290/1, Schonfeld, Letter, 17 December 1941.
102 FWPC/Marthe.
103 Ibid.
104 FWPC/Elsie.
105 Ibid.
106 FWPC/Hans.
107 FWPC/Ani, Correspondence, 17 June 2008.
108 FWPC/Marthe.
109 WHMA/KC/RG-50.002*43.
110 Braber, *Jews in Glasgow*, 203.
111 FWPC/Hans.
112 Ibid.
113 FWPC/Ariel.
114 WHMA/KC/RG-50.002*43.
115 FWPC/Elsie.
116 Ibid.
117 Ibid.
118 Heppell, 'A Rebel, not a Rabbi', 38.

119 Steinberg, 'Jewish Education', 58.
120 Abrams, *Caledonian Jews,* 53; Steinberg, 'Jewish Education', 58.
121 See Abrams, *Caledonian Jews.*
122 Ibid.
123 Ibid., 170.
124 Braber, *Jews in Glasgow*, 142.
125 FWPC/Benson.
126 FWPC/Elijah.
127 FWPC/Rachel.
128 FWPC/Hans.
129 WL/BL/25.
130 Collins, *Be Well!,* 70.
131 WL/BL/137.
132 MCPC/Drew, Letters, 14 January 1939.
133 FWPC/Edna.
134 WL/BL/103.
135 MCPC/Drew, Letters, 25 April 1940.
136 Ibid.
137 MCPC/Drew, Letters, 25 April 1940.
138 FWPC/Elijah.
139 Ibid.
140 FWPC/Abaigael.
141 FWPC/Josephina.
142 WL/BL/103.
143 WHMA/USC: 43138.
144 SJA/SOC0004, Fay Cohen Stein, Memoir, 5 January 1995.
145 Ibid.
146 HLSC/MS183/384.
147 Ibid.
148 FWPC/Jacob.
149 WL/BL/103.
150 Baerbel Laufer, 'Memories', in *Whittingehame Farm School Reunion*, Brochure, 38.
151 MS116/157/AJ396/5, Minutes, 21 March 1939.
152 See Chaim Bermant, *Lord Jakobovits; the Authorised Biography of the Chief Rabbi* (London: Weidenfeld & Nicolson Ltd, 1990).
153 HLSC/MS183/384/F1, Booklet 'Bloomsbury House; The care of German and Austrian Refugees'.
154 Collins, *Aspects of Scottish Jewry,* 33.
155 Collins, *Second City Jewry*, 77.
156 See Abrams, *Caledonian Jews.*

157 HLSC/MS183/384/F2.

158 HLSC/MS183/53/2/1, Letter, 6 February 1940.

159 Steinberg, 'Jewish Education', 27.

160 *Jewish Chronicle,* 12 January 1940.

161 HLSC/MS183/384, Minutes, 15 May 1941.

162 Ibid.

163 Steinberg, 'Jewish Education', 29.

164 HLSC/MS183/290/1.

165 Ibid.

166 See Kenneth Collins, 'Orthodoxy and Reform: Differing Practices in a Glasgow Jewish Victorian Family', *Korot: the Israel Journal of the History of Medicine and Science*, 11 (1995).

167 KA: QU/SUP.

168 Ibid.

169 Fast, Children's Exodus, 107.

170 Michael Meyer, *Response to Modernity: A History of the Reform Movement in Judaism* (New York, 1988), 54–5.

171 MS183/344/10, Schonfeld (1944) 2/3.

172 Ibid.

173 FWPC.

174 FWPC/Jan.

175 FWPC/Josephina.

176 John Simon Oswald, 'Reformed Judaism', *The Jewish Quarterly Review*, 6, 2 (January 1894), 262–77.

177 Ibid., 265.

178 Stephen Poppel, *Zionism in Germany 1897–1933; The Shaping of a Jewish Identity* (Philadelphia, 1977), 41.

179 WL/BL/3.

180 Ibid.

181 Braber, *Jews in Glasgow,* 199.

182 NYPL/*Hashannah, 5718 (Jewish year); The Scottish Jewish Year Book 1957–58* (Glasgow, 1958); Braber (2007), 158; Collins, *Aspects of Scottish Jewry,* 30.

183 FWPC; KA: QU/SUP.

184 HLSC/MS183/384/F1.

185 Jehuda Reinharz and Walter Schatzberg (eds), *The Jewish Response to German Culture; From the Enlightenment to the Second World War* (London: University Press of New England, 1985); Sybil Oldfield, '"It is Usually She": The Role of British Women in the Rescue and Care of the Kindertransport Kinder', *Shofar: An Interdisciplinary Journal of Jewish Studies*, 23 (Fall, 2004), 68.

186 Steinberg, 'Jewish Education', 46–7.

187 Tydor Baumel, 'Twice a Refugee', 179.

188 Braber, 'Jews in Glasgow', 159.

189 Ibid.

190 *Jewish Chronicle*, 9 May 1941.

191 Such as *Allgemeine Zeitung des Judentums.*

192 Steinberg, 'Jewish Education', 53.

193 WHMA/USC: 43932.

194 FWPC/Levi.

195 Bermant, *Troubled Eden,* 28.

196 Ibid., 42; See also Daiches, *Two Worlds.*

197 Bermant, Troubled Eden, 74.

198 Ibid., 58.

199 Braber, *Jews in Glasgow*, 199: Garnethill possessed a mixed choir, performed services in English, shortened services, introduced new prayers, omitted certain ceremonies and allowed the congregation to mix.

200 Ibid., 157.

201 Collins, *Aspects of Scottish Jewry,* 35.

202 Bermant, *Troubled Eden*, 74; Kölmel, 'Problems of Settlement', 251.

203 FWPC/Edna.

204 FWPC/Isabel.

205 Kölmel, 'German-Jewish Refugees in Scotland', in Collins (ed.), *Aspects of Scottish Jewry*, 73.

206 Ibid.

207 Gordon, *Hitler, Germans and the 'Jewish Question'*, 9.

208 Ibid.

209 MCPC/Drew, Letters, 14 January 1940.

210 Jehuda Reinharz and Walter Schatzberg (eds), *The Jewish Response to German Culture; From the Enlightenment to the Second World War* (London: University Press of New England, 1985).

211 Jack Werthheimer, *Unwelcome Strangers; East European Jews in Imperial Germany* (Oxford: Oxford University Press, 1987), 149.

212 Collins, *Aspects of Scottish Jewry,* 59. Over 50 per cent of Jews in Glasgow still lived in the Gorbals in 1936.

213 FWPC/Benson.

214 Heppell, 'A Rebel, not a Rabbi', 38.

215 GJA: Chaim Bermant, 'Memoir', 1979, in *Tenth Anniversary Magazine; Patterns and Images of Jewish immigration in Scotland* (Glasgow, 1997), 9.

216 Tamar El-Or, 'Power/Knowledge/Gender: The Oranges-and-Grapefruit Debate', in Peskowitz and Levitt (ed.), *Judaism since Gender,* 65.

217 Collins, *Second City Jewry*, 77.

218 Heppell, 'A Rebel, not a Rabbi', 44.
219 FWPC/Edna, Batya, Abaigael.
220 Cooper and Morrison, *A Sense of Belonging*, 93.
221 FWPC/Rachel.
222 FWPC/Elijah.
223 GJA/Bermant, 'Memoir of an Eastern-European immigrant to Glasgow', 10.
224 FWPC/Rachel.
225 Ibid.
226 FWPC/Hans.
227 Ibid.
228 FWPC/Jan.
229 *Hashannah, 5718 (Jewish year); The Scottish Jewish Year Book 1957–58,* (Glasgow: Unknown, 1958), 49.
230 FWPC/Jan.
231 FWPC/Rachel.
232 FWPC/Jan.
233 Braber, *Jews in Glasgow*, 145.
234 WL/BL/103.
235 FWPC/Rachel.
236 FWPC/Ariel.
237 WHMA/USC: 43932.
238 MCPC/Drew, Letters, 21 August 1939.
239 FWPC/Nathan.
240 FWPC/Abaigael.
241 FWPC/Elijah.
242 WHMA/USC: 43932.
243 FWPC/Benson.
244 MCPC/Lucy Laqueur, 'A Matron Remembers', in *Whittingehame Farm School Ltd*, Brochure, 17.
245 MCPC/Drew, Letters, 14 January 1940.
246 FWPC/Levi.
247 FWPC/Edna.
248 Ibid.
249 FWPC/Rachel.
250 Berger, 'Jewish Identity and Jewish Destiny', 85.
251 FWPC/Elijah.
252 Ibid.
253 WL/BL/137.
254 WL/BL/25.
255 Cooper and Morrison, *A Sense of Belonging*, 26.

256 Ibid.

257 WHMA/USC: 43932.

258 Evelyn Cowan, *Spring Remembered: A Scottish Jewish Childhood* (Edinburgh: Southside Press, 1974).

259 See Chapter 1.

260 FWPC/Rachel.

261 FWPC/Rachel, Benson.

262 GJA/SOC0002, 'List of names of refugee boys attending Garnetbank Primary School in 1939'.

263 FWPC/Jan.

264 David Limond, 'Locality, Education and Authority in Scotland: 1902–2002 (Via 1872), *Oxford Review of Education*, 28, 2/3, (June – September, 2002), 360.

265 Collins, *Be Well!*, 6.

266 Collins, *Aspects of Scottish Jewry*, 30.

267 HLSC/MS116/157/AJ396/5.

268 MCPC/Drew, Letters, 25 April 1940.

269 MCPC/Drew, Letters, 14 January 1940.

270 Ibid.

271 Ibid.

272 MCPC/Drew, Letters, 25 April 1940.

273 *Haddingtonshire Courier*, 6 January 1939.

274 Ibid.

275 HLSC/MS183/384.

276 *Jewish Echo*, 6 January 1939.

277 HLSC/MS183/384/1.

278 See Stachura, *The German Youth Movement*.

279 Proctor, '(Uni)Forming Youth', 103–34.

280 FWPC/Levi, Edna; see also Stachura, *The German Youth Movement*.

281 NYPL/Hashannah.

282 *Jewish Echo*, 2 March 1939.

283 WHMA/USC: 31378.

284 Silberstein, 'Toward a Postzionist Discourse', 93.

285 See Michael Berkowitz, *Zionism Culture and West European Jewry before the First World War* (New York: Cambridge University Press, 1993); HWZOA, *Hadassah, the Women's Zionist Organisation of America; Hadassah and Youth Aliyah* (unknown place, 1935).

286 WL/BL/25.

287 Braber, *Jews in Glasgow*, 178.

288 Ibid.

289 FWPC/Edna.

290 FWPC/Levi.

291 Ibid.

292 FWPC/Elijah.

293 FWPC/Benson.

294 BL/WL/3.

295 Ingrid Gassman, in Leverton and Lowensohn (ed.), *I Came Alone*, 117.

296 KA: QU/SUP.

297 Ibid.

298 Ibid.

4

Creating New *Olim* in Scotland: The Limitations of a Zionist Endeavour

The care experience of the Kindertransportees was influenced by a wide variety of social, cultural, economic and political factors. Zionism (an international movement that supported the re-establishment of a Jewish homeland in *Eretz Yisrael*) was perhaps the most significant political influence for many of the Kindertransportees, particularly those who were sheltered in Jewish-led residential care facilities. These facilities often utilized and coordinated their welfare efforts with various Zionist groups. As a result, they endorsed the Zionist philosophy in care agendas. At the forefront of this exploit for Kindertransportees were the pre-*hachsharot* training farms.

The *hachshara* movement had emerged at the beginning of the twentieth century in Germany in response to the desires of the Zionist movement for the creation of a generation of Jewish youth suitable for settlement in *Eretz Yisrael*. This was led by Recha Freir's Youth Aliyah, which endorsed rigorous physical and mental training of German-Jewish youth.[1] The central objective of a *hachshara* was to recreate a *kibbutz* and in doing so, provide all the necessary training and preparation for Jewish youth before they migrated to *Eretz Yisrael*. The pressures of Fascism and the surge of anti-Semitic sentiment across Germany re-energized and internationalized the *hachshara* movement. Before 1938, *hachshara* training had been reserved for a select few of the most ardent Zionist German-Jewish youth who had for many years worked towards admittance. However, the movement increasingly encouraged all suitable Jewish youth to take part in order to enable them to leave Greater Germany.

The key aim of the movement by the late 1930s was to relocate *hachsharot* from Greater Germany to temporary host nations in order that Jewish youth could safely continue their preparation for *Aliyah*. Subsequently, by 1939, the *hachsharot* centres had expanded enormously, and by 1 March 1940, there were over 2,000 refugee youths in such camps training for *Aliyot* to *Yishvo* (the pre-state

Jewish community in *Eretz Yisrael*).[2] Students now included Austrian, Czechoslovakian and Polish youth. *Hachsharot* centres were relocated to a number of countries, including Switzerland, Holland, Belgium and Britain.

The Jewish community in Britain responded to this development and aided the establishment of a number of *hachsharot* and pre-*hachsharot* centres across the country, including Great Engham Farm in Kent, Llandough Castle and Gwrych Castle in Wales, Bydown Farm in Devon, Millisle Refugee Farm in County Down, Northern Ireland, and Whittingehame Farm School, which operated from 1939 until 1941 when it was relocated to Polton House, both in Scotland. A number of adult education facilities in agriculture had been opened to refugees in the north of England, such as Bachad's centre of learning in Manchester, 'to which the agricultural workers in groups dotted over the country are drafted for a few weeks of concentrated study'.[3] However, the majority remained located in the southern regions of England.[4] Whittingehame and later Polton House were the only Scottish pre-*hachsharot* in operation during World War II. According to questionnaires, Scotland's pre-*hachsharot* sheltered an estimated 23 per cent of Scotland's Kindertransportees, and it was at these facilities that the Kindertransportees' connection with Zionism was most proactively nurtured.[5]

Figure 18 was taken at Whittingehame and captures three Kindertransportees undertaking an aspect of their agricultural work. The photograph offers an intriguing snapshot of the experience of living on a pre-*hachsharot* in Scotland. While the central figure seems to be smiling, he also appears to be cold, wearing only shorts and a light jumper, while being surrounded by snow during a Scottish

Figure 18 Kindertransportees feeding chickens at Whittingehame Farm School. *Source*: MCPC/Drew, photographs.

winter. In light of these difficult working conditions, did the Kindertransportees really associate their daily tasks with their future Zionist ambitions?

Their official purpose for feeding the chickens was to become successful *Olim* (those who make *Aliyah*). However, the Kindertransportees' personal interpretation of their daily life and reasoning for undertaking demanding chores is often expressed in testimonies as something completely different. Kindertransportees recall their experiences at Whittingehame with nostalgia for their extended childhood at a comfortable 'British boarding school', pride in their participation in the British war effort, 'digging for victory' on the home front, or antagonism over being remanded in an isolated 'internment' camp for undesirable 'alien' youth.[6] Were these Kindertransportees really motivated or inspired by Zionism?

Zionist foundations

The establishment of the Whittingehame care scheme was informed by Zionism and developed by a substantial Zionist support network. When Whittingehame was first opened, it was recorded as a prestigious, pioneering endeavour and a model for the pre-*hachsharot* programme in Britain. The physical appearance of Whittingehame – the grand house and large surrounding estate – meant that the scheme was an extremely ambitious Zionist plan (Figure 19). The school was

Figure 19 Whittingehame Farm School.
Source: MCPC/Drew, Photographs.

reported by the *Jewish Echo* as 'the largest project undertaken' and 'one of the leading experiments of its kind'.[7]

The aim of the scheme was *Halutzic* (preparing members for emigration to Palestine), but it did not endorse *Aliyah Bet* (illegal immigration), the strategy of the World Zionist Congress in 1939.[8] Instead, Whittingehame adhered to the practices advocated by Youth Aliyah and established a strategy of enabling students to gain entry to Palestine on the merit of attending recognized educational institutions. The two-year agricultural training programme was designed to enable the residents to qualify for the British Mandatory Government in Palestine's immigration certificate, which favoured agricultural skills and a knowledge of Hebrew. Youth Aliyah disseminated these certificates to youth under 16. The limited immigration quota was allocated based on the presumed 'economic absorptive capacity' of Palestine.[9] The residents were to be given both practical and cultural training 'to prepare for further emigration overseas, particularly to Palestine'.[10]

Within this Zionist training framework, Whittingehame and Polton House were deemed pre-*hachsharot* because the youth admitted tended to be between 14 and 17, below the age of eligibility for actual adult *hachshara* training.[11] The intention was still to fulfil the Zionist movement's key objective of training new *Olim,* but their role as pre-*hachshara* training farms meant that they were to offer the Kindertransportees only an introduction to life on a *hachshara* and in turn life on a *kibbutz* in *Eretz Yisrael.* After completing the 2-year training programme, the residents would either transfer to *hachsharot* centres across Britain or have qualified for a Youth Aliyah permit for entry to *Eretz Yisrael.*

The school had the capacity to accommodate 200 and opened with 160 young people.[12] There were up to 70 girls and 12 staff members.[13] The scheme was connected to the plans for the Garnethill hostel in Glasgow. The 30 boys in the hostel of ages 12–16 would 'not receive any practical training, but when they reach the age of 16 or 17 they may go on to Whittingehame House to learn agriculture'.[14] In the hostel, the Kindertransportees received Hebrew instruction twice a week and undertook physical training and boxing lessons with Sergeant Major Strathdee. The intention was to begin to prepare the boys for the demands of a pre-*hachshara* and later adult *hachshara* training at an early age. In doing so, the scheme took a long-term approach to the integration of Kindertransportees into the Zionist movement.

The aims and ambitions of the Whittingehame scheme were shaped by the goals and agendas for Zionist youth of prominent personages from within the international Zionist movement. The donation of the Whittingehame Estate was prompted by the activities of the Zionist movement. Handler, formerly the leader of Bachad, recalls that it was the joint effort of Hechalutz, Bachad, Habonim and Bnei Akiva, who 'all worked together' to establish Jewish centres for the Kindertransportees.[15] With the aid of key personages, including Chaim Weizmann, Simon Marks and Otto Schiff, Handler recalls that 'we used our political know-how' to acquire funds and resources to establish *hachsharot* in numerous places across Britain, including 'Thaxted. . . . Gwrych Castle. . . . Rosset. . . . St Asser. . . . Whittingehame, all over'.[16] Cohen Stein supports this assertion and recorded in her memoirs that she believed Weizmann 'prompted' the donation of the Balfour estate by Lord Traprain, Lord Balfour's nephew, to the Edinburgh Hebrew congregation for the care of the refugee youth.[17]

Lord Traprain offered the estate as a symbolic gesture to his uncle Lord Balfour's 'Balfour Declaration' of 1917, which endorsed the return of the Jews to Zion. The significance of this connection was not lost, and Whittingehame was often perceived as an important symbol of the progress of the Zionist movement. In 1944, Norman Bentwich recorded the significance of this connection in the psyche of Jewish Zionism, which led to Whittingehame possessing 'a peculiarly romantic association'.[18]

Highly positioned personages within the international Zionist movement were involved in directing the foundations of the scheme. Drew recorded that 'Mr Shattner' led activities of Youth Aliyah in Britain and also became a governor of Whittingehame, visiting the facility in order to allocate certificates to the Kindertransportees.[19] Chaim Weizmann, the leading British Zionist and future founder and President of Israel, was a key figure involved in the founding of Whittingehame. Weizmann had previously visited Glasgow in 1906 to advocate a policy of gradual colonization of Palestine.[20] Lord Traprain was active in the development of *Eretz Yisrael* into an independent state.[21] Both Weizmann and Traprain adopted a vested interest in the Whittingehame scheme and linked it to their international efforts intended to forward the Zionist movement.

Prominent female Zionists also played a vital role in the Whittingehame scheme. They took a leading role in generating financial support for the scheme and a small number offered guidance within the school. Vera Weizmann, Chaim Weizmann's wife, was an important figure and played a central role in the planning and overseeing of the school. She advocated that Whittingehame 'should be run like a *kibbutz* in Palestine where, it was hoped, the children would eventually go'.[22] After the school opened, she made a number of inspections, at which time she is recalled as having imposed her will upon both the cook and the governors to remedy the catering problems there.[23] Her interaction at this time remained restricted to the adult community involved in Whittingehame and she offered little individual connection to Zionism for the individual Kindertransportees, but her presence gave Whittingehame prestige and importance as a pre-*hachshara*.

Zionism remained the dominant political ideology for Jews in Scotland, most especially in Glasgow.[24] Support of the Whittingehame scheme became an expression of this Zionist commitment. This meant that a particular regional Zionist community informed the scheme.[25] Scotland possessed a particular type of Zionist preference. This did not favour the religious Mizrahi or left-wing Poalei Zion (workers of Zion) groups. Scottish Zionism remained in the most part supportive of the 'centrist general Zionists'.[26] This was an orientation that appealed to the Jewish communities in the diaspora for the reason that it required oral support and financial assistance, but did not demand the disbandment of secular practices or a pledge to migrate. The regional approach to Zionism was not revolutionary or sectarian and as a result, Whittingehame adopted a far more secular, liberal and mild approach to Zionism. The regional branch of the Women's International Zionist Organisation (WIZO) was critical in the financial support of the school.[27] Members organized fund-raising events, such as tea parties, many at the home of 'Mrs John Levinson', and events such as the Whittingehame Open Day.[28]

However, despite the instigation and support of Scotland's pre-*hachsharot* by the Zionist movement, the bureaucratic management and organization of the scheme were overseen and governed by a network of non-Zionist philanthropic organizations. These operated under the auspices of the CC in London.[29] In Scotland, on a regional level, these included the SNCR and the JCGR, as well as locally based organizations, most notably the ERC and the GRC. These local committees coordinated efforts with the pre-existing Jewish representative body, the GJRC, along with other local philanthropic groups and personages, to oversee the running of the care scheme and supervise the Kindertransportees in Whittingehame.

The beneficiary of Lord Traprain's lease of the family estate was notably not made to a Zionist organization, but to the Edinburgh congregation of the Salisbury Road Synagogue. The ERC, consisting predominantly of members from this congregation, in turn presented a proposal to the CC in London for approval and financial backing to utilize the estate. The CC then sent representatives from London to assess the estate's suitability and the scheme's feasibility.[30] In December 1938, after the estate had been deemed suitable, a meeting was arranged in London. Numerous representatives of interested parties joined the CC at the meeting to formalize the plan.[31]

Whittingehame was subsequently formulated and founded at a meeting in London under the jurisdiction of the CC. A combination of Jewish, refugee and Zionist-orientated groups attended the meeting and recorded its formulation as a beacon for British Zionism.[32] However, Zionist representatives in attendance only included a small number of members from a limited collection of international Zionist organizations: Habonim, The Federation of Women Zionists of Great Britain and Ireland, Youth Aliyah and B'nai B'rith. Furthermore, it becomes apparent at this early stage that English Zionist organizations dominated the formulation of the scheme, rather than Scottish groups.

Following the creation of the Whittingehame scheme, the role of Zionist organizations became intermittent and often limited. Zionist organizations never monopolized the scheme and other priorities preoccupied their activities. The Jewish migrant pandemic overwhelmed the multitude of Zionist organizations. Eva Michaelis of Youth Aliyah records the precedence for aiding Zionist youths who remained trapped within Greater Germany and in imminent danger.[33] As a result, non-Scottish international organizations often had limited time or resources to stay in close contact with residents. Handler recalls the logistic problems involved in keeping in touch with the boys and girls at Whittingehame, especially during the Blitz when travelling from London became very difficult.[34]

These preoccupations and logistical problems meant that representatives of the Zionist movement did not challenge the CC's jurisdiction or make efforts to take official control of the scheme. Instead, it remained firmly under the governance of the CC and its representative regional welfare network. Whittingehame became a registered company of the CC's head office in Bloomsbury House, London. The ERC in cooperation with the Edinburgh Hebrew congregation of Salisbury Road Synagogue were the main bodies involved in managing and governing Whittingehame. A small number of local personages dominated these organizations and the leadership of the scheme. Disputes and problems that arose within the school were directed for resolution first to the ERC and then, if necessary, to the CC.[35] The CC authorized supplies and allocated students for Whittingehame, who were then convoyed to Scotland, under the supervision of the ERC. The appointment and removal of staff was dictated by the ERC with final approval from the CC.[36]

The CC and its network of welfare service providers were not, however, devoid of Zionist influences. Zionist organizations utilized the infrastructure and services of the CC to further schemes with Zionist agendas, and actually worked under the guise of the CC to supervise these schemes. As a result, despite the detachment of the actual Zionist movement from many schemes for refugees in an official capacity, Zionism became a governing ideology colouring residential centres such as Whittingehame.

A significant number of organizations of the Zionist movement relocated to Britain and centralized their activities at the CC's head office at London's Bloomsbury House under the umbrella of the CC. Youth Aliyah established its head office there after 1938 and subsequently coordinated its activities with those of the CC. Because the purpose of Whittingehame was to afford the Kindertransportees an opportunity to gain Youth Aliyah certificates for entry to Palestine, Youth Aliyah did remain involved in Whittingehame after it was established.[37] Handler recalls the utilization by his organization, Bachad, of the CC's welfare network and the financial services of the Central British Fund (CBF) to instigate Bachad-inspired schemes.[38] The Zionist and non-Zionist organizations were both working to aid the refugees and inevitably, living in such proximity, their work overlapped with many efforts being coordinated.

Many of the CC's key workers and leaders of sub-committees were also important figures in the Zionist movement. Volunteers and employees frequently worked within a number of different offices and represented more than one organization. Lola Hahn Warburg worked within Bloomsbury House as a representative for both Youth Aliyah and the RCM.[39] This formed a number of links between the objectives and efforts of both offices.[40] Handler, who at the time was also the leader of Bachad, formed the Jewish Agricultural Committee (JAC) under the auspices of the CC. He recalls his desire to aid the Zionist's objective to support the activities of new *Olim*, while at the same time undertaking the CC's primary objective of establishing self-supporting refugees and self-sufficient agricultural centres in Britain.[41] Whittingehame, along with a number of other Kindertransportee care initiatives, also came under the auspices of the JAC.[42]

Thus, through the guise of a CC's refugee committee, the Zionist movement did have an important governing role in the management of Whittingehame. The extent to which Bachad members dominated the agricultural committee is not clear and the melting-pot character of Bloomsbury House makes it very difficult to pinpoint exactly which office was responsible for certain decisions made, particularly those which may have fallen across the jurisdiction of a number of offices. Nevertheless, the CC was an umbrella organization encompassing both Zionist and non-Zionist inspired offices. The Zionist organizations did not direct its initiatives, but they certainly had a voice in its activities and a say on leading figures within its infrastructure.

The pre-existing regional Jewish welfare and representative organizations of Glasgow, responsible for managing the CC's initiatives in the region, also possessed a heavily weighted membership of Zionist supporters. The popularity of Zionism among its members meant that by 1939 the main governing bodies had pledged support for Zionist rhetoric. The GJRC had publicly endorsed Zionism at the 1918 mass Zionist meeting in Glasgow.[43] The GJRC was responsible for the care of over 200 of the Kindertransportees in Scotland and played a vital role in the direction of Whittingehame.[44]

The local committees responsible for overseeing the day-to-day maintenance of Whittingehame also possessed a close relationship with the Zionist movement. The Glasgow and Edinburgh Jewish congregations of Garnethill and Salisbury Road, respectively, constituted the two dominant Scottish communities involved in the CC's regional refugee welfare network and the Whittingehame scheme.[45] Members of Edinburgh's Hebrew congregation filled the bulk of leading roles within the ERC and Whittingehame's governing board. Both were sympathetic to the Zionist agenda. Rabbi Daiches, the rabbi of Salisbury Road, had pledged his support for Zionism in the 1920s.[46] The Garnethill Synagogue's congregation dominated the GRC, which also aided the Whittingehame scheme. Their minister, Rev E. P. Phillips, had been a member of the Glasgow Chovevei Zion (an organization for the financial assistance of settlement in Palestine) and declared his support for Zionism in 1904.[47]

In summary, it seems that following the initial involvement in instigating the scheme, Zionist organizations did have some influence on the management of Whittingehame, but that this arrived under various guises. Zionists infiltrated the bureaucratic infrastructure of the CC and operated under the pretext of implementing CC policies. This meant that they never became the guardians or managers of Whittingehame. The bureaucratic involvement of these organizations did not reach the young people on a practical or personal basis. It is therefore essential to consider not only the inspiration and initial character of the scheme at its foundations and within its bureaucratic channels, but also how it was managed on a day-to-day basis.

Zionism in practice

The reality of Scotland's pre-*hachsharot* was that for many Kindertransportees their care experience was one in which Zionism became overshadowed by alternative agendas and ideas when translated into a practical training programme. Particular characteristics of Whittingehame determined that in practice much of the *Haluz* agenda and *hachshara* formula was absent from the approach to the daily management of Whittingehame, the environment of care provided, and the physical training and mental preparation given to Kindertransportees.

The daily management of Whittingehame was not consistently non-Zionist or Zionist in its orientation, but transcended both tendencies in varying degrees. This balance changed over time as the dominant figures managing Whittingehame on a day-to-day basis changed. The initial approach to staff selection was in line with the CC's general approach to priorities of care for Kindertransportees.[48] This frequently clashed with the CREC because it gave no precedent to religious affiliation or political aversions over skill and individual suitability.[49]

Whittingehame initially lacked an abundance of Jewish or Zionist staff members. The two dominant figures that emerge in Kindertransportees' recollections of life at Whittingehame are Maxwell, the second headmaster, and Drew, Maxwell's second in command.[50] Neither was Jewish nor was Zionist. In 1939, Drew recalls in letters to his parents of his anticipation at meeting a Jew and his mistake upon meeting Maxwell at assuming he was Jewish because of his facial features.[51] Maxwell is alleged to have declared on his arrival that he wished to manage Whittingehame as a model of 'British boarding schools'.[52] The naivety of both perceptions is indicative of the environment of care the teenagers received, which lacked understanding of Judaism or Zionism. Reverend Bernard Cherrick replaced Maxwell as headmaster. Cherrick was not only Jewish, but also an active member of the Zionist movement and a leader of Habonim.[53] He encouraged greater religious and Zionist involvement among the Kindertransportees and supported the political activities of the residents.

Whittingehame also remained receptive to the contrasting needs of non-Zionist and Zionist-inspired youth in residence. Subsequently, the character of the care environment was highly reflective of the student composition at the time. The students were consistently very mixed in character, faith, ideals and ability, but they do recall feeling a definitive distinction between those who were Zionist and those who were not.[54] Interviewees commonly base these distinctions upon recollections of youth group membership.

Zionist organizations' greatest role came through youth guidance and mentoring in the form of the youth group. Bachad was particularly dominant in the pre-*hachsharot* movement in Britain and had established a *hachshara* at Grwych Castle, Wales, exclusively for Bachad Jewish Orthodox Zionist refugee youth.[55] Unlike Bachad's pre-*hachshara* at Grywch Castle, Whittingehame was not under the auspices of any one youth Zionist organization. In contrast, Youth Aliyah, Aliyat Noar, B'nai B'rith, Mizrachi, Bachad, Habonim, Hashomer Hatzair and the Hechlalutz movement all played a role in Whittingehame. Each movement held slightly different interpretations and orientations of Zionism and the Kindertransportees had a choice of which group to join.

Bachad, Habonim and Hashomer Hatzair were the main youth movements involved in Whittingehame. Each group possessed a *Madrich* (a Zionist guidance councillor for *Olim*) to provide leadership and guidance to their members. Elijah recalls the important role of the youth groups in their daily lives at Whittingehame and the enormous role this had in indoctrinating the residents towards Zionism.[56] Hechalutz established links with these groups in order to absorb those who had completed the 2-year course in their *hachshara* centres across Britain.[57] The power of these groups lay in their ability to indoctrinate the student body by way of integrating Zionism into their daily lives and friendship groups.

The influence of the Zionist youth group upon the resident body was demonstrated in 1940 when Zionist students protested against the continued absence of *Madrichem*.[58] Approximately 6 weeks later, the Jewish Agency sent three *Madrichem* for their appropriate youth groups: Bachad, Habonim and Hashomer Hatzair, and Maxwell's position as headmaster was terminated.[59]

Yet, there continued to be an assorted collection of residents, ranging from ardent Zionist youth to non-Zionists. Scouting and the ARP were introduced as an alternative to Zionist youth groups.[60] This situation was largely due to the selection process and criteria for student admissions, which inadvertently diluted the *Halutzic* intensity of Whittingehame. Admittance was not exclusive to Zionist youth as Whittingehame effectively operated an open-door policy. This was largely dictated by the CC, which utilized Whittingehame's accommodation for the surplus of teenage Kindertransportees in Britain.[61] Kindertransportees of the appropriate age and who were willing to migrate somewhere were admitted.[62] They did not have to express any Zionist zeal or even knowledge.

In contrast to Whittingehame, Youth Aliyah's pre-*hachsharot* in Germany had enforced a tough selection process for admittance and this ensured that all the students were Zionists and sought a Zionist environment. Simmons has noted that applicants considered 'too physically weak for hard manual labour, those with psychological or educational problems, and those who were not committed to the *Halutzic* ideals of Zionism were weeded out'.[63] Following the initial scrutinizing of candidates, students would then have to pass a period of probation before being completely accepted for *Aliyah*.[64] The acceptance criteria were always linked to the demands of the *kibbutzim*, where only the strongest and most resilient were accepted into communities.[65] Only the urgency of the Jewish refugee crisis post-1945 meant that by 1959 H. Edelston could assert that 'no case was given up as hopeless; every case was taken'.[66]

The Whittingehame policy for admittance did not alter over the course of the scheme and, largely as a result of this, the affiliation of participants to Zionism weakened, particularly in later years at Polton House.[67] This was in part due to the maturation, past the maximum admittance age to Whittingehame of 17 years, of those Kindertransportees who would have been old enough before migration to Britain to participate in their local Zionist youth groups. A number of the first residents actually arrived in convoy with their youth group.[68]

In contrast, students arriving in later years were of a very young age when they first migrated and often had no prior experience of Zionism. They may also have been in hostels or foster homes isolated from any Zionist activity for a number of years in Britain. Jacob had been 'shunted around' various care homes for years before Polton House, and Debbie recalls that 'never ever in a lifetime would I move to Israel. When I went to Polton House I had never heard of Zionism'.[69] Subsequently, the surplus of teenage Kindertransportees who were sent to Whittingehame or Polton House in later years had less immediate affiliation to Zionism and demanded less Zionist-orientated care.

A number of later arrivals were psychologically unsuitable to pre-*hachsharot* training and this made the practical application of the scheme even harder. Kindertransportees who were fostered or placed in isolated care environments across Britain had often integrated into their local community in line with the CC's agenda for 'invisibility'.[70] The Kindertransportees wished to fit in and in some cases to be 'more British than the British'.[71] These Kindertransportees presented a challenge to the successful indoctrination of *Halutzic* principles. Their lifestyle expectations already opposed the Zionist preference for greater sectarianism and a manual labouring lifestyle aimed at emigration from Britain.

The management of the selection process also enabled physically unsuitable students to be admitted and led to the need to incorporate alternative training solutions that veered away from *Halutzic* ideals. These often had little involvement with Zionist activities and consequently Zionism played a limited role in the care experience of these Kindertransportees. This particularly occurred among the later arrivals because younger Kindertransportees would have been too physically immature to be vetted before migration for their strength and suitability for a pre-*hachsharot* training.[72] Little attention seems to have been given to this aspect in the selection process for Whittingehame once they were in Britain.[73]

Elijah who arrived at Whittingehame in the later years and Debbie who was sent to Polton House both found that they lacked the physical abilities needed for the training programme.[74] Elijah consequently worked with the gardener for the majority of his stay, while Debbie was found an apprenticeship as a secretary in Edinburgh for the duration of her time at Polton House. As a result, Debbie recalls having little experience of Zionism.[75]

The management of the social structure of Whittingehame was another dilution of the *Halutzic* ideals, due to its failure to disband a social hierarchy in favour of a socialist Utopia. This was largely as a result of the formal dissemination of power, which flowed down from the CC to the ERC, to the Board of Governors, to the headmaster and then to the staff of Whittingehame and Polton House. The students were influential in decision-making, but did not have a formal role within this system other than to be responsive to staff decisions and discipline.

This structure maintained clear social distinctions based along student/teacher polarization and a strict social order. Every morning the Kindertransportees would be gathered as one large group in order to be issued a roll call and were not permitted to leave the estate without permission.[76] The staff structure echoed the usual staff configuration in British or German public or grammar schools; teachers oversaw specific subject areas and some were placed as housemasters in charge of houses (large groups of young people). Jacob recalls the massive difference he found between Polton House and his later *hachshara* training in England.

> [At Polton House] we had a boss . . . an adult who was in charge and we had to do more or less what he told us to do. On *hachshara* it was more democratic and we were treated as adults. We worked just as hard or even harder. Socially it was similar, except that we knew why we were all together, to make *Aliyah*.[77]

Whittingehame's distinct hierarchy directly contradicted the *Haluz* philosophy. *Halutzic* principles were rooted in the notion of a collective force and the individual working for the group.[78] This element of the *hachshara* was faithful to the Russian influences and Bundist tendencies of the *kibbutzim*. The *kibbutzim* social order was organized within communal units, working for the benefit of the whole community. The youth, in permanent groups of about 30 or 40, acted as a *hevrat noar* (self-governing youth group).[79] Each group would receive the care and guidance of a *Madrich*. Adults overseeing the care of the youth, such as the *Madrich,* were not 'bosses', but referred to as *haverim* (comrades).[80] The foundations to this structure rested heavily on the ideals of creating a socialist

Utopia in the form of communes, which, Simmons argues, was unique to the *kibbutz*.[81]

The dissemination of power and leadership of Whittingehame undermined efforts to manage Whittingehame as a pre-*hachshara,* particularly because the CC and ERC gave little real power for administrative and financial decision-making to its staff. This was unlike in *kibbutzim,* where a *Menahel* (director) would lead the 'comrades' as well as direct policy, education and funds. Whittingehame appointed a matron and headmaster, but neither of them directed the policy or funds of the school. This responsibility remained within the jurisdiction of the CC. The general administration and decision-making also remained with the ERC. In contrast, in a *kibbutz* the *Menahel* would also lead a committee of senior staff members, called the *Hanhalah.* The matron, administrative staff and a chief *Madrich* would all be members of the *Hanhalah.* This too was absent.

The management of Whittingehame does not, therefore, appear to be completely in tune with *Halutzic* ideals or the agendas of the Zionist movement. Whittingehame was bolted to the fundamental agenda of the CC to accommodate a surplus of trans-migrant youth. This meant that its primary purpose was to accommodate youth as pragmatically as possible. As a result, the CC utilized non-Zionist and non-Jewish regional support, and catered for Zionist and non-Zionist Kindertransportees. This ultimately allowed fundamental characteristics of a *hachshara* centre to be replaced with alternative approaches to care.

Hachshara training

The environment of care, training programme and educational curriculum were also determining factors and of central importance to the schemes' *Halutzic* zeal. The Kindertransportees needed to be trained to adopt the agenda of the Zionists. This required physical and practical introduction to life as a pioneer, as well as psychological preparation of residents to a new type of lifestyle. The Kindertransportees needed to be inaugurated as *Olim.*

The environment of care could more readily be tailored to meet the requirements of *hachsharot* training. The living environment at Whittingehame did introduce Kindertransportees to aspects of the tough life of a pioneer. Despite the grandeur of the Whittingehame estate, the house was in a poor condition and lacked many of the basic amenities. The contents of the estate had been auctioned off in the early part of 1938, leaving very little if anything remaining in the house.[82] As a result of the lack of these basic facilities, the *Jewish*

Echo launched a campaign to acquire furniture and equipment.[83] The campaign noted that the Kindertransportees 'are without any comforts or luxuries and even without many necessities. The huge house is empty except for beds and a few articles of furniture'.[84] Despite these efforts, the conditions at Whittingehame received limited improvement because of wartime restrictions and financial difficulties of the CC. Kindertransportees' testimonies reflect that they felt a distinct drop in living conditions.[85] This feature of their training experience was in tune with the *hachsharot* intention of the scheme, to toughening youth to a new basic way of life.

Nevertheless, even these physical deprivations were milder in temperament than other *hachsharot* and suggest that a less potent form of Zionist training was being introduced to the Kindertransportees at Whittingehame. The Whittingehame house was large and impressively built, as well as being set in a well-established estate. Hubbers recalls her shock after attending Whittingehame for two and a half years, until July 1941, when she was sent to Bydown in Devon, an adult *hachshara* run by Bachad and supported by the major *hachshara* pioneers:

> It was so primitive it was unbelievable. I know it was war but it was just horrific, it was a very very old manor house, there was no electricity, no gas and it was rat infested. So much so that at night we had to keep the lamp burning to keep the rats away. . . . I didn't stay there very long needless to say. . . . I thought if this is what Israel is like I'll give it a miss.[86]

In contrast to the primitive state of Bydown, Bentwich who visited Whittingehame noted that 'the mansion . . . was set in a beautiful estate of woodland and tilth'.[87] Whittingehame and Polton House were both located about 5 miles south of Edinburgh in a 'flat part of the country' in 'quite a lot of acreage'.[88] Polton House was a smaller estate, but both facilities were spacious and provided the Kindertransportees with ample acreage in which to live.[89] Polton House is recalled as 'a large physical facility' with classrooms 'upstairs and downstairs' and a large recreational area maintained in the basement for the Kindertransportees' evening leisure activities.[90] Today, the Whittingehame house is a luxury estate comprising about eight apartments. Scotland's pre-*hachsharot* provided the Kindertransportees with better physical accommodation than most *hachsharot* centres could offer.

Despite the comparatively comfortable conditions to be found within Whittingehame and Polton House, their living environment did reflect an approach to the practical running of the physical facility adherent to tough *Olim* survival practices. This intended to maintain Whittingehame as a self-sufficient enterprise. This meant that the facility did not receive a regular maintenance income with which to purchase consumer items. This aspect of the scheme's management connected the Kindertransportees to Zionism in a fundamental way, teaching the rudiments of survival in *Eretz Yisrael* on a *kibbutz*.

The school was for the most part a working, self-supporting farm, which raised capital and supplies for its needs. Selling much of its produce – milk, corn and other food stuff – the students were the fundamental cogs that enabled a degree of self-sufficiency. The *Jewish Echo* reported in 1939 that 'the boys will virtually run the house themselves'.[91] Students remember a commitment among themselves to succeed in this objective and demand as little outside help as possible.[92] Hubbers recalls that 'sometimes if somebody didn't have a shirt or something well we borrowed from somebody else to give to them'.[93] All the Kindertransportees worked to keep the school operating in a manner that would allow it 'to be self sufficient as much as possible, so that we would not cost the committee a lot of money'.[94] The Kindertransportees were also expected to maintain the facility and regularly worked to repair damage to the building and its grounds. Figure 20 captures three Kindertransportees fixing what appears to be a water leak at Whittingehame.

Nonetheless, in this aspect too, Whittingehame offered a mild version of a *hachsharot* living environment. It was never 100 per cent self-sufficient, continuing to receive financial support and aid from the CC and its refugee welfare network. In 1942, the school was closed down and was found to have only £775 of debt, which was to be covered by the CC.[95] These reports underline that it was viewed at the time as a great self-supporting financial success, but this

Figure 20 Maintenance work at Whittingehame Farm School.
Source: MCPC/Drew, Photographs.

overlooked the financial backing it had received from the CC. Whittingehame had initially been provided with a £5,000 guarantee by the CC and benefited from ongoing support from the ERC.[96] Hubbers notes that 'they had to supply us with the necessaries like making sure there was enough money there for going to buy bread and what not', in addition to 'other bits, like Jam and bits and so on' that got sent down from Edinburgh by the committee.[97] The Kindertransportees often received large parcels of donated or acquired clothing. One year all the boys and girls received navy blue shorts and then white shirts for the Sabbath. Another year the ERC sent down bales of navy material for the girls to make themselves skirts.[98]

The living environment of Whittingehame flirted with fundamental aspects of life as an *Olim* and in doing so necessitated an adequate practical training course. The structure of the training programme was based upon the Youth Aliyah model and *Halutzic* principles. This operated a basic philosophy of a 'tripartite education; school-work-leisure'.[99] Recha Freier outlined the fundamental contents of *hachshara* training:

> It lay in agricultural surroundings and had as its basic idea the division of the day between study, agricultural and social activities in the same proportion as that practised in youth groups in *kibbutzim*.[100]

In Whittingehame, the Kindertransportees spent half of their working day undertaking a practical job, which included work in the fields, workshops or communal kitchen.[101] The other half of the day was spent in the classroom, where they were provided with an academic education to matriculation level.[102] The evenings were left for the students to enjoy social activities with a view towards political and cultural indoctrination. The training programme within this system required both practical training and psychological indoctrination in order to create new *Olim*.

Male and female Kindertransportees were included in most aspects of the practical training programme.[103] Practical training ranged from poultry rearing, dairy, fieldwork, forestry and market gardening (see Figures 21 and 22), to chores within the domestic sphere: cooking, cleaning and sewing. Although these roles were not exclusive to particular gender or age groups, fieldwork tended to be dominated by the physically stronger older boys and domestic servicing roles by the girls.[104] New popular approaches to *Halutzic* principles, which tended towards female inclusion in male-orientated spheres of work, were influential.[105] This meant that boys could work in the kitchen, while girls ploughed the field. Figure 23 shows a female Kindertransportee helping with manual work in the

Figure 21 Market gardening.
Source: MCPC/Drew, Photographs.

Figure 22 Male Kindertransportees undertaking forestry work.
Source: MCPC/Drew, Photographs.

grounds of the estate. Figure 24 shows male Kindertransportees working in the laundry.

Nevertheless, despite adopting a liberal approach towards gender roles, female Kindertransportees were not provided with the same range of *Olim* training opportunities as their male counterparts. Gender ideals, as well as physical determinants, informed gender ratios within certain tasks. This could mean that Zionism had a lesser role in female Kindertransportees' daily lives as they participated less in agricultural tasks. Drew's photographic archive shows the boys attending to forestry work, refilling the coal shed, driving agricultural machinery and working in the cobbler's shop. In contrast, girls can be seen

Figure 23 Female Kindertransportees undertaking physical work at Whittingehame Farm School.
Source: MCPC/Drew, Photographs.

Figure 24 Male Kindertransportees working in the laundry.
Source: MCPC/Drew, Photographs.

predominantly in the kitchens and sewing rooms. Edna recalls endless days in the sewing room and Ranita spent most of her time in the kitchen.[106] However, everybody was expected to muck in during harvest time when academic education was postponed.[107]

A common training practice on *kibbutzim* included the hiring-out of a portion of members to work on neighbouring farms or industries, or to utilize their trade skills. This brought in vital revenues of cash for the community. At Whittingehame and Polton House, residents were not sent to factories, but rather hired out to neighbouring farms.[108] Sidney Bratt grew up in a small farming town in Germany called Guttstadt. His parents were observant Traditional Jews and originated from Poland. As a child he attended Hebrew school and synagogue. His father was a trader and his family was poor. He was the only sibling of his large family to leave Germany on the Kindertransport. On arrival he was sent to Clayton reception camp, England, until 1940, before being sent to an Orthodox Jewish hostel in High Wycombe. He had been nurtured towards aspirations for emigration to Palestine and he requested to be moved to a pre-*hachsharot*. He was sent to Polton House. During his time at Polton House, he worked on a neighbouring farm and remembers that the Kindertransportees were not shielded from the rigours of an agricultural labouring life:

> One day I am looking back as after I am picking and I see it is all red back there and I am looking at my hands and I saw that my hands were all cut from the ice and snow and I didn't feel anything because they were all numb from the cold.[109]

Their earnings would then be collected for the common fund.[110]

However, not all Kindertransportees' participated with the Zionist aspect of the training programme. This was because Whittingehame adopted a flexible approach to the allocation of chores and would offer alternatives to Zionist training for certain Kindertransportees, male and female. Other than during the harvest, group leaders drawn from among the students allocated a work schedule every 2 weeks on a rotation basis.[111] Levi particularly enjoyed learning to cook and was able to remain in the kitchen for most of his training.[112] Josephina passionately recalls in interviews her dislike of domestic work and undertook fieldwork for her time at Whittingehame.[113] Nathan was already proficient at carpentry, which had been a family business, and was able to develop his skill over the course of his training rather than move into a new trade skill.[114]

In addition, because students controlled the roster, the acquisition of chores was often also felt to be responsive and conditional to popularity and friendship groups.[115] Edna, who recalls that she was not part of the popular crowd, felt plagued with the job of darning socks and stuck in an undesired role because of other people's preferences.[116] Figure 25 shows the enormity of the job of darning socks. This situation meant that the Kindertransportees were not being given an all-rounded introduction to life as an *Olim*.

The ability of Whittingehame to offer all aspects of *Olim* training and preparation was also hampered by staff shortages and external pressures. The curriculum of Whittingehame was fundamentally responsive to the individuals available to provide instruction and accordingly was not always faithful to previous *hachsharot* strategies. Instead, training was the product of

Figure 25 Mending socks at Whittingehame.
Source: MCPC/Drew, Photographs.

Whittingehame's staff members and the regional helpers who provided their skills in various areas of training.[117] In the domestic sphere the students received instruction from Mrs Laquer, who had previously been a headmistress of Frankfurt's Domestic Science College (FDSC).[118] Under Laquer's guidance, the students learnt how to manage a large house, in terms of cleanliness and other required chores. Ruth Fischel, who had previously been a senior staff member of FDSC, oversaw training in the sewing room.[119] Drew was proficient at Science and English instruction and was consequently assigned to these roles.

Regional factors and personages played a greater role than Zionism in formulating the curriculum and shaping its character on a daily basis. The Agricultural Committees of Glasgow, Edinburgh and London, along with Professor Shearer of Edinburgh University's Agricultural College, provided advice and a work strategy for successful agricultural practices in Scotland.[120] Local sources – estate workers, neighbouring farmers and friends of Lord Traprain – offered support and guidance.[121] 'Mr Malcolm', Lord Traprain's bailiff, provided the actual instruction in farming, horticulture and poultry keeping.[122] A Palestinian agricultural teacher was appointed to advise the students about the difference between agriculture in Britain and that in Palestine; however, this did not alter the regional character of the students' agricultural work.[123]

The alternative agendas of the CC were also directing the curriculum, which again meant that participation in practical instruction did not predetermine an active role or connection with Zionism. Emigration was the CC's central objective for the Kindertransportees and this was evident in Whittingehame's training programme.[124] The Kindertransportees were perceived as trans-migrants and only temporary charges. The instruction was not just intended

Figure 26 Scout ceremony.
Source: MCPC/Drew, Photographs.

for *Eretz Yisrael,* but was aimed at migration opportunities across the world. The objective was to equip a large number of dependent youths with self-supporting life skills, which could in turn enable emigration. Agricultural and trade skills were assets sought by a large number of potential target countries for migration: Australia, Canada, South Africa and the United States.[125] Britain too sought agricultural workers and such training was linked to wartime priorities to establish a self-supporting nation that could sustain itself with food if trading links were blocked.[126] Interviewees do not all immediately connect their agricultural training to a Zionist agenda.[127] Many of Whittingehame's students were passionate members of the Scouts and ARP, and many went on to active wartime service for Britain.[128] Figure 26 shows a Scout ceremony and illustrates that non-Zionist groups were vying for and dominating Kindertransportees' enthusiasm at Whittingehame.

The curriculum at Whittingehame also provided certain privileged training options and this opened alternative work and lifestyle opportunities to Kindertransportees, beyond those normally preferred to suit *Olim* lifestyles on a *kibbutz*. Kindertransportees were also being trained towards blue-collar employment. Male residents learnt carpentry, mechanics and draughtsmanship. While at Polton House, a small number of female Kindertransportees have recalled being offered white-collar training in the form of secretarial school in Edinburgh.[129] These wider training options enabled Kindertransportees to choose alternative lifestyles to that of a pioneer. Kindertransportees could settle in urban areas and utilize these alternative skill sets.[130] This also meant that a bridging link was not automatically formed between practical work and life as an *Olim*.

Education for the pioneer

The ability to connect residents to the Zionist ambitions for their future lives demanded a degree of psychological preparation. The Kindertransportees needed to be introduced to a whole new approach to life. A new psychological framework was necessary in order for them to adopt the rudiments of life as a pioneer and settle successfully into their new lives in Palestine. This required attention to a number of specific areas: academic tuition to promote relevant subject areas, political education towards support of Zionism, cultural indoctrination for the adoption of a Jewish Palestinian lifestyle and mental preparation to help them embrace a new approach to daily life.

In order to produce a surplus of eager manual labourers, it remained vital to condition the Kindertransportees to the psychological framework that accompanied life on a *kibbutz*. The Kindertransportees needed to adopt the necessary social skills in order to enable self-reliance, integration and progress in Palestine. Fundamentally, this meant that they must first accept new aspirations and lifestyle expectations. A report in 1967 by Julius Carlebach highlighted that the strategy of Youth Aliyah, which was followed by Whittingehame, aimed to 'wean' the students away from 'an academically-oriented, white collar-directed, approach to education'.[131]

This aspect of preparation was critical for Kindertransportees because many had had little or no previous exposure to manual or agricultural work. Elijah recalls that he 'had never been in contact with animals (before Whittingehame) . . . . I was scared of a cow. . . . I didn't even know it was a cow'.[132] A significant proportion of Kindertransportees arrived from urban, secular, bourgeois, professional families with high aspirations for academic progress.[133] Sixteen per cent had attended a *Gymnasium* with the intention of continuing on to university.[134] In stark contrast, *Halutzic* principles valued rural, labouring-class workers of the land. Simmons points to the initial need to teach the youth to aspire to a completely different way of life to their past aspirations and their parents' ambitions for them.[135] In 1935, the Hadassah organization of America noted a number of necessary psychological transitions for prospective *Olim:*

> There will be no possibility for them to enter the professions of their fathers . . . town boys and girls return to the land! Sons and daughters of tradesmen are becoming farmers! High school children wish to become manual workers. Daughters of doctors and lawyers are learning domestic work, infant welfare and sick nursing.[136]

Academic education was afforded a subordinate position to practical instruction and residents were discouraged from pursuing academic or professional lifestyles. Agriculture and trade skills were perceived as the most important components of the whole preparation process. This approach to the educational process incorporated a form of psychological re-education. This was by way of encouraging students to excel in practical subject areas rather than achieving academic excellence.

This educational approach began during the mild selection process in Britain for admittance to Whittingehame. The only requirement of the Kindertransportees was a willingness to migrate and an interest in practical training, rather than in academic education. This intended that the majority of students would be receptive to this balance between work and study. Kindertransportees who expressed a desire for academia were usually not sent to Whittingehame. Hubbers recalls that her friend Lotte 'did not want to go . . . she was more studious and she wanted to go somewhere she could go to school' and as a result she was not admitted.[137]

The emphasis on practical subjects meant that academic instruction tended to be poor, providing only a basic level of education in a limited number of subject areas. Kindertransportees were supported up to matriculation level, or lowers in Scotland. At Whittingehame, this did not always include the final matriculation exam. Abaigael responded to the question, 'Were you able to carry on with your academic education at all?' while at Whittingehame with a 'No.'[138]

Academic education was also disseminated along a specific hierarchy of subject areas. This gave weight to subjects that would be of use for the Kindertransportees during their migratory process. Languages were critical for Kindertransportees to adapt successfully into their new environments. This included their immediate location in Britain, requiring English, and later Palestine, where Hebrew would be needed. The Kindertransportees received lessons in 'English, History, *Evrit* (Hebrew), music and mathematics', along with any other subject areas that the staff could cover.[139] The CC's immediate concern for invisibility of trans-migrant youth meant that English was given precedence over the learning of Hebrew. Classroom posters used English as the formative language for the translations of Hebrew (see Figure 27), indicating that the Kindertransportees were first to become fluent in English. Bratt states that 'none of us spoke any English . . . all they tried to do was teach us English . . . we had to talk in English . . . and we learnt in a hurry'.[140]

Hebrew was still a main concern at Whittingehame as it remained a prerequisite for immigration certificates to Palestine, in accordance with the

Figure 27 Poster displaying translation of an English word to Hebrew.
Source: MCPC/Drew, Photographs.

British Mandate, and was therefore an essential component of the pre-*hachshara* training programme. The linguistic success of these teaching efforts is not clear because a significant number of students, especially those from Orthodox families, arrived in Britain with a good knowledge and training in Hebrew.[141] Nevertheless, a Palestinian teacher, Mr Gilboa, taught Hebrew at Whittingehame and Hebrew posters were displayed in the classrooms (see Figure 28). In Polton House, a previous student of Whittingehame called Eli Fachler oversaw the religious environment and Hebrew education.[142] The formal school assemblies at Whittingehame permitted only English or Hebrew to be used and the School's student newspaper included sections written in Hebrew.[143] Debbie attended Polton House with no prior knowledge of Hebrew and confesses in an interview that she can read it fluently.[144] Debbie has no recollection of being taught Hebrew and assumes this could only have occurred at Polton House.

In addition to an ability to communicate in their new environments, Kindertransportees were also required to show an affinity to the political and cultural landscape of Palestine. Political indoctrination was critical to forming a bridging link between manual work and the schemes *Halutzic* ideals. Youth groups and evening discussions on political matters relating to Palestine were encouraged in order to help connect residents with the Zionist cause.[145] *Madrichem* and their respective youth groups provided an important form of nurture and support for the Kindertransportees towards their new life in Palestine. The role of the youth groups, Bachad, Habonim and Hashomer Hatzair, and their *Madrichem* changed over time, but they did become central to recollections of Zionist experiences.[146]

Figure 28 Hebrew poster.
Source: MCPC/Drew, Photographs.

The Kindertransportees relied heavily upon their *Madrich* and youth group, and these social circles effectively became their support networks. This established strong friendship ties rooted in political affiliation and developed lifelong bonds for the residents with Zionism.[147] Sprinzeles reflects that the *Madrich* 'understood our problems . . . they were really our pilots, they guided us through many hardships'.[148] Within their youth groups the Kindertransportees formed *Gi'van,* or family groups, and many of these went on to adult *hachshara* training together. Kindertransportees recall feeling dependent on their group and as a result rejecting non-Zionist opportunities, such as work or education in Britain, for fear of leaving this support network.[149] These groups took a significant number of Whittingehame's students to Israel.[150]

The Kindertransportees' re-education included an introduction to the culture of Palestine and preparation for social integration. Permits for entry to Palestine required a 'good knowledge of Hebrew, Jewish History and conditions in Palestine'.[151] Whittingehame did employ both a Palestinian and a *Mizrachi* teacher to instruct the Kindertransportees in the social and cultural aspects of life in Palestine. The intention was to enable the Kindertransportees to integrate into a totally new community. Arie Eflel argued that 'food, living on a kibbutz, farm work, language – everything was different and hard to get used to'.[152]

Kindertransportees were taught to celebrate Jewish culture and being Jewish per se. This focused on the learning of all aspects of life in the *Yishvo*.[153] Jewish dances, songs and other forms of cultural celebration were taught. A regular feature in the Kindertransportees' social activities was the *Hora* dance and many recall being exposed to Yiddish songs for the first time.[154] Elijah remembers that 'there was a lot of dancing in the evening, mostly Israeli dances, Palestinian dances or Jewish dances', while Jacob reflects on being first exposed to Yiddish at Polton House.[155]

Despite these progressive steps, Whittingehame's approach to the students' acquisition of Palestinian culture was not coupled with efforts to sever their attachment to continental preferences or British tendencies. Training by Youth Aliyah promoted the severing of all links with the past in order to 'assume an entirely new physical and spiritual foundation'.[156] This, it was felt, would enable the Jew who had been living in the diaspora to disband his/her past affiliations and fully ingratiate him/herself with life as a pioneer. This concept formed an important symbolic construct about the correct type of Jew. The 'superior' Jewish pioneer, or *Olim,* and the 'inferior' diaspora Jew emerged as direct contradictions to one another. The students at these centres were encouraged to cut ties with both their parents and the secular Germanic diaspora habits, rituals and customs of their past lives. The underlining endeavour of other pre-*hachsharot* centres was to create a generation of the 'new Jew'.[157]

This formed a dichotomy between two lifestyle options. However, it was not easy to convince a surplus of trans-migrant youth, many from secular, urban, privileged backgrounds, that an agricultural, manual labouring pioneering lifestyle was preferable. Ben Halpern and Shalom Wurm argue that the whole mind-set and 'the mentality of the Jews in Germany' worked against this transition and that most viewed agricultural work as 'unskilled labour', preferring instead to learn a trade.[158] The Kindertransportees also continued to express cultural affiliations with their past lives. They were not forbidden from using German, as was the case in many hostels, such as Willesden Lane, London.[159] Subsequently, the German language was maintained within the school, despite efforts to teach English and Hebrew. The students formed a newspaper, which, along with their school journals, was predominantly written in German.[160] The *Jewish Echo* recorded on 24 March 1939 that, 'on the evening of Saturday last, a simple but impressive ceremony' was held at which 'a number of musical and other items' were 'rendered in Hebrew, German and English, by the pupils'.[161] The Kindertransportees' continental roots were also supported by a heavily weighted staff composition of Germans and Austrians. The matron was herself German, as was the cook, Miss Strauss. As a result, the customs, daily rituals and catering at Whittingehame strongly resembled the Kindertransportees' German-Jewish traditions.

*

Practical participation in the pre-*hachshara* training programme was not synonymous with inauguration into a pioneer's lifestyle. A bridging link was not automatically formed between the gruelling chores and agricultural labour they had to perform, and *Halutzic* ideals or the Zionist movement. This made it difficult to convince all Kindertransportees that the life of a pioneer was preferable to their previous lifestyles in diaspora.

Nevertheless, Whittingehame's Kindertransportees' migratory patterns do suggest that the Zionist aspirations for making *Aliyah* were translated with some success: 40 per cent made *Aliyah,* compared to 34 per cent who chose to remain in Britain and 20 per cent who went to the United States; 45 per cent of these stated 'Zionism' as their main reason for migrating to Israel.[162] The establishment by Scotland's refugee youth of their own *hachshara* training camp in Ayreshire in 1945 is also suggestive of a successful connection being formed between students and Zionism.[163] Furthermore, the overall statistic for *hachsharot* centres in Britain does suggest that in unison they were initially successful in integrating the youth into agriculture. A 1944 report of the War Committee recorded of the British refugee *hachshara* students: 'all have now finished their youth training and passed into the groups of *Haluzim,* of whom over 1,000 are taking part in food production under the County War Agricultural Committees'.[164] However, in respect to Whittingehame only 15 per cent who made *Aliyah* chose to settle in a *kibbutz.*[165] Although this is not representative of the total proportion of those who migrated, it does give some indication of the preference for utilizing non-agricultural skills and the failure to prepare the students psychologically.

Fundamentally, Whittingehame and Polton House were not catering for ardent Zionist youth, but for Jewish youth trans-migrants who themselves varied massively in their perception of Zionism. The individual response to the process of preparation was the ultimate determining factor in the role of Zionism in their day-to-day lives in Scotland. To return to the opening photograph, it seems possible that the aforementioned Kindertransportee attended to the chickens in the cold Scottish months under sufferance.

Notes

1 See *25 Years of Youth Aliyah* (London: The Children and Youth Aliyah Committee for Great Britain, 1959); Bentwich, *Jewish Youth Comes Home;* Marion Greenberg, *Youth Aliyah under Henrietta Szold* (New York: Hadassah, no date).

2 Bentwich, *Jewish Youth Comes Home.*

3 Ibid.

4 See Paul Goodman, *Zionism in England; English Zionist Federation 1899–1929* (London, undated).

5 KA: QU/SUP.

6 FWPC/Abaigael, Dena, Debbie.

7 *Jewish Echo*, 30 December 1938, 6 January 1939, 17 March 1939 and 24 March 1939.

8 Rosalie Gassman-Sherr, *The Story of The Federation of Women Zionists of Great Britain and Ireland; 1918–1968* (Oxford, 2006), 55.

9 Erica B. Simmons, *Hadassah and the Zionist Project* (Oxford: Rowman & Littlefield Publishers, 2006), 115.

10 *Jewish Echo*, 30 December 1938, 6 January 1939, 17 March 1939.

11 *Ibid.*, 10 February 1939, 24 March 1939, 31 March 1939; HLSC/MS116/157/AJ396/5, correspondence of Federation of Women Zionist.

12 *Jewish Echo*, 30 December 1938.

13 Ibid.; MCPC/Drew, Letters, 25 April 1940.

14 *Jewish Echo*, 24 February 1939.

15 WL/BL/25.

16 Ibid.; SJA/SOC/0002, Bachad Farm brochure, Letter from E. Kritsler of Bachad to Reverand Gamzu, 15 November 1949.

17 SJA/SOC/0004, Fay Cohen Stein, memoir, 5 January 1995.

18 Bentwich, *Jewish Youth Comes Home*, 89.

19 MCPC/Drew, Letters, 14 January 1939.

20 Collins, *Aspects of Scottish Jewry*, 11.

21 MCPC/Drew, Letters, 14 January 1939.

22 GJA/SOC/0004 (1995); PL/225, Meir Zev, 'Women in Zionism: An Interview with Dr Vera Weizmann', *The New Palestine*, 21 March 1924.

23 MCPC/Drew, Letters, 25 April 1940.

24 Collins, *Aspects of Scottish Jewry*, 21.

25 See Berkowitz, *Zionist Culture and Western European Jewry.*

26 Collins, *Aspects of Scottish Jewry*, 21.

27 *Edith Eder; in Memoriam* (London, undated); Collins, *Aspects of Scottish Jewry*, 21.

28 *Jewish Echo*, 10 February 1939.

29 Please see appendix 3, 4 and 5.

30 *Haddingtonshire Courier*, 9 December 1938.

31 HLSC/MS116/157/AJ396/5, Minutes of the special Committee.

32 Ibid.

33 Michaelis-Stern, *Children in the Searchlight*; See also Michaelis and Michaelis-Stern, *Emissaries In Wartime London* and *25 Years of Youth Aliyah*.

34 WL/BL/25.

35 MCPC/Drew, Letters, 21 August 1939, 25 April 1940, 9 May 1940; FWPC/Levi; Eva and Eli Fachler, *The Vow; Rebuilding the Fachler Tribe after the Holocaust*, (ed.) Yanky Fachler, based on the journals of, (not published, copyright 2003 to Yank Fachler).

36 MCPC/Drew, Letters, 21 August 1939.

37 MCPC/Drew, Letters, 25 April 1940.

38 WL/BL/25.

39 Oldfield, '"It is Usually She"', 57–70.

40 Michaelis and Michaelis-Stern, *Emissaries In Wartime*, Greenberg, *Youth Aliyah under Henrietta Szold*.

41 WL/BL/25.

42 HLSC/MS183/289/2/F1.

43 HLSC/MS116/157/AJ396/2, Letter from Glasgow Jewish Council for German Refugees; Collins, *Aspects of Scottish Jewry*, 10.

44 Ibid.

45 Kölmel, 'German-Jewish Refugees in Scotland', 20; See also Kölmel, 'Problems of Settlement', 251.

46 Collins, *Aspects of Scottish Jewry*, 20.

47 Ibid.

48 MS183/289/2/F1.

49 WL/BL/25/HLSC/MS183/344/10, 'The Child-Estranging Movement' (January 1944); HLSC/MS183/290/F1, Interview and correspondence with Herbert Morrison; HLSC/MS183/53/2/F1; See also Chapter 3.

50 FWPC/Abaigael, Ranita.

51 MCPC/Drew, Letters, 21 August 1939.

52 Ibid.; FWPC/Levi.

53 EGPC/Obituaries; *Jewish Chronicle*, 6 January 1989.

54 WHMA/USC: 43932; WHMA/USC:43138.

55 HLSC/MS183/50, Bachad Fellowship; SJA/SOC/0002, Brochure and letter.

56 FWPC/Elijah.

57 FWPC/Nathan, Ranita, Dena, Elijah.

58 Fachler, *The Vow*.

59 FWPC/Levi.

60 MCPC/Drew, Photographs; *Haddingtonshire Courier*, 6 January 1939.

61 HLSC/MS116/157/AJ396/5.

62 WHMA/USC:43932.
63 Simmons, '"*Persecuted, Uprooted*",' 120.
64 Brian David Amkraut, 'Zionist Attitudes towards YA from Germany, 1932–1939', *Journal of Israeli History*, 20, 2 (Spring 2001), 80.
65 Recha Freier, *Let the Children Come: The Early History of Youth Aliyah*, (London: Weidenfeld and Nicolson, 1961), 41.
66 H. Edelston, 'Uprooting and Resettlement, A Survey of the "YA" Program in Israel', *Journal of Educational Sociology* (April 1959), 398.
67 FWPC/Debbie, Jacob.
68 FWPC/Levi.
69 FWPC/Jacob, Debbie.
70 See also Kushner, 'The end of the Anglo-Jewish Progress Show: Representations of the Jewish East End, 1887–1987', in Kushner (ed.), 'The Jewish Heritage', 81; See also Curio, '"Invisible" children', 41–56.
71 FWPC/Noah.
72 Curio, '"Invisible" children', 41–56.
73 WHMA/USC: 43932.
74 FWPC/Elijah, Debbie.
75 FWPC/Debbie.
76 Morning drill and flag poll assembly point, photograph (EGPC/photograph) (not attributed); FWPC/Levi.
77 FWPC/Jacob.
78 http://www.jewishagency.org/JewishAgency/English/Jewish + Education/Compelling + Content/Eye + on + Israel/Israeli + Culture/Pioneering + Ideology + Halutziut.htm (June 2009).
79 Julius Carlebach, *The Future of Youth Aliyah*, Pamphlet No.20 (London, December 1968); Simmons, '*Persecuted, Uprooted*', 115.
80 *25 Years of Youth Aliyah.*
81 Simmons, '*Persecuted, Uprooted*', 115.
82 *Haddingtonshire Courier*, 28 October 1938.
83 *Jewish Echo*, 31 March 1939.
84 Ibid.
85 WHMA/USC: 43138.
86 Ibid.
87 Bentwich, *Jewish Youth Comes Home*, 90.
88 WHMA/USC: 36790.
89 Herbert Dryden in the *Edinburgh Star*, June 2003 (EGPC).
90 Ibid.
91 *Jewish Echo*, 24 February 1939.
92 FWPC/Abaigael.
93 Ibid.

94 Ibid.

95 HLSC/MS183/384/F1, minutes of the Executive of the Central Council, 27 July 1942.

96 HLSC/MS183/289/2/F1, Consolidated statement of the CC, 31 December 1939.

97 WHMA/USC: 43138.

98 Ibid.

99 Carlebach, *The Future of Youth Aliyah.*

100 Simmons, '"*Persecuted, Uprooted*",' 115.

101 WL: photograph collection, *Young refugees from Germany during their agricultural training in the UK,* 1939–45; Edelston, *Uprooting and Resettlement*, 392.

102 *25 Years of Youth Aliyah.*

103 Sarah Malchin, 'The Women Worker in Kinneret', *Hapoel Hatzair* (1913) 11–13.

104 HLSC/MS116/157/AJ396/5, minute papers, 21 March 1939; FWPC/Dena.

105 http://www.jewishagency.org/JewishAgency/English/Jewish + Education/Compelling + Content/Eye + on + Israel/Women + in + Israel; Rachel Janaith, 'At Work', in Rachel Katznelson-Rubashow (ed.), *The Plough Woman: Memoirs of the Pioneer Women of Palestine*, (Westport, 1976); Maimon, *Women Build a Land*, (Place/date unknown), 23. http://www.jewishagency.org/JewishAgency/English/Jewish + Education/Compelling + Content/Eye + on + Israel/Women + in + Israel.

106 FWPC/Edna, Ranita.

107 MCPC/Drew, Letters, 21 August 1939.

108 HLSC/MS183/50; WHMA/USC: 36790; EGPC: Diaries, journals and memoirs; MCPC/Drew, Letters, 25 April 1940.

109 Ibid.

110 FWPC/Josephina, Abaigael.

111 FWPC/Dena.

112 FWPC/Levi.

113 FWPC/Joesephina.

114 FWPC/Nathan.

115 FWPC/Edna.

116 FWPC/Elijah, Edna, Levi, Dena.

117 Bentwich, *Jewish Youth Comes Home*, 89.

118 FWPC/Edna.

119 WHMA/USC: 43138.

120 *Jewish Echo*, 17 March 1939; HLSC/MS116/157– AJ396/5, meeting notes, 21 March 1939, 3.

121 SJA/SOC/0004, memoir, 5 January 1995.

122 Ibid.

123 Jewish Echo, 31 March 1939.

124 HLSC/MS183/289/2/F1, minutes of the Central Council, 1 May 1940.
125 Ibid., 25 April 1940.
126 See Finlayson, *Citizen, State and Social Welfare.*
127 EGPC/Journals; FWPC/Debbie.
128 MCPC/Drew, Letters, 25 April 1940; MCPC/Drew, photographs; FWPC/Abaigael.
129 FWPC/Debbie.
130 FWPC/Edna, Levi.
131 Carlebach, *The Future of Youth Aliyah.*
132 FWPC/Elijah.
133 KA: QU/SUP.
134 Ibid.
135 Simmons, '"Persecuted, Uprooted",' 115.
136 PL/RG1/B 21/F130, HWZOA, *Hadassah and YA* (1935).
137 WHMA/USC: 43138.
138 FWPC/Abaigael.
139 Ibid.; NA/ED10/278, 'The problems faced by Jewish 'Kindertransport' refugee schoolchildren', 1943–44.
140 WHMA/USC: 36790.
141 FWPC/Levi.
142 Ibid.
143 EGPC/School newspapers.
144 FWPC/Debbie.
145 FWPC/Edna.
146 Ibid.
147 FWPC/Levi, Elijah, Nathan, Edna, Jacob.
148 WHMA/USC: 43932.
149 FWPC/Elijah.
150 FWPC/Nathan, Edna, Ranita, Elijah, Dena, Benson; KA: QU/SUP.
151 HLSC/MS183/289/2/F1.
152 Arie Eflel, 'The First Youth Group', in Meir Gottesman (ed.), *Out of the Fire* (London: unknown publisher, 1979), 24.
153 HLSC/MS183/344/10, *The Child Estrangement Movement'; An Expose on the alienation of Jewish Refugee Children in GB from Judaism*, Pamphlet, January 1944; *25 Years of Youth Aliyah* (1959); FWPC/Baisha; http://www.jewishagency.org/JewishAgency/English/Jewish + Education/Compelling + Content/Eye + on + Israel/Israeli + Culture/Pioneering + Ideology + Halutziut.htm.
154 FWPC/Ranita; MCPC/Drew, Letters, 25 April 1940.
155 FWPC/Elijah, Jacob.
156 Arie Appel, 'One year at Ein Harod', in Gottesman (ed.), *Out of the Fire*, 31.
157 PL/RG1/B21/F130, (1935), 132.

158 Ben Halpern and Shalom Wurm (eds), *The Responsible Opinion: The Life and Times of Giora Josephthal* (New York: Schocken, 1966), 95–6.

159 HLSC/MS183/384, booklet, CBF, *Bloomsbury House; The Care of German and Austrian Refugees* (London, 1942).

160 EGPC/*Iton Reidah,* school newspaper, 20 April 1941; EGPC/Journals and school newspapers.

161 *Jewish Echo,* 24 March 1939.

162 KA: QU/SUP.

163 HLSC/MS183/50, Bachad Fellowship, 68; *Glasgow Herald,* 'Glasgow Bnei Akivah Camp', 20 July 1945; See also *Sunday Mail,* 25 July 1945, 'Jew Refugees planning a new Palestine'.

164 See Bentwich, *Jewish Youth Comes Home.*

165 KA: QU/SUP.

5

Narrating Life Stories: The Long-term Impact of a Residential Upbringing

> My whole world was only a machine. There was no sun, no nature – no happiness . . . music was always my refuge – support – and friend. It had become intolerable. The great emptiness and loneliness crushed me. There were always tears . . . there is no real life any more in me . . .
>
> [I have a] hysterical mental illness, which is like a cancer of the brain, heart and soul . . . it decays my inside and I cannot stop it. I know happiness comes from inside and from nowhere else. In this illness – all happiness from outside cannot touch your inside.[1]

Between 1938 and 1945, residential care was the most common form of care for dependent minors. Although the benefits of the family unit as opposed to residential care continued to be debated, a child-centred family approach to remedy social problems only arrived post-war with the 1948 Children's Act.[2] Prior to this, priority was not given to maintaining the family unit over seeking the removal of the deprived child.[3] This was true despite Scotland's long-standing preference for use of foster care or boarding out rather than that of institutional facilities.[4] The CC had also prioritized foster care for all Kindertransportees, yet the number of homes available was always limited. This led to the prevalent use of residential care rather than that of the family unit for Kindertransportees.

Subsequently, 67 per cent of Kindertransportees experienced residential care in Britain. This figure mirrors those found within wider Scottish child welfare trends. In Scotland, in 1949, only 35 per cent of Scottish children in care were in private foster homes.[5] In the inter-war years, 275 institutions existed for homeless children and youth in Scotland.[6]

The residential facilities into which the Kindertransportees were placed in Scotland were diverse. Table 10 displays an array of residential facilities recorded to have been used for Kindertransportee care in Scotland. These included trans-

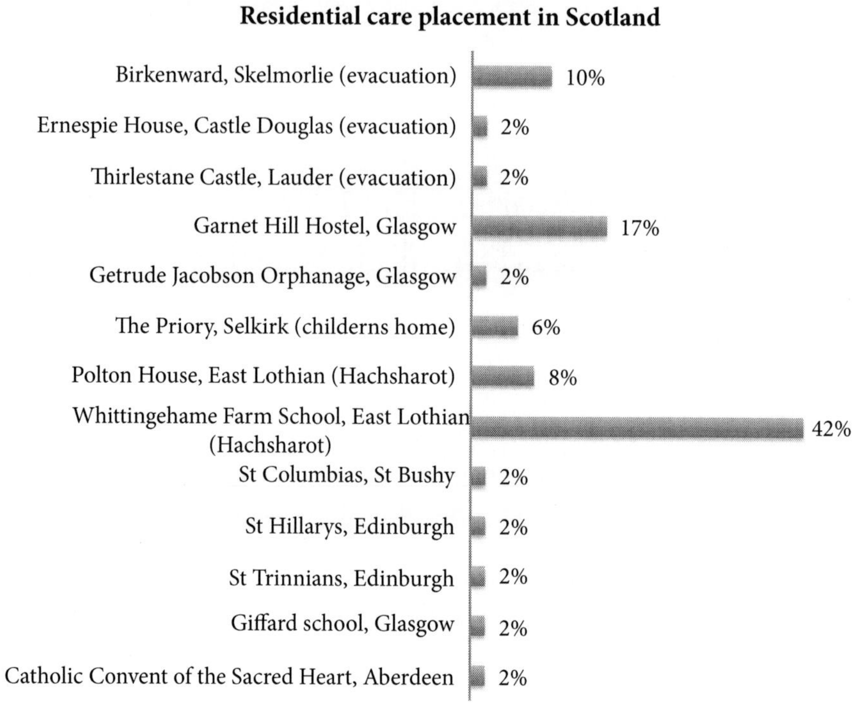

Table 10 Residential care placement in Scotland.
Source: KA: QU/SUP.

migrant hostels, British boarding schools, Catholic convents, voluntary or state-led children's homes or orphanages, evacuation centres and Zionist-inspired pre-*hachsharot* training farms.[7]

In 1946, James Clyde, along with a number of colleagues, produced the 'Report of the Committee on Homeless Children' (Clyde Report) for Scotland.[8] This, along with its English and Welsh counterpart entitled the 'Report of the Care of Children Committee' (Curtis Report) chaired by Dame Myra Curtis, offered a critical evaluation of the standard of care being provided for children in British residential welfare facilities and conceded errors were being made in approaches to the nurture of the deprived child.[9] The Clyde Report's criticism included opposition to the placement of deprived children in Poor Law institutions, the large size of residential facilities, their reliance on voluntary and untrained staff, the lack of inspection and the 'uniformity, the repression, the impersonality of these cold and forbidding abodes'.[10] The Curtis Report came to similar conclusions.

These reports represented the culmination of a growing shift in thinking about the needs of a child and what constituted health and well-being.[11] Both reports outlined that their key objectives were to rectify the inadequate substitution of a normal family and home life currently being provided for children in residential care:[12]

> The lessons, which above all else the war years have taught us is the value of home. It is upon the family that our position as a nation is built, and it is to the family that in trouble and disaster each child naturally turns. It is the growing awareness of the importance of the family, which has largely brought into prominence the problem of the homeless child. How then is the family to be re-created for the child who is rendered homeless?[13]

The growing body of research on these issues – including that done by John Bowlby, Susan Isaacs, James Robertson, Mary Ainsworth and Anna Freud – argued that nurturing experiences during the formative years of childhood had a long-term impact on physical and mental well-being.[14] They argued that it was imperative to care not only for the physical needs of the child, but also for its mental and emotional requirements in order to avoid deficiencies and future problems for society, such as juvenile delinquency and psychological weakness.

They criticized popular approaches for focusing only on physical needs and adhering to John Watson's Behaviourism theories.[15] They prescribed new preventative approaches to tackling deprivation and depravation, which included more sympathetic care of the individual's emotional needs. In doing so, they drew light on the common features that an institutional upbringing, between 1938 and 1945, was likely to include and highlighted the common emotional responses of individuals placed in these care scenarios.

The findings of these reports have been echoed in Kindertransportee testimonies. A wide array of diverse and complex reactions to a residential upbringing can be identified within Kindertransportee narratives.[16] It is important to note that these were also shaped by an array of external factors, including pre-migration experiences in Greater Germany, such as early socialization, exposure to stigmatism, community of origin, family dynamics, age of migration and even conditions of departure and transportation.[17] Furthermore, a wide variation of experience existed within one care scenario.[18] Friendship dynamics, religious orientation, financial circumstances, staff characteristics and physical environment, including geographic location, varied within each care facility at different points in time.[19]

Nonetheless, Kindertransportees use their experiences of residential care as important variables in their life experience to construct their personal narratives. Kindertransportees attach far-reaching ramifications to this particular life event and use the episode to explain their unfolding lives. These memories are used to make sense of their lives.[20] Kindertransportees' experiences of residential care introduced a new connection to and understanding of elements of their lives before migration; it renegotiated the immediate role of these features in their lives during the war, and impacted upon how these would be translated or understood in later years within the context of broader life stories.

Kindertransportees' personal testimonies that have been published and previously highlighted often emphasize suffering, perseverance and survival.[21] These reflect a close relationship with public narratives and popular historical consciousness.[22] They echo dominant Holocaust narratives, concerned with Jewish survival and victimhood, as well as popular Kindertransport narratives, which emphasize endurance and achievement. These point to the happy ending for Kindertransportees.[23] Academic interpretations of these examples have ignored alternative narratives, which include mild depression or Kindertransportees who experienced problems silently as a result of their care experiences. They instead draw a picture in which a small number of extreme cases are mentioned, while the general consensus of a positive migration experience is reiterated.

Scotland's Kindertransportee narratives, relating to experiences in and personal reactions to life within residential facilities, do not fit into this tidy positive framework. Kindertransportees' narratives reflect significant parallels with British public narratives that relate to the Scottish deprived child in care. Kindertransportees reiterate popular themes or ideas about the deprived child's life in institutional care.

Growing up in an institutional environment

The Clyde Report concluded that prior to 1946 too much emphasis was placed upon removing the deprived child from dysfunctional homes and placing them in 'approved schools' or other institutions.[24] This meant that they were forced into unfamiliar and unknown living environments.[25] Kindertransportees remember that the residential care environment represented an introduction to a completely new lifestyle and led to a degree of culture shock. The Kindertransport Association's 2007 questionnaire suggests that few Kindertransportees had any prior experience of residential care before they migrated to Britain.[26] None state that they boarded at school and only one had experience of a Jewish orphanage.[27] The majority had lived in a private nuclear family environment. Most of these had been small family circles: 22 per cent of Kindertransportees had been only children.[28] Upon arrival in Britain, Ruth Jackson was sent to a boarding school in Epping Forest, England. She recalls her shock at the boarding school dormitory life and her first night spent in 'floods of tears':

> I had to go to bed in this forlorn dormitory, and I couldn't go to sleep, and I just lay there under the bedclothes sobbing away and thinking why on earth did I have to come here.[29]

A key objection raised by the Clyde Report was that residential facilities' primary concern was only to provide shelter, rather than to offer any additional comforts.[30] As a result, most Kindertransportees remember adapting to a completely new, frequently worse, physical living environment. Kindertransportees often came from a relatively privileged background and social class in which they had enjoyed a degree of wealth. Many were from middle-class families. In contrast, the Scottish child in care usually came from Scotland's urban working classes and prior to residential placement had often already experienced a home environment that was overcrowded and lacked necessities.[31]

Between 1938 and 1945 there existed an understanding that mental and physical health were related; however mental health continued to be remedied by physical provisions.[32] The Clyde Report argued that 'the answer is certainly not to be found in the large institution' and recommended new limitations to be imposed upon the size of facilities and the number of children they accommodated.[33] It also argued that the basic standard of the accommodation and living environment was inadequate. Kindertranportees remember feeling that the institutional environment lacked important characteristics they associated with past home lives: creature comforts, private sleeping quarters, intimate dining areas or socially integrated upbringings. Residential facilities, such as Whittingehame, Garnethill hostel and Polton House, are recalled as having provided a large, impersonal, temporary and community-orientated environment, with greater emphasis on public rather than on private approaches to daily life.[34]

A communal structure to the living environment characterized these large institutions. Kindertransportees, along with the Clyde Report, felt that this trait alone contradicted the intimacies of previous family-based lifestyles.[35] This is most often remembered in the form of communal dormitories and dining areas.[36]

Few Kindertransportees had previously shared their bedroom before migration and some had never slept away from their parents.[37] The Kindertransportees were not familiar with the large dormitory, which lacked privacy and personal space.[38] Edna struggled to adapt to dormitory life:

> I was put into a huge, huge bedroom, with 12 beds in it and between the beds was a very small space. I didn't feel comfortable with that. I [was] used to my own room, my room. All of a sudden no privacy and I was not used to that sort of thing.[39]

Jackson struggled with the lack of privacy.[40] Fry recalls that in the Garnethill hostel there was never a quiet place to study or be alone.[41] The crowded atmosphere of dormitories could prove to be a lonely experience. One Kindertransportee recalls that he was 'badly bullied by everyone. . . . Oh how miserable I was. How lonely I felt'.[42] Edna reflects that she found it impossible to make any friends living within the large crowd of residents at Whittingehame.[43]

The Clyde Report also recommended that the standard of facilities be raised beyond basic needs.[44] Kindertransportees argue that facilities lacked even basic comforts. Glasgow's Garnethill hostel is recalled by Kindertransportees as lacking necessities, space and any home comforts.[45] Fry recalls that Garnethill hostel's dormitories were very cold: 'the heating was quite inadequate, I had a lot of frostbites'.[46] Hubbers recalls that the condition of Whittingehame was extremely basic, large and impersonal.[47]

Murphy has highlighted that a prevalent narrative to emerge among former children in care in Australia refers to poor food conditions in institutional facilities.[48] This prevalence also emerges in the Scottish story. The culinary provisions are remembered as being unimaginative and of poor quality. One Kindertransportee, Elijah, remembers that Whittingehame provided 'ordinary food, porridge nearly every day in the morning, egg, bread, bit of cheese . . . the food was very monotonous and simple'.[49] These issues were largely due, as Chapter 2 has argued, to the circumstances of war and also philanthropic agendas to cater for the perceived needs of the working-class child in care. Nevertheless, these conditions of care are remembered by Kindertransportees as having been in stark contrast to the home comforts they had experienced in their past family environment.

It was only after the 1948 Children's Act that efforts were made to prevent the segregation of children in care from the community.[50] Prior to this, institutions tended to be established in rural areas, outside of a town or village. The pre-*hachsharot,* evacuation centres, boarding schools, convents and children's homes were often in remote locations within secure grounds. Subsequently, institutions could isolate residents from any form of outside social engagement. In interviews, Kindertransportees place emphasis upon the cloistering experience of an institutional living environment.[51]

This situation challenged the balance between a private and public daily life usual in a middle-class German family. Kindertransportees in residential care grew up without a normal frame of reference acquired within a socially integrated family environment.[52] Handler, the leader of Bachad, recorded his concerns for the ability of youth, isolated in agricultural training facilities, to readjust to life in society and become useful citizens in Britain.[53] Elsie felt 'cloistered' within the Catholic Convent of the Sacred Heart, in Aberdeen, and felt completely cut off from the outside world.[54] She remembers that on leaving her convent she lacked any understanding of money or an ability to organize her own life.

Experience of nurture within a residential facility

Although Britain was experiencing a gradual shift towards a new open-minded and democratic perspective within theories concerning the most suitable approach to raising the deprived child in care, little development occurred within the actual day-to-day management of residential care centres until after 1948.[55] Advances in psychology, the arrival of psychiatry and psychoanalysis from Austria, and the work of the Child Guidance Clinics had had limited influence upon residential care in Scotland during the inter-war period.[56] It was only after wartime experiences, most notably evacuation, that these new ideas became influential.[57] Even then changes were particularly slow to take root in Scotland, as opposed to England, with a continued adherence to Behaviourism.[58]

As a result, in 1946, the Clyde Report concluded that the nurturing experience of the deprived Scottish child, living within a residential facility, was distinctly marked by a lack of attention to individual needs, emotional development and psychological problems.[59] Replenishing the absence of individual care was a central feature in the 1948 Children's Act, which called for greater levels of 'personal care of the individual'.[60] Hugh Cunningham has argued that care in residential facilities was distinguishable by its 'regimentation, firm discipline, ghastly food and a lack of care on an individual basis'.[61] The large size of facilities and the limited level of staff available often made it unfeasible to respond to individual needs.

Kindertransportees also argue that in residential facilities individual care strategies remained the exception rather than the rule. This tendency is remembered as having given little continuity to ritual celebrations for the individual child. Personal celebrations, such as birthdays, tended to be overlooked within residential care. Kindertransportees at Whittingehame do remember visiting Lady Traprain for afternoon tea on their birthdays.[62] However, this would occur on a group basis, inclusive of all children with nearby birthdays.

Ranita was born in Berlin. Her Jewish family was very religious and originated in Russia. On arrival in Britain, she was sent directly to Whittingehame. She remembers that at Whittingehame:

> No you did not celebrate your birthdays. . . . Lady Traprain used to invite us for our birthday parties to her house and there she looked after us very well.[63]

The contradiction in this statement suggests that the dominant impression was that personal birthday celebrations were overlooked. The likelihood is that, for the most part, Kindertransportees experienced a sharp break from past personal rituals for celebrating their special day, with presents, birthday cakes and extravagant gestures absent. Elijah recalls of birthdays: 'there wasn't really a big to-do about birthdays . . . it was a big group and the big group was divided into smaller parts, who were friendly and did things together, but things like birthdays I did not take part in any birthday parties'.[64] The rarity of individual attention meant that when individual favours were given, jealousy and hostility could be provoked among the residents.[65] Drew, a teacher at Whittingehame, wrote to his own parents of the clannish 'communal spirit' that prevented Kindertransportees from accepting individual attention when it was available because of fear of group hostility.[66]

Another key criticism raised by the work of researchers, such as James Robertson and Mary Ainsworth, was that residential facilities lacked understanding or concern for the emotional development of the minor in care.[67] The CC only began to make efforts to cater for the Kindertransportees' emotional needs after 1941 and these efforts tended to be concentrated on spiritual rather than on emotional needs.[68] Jewish evacuees were initially spared little thought for their cultural and religious requirements.[69] There existed a persistent ignorance to expressions of emotional needs by caregivers during evacuation.[70] This was particularly true in response to problems such as bed-wetting, which tended to be punished. National hysteria emerged in Scotland with regard to evacuee bed-wetting.[71]

This trend was also customary in the initial process of placing minors in care facilities. Placement strategies were often subject to time restrictions and pressures to find a care solution. The Clyde Report noted that there existed a perpetual surplus of minors to foster homes and other available placements.[72] This meant that organizations had to prioritize the caregiver's needs over the minor's requirements.[73] The placement of Kindertransportees in residential facilities is frequently remembered as having overlooked individual suitability. Kindertransportees frequently point to the CC's haphazard strategies for care placement as examples of the failures to account for their emotional needs.[74] Little thought seems to have been given to keeping siblings together. Kindertransportee Grenville recalls that on arrival to Britain he was separated from his brothers: 'I didn't know what happened to them'.[75]

This trend was also marked by the way in which the minors were included in the allocation process as objects of adult inspection rather than as individuals making their own choices. Little effort was made to shelter the child in care from the process of selection for care homes. This was true both for foster and for residential placements. Kindertransportees have recalled the 'cattle market' process of finding care placements, whereby they would be paraded in front of would-be foster parents.[76] Kindertransportees refer to these parades at Dovercourt as 'pick a child' days.[77] Karen Gershon, who was thereafter sent to Whittingehame, recorded her impressions of this selection process in a poem entitled 'The Children's Exodus':

> . . . but mealtimes were a market-place
> when sudden visitors could choose
> although we were not orphaned yet
> a son or daughter by their face . . .[78]

Similar cattle market occurrences were found during the selection process for billeting evacuees and for distributing minors to foster homes during the process of 'boarding out'.[79] Kindertransportees were often sent on to residential facilities because the CC had been unable to find them a foster home. This meant that such Kindertransportees often felt a sense of failure at having not been picked.

Once in residential care, little attention is remembered as being given to meet emotional needs. The work of the Child Guidance Clinics and the Tavistock Centre sought to introduce the relevance of recreating the 'psychological family' upbringing and the importance of the feeling of a home life for the child in care.[80] The Clyde Report supported these ideas and criticized the absence of a single guardian figure, the lack of adequate staff, and the 'insensitive' or 'excessive' disciplinary approach to care.[81] Bowlby's research through the 1940s developed related 'attachment theories' and sought to explain the problem of 'maternal deprivation', which, he argued, could impact negatively upon the child in care.[82] Bowlby attributed subsequent mental health problems to the continued lack of concern within institutions for maternal or paternal support for the emotional needs of a child.[83] These ideas developed into the 1960s with debates concerning 'separation anxiety', as well as the importance of the mother-child relationship.[84]

The notion of the central importance of 'family' to the child was also new and was only incorporated within welfare services in Scotland after the war.[85] Caregivers had not yet adopted attachment theories.[86] This meant that the legacy of the boarding school and other British institutions was felt to have marginalized the role of the family in the minors' lives.[87] In 1944, Presland reflected that 'in the best circumstances it is not easy for an organization to be an adequate substitute for the profoundly significant life of a family'.[88] As a result, there existed a 'cultural and emotional no-man's-land' for minors in care.[89]

Kindertransportees support these arguments as they stress that the nature of such care and supervision meant that few felt they had found a parental substitute to provide maternal or paternal love and support. The root of this problem lay in the inability of residential care to recreate the 'mother-child' relationship for the child's development process.[90] Kindertransportees pinpoint the significance of not having a mother figure in residential care. Edna has stressed that a 'love starved' resident body characterized Whittingehame, due to the 'legacy of having no mother'.[91]

The matron in these facilities was meant to provide a degree of maternal support, yet is often recalled by Kindertransportees as unsupportive and lacking any mothering attributes. In May 1939, Kindertransportee Alfred Batzdorf wrote a letter to 'my future wife'.[92] In the letter he described his problematic relationship with his matron, who he described as not maternal. Josephine describes her matron in Scotland as someone who was 'not sentimental . . . the most awful woman, she was so nasty to the children and she hated me . . . she was horrible'.[93] Elijah also offers an unfavourable impression of the same matron: 'I didn't like her . . . she didn't help us'.[94] Sprinzeles too felt that this matron lacked 'softness' and a 'kind touch'.[95] She believes that although the teachers were 'very kindly', the Kindertransportees lacked mothering, particularly from the matron. One Kindertransportee living in a hostel recalls that their matron had 'no idea' and they subsequently 'suffered greatly in that atmosphere . . . the atmosphere in the hostel was more often than not very unhappy'.[96]

It is important to note that the un-mothering atmosphere of many residential facilities was certainly not universal. In contrast, Elsie remembers a close family feeling at her convent school in Aberdeen and a close relationship with the nuns.

> That was my family really, the nuns, other people have one mum, but I had a whole bunch, with one or two who became really surrogate mums . . . really loving and kind, one in particular I felt as close to almost as I had to my mother . . . she would tuck me in at night and I do recall having crying attacks, and I never seemed to know why I was crying but I couldn't stop. She would kneel at my bedside and stroke my hair until I fell asleep, she was the most mothering of them all.[97]

Nevertheless, a recurring complaint by interviewees is that not only did supervisors fail to 'mother' the minors in residential facilities, but they also tended to remain at a formal distance. The Clyde Report highlighted that due to a variety of factors, residential facilities were often plagued with a poor-quality and limited pool of staff. This afforded minors minimal contact time with an adult caregiver. Supervisors are remembered as having spent little time with the Kindertransportees outside of the classroom. Edna recalls that in Whittingehame supervisors constantly retreated to the staff room and rarely interacted with the students outside of the training course:

> We were all traumatised without being able to admit it. Cidy Levi, I went to her once and I asked her why did she always go to the staff room for tea and not with us, she said because we were scared of you . . . they all had tea in the staff room. In those days there were no therapeutic methods . . . . No one knew how to empathise with us.[98]

Sprinzeles was also at Whittingehame and felt that although teachers were 'very kindly', they never developed a close relationship or bond with the residents.[99]

Without a maternal or paternal figure and lacking close constant supervision from staff, the Kindertransportees felt that they lacked adequate guidance as maturing adolescents. Robertson has argued that residential facilities were particularly concerned to curtail the sexuality of the minor and most especially to prevent habitual masturbation.[100] Scottish schools and residential facilities did not routinely provide sexual education during this period.[101] This role continued to be allocated to the family as part of parental responsibilities. However, in residential care, minors did not possess this option and there seems to have been no effort to provide a guidance substitute. Subsequently, there was a resounding silence from caregivers for sexually maturing Kindertransportees.

The absence of advice about puberty and sexuality is recalled by some Kindertransportees as a major problem during maturation. This was especially felt while they tried to understand the changes that were occurring to their bodies and minds. Kindertransportees felt that they lacked advice and guidance during pivotal periods in their pubescent development. Elijah recalls his first encounter with wet dreams as a young adolescent at Whittingehame and the matron's inability to help or advise him:

> Boys aged 13 and 14 have all sorts of problems, they don't know what is happening to them, sexually and things like this, but she would never give advice. . . . I remember my pants were covered with masturbation . . . and I wanted her to tell me that this is not a terrible thing, try not to do it, but it is a thing that happens to youth of your age . . . she was of no help whatsoever. Her important part was that the rooms were clean, that we washed properly. . . . She was not a very helpful person.[102]

This situation was not unique to Scotland. Leslie Brent attended Bunce Court and recalls that sex education from Ann Essinger was unhelpful: '[Ann Essinger] once told a group of boys whom I was one "If you ever have sexual urges come up on you, just go and have a cold shower". That was the only sex education I ever received'.[103]

As a result of the perceived limited availability of adult supervision, maternal support or individual nurturing from a qualified member of staff, Kindertransportees stress that they learnt to become dependent on alternative means of support. Mahood refers to this pattern of group behaviour as the development of 'sub-cultural psychological support'.[104] This became a common feature among Scottish children in residential institutions. For the most part, this led to a heavy dependence on friendship ties for guidance and support. Kindertransportees also frequently recall relying on one another to learn about life and cope with emotional developments. Sprinzeles remembers that 'we nurtured ourselves, we comforted ourselves . . . we would comfort each other . . . we were a clique within ourselves, the girls who lived within that room'.[105]

The 'family group' emerged in conjunction with this shift from blood kinship ties to friendship group bonds. This was a powerful bond rooted in friendship cliques or youth groups. Josephine states: 'What you did if you were clever was you got yourself a little group together . . . you got your circle, your little cliques'.[106] Within these groups, Josephine notes that 'there was always someone who clung to you'. Drew wrote that 'it is difficult to convey to an outsider this communal spirit which demands that all should have exactly the same considerations . . . to be different is to be a traitor'.[107] He suggests the clannishness of these cliques. This could mean that social groups would keep very much together and often clashed with alternative groups.[108] In 1939, Batzdorf wrote to his 'future wife' about his trauma and depression after the age of 16 when his group was relocated.[109] Such bonds could be long-standing and challenge previous understandings of a family bond.

Youth groups emerged as a particularly important type of family group. This was especially true for Kindertransportees in pre-*hachsharot*, such as Whittingehame and Polton House. These residential facilities utilized youth groups to create a long-term bond between residents.[110] Bachad, Habonim, Hatzair Hashomer and the Scouts emerged as the most popular group choices. These groups created extremely powerful long-standing peer-group ties among Kindertransportees. Elijah rejected an educational opportunity because he did not want to be separated from his Habonim group at Whittingehame.[111] The Zionist youth groups would leave their pre-*hachsharot* centre together to join an adult *hachsharot* affiliated with their Zionist group.[112] Later, within these adult centres, *Gar'in* (commonly known as family groups) were formed. It was in these groups that Kindertransportees would make *Aliyah* and establish a *kibbutz* community. Dena, Elijah and Ranita, among others, all followed their Zionist youth group from Whittingehame to an adult *hachsharot* and then on to Israel.[113] These groups transformed the meaning of family from the nuclear family to the friendship group.

Implications of residential care for broader life stories

A central concern for the Child Guidance Clinics as well as for the Tavistock Centre was the psychological implication for youth who had grown up, or were still growing up, in a welfare facility. By way of evaluating the weaknesses in current approaches, researchers, such as Bowlby, highlighted a number of key repercussions that could be expected in the mental health of such minors. These categories sought to replace previous ideas that defined a mentally unwell child as 'abnormal', 'victim' or 'threat'.[114] They established new conditions specific to children. These included 'disorders of personality', 'behaviour disorders', 'habit disorders', 'Glycopenic' disorders, 'psychoneuroses', 'psychoses' and 'epilepsy'.[115] These categories represented the perceived full spectrum of problems, beginning with timid or irritable behaviour and progressing to sexual promiscuity, bed-wetting, insomnia, hysteria or phobias, and culminating in schizophrenia or mental deficiency. Kindertransportees attach themselves to these categorizations and make similar direct links between residential care and their psychological health.

Prior to the Clyde Report, the Scottish Advisory Council reported specifically on the treatment and rehabilitation of juvenile offenders.[116] Their report investigated the relationship between Remand Homes and Approved Schools with the juvenile delinquent. The report is reflective of the concern that existed for juvenile delinquency and the impact of unsuitable care for the future mental health of the deprived child.[117] This does not wish to suggest that juvenile delinquency emerged as a dominant personal repercussion of the nurturing experience of life in care, rather that the Kindertransportees themselves testify to having experienced various degrees of adolescent rebellion and bad behaviour due to their institutional upbringing.

This element of their upbringing has been perpetually ignored and at times purposefully overlooked despite the fact that it tallies closely with wider British narratives about the child in institutional care. Zoe Josephs' research has also challenged the 'happy-ever-after' Kindertransport narrative, which overlooks the role of delinquency in their care experience.[118] The Kindertransportees were not immune to behaving badly, and the CC was aware of the potential and existing problems of anti-social behaviour among their charges. In 1939, the Nottingham Hebrew Congregation wrote to the secretary of the Chief Rabbi's Emergency Fund that Kindertransportees were proving difficult to manage. In the letter they explain their belief that one particular girl is responsible for 'rousing' anti-social behaviour among nine other residents of their hostel:

> She is a girl of very strong will and personality, the other girls look to her as to a leader, and she is exerting a most disturbing influence on them. . . . She is hysterical and rouses hysteria in the other children. She disturbs the dormitories at night and collects the girls in her bedroom.[119]

At the Annual Refugee Conference in 1942, attention focused on the problems of housing 'adolescents' and schemes were devised for the most suitable methods of management for these minors.[120]

Kindertransportees' testimonies support the hypothesis that they did not always behave well while in residential care. Drew wrote to his parents concerning incidents of bullying at Whittingehame.[121] He also described his frustration about truancy among Kindertransportees at Whittingehame and his inability to force attendance of his classes: 'it was customary for a master to lose one by one his class through the open window . . . to have three people turning up out of class of 20'.[122] A popular tale by interviewees is of other residents disregarding staff authority and school rules while exiting classrooms via windows.[123] Drew photographed Kindertransportees undertaking pursuits that seem to capture these stories.[124] The matron of Whittingehame also remembered incidents of 'unruly behaviour', including one resident destroying the electrical equipment in the sick room, while others were regularly playing truant.[125] Edna describes incidents at Whittingehame when fellow residents vandalized the estate's property.[126] In correspondence with his parents, Drew concluded unfavourably upon the temperament of the Kindertransportees: 'they are very volatile'.[127]

Kindertransportee bad behaviour was not unusual and occurred in other residential facilities across Scotland and throughout Britain. Flesch recalls similar behaviour of Kindertransportees during their evacuation in the south of Scotland:

> Fighting with them all the time. . . . This was a lovely house in its own grounds. . . . And there was a big greenhouse. One day we decided to take bricks and smash it to pieces. Things like that, you know. Screwed up.[128]

Jayson recalls Kindertransportee behaviour at the Millsie camp in Ireland: 'the refugee children would not behave correctly. . . . Sonia would not put her hand out when she was asked . . . she got hold of the cane and she snapped it'.[129]

Kindertransportees were also prone to fighting one another. This was a particular problem within residential facilities specifically established for Kindertransportees, where social groups were formed based on national origins. In Whittingehame, Dena recalls that Viennese and German children fought one another.[130] In Bunce Court, Brent was shocked by similar clashes between German and Austrian refugees:

> I was absolutely dumbfounded and disturbed, deeply disturbed by the fact that there was a huge amount of rivalry between the Berlin and the Viennese boys, less boys, the older ones. . . . there were actually knife fights between them.[131]

Legarreta has argued that similar divisions emerged among the Basque minors in Britain and that these could also lead to extreme cases of violent confrontation.[132]

Bad behaviour and rebellion is often connected by Kindertransportees to their emotional upset during the period due to residential care. A dominant issue is frustration at having lost or missed out on an important part of life due to the characteristics of the institutional environment. A key feature is the sense of having lost 'home' and 'family'. Initially homesick, Kindertransportees argue that their sense of loss was perpetuated by the living environment and nurturing experience within residential facilities. They felt that they were not provided with a substitute 'home' and that this led to their gradual alienation from a 'normal' home life. As a result, as Kushner has argued, the notion of 'home' has become a symbolic and idealized construct, which possesses qualities of safety, love and warmth.[133]

Detaching the child migrant from 'home' life could lead to negative psychological consequences.[134] Kindertransportees stress their sense of bereavement for these crucial elements within their lives.[135] One Kindertransportee recorded at the time his acute awareness of lacking his own family, which led to envy and a sense of hostility towards other people's families.[136] Rachel's narrative dwells on her lost family, especially when she compares her situation with the solid roots her husband enjoys with his extended family in America.[137] Kindertransportee Batzdorf wrote, 'I have become selfish, I want my "home" and if I cannot find that in the community, I will withdraw from it'.[138] In a diary written in July 1939, a Kindertransportee living in a hostel recalls his frustration and sadness that he was not 'At Home'.[139] Another Kindertransportee states:

> The fact of not having a home was of paramount importance. A school is not a home; other people's houses are not home.[140]

Collated testimonies of Kindertransportees by Gershon also express the paramount importance attached to having or not having a home.[141]

Kindertransportees explain that their response to this situation has been a preoccupation with finding a permanent 'home'. This is most often in the form of an initial desire to establish permanency, belonging, community membership and family roots.[142] Kushner has also argued that great importance has been placed by Kindertransportees on reconstructing a 'home'.[143] The notion of 'family', and for many the idea of the 'Jewish family', has also dominated reconstruction efforts. The process of re-imagining, recreating and re-engaging with a 'home' or 'family life' is often remembered as a difficult challenge.

The physical aspects of 'home' and 'family' are recalled by Kindertransportees as being easier to recreate, namely a permanent place of belonging and physical roots. This led Kindertransportees to choose to settle in permanent private houses at a young age.[144] Procreation also dominated many Kindertransportee narratives.[145] The desire for a large family with many children, grandchildren

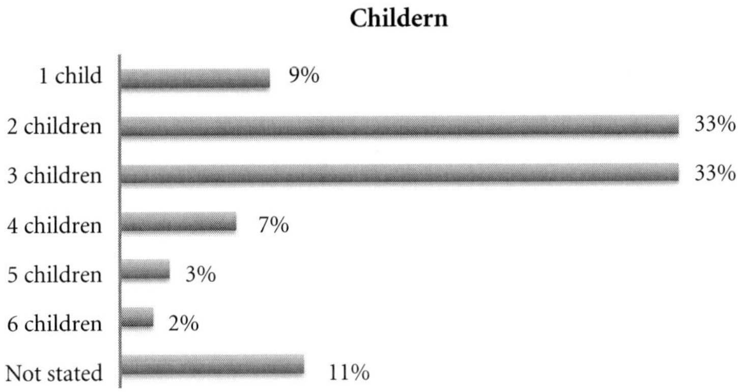

Table 11 Level of procreation.
Source: KA: QU/SUP.

and great-grandchildren is described as a source of continuity and essential for a perceived 'Jewish family life'.[146] Table 11 illustrates the trend among Kindertransportees to procreate and establish large families.

By having children soon after marriage, most Kindertransportees now have large numbers of grandchildren and great-grandchildren. One Kindertransportee interviewed had 6 children and now enjoys 28 grandchildren and over 30 great-grandchildren.[147] Another, who had 4 children, now has 12 grandchildren and 11 great-grandchildren.[148] This trend does correlate with the wider post-war baby boom in Britain, whereby young couples were getting married earlier and having families sooner. In comparison, the average British woman born between the mid 1930s and the early 1940s would have 2.4 children.[149] Nevertheless, for Kindertransportees, establishing a family is presented as a form of emotional recovery from institutional care.

This aspect of the Kindertransportees' emotional response is closely entwined with their reaction to the Holocaust. Procreation is also explained by Kindertransportees as a form of political resistance, allowing Kindertransportees to 'beat Hitler' and Nazi ambitions to exterminate the Jewish people.[150] Margot Goldberg explains that 'where life continues, death is denied' and points to the importance of procreation in the family.[151] It also provided a tool to resolve guilt for having gained a place on the Kindertransport and survived the Holocaust.[152] Nevertheless, for Kindertransportees from residential care, recreating a family unit represented a form of personal restitution. They were establishing something that had not otherwise been provided.

The intimate aspects of daily life in a family environment are recalled as having been harder to recreate. The 'Jewish family' is frequently idealized by interviewees and portrayed as a central ingredient to a perceived 'good life'.[153] However, this is often felt to be unattainable by Kindertransportees, who express the feeling that their institutional upbringing and care environment has made them unfamiliar with essential aspects of a 'Jewish family life'. This has meant that the Kindertransportees draw heavily upon their memories of their past Jewish family lives and reinterpret these as prerequisites for the sought after 'Jewish family life'. These are often nostalgic and idealistic.

Josephine found the process of reconstructing a normal home life exceptionally difficult after growing up in a residential facility.[154] The mundane Jewish habits, customs and rituals observed in a private domestic setting were rarely continued in residential facilities. In institutional care, engagement with Judaism became rooted in the public domain. This meant that social, cultural or political aspects of a Jewish life substituted intimate day-to-day private Jewish rituals or even piety per se.[155] This could halt Kindertransportees' learning process of Jewish traditions and cause confusion about the role of Judaism in the home environment.[156]

Without this frame of reference, Kindertransportees often struggled to recreate or re-imagine the prerequisites for a 'Jewish family' in later life. Ester Golan, originally Ursula Dobkowsky, lived in Glogau, Selisia, in Germany, with her Jewish and Zionist parents.[157] She was sent from Berlin, via the Kindertransport, to Whittingehame. After completing her 2 years at Whittingehame, she was sent to a domestic work placement in rural East Lothian. She has recorded her struggle to recreate family rituals, celebrations and festivals from her memory of life before the Kindertransport. The battle to re-engage with this aspect of Jewish piety left Golan 'yearning for a real Jewish home life'.[158] Interviewees have subsequently expressed the development of severe homesickness, loneliness and insecurity about belonging due to their inability to recreate the perceived 'Jewish family'.[159]

Alternatively, for some Kindertransportees whose families survived the Holocaust, they found that they were unable to re-engage with 'family life'. The experience of self-governance and communal life in an institutional environment was identified as causes for minors finding it difficult to readjust to a small patriarchal or matriarchal family environment.[160] Guske has argued that Kindertransportees underwent a process of 'parentification', shouldering adult burdens and expectations.[161] This process made it difficult to form traditional parent/child relationships with their parents.[162] Tara Zahra has shown that displaced children remaining in continental Europe also struggled in the process of readjusting to life with biological families and past lives.[163]

The lack of affection and love in institutions has also been attributed by Kindertransportees to problems experienced with re-engaging with parents, depending on others, or forming new close relationships in later life. Debbie struggled in later life to form a mutually dependent relationship with her husband.[164] Josephine believes that living in a community collective environment hampered her ability to reconstruct and readapt to a family life.[165] It is important to note that the process of reconnecting could also be hampered by many other factors that had arisen during separation, including linguistic differences.[166]

In addition to anxieties about the lack of a 'home' and 'family' life, the Kindertransportees also explain that they developed a wide range of other emotional problems that they link to the broad experience of growing up in residential care. Hamilton and Benz make a link between 'separation' and 'trauma', and argue that 'behavioural anomalies' arose among such children.[167] Guske has argued that three distinctive behavioural features arose, dependent on age at departure, within the Kindertransportee group. She believes that those aged between 1 and 4 developed 'neurotic characters' suffering from a lack of inhibition, anxiety and guilt; Kindertransportees between the ages of 4 and 10 experienced anxiety disorders and phobias, while those aged 10–18 suffered from 'chronic reactive depressive symptoms'.[168]

In contrast, Hamilton's 1985 'retrospective study' of 300 Kindertransportees recorded overarching problems ranging from depression, relationship problems, extreme insecurity, fear of abandonment and restlessness.[169] Hamilton has also identified among refugees a particular desperation to please and a chameleon-like approach to new living environments.[170] Curio has pointed to the regression of the child migrant in some circumstances, including learning difficulties, anti-social behaviour and a reversion to bed-wetting.[171]

The Kindertransportees' testimonies connect a variety of perceived psychological changes and emotional problems to their residential upbringing. The CC was aware of psychological problems afflicting many of the refugee adolescents at the time. In 1942, at the Annual Refugee Conference, it was agreed that there was a 'need for after care work for adolescent refugee girls, for native nurses to treat refugee mental cases'.[172]

By the close of war, it was increasingly recognized that the community-orientated and cloistered character of institutional life could lead to the development of unusual characteristics, which made it difficult for integration back into a normal life in society. Ellis noted that there were problems of the 'psychological effects of community life'.[173] Kindertransportees suggest that they share these anxieties. One Kindertransportee enjoyed the community life at Polton House, but claims to be crippled in later life by agoraphobia due to this experience.[174] She associates this with her fear of unfamiliar and crowded environments that are filled with unknown faces and independent life choices.[175] Now in her 80s, she explains that her psychological illness has made it difficult to form new relationships and establish a stable family life.

Kindertransportees have also suffered from severe debilitating forms of psychological and even schizophrenic illness. Ranita states that at Whittingehame, 'some of them were a little cracked, there was a girl she used to draw but she talked an awful lot of nonsense'.[176] Jayson suggests that these mental problems were widespread, recalling them as they occurred at the Millsie camp:

> We never had any psychological advice, they just left us to it. So if anyone was slightly crazy, if anything they were encouraged, so we didn't get any saner. This was particularly unfortunate for the grown-ups who were in a far worse psychological state than we children were.[177]

In most instances, severely disturbed minors would be returned to the CC in London. Hahn-Warburg recorded one incident at Bloomsbury House when she had to deal with a troubled minor.

> A boy of 18 or 19 came to see me. Nobody else at Bloomsbury House wanted him in the building. He was aggressive and undisciplined. I invited him in. When I was behind my desk, he jumped up suddenly, took out a knife and cut the telephone wire. Then he opened the window and started climbing out on the ledge. . . . Eventually, I persuaded him to go with me to hospital. There was a doctor I knew who would help him get into a special home.[178]

Severe psychiatric illness could sometimes lead to long-term institutionalization. Psychological breakdowns were not uncommon among young migrants.[179] Turner notes that by 1945 36 young trans-migrants were cared for in mental asylums and a number suffered schizophrenia and suicidal tendencies.[180]

Despite the significant presence of emotional problems, or more severe depression, Kindertransportees also stress that they survived the ordeal and are 'survivors'. This aspect of their personal narrative is most closely connected to the public Kindertransport narrative, which emphasizes endurance and achievement, despite the odds. They stress that they emerged from residential care with independent, self-reliant and ambitious approaches to life. Kindertransportees often attribute this to their unaccompanied circumstance in Britain and perceived parental expectations from Greater Germany. Yet, they also place relevance upon their care within residential facilities, which

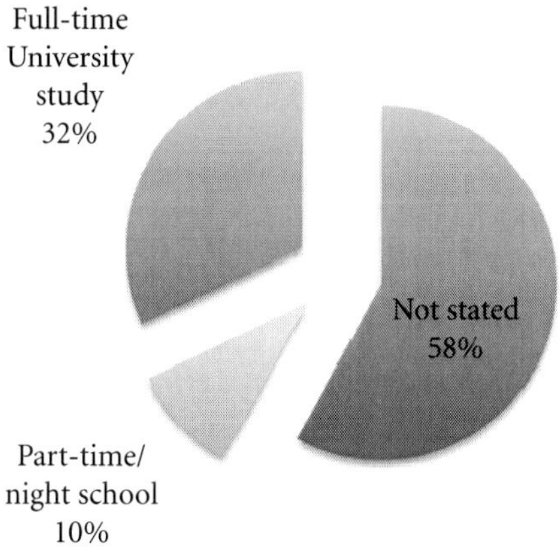

Table 12 Further education.
Source: KA: QU/SUP.

sought to prevent idleness and emphasized to residents that they must become independent and self-sufficient by the age of 14.[181]

Kindertransportees recall demanding working lifestyles from a young age and a tendency for pursuing further education alongside these busy schedules. Table 12 indicates the disproportionately high level of further education among Kindertransportees. The KA: QU/SUP suggests that 11 per cent of Kindertransportees achieved a PhD, while 20 per cent gained a BA or BSC. Ruff decided to independently take his Scottish Highers after the war and later gained a bursary from the University of Glasgow.[182] He then went on to acquire a PhD. Warton replenished his missed education at night school while undertaking his apprenticeship. This enabled him to gain a place at the University of London and Glasgow School of Art.[183]

*

The Kindertransportees' residential upbringing is felt to have had an important bearing upon their broader life stories. What is clear is that the 'happy ever after' storyline does not represent the complex narrative that emerges. Personal narratives focus on 'loss, abuse, suffering and survival'.[184] However, in contrast to Murphy's findings for Aboriginal minors in Australian care homes, Kindertransportees rarely detail overt or extreme abuses – physically or psychologically – but rather emphasize neglect and insufficiencies in provisions. Nevertheless, the 'survivor' is central to these life histories. Murphy explains that this includes the formation of the 'legacy' of a residential childhood, whereby subsequent childhood injuries become publically recognized as the cause for transforming them into 'survivors'.[185]

Kindertransportees use their experience of residential care to explain the way in which their lives have unfolded. These experiences are positioned as the catalyst and cause of later life failures or successes. They offer an explanation for future personal problems or social dilemmas and have become a shared denominator that can be used to make sense of their lives. The subsequent patterns that have emerged within these personal narratives reflect a close relationship with public narratives and popular historical consciousness.

The overarching 'survivor' storyline correlates with popular Holocaust narratives, which focus on Jewish survival against all the odds. Personal narratives also link to popular Kindertransport narratives that stress endurance and achievement. However, they do not dwell on specific Jewish victimhood. Neither do they support the 'thankful' or 'celebratory' perception of their time in Britain as Kindertransportees. Instead, they reflect a closer correlation to public narratives in Britain concerning the difficult experiences of the deprived child in institutional care during this period.

In summary, the Kindertransportees' experiences of life in a residential facility, and the subsequent life histories that they connect to this upbringing, mirror narratives and records concerning the Scottish deprived minors' experiences of life in institutional care homes. These findings should not be interpreted in sensational terms, but they do show that the 'happy-ever-after' Kindertransport narrative is naïve and overlooks the wide array of ramifications that residential care in Scotland had upon all its residents' lives and their subsequent life histories.

Notes

1 MCPC/Drew, Letters, 16 May 1943.
2 Anne-Marie Ambert, 'An International Perspective on Parenting: Social Change and Social Constructs', *Journal of Marriage and Family*, 56, 3 (August 1994), 529–43.
3 Hendrick, *Child Welfare*, 136.
4 Cunningham, *Invention of Childhood*, 194; Abrams, *The Orphan Country*, 2, 20,
5 Thoburn, 'Trends in Foster Care and Adoption', 121.
6 Cunningham, *The Invention of Childhood*, 192.
7 Ibid.; See also Turner, ... *And the Policeman smiled*.
8 House of Commons Parliamentary Papers (HCPP): Scottish Home Department, 'Report of the Committee on Homeless Children' (Clyde Report), *Parliamentary Papers*, 1946, Cmd. 6911, vol.X.755.

9 HCPP/Home Department, 'Report of the Care of Children Committee' (Curtis Report), *Parliamentary Papers*, 1946, Cmd. 6922, vol.X.559.
10 Holman, 'Fifty Years Ago', 204; Clyde Report, 15.
11 Harry Hendrick, *Child Welfare: Historical Dimensions, Contemporary Debate* (Bristol: The Policy Press, 2003), 133.
12 HCPP/Clyde Report, 3.
13 Ibid., 14.
14 David Howe, Marian Brandon, Diana Hinnings and Gillian Schofield, *Attachment Theory, Child Maltreatment and Family Support; A Practice and Assessment Model* (New York: Palgrave, 1999), 13.
15 Hendrick, *Child Welfare*, 140; See David Cohen, *J. B. Watson: The Founder of Behaviourism: A Biography* (London: Routledge, 1979).
16 Benz, 'Traumatization through Separation', 86; Kröger, 'Child Exiles', 11.
17 Ibid.
18 Tydor Baumel, 'Twice a Refugee', 176.
19 WL/BL/74.
20 Murphy, 'Memory, Identity and public narrative'.
21 See Leverton and Lowensohn, *I came alone*; WL/1368/2/1, Notes, letters and memoirs collected for Bertha Leverton's publication 'I came alone', 1989–2000.
22 Ibid., 307.
23 Kushner, 'The Kinder: A Case of Selective Memory?', 145.
24 Holman, 'Fifty Years Ago', 204; Hendrick, *Child Welfare,* 124.
25 Thoburn, 'Trends in Foster Care and Adoption', 121; Hendrick, *Child Welfare*; See also Roger Bullock, 'The Children Act 1948: residential care', in Stevenson (ed.), *Child Welfare in the UK*, 156.
26 KA: QU/SUP.
27 Ibid.
28 Ibid.
29 WL/BL/69.
30 HCPP/Clyde Report, 14.
31 Lynn Abrams and Callum G. Brown (eds), *A History of Everyday Life in Twentieth-Century Scotland* (Edinburgh: Edinburgh University Press, 2010), 51.
32 Hendrick, *Child Welfare,* 99.
33 Ibid.
34 FWPC/Edna, Debbie; WHMA/USC: 31378.
35 Ibid., 15. For information concerning German Jewish family lives pre-migration see Kaplan, *Jewish Daily Life in Germany;* Ruth Kluger, *Landscapes of Memory: A Holocaust Girlhood Remembered* (New York: Bloomsbury Publishers, 2003).
36 FWPC/Levi, Elijah, Dena.
37 FWPC/Debbie.

38 FWPC/Edna.
39 Ibid.
40 WL/BL/69.
41 WHMA/USC: 31378.
42 Gershon, *We Came as Children*, 84.
43 FWPC/Edna.
44 Holman, 'Fifty Years Ago', 204.
45 WHMA/USC: 31378.
46 Ibid.
47 WHMA/USC: 43138.
48 Murphy, 'Memory, Identity and public narrative', 306.
49 FWPC/Elijah.
50 Hendrick, *Child Welfare,* 136.
51 FWPC/Abaigael, Dena, Levi, Elijah.
52 Hammel, 'Representations of Family in Autobiographical texts', 129.
53 WL/BL/25.
54 FWPC/Elsie.
55 Hendrick, *Child Welfare,* 112.
56 Urwin and Sharland, 'From bodies to minds', 180.
57 Welshman and Stewart, 'The Evacuation of Children in Wartime Scotland', 102.
58 Hendrick, *Child Welfare,* 100; See also Deborah Thom, 'Wishes, anxieties, play and gestures: Child guidance in inter-war England', in Cooter (ed.), *In the Name of the Child,* 215; Cunningham, *Invention of Childhood,* 197.
59 HCPP/Clyde Report, 24.
60 Hendrick, *Child Welfare*, 139.
61 Cunningham, *Invention of Childhood,* 193.
62 FWPC/Abaigael.
63 FWPC/Ranita.
64 FWPC/Elijah.
65 FWPC/Edna, Josephine.
66 MCPC/Drew, Letters, 14 January 1939.
67 David Howe, *Attachment Theory,* 13.
68 Tydor Baumel, *Twice a Refugee*, 179.
69 See Gottlieb, *Men of Vision.*
70 Macnicol, 'Effect of the Evacuation', 3–31; Welshman, 'Evacuation and Social Policy', 28–53.
71 Abrams, *The Orphan Country*, 173.
72 HCPP/Clyde Report, 15.
73 Buck, 'Feeding A Pauper Army', 312; See also Kushner and Know, *Refugees in an Age of Genocide*, 126–216.

74 Tydor Baumel, 'Twice a Refugee', 176.
75 WL/BL/150.
76 Gershon, *We Came as Children*, 40.
77 FWPC/Sarah, Noah, Abaigael.
78 Gershon, *We Came as Children*, 173.
79 Tydor Baumel, 'Twice a Refugee', 176; Abrams, *The Orphan Country*, 57.
80 Hendrick, *Child Welfare*, 99; Hendrick, 'Children's emotional well-being and Mental Health in Early Post-Second World War Britain: The case of Unrestricted Hospital visiting', in M. Gijswijt-Hofstra and Hilary Marland (eds), *Cultures of Child Health in Britain and the Netherlands in the Twentieth Century* (New York: Rodopi, 2003), 214.
81 Hendrick, *Child Welfare*, 133.
82 Howe, *Attachment Theory*, 12.
83 See Inge Bretherton, 'The Origins of Attachment Theory: John Bowlby and Mary Ainsworth', *Development Psychology*, 28 (1992), 759–75.
84 Hendrick, 'Children's emotional well-being', 213.
85 Abrams, *The Orphan Country*, 54.
86 Barnett, 'The Acculturation of the Kindertransport Minors', 100–10.
87 Gopfert, 'Kindertransport: History and memory', 22.
88 Presland, *A Great Adventure*, 21.
89 Abrams, '*The Orphan Country*', 59–60.
90 Ibid., 59.
91 FWPC/Edna.
92 Batzdorf in *ROK*, 28.
93 FWPC/Josephine.
94 FWPC/Elijah.
95 WHMA/USC: 43932.
96 Gershon, *We came as children*, 81.
97 FWPC/Elsie.
98 FWPC/Edna.
99 WHMA/USC: 43932.
100 Robertson, 'The home as a nest', 420.
101 See Johnston, 'Compulsory Day Continuation Classes'.
102 FWPC/Elijah.
103 WL/BL/72.
104 Mahood, *Policing gender*, 150.
105 WHMA/USC: 43932.
106 FWPC/Josephine.
107 MCPC/Drew, Letters, 14 January 1940.
108 FWPC/Elijah.

109 Batzdorf in *ROK*, 28.
110 FWPC/Levi, Elijah, Nathan, Edna, Jacob.
111 FWPC/Elijah.
112 FWPC/Nathan, Ranita, Dena, Elijah.
113 FWPC/Nathan, Edna, Ranita, Elijah, Dena, Benson; KA: QU/SUP.
114 Hendrick, *Child Welfare,* 7, 13.
115 Ibid., 104.
116 HCPP/Clyde Report, 4.
117 Holman, 'Fifty Years Ago', 204.
118 Zoe Josephs, *Survivors; Jewish Refugees in Birmingham 1933–1945* (Birmingham: Denali Press, 1988).
119 HLSC/MS183/52/F2, Letter from the Nottingham Hebrew Congregation's Rev Dr S. Goldman, 16 January 1939, to the secretary of the Chief Rabbi's Emergency Fund.
120 HLSC/MS183/384/F1, Report of Annual Refugee Conference held at Birmingham, 18–19 January 1942.
121 MCPC/Drew, Letters, 14 January 1940.
122 MCPC/Drew, Letters, 9 May 1940.
123 FWPC/Edna, Abaigael, Dena.
124 MCPC/Drew, Photographs.
125 Gershon, *We Came as Children,* 78.
126 FWPC/Edna.
127 MCPC/Drew, Letters, 25 April 1940.
128 WL/BL/137.
129 WL/BL/26.
130 FWPC/Dena.
131 WL/BL/72.
132 Legarreta, *The Guernica Generation*, 101.
133 Kushner, 'The Kinder: A Case of Selective Memory?', 157.
134 Benz, 'Traumatization through Separation', 89.
135 FWPC/Edna.
136 Anonymous, 'A Diary for Susie', in *ROK,* 18.
137 FWPC/Rachel.
138 Alfred Batzdorf, 'Letter to my future wife', 5 May 1939, in *ROK,* 28.
139 Anonymous, 'A Diary for Susie', in *ROK* (1999) 18.
140 Gershon, *We came as children,* 152, 153, 160.
141 Ibid.
142 FWPC/Edna.
143 Kushner, 'The Kinder: A Case of Selective Memory?', 157.
144 FWPC/Rachel, Edna.

145 FWPC/Edna.

146 http://golanes.blogspot.com, viewed 25 April 2008.

147 Ibid.

148 Ibid.

149 www.bbc.co.uk/news/health-11960183; see also www.Statistics.gov.uk/statbase/Product.asp?vlnk = 14408 (both viewed 23.05.2011).

150 FWPC/Edna.

151 Margot Goldberg, 'Honors', in *ROK*, 64.

152 Ibid.

153 FWPC/Noah, Edna.

154 FW/PC: Josephine.

155 FW/PC: Edna.

156 FW/PC: Elijah.

157 http://golanes.blogspot.com, viewed 25 April 2008.

158 Ibid.

159 FWPC/Edna; See also Gershon's collection of published poems, including *Collected Poems* (England, 1990).

160 HCPP/Clyde Report, 31.

161 Iris Guske, *Trauma and Attachment in the Kindertransport Context: German-Jewish Child Refugees' Accounts of Displacement and Acculturation in Britain* (Cambridge: Cambridge Scholars publishing, 2009), 27.

162 Kröger, 'Child Exiles', 18.

163 Tara Zahra, 'A Human Treasure': Europe's Displaced Children between Nationalism and Internationalism', *Past and Present*, 6 (2011), 344.

164 FWPC/Debbie.

165 FWPC/Josephine.

166 Ibid.

167 Benz, 'Traumatization through Separation', 98; See Vernon Hamilton, *A Retrospective Study of Child Refugees from Nazi Germany* (UK, 1985).

168 Guske, *Trauma and Attachment*, 19.

169 *Ibid.*; See also Curio, '"Invisible" children', 24.

170 Hamilton, *A Retrospective study.*

171 Curio, '"Invisible" children', 54.

172 HLSC/MS183/384/1, Report of Annual Refugee Conference held at Birmingham, 18 and 19 January 1942.

173 Ellis, 'Effects Of War On Child Health', 243.

174 FWPC/Debbie.

175 Ibid.

176 FWPC/Ranita.

177 WL/BL/26.

178 Lola Hahn-Warburg, cited in Turner, ... *And the Policeman smiled, 230–1.*

179 Turner, ... *And the Policeman smiled*, 228.

180 Ibid.

181 See Chapter 2.

182 WL/BL/50.

183 WHMA/USC: 23855.

184 Murphy, 'Memory, Identity and Public Narrative', 299.

185 Ibid., 303, 305.

6

Imagining Scotland: The Scottish Legacy after Migration

> I always say I am a product of three peoples, or ethnicities, or nations that have been screwed throughout history, the Scots, the Czechs and the Jews.[1]

The KA's new database suggests that 800 children were sent to Scotland via the Kindertransport.[2] Of those surveyed, by 1950 few remained within the Scottish borders. Only 13 per cent of these Kindertransportees remain in Scotland today.[3] Eighty-seven per cent migrated and can now be found across the world, as far from Britain as Canada, Nepal and New Zealand.[4] The majority did, however, adhere to three preferred destinations: 34 per cent migrated south to England, 23 per cent went to the United States and 25 per cent to Israel. Table 13 shows the ratio of Scotland's Kindertransportees across the world.

That 87 per cent of Scotland's Kindertransportees chose to migrate from Scotland does not, however, signify a definitive lack of relevance to their Scottish experience. In fact, despite some Kindertransportees feeling alienated or ambivalent towards Scotland, many express a strong sense of connection towards the country. Most of these Kindertransportees had spent much of their formative years in Scotland and express their sense of attachment and loyalty to Scotland. Benson, who now lives in Israel, claims in the opening statement that he is the product of 'three peoples' and notably lists Scots first. In doing so, he indicates that a perceived affinity with Scotland is not dependent upon a continued geographic connection to Scotland.

Yet, if Scotland is an important feature or concept for Kindertransportees, then why did the majority choose to migrate from Scotland? Scotland's Kindertransportees have become part of the Scottish diaspora experience. They continue to reiterate an affinity towards Scotland, yet continue to live outside of Scotland. They explain that their migration choices reflect a complex

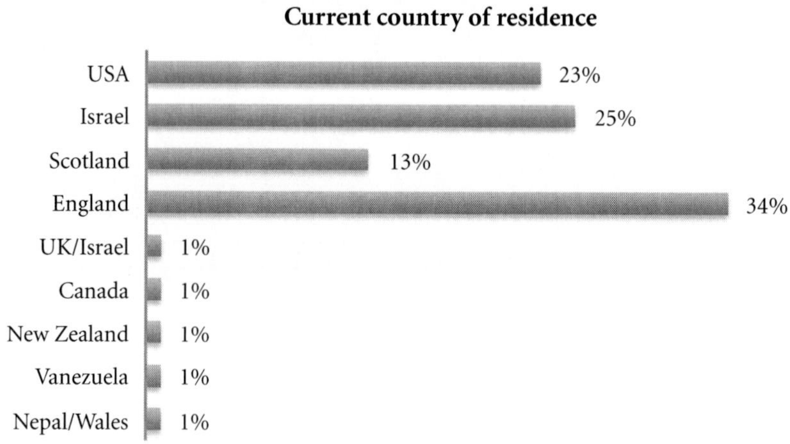

Table 13 Current country of residence.
Source: KA: QU/SUP.

collection of motivating factors, rather than a simple decision not to live in Scotland.

Members of a Scottish diaspora

Kindertransportees express a belief that they possess a distinct Scottish affiliation, regardless of whether they remained within Scotland's geographic territory. Combes, Hibbert, Hogg and Varey all argue that the strength of these associations is not dependent upon geographic location, nor is it necessarily related.[5] It is instead connected to one's sense of a collective identity and this does not require residence in Scotland.

Kindertransportees explain their sense of attachment to Scotland in ambiguous terms and emphasis clichéd symbols of 'Scottishness'.[6] Figure 29 shows the relevance of 'Scotland the brand' upon Kindertransportees' perception of Scottishness. In the photograph, Kindertransportees at Whittingehame have dressed up as 'Scots'. They have chosen to wear kilts to represent Scottishness. This suggests that ideas about 'Highlandism' form the basis of their construction of the imagined community of Scotland.

Highlandism is based on invented traditions and relies heavily upon 'retrospective cultural apparatus', most notably drawn from distorted perceptions of Highland culture.[7] Hugh Trevor-Roper refers to this Highland-based construction of Scottishness as a 'retrospective invention' and a modern apparatus that possesses 'great ambiguity'.[8] R. Nicholson also offers an important

Figure 29 Kindertransportees in kilts.
Source: MCPC/Drew, Photographs.

insight into the construction of 'Scottishness' drawn from imagined Highland traditions.[9] This process, Nicholson argues, crystallized as a reaction against the 1707 Act of Union. This has meant that symbols of Scottishness express a distinct non-English character. Over time these symbols of Scottishness have become deeply rooted in the public imagination of Scotland.

Scotland's migrants adopted these ideas about the centrality of Highlandism to a connection to Scotland.[10] This has developed into the establishment of a Scottish heritage culture in foreign countries, including the establishment of ethnic institutions – Burns' clubs, pipe bands or Caledonian clubs – or Scots language and idiom.[11] This apparatus is used to distinguish themselves 'firmly' from English migrants.[12] Kindertransportees who migrated from Scotland also explain their appropriation and enthusiasm for specific Scottish 'traditions' or cultural habits. These include public displays of 'Scottishness', such as celebrating Burns' Night, wearing tartan, drinking whiskey. Despite leaving Scotland, Benson still feels that he is equally the product of the Scots as much as he is the Czechs and the Jews. He states: 'I have very good and close feelings to my Scottish heritage and my Czech'.[13] Kindertransportees also underline their distinct Scottish language and idiom.[14] Jan recalls that by 1945 she had acquired a 'broad Scots accent'.[15] Jan, like many others, prefers to emphasize her Scottish accent rather than her German one. Marthe, who has remained in Ayrshire, states that, 'och yeah, I do feel Scottish . . . all my children live in Scotland'.[16]

Kindertransportees advocate Scottish nationalist sentiments. These Kindertransportees can sometimes express an inherent disdain for England and even the 'English Kinder'.[17] Scotland's Kindertransportees have even established this national divide with regard to commemorative events and reunions of the Kindertransport.[18] The emergence of SAROK, Scotland's own national Kindertransport Association, perhaps best articulates the depth of the Scottish legacy upon the Kindertransportees who were placed north of the border.

They use the term *Sassenach* to derogatively differentiate the English other. Upon meeting me, one interviewee, who now lives in the United States, expressed her disappointment that, in spite of coming from Edinburgh University, I was not actually Scottish, but explained that despite my unfortunate English origins I was a 'nice *Sassenach*' and welcome in her home.[19] For these Kindertransportees, the meaning of being Scottish remains heavily charged in their imagination. Elsie, who now lives in the United States, proudly asserts an abundance of perceived Scottish national sentiments, prejudices and cultural peculiarities:

> It feels familiar hearing the Scottish accent. . . . A really warm feeling about anything to do with Scotland.
>
> I am somewhat prejudiced . . . how can you grow up in Scotland otherwise, but you are a nice *Sassenach,* but I was never exposed very much to English people.[20]

Those who could not or did not wish to remain in Scotland frequently point to an underlining connection with the Scottish diaspora community and followed uniquely Scottish migration routes and settlement areas. Areas with a large Scottish contingency in Israel were particularly popular with Kindertransportees who had undertaken pre-*hachsharot* training in Scotland. Among the founders of *Kfar* Hanassi and *Kibbutz* Amiad were a significant number of Glaswegian Jews. These Kindertransportees' life narratives are constructed in a way that firmly attaches them to a wider Scottish diaspora migration story and in doing so advocates a strong Scottish affiliation.

Resident Kindertransportees of 'Scottish' settlements argue that their new community continues to resonate a Scottish connection to the present day. Enclaves of Scottish migrants commonly form various public institutions for the expression of their Scottish 'ethnocentrism'.[21] Expressions of national identity can include parades, memorials, folklore, popular heroes/heroines and national recreations.[22] *Kibbutz* Amiad organized annual Burns' Nights until the 1980s and one resident believes that there is still a strong Scottish influence on the character of the *Kibbutz*, including accent, humour and other specifically 'Scottish' cultural peculiarities.[23]

The seeming contradiction that exists within this narrative – expressions of a strong ethnocentric attachment to Scotland, juxtaposed with the decisions not to live in Scotland – is explained by Kindertransportees as arising from a number of additional factors. One of these is that Kindertransportees were responsive to factors driving migration from Scotland per se. Kindertransportees were part of Scotland's economic emigration. Economic difficulties of the area were a particularly important factor driving Scottish youth into diaspora circumstances.[24] Economic reasons factored highly in the Kindertransportees' decision-making for migration. Because of a lack of financial support, Kindertransportees had to be self-supporting and financially astute. This meant that the desire for better jobs and greater economic opportunities dominated the plans of many after the war. Eight per cent of the Kindertransportees state that they migrated for opportunities: work, economic gain and educational advancement.[25]

Economic migrants tended to follow financial opportunities south of the border or overseas. Kindertransportees who remained in Scotland tended to gravitate towards either Glasgow (67%) or Edinburgh.[26] However, the majority left Scotland and moved to large cities, especially to London. The United States also offered greater financial rewards. Twenty-eight per cent of those who migrated to the United States did so for opportunities pertaining to either monetary or material gains, work or educational opportunities.[27] Twenty per cent of these migrated specifically to take advantage of educational opportunities.[28] For whatever reason, education emerges as an important draw for Kindertransportees' resettlement choices. In tandem with educational advancement, the desire for economic betterment equated to 40 per cent of Kindertransportees who migrated for better opportunities.[29] Business promotions directed Bert to Venezuela, where he worked as regional manager of a large company until retirement.[30]

The Kindertransportees' decision to migrate overseas was therefore not automatically linked to a desire to leave Scotland. Instead, it reflected the Kindertransportees' pragmatic approach to their lives after 1945. Elsie states:

> I would probably have gone wherever I could make a living, I had learnt that there was a relationship between where you lived, what you do and how you survive, I think my first thing if things had gone normally and there was a teaching job in Scotland I would have gone there . . . it's just a matter of history and familiarity . . .

> you don't expose yourself more than you have to, to stranger things. I had already had plenty of experience of being uprooted and I would have had to make still another adjustment. I would never have said "no, I could never go to England".[31]

Bauer reiterates this point as she explains the sharp improvement in lifestyle after migrating to the United States: "during the war we were permitted one pat of butter once a week . . . in Ellis Island we had all the butter we could eat . . . in Ellis Island we had napkins everyday . . . the contrast was so big".[32]

Patterns of trans-migration

The status of the Kindertransportees in Britain – unaccompanied trans-migrant youth or children – and the circumstance this afforded them in Scotland, determined important characteristics of their post-war settlement choices, namely an inability to feel truly Scottish and a subsequent tripartite migration narrative. The terms and conditions of the Kindertransportees' entry to Britain had always been that they were migrants in transit.[33] Between 1938 and 1945, neither the CC nor the general public ever discarded these terms or the notion of this trans-migration eventuality. In February 1939, *The Times* assured its readers of the new arrivals' 'ultimate emigration elsewhere'.[34] In 1944, with the close of war in sight, attention returned to the migratory choices of the trans-migrants. In March 1944, an article in the *Scotsman* placed emphasis on the imminent return of refugees to their homelands.[35]

The Kindertransportees were also aware of this expectation for their departure from Britain. One former member of the Kindertransport, Elsie, remembers in an interview that she felt she was 'luggage in advance', never collected for her onward journey.[36] Another interviewee, Dena, states that her time in Scotland was always based on the need to gain certificates to get to Palestine, where she had 'always wanted to go'.[37] Their status, reception, and care in Scotland encouraged the Kindertransportees to feel like visitors and temporary migrants, not as permanent immigrants.

The notion of being an outsider or non-Scot pervades Kindertransportees' life narratives, even those who have remained in Scotland their whole lives. These Kindertransportees continue to emphasize that although they hold a strong affinity to Scotland, they are not Scottish and never will be. Kindertransportees reiterate the 'birth, blood and belonging' identity of 'real' Scotsman.[38] This is explained as a more decisive Scottish identity and one that they do not feel able to claim. As Richard Kiely, Frank Bechhofer and David McCrone have argued, the issue of 'born and brought up' is a powerful ideology, which is felt by immigrants to prevent them from being able to become Scottish.[39] Kindertransportees make reference to their non-Scottish surnames, which lack 'Mc', to distinguish their lack of 'real' Scottish authenticity. Rachel, who still lives in Scotland, explains:

> I can't say I am Scottish because I don't belong to the McDonalds, the McClouds, the McCandels. . . . I always felt an outsider, I always felt that I had to be very careful and I never felt part of it, I couldn't, I knew I was a refugee and I knew there were limitations to what I could expect and what I could demand.[40]

Kindertransportees suggest that they would feel fraudulent if they claimed to be Scottish and that they could never tick all the social and cultural boxes they feel are necessary to qualify. Rachel believes that possessing foreign accents and customs bar her from being a real Scot.[41] Rachel states that, although she could never lay claim to being 'Scottish', she does say, 'I am British'.[42] This trend has also become apparent among English Kindertransportees. They express the belief that being 'British' is less demanding for foreign-born citizens.[43]

The desire to belong and to feel like a true national citizen or community member has also had a central bearing on the Kindertransportees' broader life stories. Kindertransportees who went to the United States stress the privileged position they enjoyed joining an immigrant country, which allowed them to shed their refugee status at an early stage.[44] In contrast, Kindertransportees who remained in Britain express their frustration at being considered outsiders, believing that they never truly integrated.

That the Kindertransportees felt they were both officially and socially considered non-Scots ensured that, despite holding a strong affinity for Scotland, many Kindertransportees chose to migrate. Repatriation to Germany or Austria was not a popular migration option. Instead, the Kindertransportees' intended migratory route was predominantly focused on new destinations, rather than returning to their homelands. Interviewees explain that by 1945 they had become dislocated from their homelands and did not wish to return. Elsie no longer felt 'at home there anymore'.[45] Ariel, like many other Kindertransportees, had left Vienna at a very young age and felt that he had not formed any attachment to the city.[46] Kindertransportees had also often lost their mother tongue and felt unable to return to a linguistically foreign community. Isabel lost her ability to speak German and struggled to engage with German people in later life.[47] Elsie recalls: 'I had lost my German totally, completely, I couldn't read it, I couldn't understand it, I couldn't speak it, so I couldn't even read my parents' letters'.[48]

Fear and loathing is another given reason for their desire not to return to their original homelands. When Isabel did make a return trip, she was preoccupied with evaluating people and their likely roles during the Holocaust.[49] As a result, few Kindertransportees took the opportunity to return to their countries of origin and instead waited for alternative onward migration opportunities.

The long process of waiting for visas meant that Kindertransportees often grasped the first opportunity for further migration. The attainment of the necessary visa or immigration certificate enabled Kindertransportees to fulfil their parents' prearranged plans to meet in America or make *Aliyah* to Palestine or later Israel. Six per cent of Kindertransportees who went to the United States did so purely because they received their visa.[50] Many of the Kindertransportees had been registered for a US visa before they came to Britain on the Kindertransport. Their time in Scotland has sometimes been recalled as a form of purgatory, awaiting a judgement to enable them to move on to their next life in a new country. Elsie's parents had placed her on a visa waiting list for the United States, which took ten years to arrive.[51] She recalls that at 'times I felt a little edgy when I realised this (waiting) could go on forever'.[52] The inability to acquire the necessary documentation meant that the Kindertransportees' migration occurred over a long timescale. Levi remembers that quite a few Kindertransportees received their affidavit for the United States or Palestine and left between May and June 1941.[53] Others, such as Elsie, were not able to leave until the late 1940s.

The trans-migrant basis of the Kindertransportees' status in Britain developed a tripartite pattern to their migration story. Kindertransportees often reflect on their three lives: before, during and after the Kindertransport. They began their migration earlier than most Holocaust survivors and most Kindertransportees stayed in Britain for many years before onward migration. This meant that the British part of their passage remained an important element of their story. The opening quotation to this chapter, which is taken from an interview, explains the importance of the tripartite migration experience. Benson, who migrated to Israel, believes he is not only a Czech, but also equally a Scot and a Jew or Israeli.[54] Another Kindertransportee narrates her life story in three neat packages:

> I have my Austrian life, my Scottish life and my American life. . . . My first ten years in Austria were one life, then in Scotland I had another life completely, you just got picked up out of one life and dumped into another, and then coming to America that was my third life, which seemed to have very little to do with either life one or two.[55]

The tripartite structure of their migration, as mentioned previously, has developed disjointed and unattached sections to their lives. Kindertransportees reflect on the lack of overarching continuity across their lifespan. Elsie, who narrated her Austrian, Scottish and American lives as three defining eras, notes that her greatest remorse is the lack of continuity compared to her husband's life:

> I miss the continuity in my life very much and as I get older perhaps even more. . . . I do not know anyone from my first life except my cousin, but nobody has known me throughout my three lives. . . . I have a different relationship with all these people, that's the one thing I really feel very jealous of my husband, who has a continuum, all his life of the same people and the same places. . . a normal life.[56]

This tripartite structure has also meant that the latter stage of the Kindertransportees' trans-migration journey is not usually presented by Kindertransportees as their big migration experience. Instead, it is portrayed as the conclusion to a broader story of migration beginning before the war with the Kindertransport. As such, after 1945, the initial migration was the last major relocation of 93 per cent of Kindertransportees as they chose to remain permanently rooted to that first chosen resettlement nation.[57] This pattern may be linked to the trauma of the initial migratory experience via the Kindertransport. Bauer explains that she simply could not bring herself to be uprooted again.[58]

Nevertheless, a lesser number of Kindertransportees broke this tripartite structure and made multiple migrations after 1945. The Kindertransportees were unaccompanied minors and expressed their sense of freedom and adventure during this period. In 1945, most Kindertransportees were still living independently with few commitments or geographic ties. There is a sense of 'why not' and an experiment with migration choices. Hubbers recalls her decision to go to a *hachshara:*

> I was in a couple of camps and a couple of families. In the second camp I went to, a lady came round and asked if there was anyone who was interested in going to Israel. . . . I thought yes this was a good idea I will go on *hachshara* and from there I could go to Israel.[59]

Seven per cent of Scotland's Kindertransportees made multiple migrations, while others relocated within their chosen country.[60] Multiple migrations even included transatlantic moves. These tended to be between the United States and Israel.

The presence of multiple migrations may be attributed to a lack of supervision or guidance felt by many Kindertransportees as unaccompanied minors. The migration pattern suggests a degree of confusion about where to go and a lack of clear guidance concerning how to get there. Eighty-three per cent of former members of the Kindertransport, who made multiple migrations, migrated first to Israel before deciding to go to the United States.[61] Disillusionment with the reality of the *kibbutzim* lifestyle was a contributing factor for some Kindertransportees' decision to leave Israel.[62] Israel was often seen by Kindertransportees as a tough place to live with limited opportunities outside of manual labouring.[63] The United States offered greater educational or career opportunities. One interviewee mentions how he went to the United States to study at university after becoming disillusioned with manual or labouring lifestyles in Israel.[64]

It is also apparent that many more Kindertransportees would have made multiple migrations had they been able to do so. Elsie went to the United States and immediately wished to return to Scotland or migrate elsewhere. However, she had to find employment because she lacked the money needed for her return passage.[65] She then decided to stay in the United States by the time she had managed to raise enough money. The limited level of support and financial assistance for the Kindertransportees not only kept them abroad, such as those who may have wished to return or re-migrate, but also prevented some from leaving Scotland. By 1945, 54 per cent of Kindertransportees were orphans and the majority were deemed too old to remain dependent on welfare.[66] This meant that many found they lacked a support network during the resettlement process.[67] One Kindertransportee who still lives in Scotland explains her reluctance to move due to fear and financial uncertainty.[68]

This lack of support meant that migration eventualities were often due to chance and luck. Jacob was extremely keen to gain a certificate for Palestine and make *Aliyah* during the war years.[69] However, due to miscommunication and a lack of information, he missed his opportunity. Jacob recalls Youth Aliyah explaining that they had been searching for him for many years when his name came up as a candidate for *Aliyah*. Unfortunately, contact with him was only made ten days after he passed the maximum age restriction for the certificate.

Individual preferences about where to go or not were also relevant for the Kindertransportees' migration patterns. The ability to pursue these goals was limited by a lack of resources, yet Kindertransportees still played a determining role in their resettlement plans. This point has frequently been overlooked in favour of the notion that Kindertransportees were minors led by older Jewish refugee migrants, or channelled into particular migration choices to fulfil quotas. This was the case for some Kindertransportees, yet a significant number were able to direct their own migration paths.

The Kindertransportees' role in determining migration options was often by way of refusing resettlement or travel plans. In 1947, Jacob rejected an offer to become naturalized in Britain, stating that 'it wasn't my ambition'.[70] Jacob's decision at the age of 19 went against his father's wishes. Kindertransportees who attended Scotland's pre-*hachsharot* maintained a certainty that they would not migrate to Israel and they never did. Debbie states that 'never, never, ever in a lifetime would I move to Israel. When I went to Polton House I had never heard of Zionism. . . . It had no pull for me'.[71] On the other hand, Kindertransportees astutely sought out *hachsharot* training programmes as a means for migration to Palestine. Bratt recalls that 'it was always my dream to go to Israel, to train for that and by expressing that I was transferred to a *hachshara* or training establishment for Israel'.[72]

The Kindertransportees also often chose to follow friends in migration. Due to the terms and conditions of their entry to Britain – requiring them to enter unaccompanied – and the inability of most of their parents to exit Greater Germany thereafter, the vast majority of Kindertransportees felt a parental void for the duration of the war years.[73] This made peer-group ties extremely important to them as they felt they lacked maternal or paternal support.[74] These ties played a central role in influencing the minors' settlement choices. Elijah explains that he did not question his decision to follow his friends abroad.[75] This was particularly true in migration to Israel, where *Gar'in* (family groups) made *Aliyah* together. The *Gar'in* developed from friendship ties in *hachsharot* and would eventually provide the foundations for a new *kibbutz*. Friendship groups that were formed at Whittingehame Farm School today remain together in two main settlements in Israel: *Kfar* Hanassi and *Kibbutz* Lavi.[76]

In 1945, the majority of Kindertransportees remained unaccompanied or were now orphaned. Ute Benz has pointed to the traumatic implications for Kindertransportees of their separation and loss of family or home life during the war.[77] For some, the end to the war enabled family reunions and these became dominant features in migration plans. M. Boyd has shown how 'family and personal networks' emerged as important variables for international migration choices.[78] Elsie's parents were both killed in the Holocaust, yet she felt desperate to acquire her affidavit for the United States in order to 'come to my family, the only family I had'.[79] Elsie eventually joined her 'American family' and lived with her aunt in the United States. Jacob wanted to migrate to Israel in order 'to join my brothers and my mother'.[80] Bratt recalls the negotiations that took place with his father, which brought them to the United States in 1948.[81] These decisions prioritized the need to keep the family together:

> They both approached me and said listen we don't want to stay in United Kingdom, we have relatives and you have to be with family together and we want to go to the United States, we would appreciate it if you would come with us.[82]

The importance of family reunions to migration patterns has been reflected in the statistics drawn from the recent worldwide Kindertransport survey. This has shown that family reunions were the second largest given cause for further migration (11%).[83] Forty-four per cent of Kindertransportees who migrated to the United States did so in order to be reunited with family members. Forty-six per cent of Kindertransportees were reunited with at least one parent; 64 per cent of these were reunited with both parents and the place of reunion was highly influential in resettlement decisions; of these, 49 per cent were reunited in Britain, 29 per cent in Israel and 22 per cent in the United States . These figures closely mirror the current national locations of Kindertransportees: 47 per cent in Britain, 25 per cent in Israel and 23 per cent in the United States. Of those who were reunited in the United States, they tended to resettle in close proximity to where the reunion with their parents occurred; for example, 63 per cent were reunited in New York and 25 per cent in California. Today, 42 per cent of former members of the Kindertransport live in New York and 21 per cent live in California, the two largest concentrations of Kindertransportee settlement in the United States. However, reunions did not always prescribe long-term settlement. Forty-one per cent of Scotland's Kindertransportees who were reunited in the United Kingdom were reunited in Scotland, yet only 13 per cent of Kindertransportees remained in Scotland.

For Kindertransportees whose parents had been killed, migration decisions were also often influenced by memories and nostalgic beliefs in parents' dreams and wishes for their children. This belief was particularly used in relation to migrations to the United States or Israel. Interviewees explain that their destination had always been their parents' goal. Ariel states that he went to the United States because 'that was the plan' of his parents.[84] Isabel explains that, 'I always knew I was coming to America . . . my parents had planned to come to this country and I felt that it was my duty to come to this country'.[85] In the absence of a father, Jacob's brother had influenced his migration decision:

> My eldest brother . . . growing up without my father, he was my role model and that was where I was going. He was killed two and a half months after he arrived in this country. But this role model took me and kept me in the *kibbutz* for a long time.[86]

The Kindertransportees' migration story also reflects a connection to the wider movements in population demographics, especially those movements of displaced refugees following the Holocaust.[87] Their experience often prioritized choices that would provide a sense of belonging and security and enable a degree of permanency. Berger has emphasized the role of refugees' sense of permanent 'rootlessness' and their subsequent preoccupation with seeking a place of belonging.[88] These migratory objectives often lie behind reasons given for choosing to live in Israel. However, this point is not to be confused with the 'traditional diaspora experience', which Berger argues led all Jews to wait for the first opportunity to return to their homeland in Zion.[89] This was not applicable to Kindertransportees. They held a particular connection to post-Holocaust Jewish migratory patterns that drew even non-Zionists to Palestine in the search of socio-economic and political security.

For others, security and permanency were symbolized in the creation of a family. By 1945 an estimated 54 per cent of all Kindertransportees were orphans.[90] Establishing roots, by way of a new family unit or place of belonging, dominated many of the Kindertransportees' activities. Marriage constituted 5 per cent of given reasons for migration.[91] This particularly affected females. Eleven per cent of Kindertransportees who migrated to the United States did so because of marriage.[92]

As displaced persons, the Kindertransportees also sought to relocate to areas with more cultural and social familiarity to them. Cultural differences did play a role in creating problems for continental migrants settling in Scotland.[93] Some interviewees express having never felt totally at home in Scotland or familiar with Scottish culture.[94] This led to them relocating to areas popular with other refugees from Central Europe, who shared similar cultural and social backgrounds. Most Kindertransportees who remained in Scotland gravitated towards Glasgow, the hub of Jewish immigrant life in Scotland.[95] Those who migrated to England tended to opt for London. Sixty-two per cent of Kindertransportees in Britain settled in Greater London;[96] 67 per cent of these Kindertransportees moved to North London, predominantly to Middlesex and to areas surrounding Hampstead and Golders Green. This mirrored the wider Jewish refugee communities' preferences for the affordable suburbs of North London. Continental enclaves emerged in these areas.[97] Kindertransportees' affinity to other Jewish refugees is also underlined by their preference for marriage partners: 30 per cent married a Holocaust survivor and 40 per cent of these are stated to be fellow Kindertransportees.[98]

The trends that emerge in the Kindertransportees' post-war migration are also reflective of general post-war demographic shifts around the world. This was very much linked to ideological goals for a better life in the aftermath of the war. This drew a substantial number of Scots to locations across the world, such as Australia and New Zealand. Kindertransportees who took these routes express the importance of this geographical separation of their new 'home' from associations of war. Five per cent of Kindertransportees migrated to alternative destinations to England, Israel and the United States, instead choosing Nepal, South America, New Zealand and Canada. One Kindertransportee chose Ottawa in Canada as an experiment for a new life and another migrated to New Zealand to escape the associations of war and violence with Europe.[99]

Ideological commitments, such as communism, pacifism and Zionism, drew Kindertransportees to new countries that offered to meet their Utopian ideals. Nineteen per cent of Scotland's Kindertransportees stated that Zionism was their main reason for migration. Unsurprisingly, all of those who stated 'Zionism' as their reason for migration chose to make *Aliyah* to Israel. Zionism had a significant support network among Scotland's Jews.[100] Kindertransportees were commonly nurtured towards a Zionist-inspired lifestyle and a significant number underwent the two-year training programme at one of Scotland's pre-*hachsharot*. Chapter 4 has shown that this did not automatically infuse Zionist zeal into all trainees. Nonetheless, it did lead a significant number of Scotland's Kindertransportees to choose to migrate to Israel, sometimes temporarily, based on their humanitarian or Zionist beliefs. Some went to aid the influx of destitute Holocaust survivors, while others wished to help establish the infrastructure needed for the new nation. This included founding a *kibbutz* and offering specific skills in other fields, such as nursing gained during the war.[101] Between 1947 and 1953, Kindertransportees also volunteered for the Israel Defence Forces.[102]

The desire to dislocate themselves from being Jewish was also important in some Kindertransportees' migratory choices. Kindertransportees explain that this was because they feared the return of anti-Semitism in the future and sought to protect their new families from undue persecution and social insecurity. Debbie does not want her children to be Jewish.[103] She still fears for the inevitable impact of anti-Semitism in the future and has distanced herself and her family from other Jewish communities in London. Kindertransportees in Britain and the United States often relocated to areas isolated from Jewish communities. In England, locations such as Yorkshire, Cambridgeshire, Worcestershire and Henley-on-Thames were chosen, where Kindertransportees sought little or no participation with the nearest Jewish community.[104] In the United States, individual Kindertransportees settled in areas with limited Jewish activity, including Brewer in Maine, Beachwood in Ohio, Highland Park in Illinois and Reading in Pennsylvania.[105]

*

Scotland experienced a mass exodus of Kindertransportees after 1945. However, these statistics should not be interpreted as an indication of Scotland's limited influence on the Kindertransportees' future lives. Kindertransportees not only express a celebratory connection to ambiguous clichéd symbols of Scottishness, but also reveal the importance of England as the distinct demarcation of not being Scottish. Kindertransportees express a prevalence of Scottish nationalist sentiments. In interviews, Kindertransportees have utilized the Gaelic term *Sassenach* to refer derogatively to an English person as an inferior outsider or a non-Scot.[106]

The complexity of their forced migration story, however, has meant that, despite this loyalty, most feel unable to proclaim that they are Scottish. Instead, Kindertransportees' proclaim 'Britishness' and reflect a deep-rooted insecurity about membership and belonging. The idea of being 'truly Scottish', having been both born and brought up within Scotland, prevents Kindertransportees from feeling able to ascribe themselves a complete Scottish identity.[107] The Kindertransportees make a distinction between 'feeling Scottish and definitively saying "I am Scottish" '.[108]

A desire to counter these insecurities and displacement issues became central to many Kindertransportees' migration and resettlement decisions. These often prioritized family reunions, daily stability, permanency, roots, belonging and a sense of membership to a group, over an immediate Scottish connection. These priorities drew many Kindertransportees from Scotland, but not necessarily from the concept of being part of a Scottish people. Bermant once noted that 'when Scottish Jews assimilate they tend to become Anglicised rather than Scotticised'.[109] This does ring true for Kindertransportees who have remained in Scotland and who struggle to attribute to themselves true Scottish membership. Yet for those who left Scotland it seems that they have clung more closely to the idea of having been 'Scotticised' and it was this legacy of having once been part of Scotland that emerges as the most profound Scottish inheritance for the Kindertransportees.

Notes

1 FWPC/Benson.
2 KA: QU/SUP.
3 Ibid.
4 KA: QU/SUP.
5 Combes, Hibbert, Hogg and Varey, 'Consuming Identity', 328.
6 Ibid., 331.
7 Eric Hobsbawm, 'Introduction: Inventing Traditions', in Hobsbawm and Ranger (eds), *The Invention of Tradition*, 12; Hugh Trevor-Roper, 'The Invention of Tradition: The Highland Tradition of Scotland', in Eric Hobsbawm and T. Ranger (eds), *The Invention of Tradition* (Cambridge: Cambridge University Press, 1983), 15.
8 Trevor-Roper, 'The Invention of Traditions', in Hobsbawm and Ranger (eds), *The Invention of Tradition*, 15.
9 R. Nicholson, 'From Ramsay's *Flora MacDonald* to Raeburn's *MacNab*: The Use of Tartan as a Symbol of Identity?', *Textile History*, 36, 2 (2005), 146.
10 Angela McCarthy, 'Scottish National Identities among Inter-war Migrants in North America and Australasia', *The Journal of Imperial and Commonwealth History*, 34, 2 (June 2006), 201.
11 Ibid., 202.
12 McCarthy, 'Scottish National Identities', 202.
13 FWPC/Benson.
14 Ibid., 202.
15 FWPC/Jan.
16 FWPC/Marthe.
17 FWPC/Rachel.
18 FWPC/Rachel, Elsie.
19 FWPC/Elsie.
20 Ibid.
21 Combes, Hibbert, Hogg and Varey, 'Consuming Identity', 329.
22 Anthony Smith, *National Identity* (London: Penguin, 1991).
23 FWPC/Benson.
24 Berthoff, review of Hollingsworth, 'Migration'.
25 KA: QU/SUP.
26 Ibid.
27 Ibid.
28 Ibid.
29 Ibid.
30 FWPC/Bert: Memoir.
31 FWPC/Elsie.

32 WHMA/SC:RG-50.166*03.
33 Curio, '"Invisible" children', 41–56.
34 *Times*, 9 February 1939.
35 *Scotsman*, 21 March 1944.
36 FWPC/Elsie.
37 FWPC/Dena.
38 Richard Kiely, Frank Bechhofer and David McCrone, 'Birth, blood and belonging: identity claims in post-devolution Scotland', *The Sociological Review*, 2005, 150–171.
39 Ibid., 156.
40 FWPC/Rachel.
41 Ibid.
42 Ibid.
43 FWPC/Noah.
44 FWPC/Jan, Isabel.
45 FWPC/Elsie.
46 FWPC/Ariel.
47 FWPC/Isabel.
48 FWPC/Elsie.
49 FWPC/Isabel.
50 KA: QU/SUP.
51 FWPC/Elsie.
52 Ibid.
53 FWPC/Levi.
54 FWPC/Benson.
55 FWPC/Elsie.
56 Ibid.
57 KA: QU/SUP.
58 WHMA/SC/RG-50.166*03.
59 WHMA/USC: 43138.
60 KA: QU/SUP.
61 Ibid.
62 FWPC/Rachel, Edna.
63 FWPC/Rachel, Edna and Abaigael.
64 FWPC/Benson.
65 FWPC/Elsie.
66 KA: QU/SUP.
67 For further details about Scotland's limited welfare facilities see Finlayson, *Citizen, State and Social Welfare in Britain;* Abrams, *The Orphan Country.*
68 FWPC/Marthe.

69 FWPC/Jacob.
70 Ibid.
71 FWPC/Debbie.
72 WHMA/USC: 36790.
73 WHMA/USC: 43932; FWPC/Elijah, Edna.
74 FWPC/Edna, Elijah.
75 FWPC/Elijah.
76 See Chapter 4 for more information about Scotland's pre-*hachsharot* centres; See also Amkraut, 'Zionist Attitudes towards YA from Germany'; Edelston, "Uprooting and Resettlement"; *25 Years of YA.*
77 Benz, 'Traumatization through Separation', 85–99.
78 Boyd, 'Family and personal networks', 638–70.
79 FWPC/Elsie.
80 FWPC/Jacob.
81 WHM/USC: 36790.
82 Ibid.
83 KA: QU/SUP.
84 FWPC/Ariel.
85 FWPC/Isabel.
86 FWPC/Jacob.
87 See Mark Wyman, *DPs: Europe's Displaced Persons, 1945–1951* (Cornell: Cornell University Press, 1998); Arieh Kochavi, *Post-Holocaust Politics: Britain, the United States, & Jewish Refugees, 1945–1948* (Chapel Hill: University of North Carolina Press, 2001).
88 Berger, 'Jewish Identity and Jewish Destiny', 84.
89 Ibid.
90 KA: QU/SUP.
91 Ibid.
92 Ibid.
93 Kölmel, 'Problems of Settlement', 251.
94 FWPC/Marthe, Rachel, Gabby, Johan.
95 FWPC/Johan, Gabby, Rachel.
96 KA: QU/SUP.
97 See Berghahn, *Continental Britons.*
98 Ibid.
99 FWPC/Ruth.
100 See Braber, *Jews in Glasgow;* Collins, *Aspects of Scottish Jewry;* Collins; *Second City Jewry.*
101 FWPC/Rachel.
102 FWPC/Rachel, Edna.
103 FWPC/Debbie.

104 KA: QU/SUP.

105 Ibid.

106 FWPC/Rachel, Elsie.

107 Kiely, Bechhofer and McCrone, 'Birth, blood and belonging', 152.

108 Ibid., 164.

109 Bermant, 'Memoir of an E-European immigrant to Glasgow', 59.

Appendix 1

The Kindertransport Association's Worldwide Kindertransport Questionnaire[1]

1

KINDERTRANSPORT SURVEY

'Making New Lives in Britain'
January 2007

PART 2: QUESTIONNAIRE

1. Kindertransportee Details

Date of Birth: 15 | 06 | 27 (DD MM YEAR)

Town & Country of origin: BERLIN, GERMANY

Original nationality (eg German, Austrian, Czech): GERMAN

Male ☑ Female ☐

Parents' religious affiliation (eg Jewish Orthodox, Liberal, other): JEWISH – LIBERAL

Current location (town, country): WEYBRIDGE, GB

Current nationality (eg British, American, German, Czech): BRITISH

Current religious affiliation (Jewish Orthodox, Liberal, other): JEWISH REFORM

2. Departure on Kindertransport

Point of departure: BERLIN

Travelled via (eg Holland, Hamburg): HOLLAND

Date of departure: 01 | 12 | 38 (DD MM YEAR)

Details of any accompanying brothers or sisters:

Age....... Male ☐ Female ☐
Age....... Male ☐ Female ☐ NONE
Age....... Male ☐ Female ☐

3. Arrival in Britain

Place(s) of arrival: Port (eg Harwich): HARWICH
Main Railway station (eg Liverpool Street): ....

Age on arrival (years): 11 ½

Date of arrival: 02 | 12 | 38 (DD MM YEAR)

Separated from siblings Yes ☑ No ☐

6. Evacuation & Internment

i. Were you evacuated Age .... Yes ☐ No ☑

Location/ Lodged with..

ii. Were you interned Age .... Yes ☐ No ☑

How long for..

Location/ Name of Ship if applicable ....

7. Education

Type of school prior to emigration HÖHERE SCHULE DER JÜDISCHEN GEMEINDE, BERLIN

School(s) attended in Britain ...GREEN PARK COLLEGE, BATH.............

.... Age at leaving School....16..........

Further & Higher Education: institution/college/university ..../...........................

....

Please *circle*: full time/part time/night school/technical training/other ....

Scholarships/bursaries, qualifications, diplomas, degrees, awards, civil decorations, etc.

....

....

8. Employment and War Service

Unpaid domestic work in the home Yes ☐ No ☑

Type(s) of paid employment..

Age began work.................................

War work (incl. nursing, fire service, other) 1 YEAR AMBULANCE DRIVER

Did you work for yourself Yes ☐ No ☑

Trade/Profession/highest position achieved...

....

Voluntary activities (eg Home Guard, ARP, fire watching) ....

Did you serve in the forces/other uniformed service Yes ☑ No ☐

Branch and length of service RASC, 3½ YEARS

Were you posted abroad Yes ☑ No ☐

Where.........EGYPT – MIDDLE EAST LAND FORCES

Final rank ..T/CAPT............. Military decorations...

9. What was the fate of your parents

Father .....SUICIDE, BERLIN 1942

Mother.......DIED, CANCER, 1933

If you were re-united, when and where............/...................................

BROTHER – AUSCHWITZ, 1943

Note

1 Example questionnaire used with permission from Joseph (FWPC).

Appendix 2

Kindertransport Associations' New Database (KA: QU/SUP)[1]

Ref	Day of birth	Month of birth	Year of birth	Town of origin	Country of origin	Original nationality	Gender
33	27	2	31	Frankfurt am Main	Germany	German	F
313	18	7	23	Hamburg	Germany	German	F
325	12	8	25	Vienna	Austria	Austrian	M
396	8	12	31	Kassel	Germany	German	F
412	5	12	25	Dusseldorf	Germany	German	F
438	3	3	34	Vienna	Austria	Austrian	M
2210	8	25	26	Berlin	Germany	German	F
19	31	8	25	Vienna	Austria	Austrian	F
223	29	5	30	Hannover	Germany	German	F
330	11	7	21	Berlin	Germany	German	F
443	23	2	24	Nuremberg	Germany	German	M
532	25	8	30	Ruhla	Germany	German	F
1074	25	2	34	Hronov	Czechoslovakia	Czech	M
1143	14	5	26	Koenigsberg	Germany	German	F
1145	19	8	24	Koenigsberg	Germany	German	F
1147	3	8	21	Koenigsberg	Germany	German	F
2085	31	8	33	Vienna	Austria	Austrian	M
2111	23	5	23	Vienna	Austria	Austrian	M

Note

1 http://www.ajr.org.uk/kindersurvey.

Appendix 3

A Selection of Biographies from Interviewees

Frances Williams' private collection (FWPC):

1 Benson

Born in 1934 in a small town near Prague called Ranov, Czechoslovakia, his father managed a textile factory. His family was not religious, but totally secular and non-practising. Benson considers himself to be one of Nicholas Winton's saved 'children'. An elderly Jewish and Zionist lady in Glasgow fostered him for the duration of the war. He felt totally absorbed into the family. He spoke Yiddish to his foster family on arrival as a means to communicate. He did find himself in a more pious Jewish environment and he struggled to adapt to his new Orthodox Jewish upbringing and education in Glasgow. He joined Habonim and eventually went on *hachshara* training to reading. He made *Aliyah* and became a founding member of *Kibbutz* Amiad. He tried to preserve Scottish traditions in later life. He currently lives in *Kibbutz* Amiad, Israel.

2 Ariel

Born in 1923, he lived in Vienna, Austria. His mother was a physician and his father a banker and lawyer. He came from an observant Jewish family, but with no Zionist connection. Ariel attended a gymnasium and intended to go to university. His father was sent to Dachau before he was sent on the Kindertransport. In Edinburgh, a non-Jewish male Danish immigrant fostered him. His foster father purchased tickets for his parents to go to Shanghai, China. This secured the release of his father from Dachau. On route to Shanghai his parents arrived in Britain and gained asylum. His parents thereafter worked as domestics in England. He joined his parents in Birmingham in July 1939. He was later interned with his father. They were then separated and he was sent to York internment camp. In 1940 he migrated with his parents to the

United States. He joined the army and this helped him gain a BA and MA. He focuses much of his narrative on pre-migration wider historical events and then his personal life after migrating to the United States. He currently lives in Maine, USA.

3 Isabel

Born in 1925 in Germany, she first lived in a small town called Korb and later moved to a small agricultural village. She came from a large, yet poor, Conservative Jewish family. Her father led a strictly patriarchal family unit and worked as a cattle dealer, while her mother was a housewife. After the Nazi party came to power the family moved to a big city and later sent the children to Aachen. In March 1939, she and her two sisters departed on the Kindertransport. She was separated from her siblings on arrival and sent to a number of different foster homes in England. She was later evacuated with one of her foster mothers to Kemnay, Scotland. They eventually returned to London. In 1947 she migrated with her siblings to the United States. Her parents did not survive and this prompted her to take on a maternal role with her younger sisters. She currently lives in Silver Spring, USA.

4 Jan

She lived with her Polish parents in Frankfurt, Germany. Her wealthy family ran a fabric and menswear business, and she was brought up by a maid. Her family was Orthodox Jewish. Her Father tried to organize for the whole family to migrate to Palestine. When this failed, he secured a foster family for her in Glasgow. She used the Kindertransport to reach this pre-arranged destination. A wealthy Orthodox family in Pollokshields, Glasgow, initially fostered her, before she was evacuated to the countryside with her school. Her guardian removed her from the school in order for her to provide domestic help at home and to work in his garment factory. She was later asked to leave by her guardian. She wanted to continue schooling. The Glasgow Jewish committee offered her accommodation in a hostel in Glasgow. She rejected this offer due to its poor living conditions. Instead, she moved to London and worked for the Agudas World Organisation to save money for her passage to the United States. She later became a fashion buyer in New York. She was reunited with her parents in the United States, but struggled to readjust to life with them. She currently lives in New York, USA.

5 Marthe

Marthe grew up in Kassel, Germany. Her father worked for a Jewish social care organization. She had a Jewish upbringing. Her father was arrested. Her parents escorted her to Hamburg, where she joined the Kindertransport and took a boat to Britain. Her Christian foster family in Britain was pre-arranged. On departure she was 6 years old. She lived in Edinburgh with her foster family before being evacuated with her school. She experienced xenophobia in Scotland. Her aunt escaped to Britain and stayed with her foster family for 6 months before migrating to the United States. Her Christian foster parents later moved to the Pentland hills. She experienced a Christian social life in Scotland and feels she has forgotten everything about Judaism. She feels she has adopted Scotland as her homeland and currently lives in Ayreshire, Scotland.

6 Elsie

Born in Vienna in 1928, she grew up in a little village on the Czech border until 1938. She felt unaware of her Jewish ancestral links until she became socially ostracized. Her parents had converted to Catholicism and adhered to mainstream Christian rituals. She attended a Catholic convent school before migration. Her father managed a sugar factory, while her mother was a housewife. Her Catholic aunt arranged for her to be sent to a Catholic convent in Aberdeen, Scotland. She grew up in the convent for 16 years. She recalls the cloistered environment during term time. In the holidays she was sent to various care homes. She wanted to become a nun, but was advised by the nuns to explore life first. She received her affidavit 10 years after applying and migrated to the United States. She feels that she has lived three separate lives. While she still feels bonded to Catholicism and to Scotland, she married a Jewish man and now lives as a Jew in the United States.

7 Rachel

Rachel lived in Berlin and came from a political and Orthodox Jewish family. After 1935, she was expelled from her school and sent to a Jewish school. Her father was arrested and sentenced to hard labour. She recalls the impact of *Kristallnacht*. At the age of 13 she left on the Kindertransport. On arrival she was sent to Dovercourt reception camp. She recalls the selection process being traumatic. She was eventually sent with 13 others to a boarding school in Edinburgh. She was then sent to a poor Jewish foster home before being transferred to a wealthier Jewish family, where she worked as a maid. She felt animosity against her from *Ostjuden* Jews in Scotland. She later moved to Peebles to look after evacuated children and then to Glasgow where she lived at the Quaker's Renford Street hostel. She became involved in the Christian community and felt pressured to convert. She was helped to complete her education to the level of Highers. The hostel closed so she decided to train as a nurse. While in Glasgow she was a member of the Sauchihall youth club. She was not a Zionist, but decided to migrate to Palestine to help Holocaust survivors after qualifying as a nurse. She later returned to Scotland, where she was reunited with her mother. She currently lives in Glasgow, Scotland.

8 Debbie

Born in Frankfurt, she lived in Berlin and attended a Jewish School. She recalls no exposure to or experiences of anti-Semitism. Her parents were non-Orthodox Jews. She had a pre-arranged foster placement with an Ultra-Orthodox Jewish family in London. She was later evacuated with her school to Windsor until 1942. At age 14 she was sent to Polton House, Scotland. She does not feel she was ever exposed to Zionism at *the hachshara* centre. At Polton House, she was allowed to pursue secretarial training in Edinburgh rather than undertake agricultural training. She recalls the enjoyment and adventure of her time at Polton House. In later life she has suffered from depression and agoraphobia. She currently lives in London, England.

9 Jacob

Jacob arrived from Herlingham (near Ulm), a small village in southern Germany. His parents were not religious, but he did attend a Jewish boarding school until *Kristallnacht*. In 1938, his brothers were sent to Palestine. His parents were divorced and he lived with his mother. In May 1939 he departed on a Kindertransport. He was sent to a number of Jewish hostels in England: one in Westgate, one in South Croydon, which was run along very Orthodox lines, and another in Eaton Avenue, London. Aged 12, he was evacuated and randomly selected for billeting to a foster lady. He recalls feeling stigmatized because he was from a better social and economic background. He felt isolated from any Jewish community and pressured to anglicize and adopt a British accent. His father escaped to Britain, but was interned. Jacob requested to be transferred to a Jewish and Zionist environment. He was sent to Polton House, Scotland. After Polton House he joined an adult *hachsharot* in England. He missed out on a Youth Aliyah permit because of inadequate information and communication. In 1947 he rejected the opportunity to become a British national and, after working with Holocaust survivors in Europe's DP camps, he made *Aliyah bet* (illegal emigration) to Palestine. He currently lives in *Kfar H*anassi, Israel.

10 Abaigael

Born in 1925 in Vienna, Austria, she had a Traditional Jewish upbringing. Her parents ran a perfumery, and she attended the local gymnasium. She feels she was protected from anti-Semitism, but recalls seeing Hitler during a procession in Vienna. Her father was arrested and sent to Dachau. She left school to help her mother in the perfumery. She was later sent to a Jewish school. The perfumery was ransacked on *Kristallnacht.* She departed on the Kindertransport to Harwich and was taken to a reception camp. Along with her friend from Austria, she was chosen to live with a poor non-Jewish foster family from Lincoln. The family could not afford to keep them, so they were sent to Dovercourt reception camp. She was then separated from her friend and sent to Whittingehame Farm School, Scotland. She was not involved in the Zionist groups, but instead joined the Scouts. In 1941, she was sent to an adult *hachsharot* in Devon, at which point she decided she did not want to live a pioneer's lifestyle. She moved to London and worked as a dressmaker. She was reunited with her father in Vienna in 1947. She currently lives in Middlesex, England.

11 Dena

She was born in 1924 in Poland, but lived in Vienna, Austria. Her parents were Orthodox Jews. She attended the local gymnasium until the Anschluss, when she moved to a Jewish Zionist school. Her siblings had migrated to Britain, where they worked as agricultural labourers. Her father was taken to Dachau and died in 1938. She departed on the Kindertransport in 1938. On arrival she was sent to Lowestoft, before being taken to Whittingehame Farm School. She was among the first residents to arrive at Whittingehame and worked to clean and prepare the facility for its opening. She became a member of the Habonim Zionist youth group. She went on to join two adult *hachsharot in* England. She currently lives in *Kfar* Hanassi, Israel.

12 Josephine

Josephine came from Berlin, Germany. Her parents were non-observant Orthodox Jews. She attended a religious Jewish school. She departed on the Kindertransport age 16. Her care at Whittingehame Farm School was arranged before her migration to Britain on the Kindertransport. After Whittingehame, she went on to join the David Eder farm, an adult *hachsharot in* England. She migrated to Palestine with Youth Aliyah, where she later joined the British Army. She returned to England, but found it difficult to integrate into British Jewish communities. She currently lives in London, England.

13 Levi

Born in Berlin, Germany, to Polish parents, he had an Orthodox Jewish upbringing. He attended religious Jewish school and was fluent in Yiddish and Hebrew. In October 1938, his father was expelled as a Polish Jew. He recalls the impact of anti-Semitism on his family, friends and the Jewish community. He was a member of a Bachad Zionist youth group. Under the auspices of Youth Aliyah and B'nai B'rith he departed on the Kindertransport. On arrival he was sent to Whittingehame Farm School. He was expelled after campaigning against the absence of Madrichem, but was swiftly allowed to return. He left in 1941 and went to an adult *hachsharot* in Buckingham, England. He later became a staff member of Polton House, Scotland. He then joined the army and later established a Kosher butchers in Luton, England. He made *Aliyah* in 1972 and now lives between Jerusalem, Israel and Golders Green, London, England.

14 Elijah

Born in 1924 in Warsaw, Poland, he had a non-Orthodox Jewish upbringing. Aged 5, his parents moved the family to Danzig, Germany. He attended a Polish school, before being expelled in 1937 for being Jewish. Because no Jewish school existed, his education ended. His family was very poor, so his Father stayed in Poland to work in order to earn money. He was a member of a Zionist youth group in Danzig. He departed on the Kindertransport with one of his sisters. He was fostered by a very Orthodox Jewish family, but struggled to integrate into the strict Orthodoxy of Anglo-Jewry. As a result, he ran away from this foster home and was sent to Whittingehame Farm School. He became a member of the Habonim Zionist youth group. He felt stigmatized by other Kindertransportees because of his Polish heritage. He later joined two adult *hachshara* in England.

He made *Aliyah Bet* to Palestine and became a founding member of *Kfar* Hanassi. He currently lives in *Kfar* Hanassi, Israel.

15 Nathan

Born in 1924 in Vienna, Austria, Nathan came from an observant Orthodox Jewish family. He attended a non-denominational school before being forced to leave because he was Jewish. He departed on the Kindertransport and was sent to the Dovercourt reception camp. He was then sent to Whittingehame Farm School. He was later interned for four months before returning to Whittingehame Farm School. He became a member of the Bachad Zionist youth group. After Whittingehame, he went with his Bachad youth group to an adult *hachshara* in Wales. They made *Aliyah* together and he helped to found Kibbutz Lavi, Israel. He currently lives in Kibbutz Lavi, Israel.

16 Ranita

Born in Berlin, Germany, she came from a very religious Russian Jewish family. She departed on the Kindertransport and was sent directly to Whittingehame Farm School. She became a member of the Bachad Zionist youth group. After Whittingehame, she decided to go to London to join her two sisters. She worked in Welling Garden city. She currently lives in *Kibbutz* Lavi, Israel.

17 Edna

Edna came from an Orthodox German Jewish family. She places great emphasis within her narrative upon the friendship that existed between her mother and Recha Freier of Youth Aliyah. She departed on the Kindertransport to Whittingehame Farm School. She became a member of the Bachad Zionist youth group. After Whittingehame, she was sent to a domestic work placement in rural Scotland, where she felt very isolated. She made *Aliyah* and lived on a *kibbutz* with her husband. However, she decided she did not want to live on a *kibbutz* and currently lives in Jerusalem, Israel.

18 Johan

He was born in 1924 in Nuremburg, Germany. His father was non-Jewish. He attended the Realschule Furth. In May 1939 he departed on the Kindertransport and was fostered by a Jewish lady in Glasgow. He was later evacuated to a farm in Perth, Scotland. He returned to Glasgow after Perth became a protected area. After failing to register as an alien at the age of 16, he was interned on the Isle of Man. He worked as a cook in the camp, before being released and sent back to Glasgow. In Glasgow, he continued to work as a chef and later became a Jewish caterer. He was a member of the Sauchihall Street youth club in Glasgow. He currently lives in Glasgow, Scotland.

19 Bert

Born in Prague, Bert's Jewish family originated in Poland and was Ultra-Orthodox. In 1934, his grandmother sent him to Vienna to live with his uncle and aunt. In May 1939, he departed on the Kindertransport and was sent to the Jewish Gertrude Jacobson Orphanage, Glasgow. He was later evacuated to the Birkenward hostel in Skelmorlie, Scotland. He eventually migrated to the United States to join his family. He joined the US Army and later went to an American University in Mexico City. Due to work opportunities, he moved to Peru and became the manager of Johnson and Johnson. He currently lives in Venezuela.

Washington DC's Holocaust Memorial Museum's archive:

20 Lola L. Sprinzeles (nee Schneider)

Born in 1929 in Vienna, Austria, her family were observant Conservative Jews from Austria-Hungary, an area that later became part of Poland. She experienced a very patriarchal upbringing. Her father was a teacher and ordained Rabbis. She went to a fee-paying Jewish high school. She recalls the impact of anti-Semitism upon her friends and family. In 1938, her brother made *Aliyah Bet* to Palestine. On *Kristallnacht* her father was arrested and taken for forced labour, while the family home was confiscated. She was sent on the Kindertransport, but remained adamant that she did not want to be fostered. She believes she chose to go to Whittingehame Farm School. She was then sent to an adult *hachshara,* but chose to attend high school independently in Manchester. She later volunteered as a nurse for the Jewish army in Israel. In 1948 she became a British citizen. She was reunited with her parents in Israel. She returned to England, but later migrated to the United States to pursue an academic education. She currently lives in New York, USA.

21 Sidney Bratt

Born in 1928 in Guttstadt, a small farming town in Germany, his parents originated in Poland. He came from an observant Traditional Jewish family and attended Hebrew school and the synagogue. His family was poor and uneducated. His father was a trader. His father was arrested on *Kristallnacht* and he did not see him again for 3 years. Bratt recalls anti-Semitism in Germany and the pre-occupation of the Jewish community to emigrate. He moved to a Jewish school and then later went from Berlin on the Kindertransport. He was the only sibling in his family to leave. Until May 1940, he was sent to a reception camp in Clayton, Suffolk. In August 1939, his father migrated to England, but was sent to an internment camp. Bratt was eventually sent to very Orthodox hostel in High Wycombe. He felt that it was too religious. He had been nurtured with aspirations for emigration to Palestine so he requested to go to a pre-*hachsharot*. He was sent to Polton House. After the war he moved to London to join his father. He trained as a mechanic and migrated to the United States in 1948. He currently lives in Reading, USA.

22 Hano Fry

Born 1924 in Hamburg, Germany, his parents were non-practicing and not affiliated to any religion. His parents divorced when he was young, after which his mother and stepfather raised him. His stepfather was an Orthodox Jew, but non-observant. They moved to a large apartment in Berlin and he attended the gymnasium. He was a member of Jewish youth clubs. He had a pre-arranged foster placement with a parson of the Church of Scotland in Scotland, while his brother was sent to members of the Plymouth Brethren sect, near Clydebank. He believes his brother became very isolated and cloistered living within the Plymouth Brethren sect. Fry was thrown out of his foster home because he would not work or convert. He was sent to Garnethill hostel, Glasgow, and attended the Paisley Technical College to complete his matriculation. Fry currently lives in England.

23 Michael Warton

Warton was born in 1925 in Könnigsberg, East Prussia (later becoming part of Germany and now a part of Russia). His father was a successful horse merchant. His parents were Orthodox Jews and he received an observant

Jewish upbringing. He was enrolled in the local gymnasium until he was forced to leave because of anti-Semitism, after which he moved to a Jewish school. He attended Hebrew school three times a week, along with the local Temple twice a week. Warton experienced bullying and anti-Semitism before his departure. His Zionist mother had always sought to focus the family towards migration to Palestine. Nevertheless, through connections with one of their synagogue's cantors, who had already emigrated, his father was able to arrange a foster care placement for him in Scotland. His father was arrested on Kristallnacht, but returned the following morning. In February 1939, Warton left on the Kindertransport from Berlin with his sister and two cousins. They were all sent to a reception camp for 2 days before their sponsors from Glasgow came to collect them. Once in Glasgow they were separated. Warton was sent to live with a wealthy Jewish man. His sister lived with the cantor, while his cousins were placed with the cantor's relatives. He attended the local grammar school. In Glasgow he felt stigmatized as a refugee. He was evacuated to Ayr. Aged 15, he took an apprenticeship in a furniture factory in Glasgow. During his apprenticeship he lived in a hostel and attended night school. From 1945 he worked in London. In 1947 he migrated to Chicago, USA. Today he is an Athiest Jew and currently lives in Highland Park, Illinois, USA.

24 Walter Nachtigall

Born in Vienna, Austria, he came from an observant Jewish family. The Nazis ransacked his family home and sent his father to Dachau. Aged 8, he left Austria with his sister on the Kindertransport. In Edinburgh, they were both fostered; Nachtigall by a Jewish physician, while his sister was fostered separately by another Jewish family. In his foster home, he experienced very poor conditions and slept in a storage room with minimal creature comforts. When the physician went on holiday he was sent by the Fresh Air fund to a Christian family in Disert, Scotland. The new family was poor, but provided a loving home. Due to the subsequent evacuation of Edinburgh he remained with the family for the duration of the war. He felt isolated from other Jews in Disert, but believes he was given support to maintain his knowledge of his Jewish heritage. His parents escaped and rejoined them in Glasgow, Scotland. They migrated to the United States.

Glossary

Aliyah - To return to Eretz Yisrael.

Aliyah Bet - Illegal immigration.

Bachad - A Zionist youth movement. Abbreviation for Brit Chalutzim Datiim or Union of Religious Pioneers. Bachad incorporates Orthodox observance of religious commandments with Zionist pioneering.

Chalutzic - Preparing members for emigration to Palestine.

Chalutzim - Young pioneers.

Chaverim - Comrades.

Eretz Israel - Pre-state of Israel.

Gar'in - Group of Olim who will make Aliyah together.

Habonim - A Zionist youth movement. Meaning The Builders. Little religious observance encouraged. Characterized by its Socialist Zionist approach.

Hachshara - Agricultural training and Aliyah preparation centre for Jewish youth.

Hachsharot - Plural Hachshara.

Hashomer Hatzair - A Zionist youth movement. Meaning The Young Guardsmen. A politically orientated, far-left, socialist and non-religious Zionist group. At Whittingehame Farm School, it was an amalgamation of Dror, Poalei Zion, Hechalutz Hatzair and other smaller far-left groups.

Halutzim - Pioneering generation.

Haluz - Philosophy of pioneering youth movement.

Halutzic - Pioneering ideology.

Hechalutz - A Zionist youth movement. Meaning The Pioneer. The worldwide federation of Zionist youth, which supported various youth movements in order to aid their pioneering efforts.

Hevrat noar - Self-governing youth group.

Israelitische Kultusgemeinde - Jewish Synagogue Association, based in Austria. Aided the IAC by overseeing the organization and selection process of the Kindertransport in Austria.

Kashrut - Jewish dietary laws.

Kindertransport - Organized transport of refugee children from Nazi occupied territory to Britain.

Kindertransportees - Minors allocated a place on the Kindertransport.

Maccabi Youth - An international Zionist-inspired Jewish sports organization.

Madrich - Youth leader.

Menahel - Director.

Metapelet - Housemother.

Olim - Those who make Aliyah.

Reichsvertretung der Juden in Deutschland - Jewish organization in Germany. Aided the IAC by overseeing the organization and selection process of the Kindertransport in Germany.

Sassenach - Gaelic term meaning Anglo-Saxon. Used by Kindertransportees in Scotland to derogatively describe an English person.

Yishuv - The pre-state Jewish community in Eretz Yisrael.

Zionism - International political movement that originally supported the reestablishment of a homeland for the Jewish People in Palestine.

Bibliography

Primary sources

a Unpublished primary sources

Association of Jewish Refugees/Kindertransport Association Archive (KA: QU/SUP)
Kindertransport Association/Association of Jewish Refugees, Worldwide Questionnaire database, which includes 87 respondents who were placed in Scotland out of 1026 returned questionnaires.
Hartley Library Special Collection (HLSC)
MS116/157/AJ396, Papers of Cissi Z. Rosenfelder.
MS116/157/AJ396/5, Papers of the Central Council for Jewish Refugees.
MS183, K.Robson, Papers of Rabbi Solomon Schonfeld, c.1900–88.
MS173, Archives of Jewish care, 1757–1989.
MS225, Archives of the Jewish Chronicle, 1841–1990.
House of Commons Parliamentary Papers (HCPP)
Scottish Home Department, 'Report of the Committee on Homeless Children', *Parliamentary Papers*, 1946, Cmd. 6911, vol. X.755.
English Home Department, 'Report of the Care of Children Committee', *Parliamentary Papers*, 1946, Cmd. 6922, vol. X.559.
Imperial War Museum, Oral History Collection (IWM)
Handler, Arieh, Interview ref: 23830, 12 September 2002.
Leo Baeck and YIVO Centre for Jewish History, New York (LB/YIVO)
MSS590–591; 593–606, MSF 57, Reel 57, microfilm collection.
Benedikt, Lucie, AHC251.
Kovacs, George Joseph, ref: AHC3168.
Rybeck, Erika, ref: AR11522.
Subak-Sharpe, Gerald Emil, Poems and manuscript collection, ref: MS739/AH3138.
Uri, Max, ref: MS1341.
New York Public Library; Jewish Institute (NYL)
PWC.N.C.I1-7, 'Palestine; A Collection of Pamphlets'.
National Archives, Kew, England (NA)
ED10/278, The problems faced by Jewish 'Kindertransport' refugee schoolchildren who show particular academic talent, 1943–44.
HO213/49, Jewish Refugee Committee, 1942.

PREM/4/89/2, William Beveridge, 'Social Insurance and Allied Services', Report, 1 December 1942.

Parkes Library, Southampton University (PL)

Michaelis Stern, Eva, 'Children in the Searchlight', Jerusalem, May 1946 (unpublished transcript).

Private papers of Ester Golan (EGPC)

Anonymous, *New Start; Whittingehame Farm School LTD*, Whittingehame Farm School Limited publicity brochure.

—, *Jewish Youth on the Land; at Whittingehame Farm School*, Whittingehame Farm School Ltd publicity brochure.

—, *How Jewish Youth in Britain regains new life on the land*, published by *Hechaluz* (1942).

—, *Women Build a Land* (Place/date unknown).

Barnett, Ruth, *By the Rivers of Babylon: A Kindertransportee's Experience of Uprooting, Exile and Reconciliation* (unknown).

Borchardy, Lucy, 'Merchant Marine Hachshara in Hamburg (1935–38) "The only Jewish female ship owner in the world"' (unpublished transcript).

Fachler, Eva and Eli 'The Vow; Rebuilding the Fachler Tribe after the Holocaust', (ed.) Yanky Fachler, based on journals (not published, but copyright 2003 to Yank Fachler).

Golan, Ester, letter of rejection from the Director of placements for the American adoption scheme.

(The following documents relate to Whitingehame Farm School).

Kindertransportees' school reports.

Letters and correspondence papers with Countess Jean Balfour, Eva Michaelis, Mike Challis and surviving Kindertransportees.

Newspaper clippings.

Official documents.

Private diaries and memoirs written by Kindertransportees.

Publicity brochures.

Questionnaire collection, including memoirs of Kindertransportees, 1989.

Questionnaire supplementary documents provided by Kindertransportees, 1989.

Religious event programmes.

School inspector's report.

School work, including school journals written by Kindertransportees.

School newspapers.

Secular event pamphlets.

Songs and poems written by the Kindertransportees.

Speech transcripts from the 1989 reunion.

Transcripts of school plays.

Reunion documents for Whittingehame Farm School's Kindertransportees.
Golan, Ester, analysis of Whittingehame Farm School questionnaire, 1989.
Collection of photographs.

Private collection of Mike Challis (MCPC)

Letters from William Farinton Drew to his parents, August 1939 – May 1943.
Newspaper clippings.
Photograph collection, containing over 400 negatives taken by Drew at Whittingehame Farm School, 1939–41.
Whittingehame Farm School Ltd, brochure (no date).

Private Collection of Frances Williams (FWPC)

Correspondence with Kindertransportees.
Heiman, Ruth K., 'Kindertransport questionnaire', Summer 2006.
Herner, Henry, memoir, received June 2009.
Interviews by Frances Williams with 30 Kindertransportees formerly placed in Scotland. Now located in Israel, Britain and the United States (pseudonym have been used throughout the thesis).
Interviews by Frances Williams with seven Kindertransportees formerly placed in England.
Interview with former Israeli *Kibbutznik*.

Scottish Jewish Archives, Glasgow (SJA)

POL0001, 'Jewish Refugees in East Lothian' (unpublished transcript).
POL.BAC/0001, Documents of Bachad and register of refugees at Garnethill Hostel (undated).
SOC0002, List of names of refugee boys attending Garnetbank Primary School, 1939; Bachad Hachsharot brochure; Bachad correspondence, 15 November 1949.
SOC0004, Register of Refugee Children, 1938; Correspondence of Whittinghame Farm School Kindertransportees; Memoir of Mrs Seftor; Memoir by Fay Cohen Stein.
SOCCK0005, Photographs and cuttings relating to Whittinghame Farm School.
(No reference no.) Unknown newspaper clipping, 'House on the Hill', 25 February – 3 March 1989.
(No reference no.) Cowen, Jack, recollections of the first years of the Gertrude Jacobson Orphanage, 24 September 1995.
(No reference no.) Ernespie House reunion documents.
Tenth Anniversary Magazine; Patterns and Images of Jewish immigration in Scotland (Glasgow, 1997).

Washington DC's Holocaust Memorial Museum's archive (WHMA)

Kean College New Jersey Collection (KC) oral history archives: Two relevant interviews found.

USC Shoah Foundation Institute (USC) oral history archive: Nine relevant interviews found.

Slate collection (SC) oral history archive: One relevant interview found.

Wiener Library London (WL)

1368/2/1, Notes, letters and memoirs collected for Bertha Leverton's publication 'I came alone', 1989–2000.

1368/2/2/1-166, 13 boxes of testimonies and other correspondence, entitled 'Reunion of the Kindertransport Documents 1987–2002'.

Association of Jewish Refugees (AJR) oral history archive: 38 relevant interviews found within Bea Leckowitz's collection of 150 interviews with Holocaust survivors (WL/BL).

Photograph collection of Kindertransportees.

b Published primary sources

Anonymous, *A Defence of the Alien Immigrant* (London: London Committee of the Deputies of British Jews, 1904).

—, *Hadassah, the Women's Zionist Organisation of America; Hadassah and Youth Aliyah* (Unknown, 1935).

—, *Hashannah, 5718 (Jewish year); The Scottish Jewish Year Book 1957–58* (Glasgow: Unknown, 1958).

—, *Memorandum on Children's Homes* (Edinburgh: His Majesty's Stationary Office, 1959a).

—, *25 Years of Youth Aliyah* (London: The Children and Youth Aliyah Committee for Great Britain, 1959b).

, '50 reunion of Whittingehame Farm School Ltd', Kindertransport reunion programme.

—, *Edith Eder; in Memoriam* (London: The Women's International Zionist Organisation (WIZO), undated).

—, *Kindertransport 60 Anniversary; In Deep Gratitude to the People and Parliament of the United Kingdom for Saving the Lives of 10,000 Jewish and other Children who Fled to this Country from Nazi Persecution on the Kindertransport 1938–1939,* RoK, 15–17 (London: Unknown, 1999).

Avrays, Harry, *Not With Silver Spoon* (London: Sharon Press, 1989).

Bader, Alfred, *Adventures of a Chemist Collector* (London: Weidenfeld and Nicolson, 1995).

Bentwich, Norman, *Jewish Youth Comes Home; The Story of the Youth Aliyah, 1933–1943* (London: Hyperian Press, 1944).

—, *They Found Refuge* (London: Cresset Press, 1956).

Bermant, Chaim, *Troubled Eden; An Anatomy of British Jewry* (London: Valentine Mitchell, 1969).

—, *Lord Jakobovits; the Authorized Biography of the Chief Rabbi* (London: Weidenfeld & Nicolson Ltd, 1990).

—, 'Memoir of an E-European immigrant to Glasgow', in *Tenth Anniversary Magazine; Patterns and Images of Jewish Immigration in Scotland* (Glasgow: Unknown, 1997).

Blend, Martha, *A Child Alone* (England: Vallentine Mitchell Publishers, 1996).

Cameron, Lewis, *The Challenge of Need: A History of Social Service by The Church of Scotland 1869–1969* (Edinburgh: Unknown, 1971).

Carlebach, Julius, *The Future of Youth Aliyah*, Pamphlet 20 (London: Anglo-Israel Association, December 1968).

David, Ruth, *Child of Our Time: A Young Girl's Flight From the Holocaust* (London: I. B. Tauris, 2002).

Drucker, Olga Levy, *Kindertransport* (New York: Scholastic Books, 1992).

Dubrovsky, Gertrude, *Six from Leipzig: Kindertransport and the Cambridge Refugee Children's Committee* (London: Vallentine Mitchell & Co Ltd, 2003).

Figes, Eva, *Little Eden* (New York: Persea Books, 1988).

Fox, Anne, *Between the Lines: Letters from the Holocaust* (Atlantic City: ComteQ Publishing, 2005).

Fox, Anne and Eva Abraham-Podietz, *Ten Thousand Children: True Stories Told by Children Who Escaped the Holocaust on the Kindertransport* (New Jersey: Behrman House, 1998).

Freier, Recha, *Let the Children Come: The Early History of Youth Aliyah* (London: Weidenfeld and Nicolson, 1961).

Gershon, Karen, *We Came as Children; A Collective Autobiography of Refugees* (London: Gollancz, 1966).

—, *A Lesser Child* (London: Peter Owen Publishers, 1993).

Gissing, Vera, *Pearls of Childhood: The Poignant True Wartime Story of a Young Girl Growing Up in an Adopted Land* (New York: St Martin's Press, 1988).

Glasser, Ralph, *Growing up in the Gorbals* (London: Chatto and Windus, 1989).

Greenberg, Marian G., *Youth Aliyah under Henrietta Szold* (New York: Hadassah, no date).

Haas, Jacob de, *Palestine: A Problem In Development* (New York: Twentieth Century Press, 1924).

Harris, Mark Jonathan and Deborah Oppenheimer, *Into the Arms of Strangers; Stories of the Kindertransport* (London: Bloomsbury publishing, 2000).

Hartman, Geoffrey, *A Scholar's Tale: Intellectual Journey of a Displaced Child in Europe* (New York: Fordham University Press, 2007).

Hayman, Eva, *By the Moon and the Stars* (Auckland: Random Century New Zealand, 1992).

Johnston, Thomas (Secretary of State for Scotland), *Scottish Education Department; Compulsory Day Continuation Classes; Fourth Report of the Advisory Council on Education in Scotland* (Edinburgh: His Majesty's Stationary Office, 1943).

Knight, Rev George, 'For Christians Only – About Jews', in *Church of Scotland Jewish Mission Committee*, Booklet (Edinburgh, 1939–45).
Landa, Myer Jack, *The Alien Problem and its Remedy* (London: P. S. King, 1911).
Leverton, Bertha and Shmuel Lowensohn, *I Came Alone; Stories of the Kindertransports* (England: The Book Guild, 1990).
Levy, Herbert, *Voices from the Past* (London: Temple House Books, 1995).
Malchin, Sarah, 'About Women Worker in Kinneret', *Hapoel Hatzair* 5, 11–13: 14 (1913).
McDougall, Rev David, *In Search of Israel; A Chronicle of the Jewish Mission of the Church of Scotland* (New York: Nelson, 1941).
Neuburger, Werner, *Dark Clouds Don't Stay Forever: Memoirs of a Jewish German Boy in the 1930s and 1940s* (Maryland: Publish America, 2006).
Newman, Jacob, *Kindertransports: A Study of Stresses and Traumas of Refugee Children* (place and date of publication unknown, but c. 1992).
Prager, Peter, *From Berlin to England and back; Experiences of a Jewish Berliner* (London: Library of Holocaust testimonies, 2002).
Presland, John, 'A Great Adventure; The story of the Refugee Children's Movement', in '*Sixtieth anniversary of the Kindertransport, 1939–1999: 15–17 June 1999, London*' (London: RoK, 1999).
Roth, Milena, *Lifesaving Letters: A Child's Flight from the Holocaust* (Seattle: University of Washington Press, 2004).
Rowntree, Seebohm, 'Poverty: A study of Town Life' (Report, 1901).
Sacherin, Rosa (ed.), *Scottish Annual Reunion of Kinder: Recollections of Child Refugees from 1938 to the Present* (Glasgow: Scottish Annual Reunion of the Kinder, 1999).
Sadan, Inge (ed.), *No Longer a Stranger in a Strange Land* (Jerusalem: Inge Saden, 1999).
Samuel, Edwin, *Handbook of the Jewish Communal Villages in Palestine* (Jerusalem: The Zionist Organisation youth department, 1938).
Scottish Education Department, *Public Education in Scotland* (Edinburgh: Her Majesty's Stationery Office, 1958) (PL).
Scottish Home Department, *Memorandum on the Boarding-Out of Children* (Edinburgh: Her Majesty's Stationery Office, 1959).
Selo, Laura, *Three Lives in Transit* (London: Excalibur Press, 1992).
Wells, James, *United Free Church of Scotland; Our Jewish Mission* (Scotland: Unknown, 1905).
Zeller, Frederic, *When Time Ran Out: Coming of Age in the Third Reich* (New York: Permanent Press, 1989).

Newspapers

Cambridge Daily News.
Daily Telegraph.
Evening Standard.
Glasgow Herald.
Haddingtonshire Courier.
Hampstead and Highgate Express.

Jerusalem Post.
Jewish Chronicle.
Jewish Echo.
Lilith: The Jewish Women's Magazine.
Link.
Scotsman.
Sunday Mail.
The New Palestine.
The Times.

Secondary sources

a Articles and chapters

Alderman, Geoffrey, 'The defense of an image', in Alderman, *Modern British Jewry* (Oxford: Oxford University Press, 1992), 321–78.

Ambert, Anne-Marie, 'An International Perspective on Parenting: Social Change and Social Constructs', *Journal of Marriage and Family*, 56, 3 (August 1994), 529–43.

Anthony, Richard, 'The Scottish Agricultural Labour Market, 1900–1939: A Case of Institutional Intervention', *The Economic History Review*, New Series, 46, 3 (August 1993), 558–74.

Ashplant, T. G., review of Peter Gay, 'Freud for Historians', *History Workshop*, 27 (Spring 1989), 205–7.

—, 'Anecdote as narrative resource in working-class life stories; Parody, Dramatization and sequence', in Mary Chamberlain and Paul Thompson (eds), *Narrative and Genre* (Routledge: London, 1990), 99.

Barnett, Ruth, 'The Other Side of the Abyss: A Psychodynamic Approach to Working with Groups of People who Came to England as Children on the Kindertransporte', *British Journal of Psychotherapy*, 12, 2 (1995), 178–94.

—, 'The Acculturation of the Kindertransport Children: Intergenerational Dialogue on the Kindertransport Experience', *Shofar: An Interdisciplinary Journal of Jewish Studies*, 23 (2004), 100–10.

Benz, Ute, 'Traumatization through Separation: Loss of Family and Home as Childhood Catastrophes', *Shofar: An Interdisciplinary Journal of Jewish Studies*, 23 (2004), 85–99.

Benz, Wolfgang and Andrea Hammel, 'Emigration as Rescue and Trauma: The Historical Context of the Kindertransport', *Shofar: An Interdisciplinary Journal of Jewish Studies*, 23, 1 (Fall 2004), 2–7.

Berger, Alan L., 'Jewish Identity and Jewish Destiny, the Holocaust in Refugee Writing: Lore Segal and Karen Gershon', *Studies in American Jewish Literature*, 11, 1 (1992), 83–95.

Berghahn, Marion, 'German Jews in England; Aspects of the Assimilation and Integration process', in Gerhard Hirschfeld (ed.), *Exile in Great Britain; Refugees from Hitler's Germany* (London: Allen & Unwin, 1984), 285–309.

Berthoff, Rowland, review of T. H. Hollingsworth, 'Migration: A Study Based on Scottish Experience between 1939 and 1964', *International Migration Review*, 5 (Winter 1971), 509.

Black, Eugene, review of Tony Kushner, 'The Jewish Heritage in British History: Englishness and Jewishness', *Albion: A Quarterly Journal Concerned with British Studies*, 25, 4 (Winter 1993), 743–6.

—, review of Amy Zahl Gottlieb, 'Men of Vision: Anglo-Jewry's Aid to Victims of the Nazi Regime, 1933–1945', *American Historical Review*, 105, 5 (December 2000), 1805–6.

Blau, Joseph L., *Reform Judaism, a Historical Perspective; Essays from the Yearbook of the Central Conference of American Rabbis* (New York: Ktav Publishing House, 1973).

Boll, Eleanor S., 'Britain's Experience with Adolescents', *Annals of the American Academy of Political and Social Science*, 236 (November 1944), 74–82.

Bowlby, John, *Maternal Care and Mental Health* (London: Northvale, 1950).

Boyarin, Daniel and Jonathan Boyarin, 'Diaspora: Generation and the Ground of Jewish Identity', *Critical Inquiry*, 19, 4 (Summer 1993), 693–725.

Boyd, M., 'Family and personal networks in international migration: recent developments and new agendas', *International Migration Review*, 23 (1989), 638–70.

Breitenbach, Esther, Alice Brown, and Fiona Myers, 'Understanding Women in Scotland', *Feminist Review*, 58, International Voices (Spring 1998), 44–65.

Brenner, David, 'Promoting East European Jewry: "Ost und West", Ethnic Identity, and the German Jewish Audience', *Prooftexts*, 15, 1 (January 1995), 63–88.

Breslauer, Walter, 'Notes on Organisational Problems of German Jewry', *Leo Baeck Institute Year Book*, 14 (1969), 259–65.

Bretherton, Inge, 'The Origins of Attachment Theory: John Bowlby and Mary Ainsworth', *Development Psychology*, 28 (1992), 759–75.

Brugger, Robert J., review of Jacques Barzun, 'Clio and the Doctors: Psycho-History, Quanto-History & History', *The Business History Review*, 49, 3 (Autumn 1975), 362–4.

Bruner, Jerome and Susan Weisser, 'The Invention of Self: Autobiography and its Form', in David R. Olson and Nancy Torrance (eds), *Literacy and Orality* (Cambridge: Cambridge University Press, 1991), 129–48.

Bryder, Linda, 'Wonderlands of Buttercup, Clover and Daisies; Tuberculosis and the open-air school movement in Britain, 1907–39', in Roger Cooter (ed.), *In the Name of the Child; Health and Welfare, 1880–1940* (London: Routledge, 1992).

Buck, M. L., 'Feeding A Pauper Army: War Refugees and Welfare in Britain, 1939–42', *Twentieth Century British History*, 10, 3 (1999), 310–44.

Bullock, Roger, 'The Children Act 1948: residential care', in Olive Stevenson (ed.), *Child Welfare in the UK* (Oxford: Blackwell Science Ltd, 1999).

Cesarani, David, 'Anti-Alienism in Britain after the First World War', *Immigrants and Minorities*, 6, 1 (1987), 5–29.

Chambers, Don, 'Prelude to the Last Things: the Church of Scotland's mission to the Jews', *Records of the Scottish Church History Society*, XIX (1975), 43–58.

Collins, Kenneth, 'Orthodoxy and Reform: Differing Practices in a Glasgow Jewish Victorian Family', *Korot: the Israel Journal of the History of Medicine and Science*, 11 (1995), 54–65.

Combes, Emma, Sally Hibbert, Gillian Hogg and Richard Varey, 'Consuming Identity: The Case of Scotland', *Advances in Consumer Research*, 28 (2001), 328–33.

Curio, Claudio, '"Invisible" children; The selection and integration strategies of relief organisations', *Shofar: An Interdisciplinary Journal of Jewish Studies*, 23 (Fall 2004), 41–56.

—, 'Were unaccompanied child refugees a privileged class of refugees in the Liberal States of Europe?', in Frank Caestecker and Bob Moore (eds), *Refugees from Nazi Germany and the Liberal European States* (New York: Bergahn Books, 2010).

Dekel-Chen, Jonathan and Israel Bartal, 'Jewish Agrarianization', *Jewish History*, 21 (2007), 239–428.

Edelston, H., 'Uprooting and Resettlement, A Survey of the "Youth Aliyah" Program in Israel', *The Journal of Educational Sociology* (April 1959), 32, 8, 392–401.

Elliott, B. J., 'Early Examination of Reform in Scotland and the Crisis in History 1888–1939', *Journal of Educational Administration and History*, 1478–7431, 24, 1 (1992), 47–57.

Ellis, Richard W. B., 'Effects Of War On Child Health', *The British Medical Journal*, 1, 4544 (February 1948), 239–45.

Endelman, Todd, review of Marion Berghahn, 'Continental Britons: German Jewish Refugees from Nazi Germany', *The American Historical Review*, 94, 5 (December 1989), 1389–90.

—, 'English Jewish History', *Modern Judaism*, 11, 1 (1991), 91–110.

—, 'England – Good or Bad for the Jews?', Pamphlet, 3, University of Michigan, The Jubilee Parkes Lecture, May 2002. (2004).

Feidel-Mertz, Hildegaril, 'Integration and Formation of Identity: Exile Schools in Great Britain', *Shofar: An Interdisciplinary Journal of Jewish Studies*, 23 (Fall 2004), 71–84.

Feidel-Mertz, Hildegard and Andrea Hammel, 'Integration and Formation of Identity: Exile Schools in Great Britain', *Shofar: An Interdisciplinary Journal of Jewish Studies*, 23 (2004), 71–84.

Ferguson, Harry, 'Cleveland in History; The abused child and child protection, 1880–1914', in Cooter Roger (ed.), *In the Name of the Child*; Health and welfare, 1880–1940 (London: Routledge, 1992), 146–73.

Finlayson, Geoffrey, 'A Moving Frontier: Voluntarism and the State in British Social Welfare, 1911–1949', *Twentieth Century British History*, 1, 2 (1990), 183–206.

Ford, Mary, 'The Arrival of Jewish Refugee Children in England 1938–1939', *Journal of Immigrants and Minorities*, 2 (July 1983), 137–51.

Gillespire, Veronica, 'Working with the 'Kindertransports', in Sybil Oldfield (ed.), *This Working Day World: Women's Lives and Culture(s) in Britain 1914–1945* (London: Taylor and Francis, 1994), 123–31.

Glick Schiller, Nina, Linda Basch and Cristina Szanton Blanc, 'Immigrant to Transmigrant: Theorizing Transnational Migration', *Anthropological Quarterly*, 68, 1 (January 1995), 48–63.

Gökyiğit, Emel Aileen, 'The Reception of Francis Galton's "Hereditary Genius" in the Victorian Periodical Press', *Journal of the History of Biology*, 27, 2 (Summer 1994), 215–40.

Goldman, Aaaron, 'The Resurgence of Anti-semitism in Britain during World War II', *Jewish Social Studies*, 46 (Winter 1984), 37–50.

Gopfert, Rebekka, 'Kindertransport: History and memory', *Shofar: An Interdisciplinary Journal of Jewish Studies*, 23 (Fall 2004), 21–7.

Grant, Nigel, 'Multicultural Education in Scotland', *Comparative Education*, 19, 2, Special Number (7): Education and the Diversity of Cultures (1983), 133–53.

Guske, Iris, *Trauma and Attachment in the Kindertransport Context; German-Jewish Child Refugees' Accounts of Displacement and Acculturation in Britain* (Cambridge: Cambridge Scholars publishing, 2009).

Hammel, Andrea, 'Representations of Family in Autobiographical texts of child refugees', *Shofar: An Interdisciplinary Journal of Jewish Studies*, 23 (Fall 2004), 121–32.

Hein, Susanne, 'International Refugee Policy and Jewish Immigration', in Frank Caestecker and Bob Moore (eds), *Refugees from Nazi Germany and the Liberal European States* (New York: Bergahn Books, 2010).

Hendrick, Harry, 'Children's emotional well-being and Mental Health in Early Post-Second World War Britain: The case of Unrestricted Hospital visiting', in M. Gijswijt Hofstra and Hilary Marland (eds), *Cultures of Child Health in Britain and the Netherlands in the Twentieth Century* (New York: Rodopi, 2003), 213–42.

Heppell, Jason L., 'A Rebel, not a Rabbi: Jewish Membership of the Communist Party of Great Britain', *Twentieth Century British History*, 15, 1 (2004), 28–50.

Herlihy, David, 'Family', *The American Historical Review*, 96, 1 (February 1991), 1–16.

Hoffman, Charles, 'Absorbing Experience', *The Jerusalem Post Magazine*, 18 (March 1988).

Hogman, Flora, 'The experience of Catholicism for Jewish children during World War II', *Psychoanalytic Review* (1963), 75, 4 (Winter 1988), 511–32.

Holman, Bob, 'Fifty Years Ago: the Curtis and Clyde Reports', *Children and Society*, 10 (1996), 197–209.

Jonçich Clifford, Geraldine, review of Sudhir Kakar, 'Frederick Taylor: A Study in Personality and Innovation', *History of Education Quarterly*, 11, 4 (Winter 1971), 413–25.

Kiely, Richard and Frank Bechhofer, David McCrone, 'Birth, blood and belonging: identity claims in post-devolution Scotland', *The Sociological Review*, 53, 1 (2005), 150–71.

Kleinman, Susan and Chana Moshenska, 'Class as a Factor in the Social Adaptation of the Kindertransport Kinder', *Shofar: An Interdisciplinary Journal of Jewish Studies*, 23 (Fall 2004), 28–40.

Kölmel, Rainer, 'Problems of Settlement; German-Jewish Refugees in Scotland', in Hirschfeld (ed.), *Exile in Great Britain:* Refugees from Hitler's Germany (London: Allen and Unwin, 1984).

—, 'German-Jewish Refugees in Scotland', in Kenneth Collins (ed.), *Aspects of Scottish Jewry* (Glasgow: Glasgow Jewish Representative Council, 1987), 73–7.

Kröger, Marianne, 'Child Exiles: New Research Area?', *Shofar: An Interdisciplinary Journal of Jewish Studies*, 23 (Fall 2004), 8–20.

Kushner, Tony, 'Ambivalence or anti-Semitism?: Christian Attitudes and Responses in Britain to the Crisis of European Jewry During the Second World War', *Holocaust and Genocide Studies*, 5, 2 (1990a), 175–89.

—, 'The impact of British anti-Semitism, 1918–1945', in David Cesarani (ed.), *The Making of Modern Anglo-Jewry* (Oxford: Blackwell, 1990b), 115–37.

—, 'The Western Allies and the Holocaust: Rules of the Game in Britain, America and the Holocaust in 1944', *Holocaust and Genocide Studies,* 5, 4 (1990c), 381–402.

—, 'The end of the Anglo-Jewish Progress Show: Representations of the Jewish East End, 1887–1987', in Kushner (ed.), *The Jewish heritage in British History; Englishness and Jewishness* (London: Frank Cass & Co, 1992).

—, 'The Margins Strike Back', *History Today* (August 1996), 57–8.

—, 'The Kinder: A Case of Selective Memory?', in Tony Kushner (ed.), *Remembering Refugees, Then and Now* (Manchester: Manchester University Press, 2006a), 141–80.

—, 'Holocaust Testimony, Ethics, and the Problem of Representation', *Poetics Today*, 27, 2 (Summer 2006b), 275–95.

Lammers, Benjamin J., 'The Citizens of the Future: Educating the Children of the Jewish East End, c.1885–1939', *Twentieth Century British History,* 19, 4 (2008), 393–418.

Landrum, Robert, review of Hugh Trevor-Roper, 'The Invention of Scotland: Myth and History', *The Historian*, 73, 1 (Spring 2011), 208–9.

Limond, David, 'Locality, Education and Authority in Scotland: 1902–2002 (Via 1872)', *Oxford Review of Education*, 28, 2/3 (June–September 2002), 359–71.

Lin, Patricia, 'National Identity and Social Mobility: Class, Empire and the British Government Overseas Evacuation of Children During the Second World War', *Twentieth Century British History,* 7, 3 (1996), 310–44.

Livshin, Rosalyn, 'The Acculturation of the Children of Immigrant Jews in Manchester, 1890–1930', in Cesarani (ed.), *The Making of Anglo-Jewry* (Oxford: Oxford University Press, 1990).

London, Louise, 'British government policy and Jewish refugees, 1933–1945', *Patterns of Prejudice*, 23 (1989/90), 26–43.

—, 'Jewish Refugees, Anglo-Jewry and British Government Policy, 1930–1940', in Cesarani (ed.), *The Making of Anglo-Jewry*, 115–37.

Ludlow, P. W., 'The refugee problem in the 1930s: The failures and successes of Protestant relief programmes', *The English Historical Review*, 90, 356 (July 1975), 564–603.

MacKenzie, Donald, 'Eugenics in Britain', *Social Studies of Science*, 6, 3/4, Special Issue: Aspects of the Sociology of Science: Papers from a Conference, University of York, UK 16–18 September 1975 (September 1976), 499–532.

Macnicol, John, 'The Effect of the Evacuation of Children on Official Attitudes to State Intervention', in Harold L. Smith (ed.), *War and Social Change* (Manchester: Manchester University Press, 1986), 3–31.

—, 'Welfare, wages and the family; child endowment in comparative perspective, 1900–50', in Cooter Roger (ed.), *In the Name of the Child*; Health and welfare, 1880–1940 (London: Routledge, 1992), 244–75.

Mazlish, Bruce, 'What Is Psycho-History?', *Transactions of the Royal Historical Society*, 21 (1971), 79–99.

McCarthy, Angela, 'Scottish National Identities among Inter-war Migrants in North America and Australasia', *The Journal of Imperial and Commonwealth History*, 34, 2 (June 2006), 201–22.

Moeller, Robert, 'The Third Reich in post-war German memory', in Jane Caplan (ed.), *Nazi Germany; Short Oxford History of Germany* (Oxford: Oxford University Press, 2008), 246–305.

Moore, Peter G., 'The Next Decade', *Journal of the Royal Statistical Society*. Series A (General), 146, 3 (1983), 213–45.

Murphy, John, 'Memory, Identity and public narrative', *Cultural and Social History*, 7, 3 (2010), 297–314.

Myers, Kevin, 'History, migration and childhood: the case of refugee children in 1930s Britain', *Journal of Family and Community History*, 3, 2 (2000), 147–57.

Neumeir, Beate, 'Kindertransport: Memory, Identity and the British-Jewish Diaspora', in Monika Fludernik (ed.), *Diaspora and Multiculturalism: Common Traditions and New Developments* (New York: Rodopi B. V., 2003).

Newman, Jacob, *Kindertransports: A Study of Stresses and Traumas of Refugee Children* (place and date of publication unknown, but c. 1992).

Nicholson, R., 'From Ramsay's *Flora MacDonald* to Raeburn's *MacNab*: The Use of Tartan as a Symbol of Identity?', *Textile History*, 36, 2 (2005), 146–67.

Oldfield, Sybil, '"It is Usually She": The Role of British Women in the Rescue and Care of the Kindertransport Kinder', *Shofar: An Interdisciplinary Journal of Jewish Studies*, 23 (Fall 2004), 57–70.

Oppenheim, Michael, 'A "Fieldguide" to the Study of Modern Jewish Identity', *Jewish Social Studies*, 46, 3/4 (Summer/Fall 1984), 215–30.

Parks, Robert J., review of Jacques Barzun, 'Clio and the Doctors: Psycho-history, Quanto-history & History', *The American Historical Review*, 81, 3 (June 1976), 557.

Parr, J., 'The skilled emigrant and her kin: gender, culture and labour recruitment', *Canadian Histoical Review*, 68 (1987), 529–51.

Pedraza, Silvia, 'Family', *The American Historical Review*, 96 (1991), 1–16.

—, 'Women and Migration: The Social Consequences of Gender', *Annual Review of Sociology*, 17 (1991), 303–25.

Proctor, Tammy M., '(Uni)Forming Youth: Girl Guides and Boy Scouts in Britain, 1908–39', *History Workshop Journal*, 45 (Spring 1998), 103–34.

—, 'On My Honour: Guides and Scouts in Interwar Britain', *Transactions of the American Philosophical Society*, New Series, 92, 2 (2002), 159–80.

Rathbone, Eleanor, 'Personal View of the Refugee Problem', *The New Statesman and Nation*, 5 April 1939.

Rees, Jenny, 'Night of the Long Memories', *Daily Telegraph*, 12 July 1989.

Robertson, Priscilla, 'The home as a nest', in Lloyd de Mause (ed.), *The History of Childhood* (London: A Condor Book Souvenir Press, 1976).

Rosenmann, Stanley and Irving Handelsman, 'The Collective Past, Group Psychology and Personal Narrative: Shaping Jewish Identity by Memoirs of the Holocaust', *American Journal of Psychoanalysis*, 50, 2 (June 1990), 151–70.

Rutter, Jill, 'Learning from History: Responses to refugees 1900–89', in Jill Rutter (ed.), *Refugee Children in the UK* (New York: Open University Press, 1999).

Schulzinger, Robert, review of Jacques Barzun, 'Clio and the Doctors. Psycho-History, Quanto-History, and History', *History and Theory*, 15, 1 (February 1976), 94–103.

Segal, Lore, 'The Bough Breaks', in David Rosenberg (ed.), *Testimony: Contemporary Writers Mare the Holocaust Personal* (New York: Random House, 1989).

Sharples, Carolyn, 'Kindertransport: Terror, Trauma and Triumph', *History Today*, 54, 3 (2004a).

—, 'replies', *History Today*, 54, 5 (May 2004b), 92.

Silberstein, Laurence, 'Toward a Postzionist Discourse', in Miriam Peskowitz and Laura Levitt (eds), *Judaism since Gender* (New York: Routledge, 1997).

Simon, Oswald John, 'Reformed Judaism', *The Jewish Quarterly Review*, 6, 2 (January 1894), 262–77.

Smith, David, 'Official Responses to Juvenile Delinquency in Scotland During the Second World War', *Twentieth Century British History*, 18 (2007), 78–105.

Smith, Leonard, 'Thank God for the Kindertransport', *History Today*, 54, 5 (May 2004), 92.

Spector, Shmuel and Geoffrey Wigoder, *The Encyclopedia of Jewish Life; Before and During the Holocaust vol. 1* (New York: New York University Press, 2001).

Steahr, Thomas E., review of T. H. Hollingsworth, 'Migration: A Study Based on Scottish Experience between 1939 and 1964', *Social Forces*, 49, 4 (June 1971), 655.

Steigmann-Gall, Richard, 'Religion and the churches', in Jane Caplan (ed.), *Nazi Germany; Short Oxford History of Germany* (Oxford: Oxford University Press, 2008).

Steinberg, Bernard, 'Jewish Education in Great Britain during World War II', *Jewish Social Studies*, 29, 1 (January 1967), 27–63.

Stephenson, Jill, 'Girls' Higher Education in Germany in the 1930s', *Journal of Contemporary History*, 10, 1 (January 1975), 41–69.

—, 'Nazism, Modern War and Rural Society in Wurttemberg, 1939–45', *Journal of Contemporary History*, 32, 3 (July 1997), 339–56.

Stewart, John, 'The Scientific Claims of the British Child Guidance, 1918–1945', *The British Journal for the History of Science*, 42, 3 (September 2009), 407–32.

Strauss, Herbert, 'The Immigration and Acculturation of the German Jews in the United States of America', *Leo Baeck Institute Year Book*, 16 (1971), 63–94.

Summerfield, Penny, 'Women, Work and Welfare: A Study of Child Care and Shopping in Britain in the Second World War', *Journal of Social History*, 17, 2 (Winter 1983), 249–69.

—, 'Culture and Composure: Creating Narratives of the Gendered Self in Oral History Interviews', *Cultural and Social History*, 1 (2004), 65–93.

Thoburn, June, 'Trends in Foster Care and Adoption', in Olive Stevenson (ed.), *Child Welfare in the UK* (Oxford: Blackwell Science Ltd, 1999).

Thom, Deborah, 'Wishes, anxieties, play and gestures: Child guidance in inter-war England', in Cooter (ed.), *In the Name of the Child*, (London: Routledge, 1992), 200–19.

Trevor-Roper, Hugh, 'The Invention of Traditions: The Highland Tradition of Scotland', in E. Hobsbawm, and T. Ranger (eds), *The Invention of Tradition* (Cambridge: Cambridge University Press, 1983).

Tydor Baumel, Judith, 'Twice a Refugee: The Jewish Refugee Children in Great Britain during Evacuation, 1939–1943', *Jewish Social Studies*, 45, 2 (Spring 1983), 175–84.

Ugolini, Wendy, 'The Internal Enemy 'OTHER': Recovering the World War Two, Narratives of Italian Scottish Women', *Journal of Scottish Historical Studies*, 24, 2 (2004), 137–58.

—, 'Memory, War and the Italians in Edinburgh: The Role of Communal Myth', *National Identities*, 8, 4 (2006), 421–36.

Urwin, Cathy and Elaine Sharland, 'From bodies to minds in childcare literature; advice to parents in inter-war Britain', in Cooter (ed.), *In the name of the child* (London: Routledge, 1992), 191.

Voeltz, Richard A., review of Tony Kushner, 'Antisemitism in British Society', *Historian*, 53, 4 (Summer 1991), 794.

Volkov, Shulamit,'Die Juden in Deutschland 1780–1918', in Lothar Gall a.o. (ed.), *Enzyklopädie deutscher Geschichte*, 16 (Oldenbourg Verlag, München 1994, second edition 1999).

Wachsmann, Nikolaus, 'The Policy of exclusion: repression in the Nazi State, 1933–1939', in Jane Caplan (ed.), *Nazi Germany; Short Oxford History of Germany* (Oxford: Oxford University Press, 2008), 122–43.

Welshman, John, 'Evacuation and Social Policy During the Second World War: Myth and Reality', *Twentieth Century British History*, 9, 1 (1998), 28–53.

Welshman, John and Stewart, J., 'The Evacuation of Children in Wartime Scotland: Culture, Behaviour and Poverty', *Journal of Scottish Historical Studies*, 19 (2006), 100–20.

Williams, Bill, 'The Anti-Semitism of Tolerance', in A. Kidd and K. Roberts (eds), *City, Class and Culture* (Manchester: Manchester University Press, 1985).

Zahra, Tara, 'A Human Treasure': Europe's Displaced Children between Nationalism and Internationalism', *Past and Present*, 6 (2011), 332–50.

b Books

Abrams, Lynn, *The Orphan Country; Children of Scotland's Broken Homes from 1845 to the Present Day* (Edinburgh: John Donald, 1998).

—, *Oral History Theory* (London: Routledge, 2010).

Abrams, Lynn and Callum G. Brown (eds), *A History of Everyday Life in Twentieth-Century Scotland* (Edinburgh: Edinburgh University Press, 2010).

Abrams, Nathan, *Caledonian Jews; A Study of Seven Small Communities in Scotland* (London: McFarland and Company, 2009).

Adrendt, Hannah, *The Jew as Pariah* (New York: Grove Press, 1978).

Affleck, Gray, *Timber!; Memories of life in Scottish Women's Timber Corps, 1942–46* (East Lothian: Tuckwell Press, 1998).

Alderman, Geoffrey, *Modern British Jewry* (Oxford: Oxford University Press, 1992).

—, *Controversy and Crisis: Studies in the History of the Jews in Modern Britain* (Boston: Academic Studies Press, 2008).

Amkraut, Brian, *Between Home and Homeland; Youth Aliyah from Nazi Germany* (Alabama: University of Alabama Press, 2006).

Anderson, Benedict, *Imagined Communities: Reflections on the Origin and Spread of Nationalism* (London: Verso, 1991).

Anthony, Sylvia, *Women's Place in Industry and Home* (London: George Routledge and Sons, 1932).

Arbabzadah, Nushin, *From Outside in: Refugees and British Society: An Anthology of Writings by Refugees on Britain and Britishness* (London: Arcadia Books, 2007).

Aronoff, Myron J., *Israeli Visions and Divisions; Cultural Change and Political Conflict* (New Jersey: Transactions Publishers, 1989).

Bader Whiteman, Dorit, *The Uprooted: A Hitler Legacy: Voices of Those Who Escaped Before the 'Final Solution'* (New York: Insight Books, 1993).

Barth, Frederick (ed.), *Ethnic Group and Boundaries: The Social Organization of Culture Difference* (London: George Allen and Unwin, 1970).

Basch, Linda, Nina Glick Schiller and Cristina Szanton-Blanc, *Nations Unbound: Transnational Projects and the Deterritorialised Nation-state* (New York: St Martins Press, 1994).

Bechhofer, Susie and Jeremy Josephs, *Rosa's Child, The True Story of One Women's Quest for a Lost Mother and a Vanished Past* (London: I. B. Tauris, 1996).

Bell, Adrian, *Only for 3 months; The Basque Children in Exile* (Norwich: Mousehold Press, 1996).

Benjamin, Natalia (ed.), *Recuerdos: Basque children refugees in Great Britain* (Oxford: Mousehold Press, 2007).

Berghahn, Marion, *Continental Britons; German-Jewish Refugees from Nazi Germany* (London: Macmillan, 1984).

Berkowitz, Michael, *Zionism Culture and West European Jewry before the First World War* (New York: Cambridge University Press, 1993).

—, *Nationalism and Zionism and Ethnic Mobilisation in 1900 and beyond* (Boston: Brill, 2004).

Black, Eugene, *The Social Politics of Anglo-Jewry, 1880–1920* (Oxford: Blackwell, 1988).

Blau, Joseph L., *Reform Judaism, a Historical Perspective; Essays from the Yearbook of the Central Conference of American Rabbis* (New York: Ktav Publishing House, 1973).

Bolchover, Richard, *British Jewry and the Holocaust* (Oxford: Oxford University Press, 2003).

Braber, Ben, *Jews in Glasgow 1879–1939; Immigration and Integration* (London: Valentine Mitchell, 2007).

Bregman, Ahron, *A History of Israel* (New York: Palgrave MacMillan, 2003).

Brook, Stephen, *The Club: The Jews of Modern Britain* (London: Constable Cantor, 2000).

Caestecker, Frank and Bob Moore (eds), *Refugees From Nazi Germany and the Liberal European States* (Oxford: Berghan Books, 2010).

Caplan, Jack, *Memories of the Gorbals* (Edinburgh: Pentland Press, 1991).

Caplan, Jane, *Nazi Germany: Short Oxford History of Germany* (Oxford: Oxford University Press, 2008).

Carr, E. H., *What is History?* (London: Penguin, 1961).

Cesarani, David (ed.), *The Making of Modern Anglo-Jewry* (Oxford: Basil Blackwell Ltd. 1990).

—, *Citizenship, Nationality and Migration in Europe* (London: Routledge, 1996).

Chamberlain, Mary and Paul Thompson (eds), *Narrative and Genre* (London: Routledge, 1990).

Cohen, Asher and Bernard Susser, *Israel and the Politics of Jewish Identity* (London: John Hopkins University Press, 2000).

Cohen, David, *J. B. Watson: The Founder of Behaviourism: A Biography* (London: Routledge, 1979).

Collins, Kenneth, *Aspects of Scottish Jewry* (Glasgow: Glasgow Jewish Representative Council, 1987).

—, *Second City Jewry; the Jews of Glasgow in the age of expansion, 1790–1919* (Glasgow: Scottish Jewish Archives, 1990).

—, *Glasgow Jewry: A Guide to the History and Community of the Jews in Glasgow* (Glasgow: Scottish Jewish Archives, 1993).

—, *Scotland's Jews; A guide to the History and Community of the Jews in Scotland* (Glasgow: Scottish Council of Jewish Communities, 1999).

—, *Be Well!; Jewish Immigrant Health and Welfare in Glasgow, 1860–1914* (East Lothian: Tuckwell Press, 2001).

Colls, R. and P. Dodds (eds), *Englishness: Politics and Culture, 1880–1920* (London: Croom Helm, 1986).

Cooper, Howard and Paul Morrison, *A Sense of Belonging; Dilemmas of British Jewish Identity* (London: Weidenfeld & Nicolson, 1991).

Cooter, Roger (ed.), *In the Name of the Child; Health and Welfare, 1880–1940* (London: Routledge, 1992).

Cowan, Evelyn, *Spring Remembered – A Scottish Jewish Childhood* (Edinburgh: Southside Press, 1974).

Cunningham, Hugh, *Children and Childhood in Western Society since 1500* (London: Longman, 1998).

—, *The Invention of Childhood* (London: BBC books, 2006).

Daiches, David, *Two Worlds* (Edinburgh: Macmillan, 1957).

Dent, H., *Education in Transition* (London: Routledge, 1944).

Denton, Howard and Jim C. Wilson, *The Happy Land* (Edinburgh: Ramsay Head Press, 1991).

Despert, Louise, *Preliminary Report on Children's Reaction to the War* (New York: Macy Jr., 1942).

Deutscher, Isaac, *The Non-Jewish Jew and Other Essays* (New York: Oxford University Press, 1968).

Donzelot, Jacques, *The Policing of Families* (New York: Pantheon Books, 1979).

Durkheim, Emile (translated by J. Swain), *Elementary Forms of the Religious Life* (London: Collier Books, 2000).

Dwork, Deborah and Jan Van Pelt, *Flight from the Reich: Refugee Jews, 1933–1946* (New York: Robert W. W. Norton & Co., 2009).

Edelheit, Abraham J., *History of Zionism; A Handbook and Dictionary* (Colorado: Westview Press, 1999).

Emmanuel, Muriel and Vera Gissing, *Nicholas Winton and the Rescued Generation* (England: Vallentine Mitchell Publishers, 1982).

Endelman, Todd, *Radical Assimilation in English Jewish History, 1656–1945* (Bloomington: Indiana University Press, 1990).

—, *The Jews of Britain; 1656 to 2000* (London: University of California Press, 2002).

Engelking, Barbara, *Holocaust and Memory* (London: Leicester University Press, 2001).

Epstein A. L., *Ethos and Identity: Three Studies in Ethnicity* (London: Tavistock, 1978).

Esman, Milton J. and Itamar Rabinovich, *Ethnicity, Pluralism and the State in the Middle East* (London: Cornell University Press, 1988).

Fackenheim, Emil, *The Jewish Return into History: Reflections in the age of Auschwitz and a New Jerusalem* (New York: Schocken Books, 1978).

—, *Epitaph for German Judiasm; From Halle to Jerusalem* (Wisconsin: The University of Wisconsin Press, 2007).

Feldmann, David, *Englishmen and Jews; Social Relations and Political Culture 1840–1914* (London: Yale University Press, 1994).

Finlayson, Geoffrey, *Citizen, State and Social Welfare in Britain 1830–1990* (Oxford: Oxford University Press, 1994).

Fludernik, Monika (ed.), *Diaspora and Multiculturalism: Common Traditions and New Developments* (New York: Rodopi B. V., 2003).

Foucault, Michael, *The History of Sexuality* (New York: Knopf Doubleday Publishing, 1990).

Freud, Anna, *Infants without Families: Reports on the Hampstead Nurseries 1939–1945* (New York: International University Press, 1973).

Freud, Anna and Dorothy Burlingham, *War and Children* (New York: Medical War Books, 1943).

Freud-Kandel, Miri J., *Orthodox Judaism in Britain since 1913; An Ideology Forsaken* (London: Vallentine Mitchell, 2006).

Galton, Francis, *The Possible Improvement of the Human Breed, under the existing Conditions of Law and Sentiment* (London: Eugenics Education Society, 1909).

Gassman-Sherr, Rosalie, *The Story of The Federation of Women Zionists of Great Britain and Ireland; 1918–1968* (London: Federation of Women Zionists, 1969).

Gay, Peter, *Freud, Jews and other Germans. Masters and Victims in Modernist culture* (New York: Oxford University Press, 1978).

Gershon, Karen, *We Came as Children: A Collective Autobiography* (London: Harcourt Brace and World, 1966a).

—, *Selected Poems* (New York: Harcourt Brace and World, 1966b).

—, *The Fifth Generation* (New York: Beaufort Books, 1987).

Gill, Alan, *Interrupted Journeys: Young Refugees from Hitler's Reich* (Sydney: Simon and Schuster, 2004).

—, *Interrupted Journeys, Young Refugees from Hitler's Reich* (Pymble, NSW: Simon and Schuster, 2005).

Glazer, Nathan and Daniel P. Moyniham (eds), *Beyond the Melting Pot* (Cambridge: MIT Press, 1963).

Glick Schiller, Nina, Linda Basch and Cristina Blanc-Szanton (eds), *Towards a Transnational Perspective on Migration: Race, Class, Ethnicity, and Nationalism Reconsidered* (New York: New York Academy of Sciences, 1992).

Goodman, Paul, *Zionism in England; English Zionist Federation 1899–1929* (London: Fishburn books, no-date).

Gordon, Peter, Richard Aldrich and Denis Dean, *Education and Policy in England in the Twentieth Century* (London: Woburn Press, 1991).

Gordon, Sarah, *Hitler, Germans and the 'Jewish Question'* (Princeton: Princeton University Press, 1984).

Gottesman, Meir, *Out of the Fire* (London: unknown publisher, 1979).

Greenstein, Howard R., *Turning Point: Zionism and Reform Judaism* (California: Scholars Press, 1981).

Grenville, Anthony, *Jewish Refugees from Germany and Austria in Britain, 1933–1970: Their Image in AJR Information* (London: Vallentine Mitchell, 2010).

Grunfeld, Judith, *Shefford: The Study of a Jewish School Community in Evacuation 1939–1945* (London: Soncino Press, 1980).

Guske, Iris, *Trauma and Attachment in the Kindertransport Context; German-Jewish Child Refugees' Accounts of Displacement and Acculturation in Britain* (Cambridge: Cambridge Scholars publishing, 2009).

Halpern, Ben and Shalom Wurm (eds), *The Responsible Opinion: The Life and Times of Giora Josephthal* (New York: Schocken, 1966).

Halsey, H., A. F. Heath and J. M. Ridge, *Origins and Destinations: Family, Doss and Education in Modern Britain* (Oxford: Oxford University Press, 1981).

Handelman, Don, *Nationalism and the Israeli State; Bureaucratic Logic in Public Events* (Oxford: Berg, 2004).

Hartman, Donniel, *The Boundaries of Judaism* (London: Continuum, 2007).

Hartman, Geoffrey, *The Longest Shadow: In the Aftermath of the Holocaust* (New York: Palgrave, 2002).

Hendrick, Harry, *Images of Youth: Age, Class and the Male Youth Problem, 1880–1920* (Oxford: Oxford University Press, 1990).

—, *Child Welfare: England 1872–1988* (London: Routledge, 1994).

—, *Child Welfare: Historical Dimensions, Contemporary Debate* (Bristol: The Policy Press, 2003).

Hirschfeld, Gerhard (ed.), *Exile in Great Britain: Refugees from Hitler's Germany* (London: Allen and Unwin, 1984).

Hirschman, Elizabeth Caldwell and Donald N. Yates, *When Scotland was Jewish; DNA Evidence, Archeology, Analysis of Migrations, and Public and Family Records Show Twelfth Century Semitic Roots* (London: McFarland and Co. Inc., 2006).

Hobsbawm, Eric and Terence Ranger (eds), *The Invention of Tradition* (Cambridge: Cambridge University Press, 1992).

Hofman, Ethel G., *Mackerel at Midnight – Growing Up Jewish on a Remote Scottish Island* (Philadelphia: Camino Books, 2005).

Hollingsworth, T. H., *Migration: A Study Based on Scottish Experience between 1939 and 1964* (Edinburgh: Oliver & Boyd, 1970).

Howe, David, Marian Brandon, Diana Hinnings and Gillian Schofield, *Attachment Theory, Child Maltreatment and Family Support; A Practice and Assessment Model* (New York: Palgrave, 1999).

Hutt, C. and H. L. Kaplan (eds), *A Scottish Shtetl – Jewish Life in the Gorbals, 1880–1974* (Glasgow: Unknown, 1984).

Inglis, Ruth, *The Children's War Evacuation 1939–45* (London: Routledge, 1989).

Jenkins, Keith, *On What is History?: From Carr and Elton to Rorty and White* (Routledge: London, 1995).

Jenkins, Richard, *Rethinking Ethnicity; Arguments and Explorations* (London: Sage Publications, 1997).

Josephs, Zoe, *Survivors; Jewish Refugees in Birmingham 1933–1945* (Birmingham: Denali Press, 1988).

Kamins, Toni L., *The Complete Jewish Guide to Britain and Ireland* (New York: St Martin Griffin, 2001).

Kaplan, Harvey, *The Gorbals Jewish Community in 1901* (Glasgow: Scottish Jewish Archives, 2006).

—, *Glasgow Jewish Journeys* (not stated).

Kaplan, Marion, *The Making of the Jewish Middle Class: Women, Family and Identity in Imperial Germany* (New York: Oxford University Press, 1991).

—, *Between dignity and despair: Jewish life in Nazi Germany* (New York: Oxford University Press, 1998).

—, *Jewish Daily Life in Germany 1618–194* (Oxford: Oxford University Press, 2005).

Katznelson-Rubashow, Rachel (ed.), *The Plough Woman: Memoirs of the Pioneer Women of Palestine* (New York: Herzl Press, 1975).

Kay, Billy, *The Scottish World: A Journey into the Scottish Diaspora* (England: Mainstream publishing, 2008).

Kluger, Ruth, *Still Alive; A Holocaust Girlhood Remembered* (New York: The Feminist Press, 2001).

—, *Landscapes of Memory: A Holocaust Girlhood Remembered* (London: Bloomsbury Publishers, 2003).

Kochavi, Arieh, *Post-Holocaust Politics: Britain, the United States, & Jewish Refugees, 1945–1948* (Chapel Hill: University of North Carolina Press, 2001).

Koehn, Ilse, *Mischling, Second Degree: My Childhood in Germany* (London: Hamish Hamilton, 1978).

Koschland, Bernard, *Kindertransport: Tylers Green Hostel for Young Jewish Refugees* (London: Jewish Historical Society of England, 2007).

Kramer Lotte, *The Phantom Lane* (England: The Rockingham Press, 2000).

—, *Kintertransport, Before and After, Elegy and Celebration Elegy and Celebration: Sixty poems, 1980–2007* (Brighton: Centre for German Jewish Studies, University of Sussex, 2007).

Kranzler, David and Gertrude Hirschler (eds), *Solomon Schonfeld: His Page in History* (New York: Judaica Press, 1982).

Kushner, Tony, *The Persistence of Prejudice: Antisemitism in British Society during the Second World War* (Manchester: Manchester University Press, 1989).

—, *The Jewish Heritage in British History: Englishness and Jewishness* (London: Frank Cass, 1992).

—, *The Holocaust and the Liberal Imagination* (Oxford: Blackwell, 1994).

—, *Anglo-Jewry Since 1066: Place, Locality and Memory* (Manchester: Manchester University Press, 2009).

Kushner, Tony and K. Lunn (eds), *Traditions of Intolerance: Historical Perspectives on Fascism and Race Discourse in Britain* (Manchester: Manchester University Press, 1989).

Kushner, Tony and Katherine Know, *Refugees in an Age of Genocide: Global, National and Local perspectives during the Twentieth Century* (London: Frank Cass, 1999).

Kutner, Bob, *Over My Shoulder* (Glasgow: Pentland Press, 1995).

Landau, Ronnie, *Studying the Holocaust; Issues, Readings and Documents* (London: Routledge, 1998).

Langer, Lawrence L., *Holocaust Testimonies: The Ruins of Memory* (New Haven: Yale University Press, 1991).

Langton, Daniel R., *Claude Montefiore; His Life and Thought* (London: Valentine Mitchell, 2002).

Lassner, Phyllis, *Anglo-Jewish Women writing the Holocaust; Displaced Witnesses* (Hampshire: Palgrave Macmillan, 2008)

Lawson, Peter, *Broken Homes: Three Kindertransport Poets* (New Milford: Bergan Journals, 2008).

Legarreta, Dorothy, *The Guernica Generation: Basque Refugee Children of the Spanish Civil War* (Nevada: University of Nevada Press, 1984).

Leipman, Flora, *The Long Journey Home* (London: Bantam Press, 1987).

Lelaidier, Veronica, *Jewish Children's Experiences of Evacuation during the Second World War* (Paris conference, 1998) (Paris: Parcours Judaiques IV, 1998).

Lerman, Antony, David Jacobs, Lena Stanley-clamp, Anne Frankel and Alan Montague (eds), *The Jewish Communities of the World* (London: Unknown, 1989).

Leverton, Bertha and Shmuel Lowensohn, *I Came Alone; Stories of the Kindertransports* (Sussex, England: Book Guild, 1990).

Levin, Salmond S. (ed.), *A Century of Anglo-Jewish Life, 1870–1970* (London: United Synagogue, 1970).

Levy, Arnold, *The Origins of Glasgow Jewry, 1812–1895* (Glasgow: A. J. Macfarlane, 1949).

—, *The Origins of Scottish Jewry* (Glasgow: JHSE, 1958).

Liedtke, Rainer and David Rechter (eds), *Towards Normality?; Acculturation and Modern German Jewry* (London: Chicago University Press, 2003).

London, Louise, *Whitehall and the Jews, 1933–1948: British Immigration Policy, Jewish Refugees and the Holocaust* (Cambridge: Cambridge University Press, 2001).

MacEwen, Scott, Alison, *Gender Segregation and Social Change; Men and Women in Changing Labour Markets* (Oxford: Oxford University Press, 1994).

Mahood, Linda, *Policing Gender, Class and Family; Britain, 1850–1940* (London: UCL Press, 1995).

Marienstras, Richard, *The Jews of the Diaspora or the Vocation of a Minority* (Oxford: Oxford University Press, 1983).

Marwick, A., *Britain in the Century of Total War: War, Peace and Social Change, 1900–1967* (London: Bodley Head, 1968).

Marwick, W. H., *Scotland in Modern Times. An Outline of Economic and Social Development since the Union of 1707* (London: Frank Cass, 1964).

Mause, Lloyd de (ed.), *The History of Childhood* (London: A Condor Book Souvenir Press, 1976).

McCarthy, Angela, *Personal Narratives of Irish and Scottish Migration, 1921–65: For Spirited Adventure* (Manchester: Manchester University Press, 2007).

Meyer, Michael, *Response to Modernity: A History of the Reform Movement in Judaism* (New York: Oxford University Press, 1988).

Michaelis, Dolf (1906–82) and Eva Michaelis-Stern, *Emissaries In Wartime London, 1938–1945* (Jerusalem: Unknown, 1989).
Morris, Nathan, *Jewish Education in Time of Total War* (London: JEC Publications, 1946).
Neuberger, Julia, *On Being Jewish* (Great Britain: Mandarin, 1996).
Newman, Jacob, *Kindertransports: A Study of Stresses and Traumas of Refugee Children* (place and date of publication unknown, c. 1992).
Novick, Peter, *The Holocaust and Collective Memory: The American Experience* (London: Bloomsbury, 1999).
Oppenheimer, Deborah and Mark Jonathan Harris, *Into the Arms of Strangers* (London: Bloomsbury, 2000).
Parker, H. M. D., *Manpower: Study of Wartime Policy and Administration* (London: HMSO, 1957).
Pearl, Judea and Ruth Pearl (eds), *I am Jewish; Personal Reflections Inspired by the Last Words of Daniel Pearl* (Vermont: Jewish Lights, 2004).
Peskowitz, Miriam and Laura Levitt, *Judaism since Gender* (New York: Routledge, 1997).
Pine, Lisa, *Nazi Family Policy, 1933–1945* (Oxford: Berg Publishers, 1997).
Platt, Anthony, *The Child-savers: the Invention of Delinquency* (Chicago: University of Chicago Press, 1969).
Poppel, Stephen M., *Zionism in Germany 1897–1933; The Shaping of a Jewish Identity* (Philadelphia: Jewish Publication Society of America, 1977).
Portelli, Alessandro, *The Battle of Vale Giulia: Oral History and the Art of Dialogue* (Wisconsin: University of Wisconsin Press, 1997).
Rapaport, Lynn, *Jews in Germany after the Holocaust; Memory, Identity and Jewish-German Relations* (Cambridge: Cambridge University Press, 1997).
Reinharz, Jehuda and Walter Schatzberg, *The Jewish Response to German Culture; From the Enlightenment to the Second World War* (London: University Press of New England, 1985).
Rose, John, *The Myths of Zionism* (London: Pluto Press, 2004).
Rubinstein, W. D., *A History of the Jews in the English-Speaking World: Great Britain* (New York: Macmillan, 1996).
Rutter, Jill, *Refugee Children in the UK* (New York: Open University Press, 1999).
Sacks, Jonathan, *The Dignity of Difference; How to Avoid the Clash of Civilizations* (London: Continuum, 2002).
Samuel, Maurice, *The Plough Woman: Memoirs of the Pioneer Women of Palestine*, (Westport, Conn.: Hyperion, 1976).
Segal, Lore, *Other People's Houses* (New York: Harcourt, 1964).
Shatzkes, Pamela, *Holocaust and Rescue: Impotent or Indifferent? Anglo-Jewry 1938–1945* (New York: Palgrave, 2002).
Sherman, A. J., *Island Refuge, Britain and the Refugees from the Third Reich, 1933–1939* (London: Elek Books Limited, 1973).

Sicker, Martin, *Judaism, Nationalism and the Land of Israel* (Oxford: Westview Press, 1992).

Simmel, George, *The Web of Group Affiliation* (London: Macmillan, 1989).

Simmons, Erica B., *Hadassah and the Zionist Project* (Oxford: Rowman & Littlefield Publishers, 2006a).

—, *"Persecuted, Uprooted": Youth Aliyah and the Rescue of European Jewish Children* (Oxford: Oxford University Press, 2006b).

Smith, Anthony, *National Identity* (London: Penguin, 1991).

—, *Nationalism* (London: Frank Cass, 2001).

Sonnert, Gerhard and Gerald Holton, *What Happened to the Children Who Fled Nazi Persecution*? (New York: Palgrave Macmillan, 2006).

Stachura, Peter D., *The German Youth Movement 1900–1945; An Interpretative and Documentary History* (London: Macmillan Press Ltd, 1981).

Stargardt, Nicholas, *Witnesses of War: Children's Lives under the Nazis* (London: Jonathan Cape, 2005).

Stevenson, Olive, *Child Welfare in the UK* (Oxford: Blackwell Science Ltd, 1999).

Summerfield, Penny, *Women workers in the Second World War; Production and Patriarchy in conflict* (London: Croom. Helm, 1984).

Sword, K., N. Davis and J. Ciechanowski, *The Formation of the Polish Community in Great Britain, 1939–50* (London: School of Slavonic and East European Studies, 1989).

Taylor, A. J. P., *English History, 1914–1945* (Oxford: Oxford University Press, 1965).

Thomson, Paul, *The Voice of the past: Oral History* (New York: Oxford University Press, 1978).

Titmuss, Richard, *History of the Second World War: Problems of Social Policy* (London: HMSO, 1976).

Tosh, John, *The Pursuit of History* (Harlow: Longman, 2006).

Turner, Barry, ... *And the Policeman Smiled; 10,000 Children Escape from Nazi Europe* (London: Bloomsbury, 1990).

Tydor Baumel, Judith, *Unfulfilled Promise – Rescue and Resettlement of Jewish Refugee Children in the United States 1934–1935* (Juneau, AK: Denali Press, 1990).

Wasserstein, B., *Britain and the Jews of Europe 1939–1945* (New York: Oxford University Press, 1979).

Werthheimer, Jack, *Unwelcome Strangers; East European Jews in Imperial Germany* (Oxford: Oxford University Press, 1987).

Williams, Bill, *The Making of the Manchester Jewry, 1740–1875* (Manchester: Manchester University Press, 1976).

Wyman, Mark, *DPs: Europe's Displaced Persons, 1945–1951* (Cornell: Cornell University Press, 1998).

Zahl Gottlieb, Amy, *Men of Vision; Anglo-Jewry's Aid to Victims of the Nazi Regime 1933–1945* (London: Weidenfeld and Nicolson, 1998).

Zariz, Ruth, *Escape before the Holocaust, Migration of German Jews 1938–1941* (Hakibbutz Hameuchad: unknown, 1990).

c Unpublished articles and papers

Baumel, E. J., 'The Jewish Refugee Children in Great Britain 1938–1945', unpublished MA thesis (Bar-Ilan University, Israel, 1981).

Ben Braber, 'Integration of Jewish Immigrants in Glasgow 1880–1939', unpublished PhD thesis (University of Glasgow, 1992).

Claudio Curio, 'Verfolgung, Flucht, Rettung; Die Kindertransporte 1938/39 nach GroBbritannien', unpublished PhD thesis (University of Berlin, 2006).

Hamilton, Vernon, 'A Retrospective Study of Child Refugees from Nazi Germany', unpublished PhD thesis (University of Reading, 1985).

Hill, Paula, 'Anglo-Jewry and the Refugee children 1938–1945', unpublished PhD thesis (Royal Holloway College, University of London, 2001).

Imber, Elizabeth, 'Saving Jews: The History of Jewish-Christian relations in Scotland – 1880–1948', unpublished MA thesis (Brandeis University, 2011).

Kadosh, Sandra Berliant, '"Ideology versus Reality": Youth Aliyah and the Rescue of Jewish Children during the Holocaust Era, 1933–45', unpublished PhD thesis (University of Columbia, 1995).

Lloyd, J. M., 'The Scottish School System and the Second World War: A Study in Central Policy and Administration', unpublished PhD thesis (University of Stirling, 1979).

Smith, A., 'What Light do the Records of the Scottish Office Shed on the Planning and Implementation of the Evacuation of Women and Children in Scotland?', unpublished MSc dissertation (University of Edinburgh, 2002).

d Multimedia (web sources, broadcasts and films)

Association of Jewish Refugees' webpage relating to the Kindertransport Association's activities in Britain, www.ajr.org.uk/kindertransport.htm.

Jewish Agency for Israel, webpage detailing the pioneering ideology of Halutziut, http://www.jewishagency.org/JewishAgency/English/Jewish + Education/Compelling + Content/Eye + on + Israel/Israeli + Culture/Pioneering + Ideology + Halutziut.htm.

Jewish Care Scotland (website for the Jewish community in Scotland) http://www.jcarescot.org.uk/jewishcarewho.asp.

List of Kindertransportees brought over by Nicholas Winton, http://www.just-powell.co.uk/winton/list.htm.

'The Reunion', BBC Radio 4 (FM only), 11.15am, 12 September 2010.

'The Kindertransport Story', BBC broadcast, IPlayer 29 April 2009.
Hall, Robert, 'Czech evacuees thank their savior,' BBC News, 4 September 2009.
Harris, Mark Jonathon, *Into the arms of strangers*, film (Washington: Warner Bros. Pictures, 2001).
'WWII Rescue train trip recreated', BBC News, 4 September 2009.

Index